Kīkā Kila

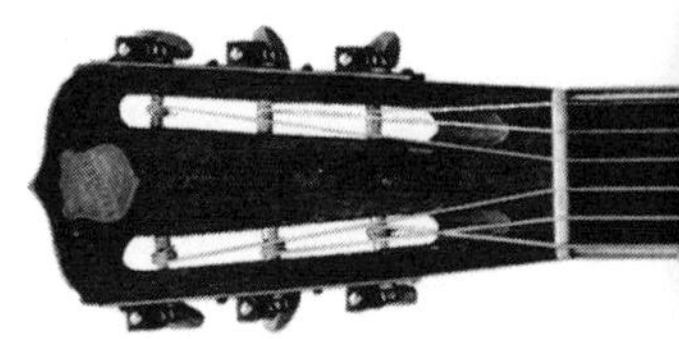

JOHN W. TROUTMAN

Kīkā Kila

How the HAWAIIAN STEEL GUITAR *Changed the Sound of Modern Music*

THE UNIVERSITY OF
NORTH CAROLINA PRESS
Chapel Hill

Published with the assistance of the Anniversary Fund of the University of North Carolina Press

Designed by Richard Hendel
Set in Garamond Premier Pro
by Tseng Information Systems, Inc.
Manufactured in the United States of America

Portions of this work appeared previously in somewhat different form in John W. Troutman, "Creating Community in the Confines of 'Fine Barbaric Thrill': Joseph Kekuku, a Hawaiian Manhattan, and the Indigenous Sounds of Modernity," *Journal of the Gilded Age and Progressive Era* 15, no. 4 (October 2015): 551–61. Portions of Chapter 6 appeared previously in somewhat different form in John W. Troutman, "Steelin' the Slide: Hawai'i and the Birth of the Blues Guitar," *Southern Cultures* 19, no. 1 (Spring 2013): 26–52. Reprinted with permission.

The paper in this book meets the guidelines for permanence and durability of the Committee on Production Guidelines for Book Longevity of the Council on Library Resources.

The University of North Carolina Press has been a member of the Green Press Initiative since 2003.

Cover image courtesy of Lani Ellen McIntire and HLC Properties, Ltd.

Library of Congress Cataloging-in-Publication Data
Title: Kīkā kila : how the Hawaiian steel guitar changed the sound of modern music / John W. Troutman.
Description: Chapel Hill : The University of North Carolina Press, [2016] | "Published with the assistance of the Anniversary Fund of the University of North Carolina Press." | Includes bibliographical references and index.
Identifiers: LCCN 2015041086| ISBN 9781469627922 (cloth : alk. paper) | ISBN 9781469659091 (pbk. : alk. paper) | ISBN 9781469627939 (ebook)
Subjects: LCSH: Hawaiian guitar—History. | Music—Hawaii—History. | Music—United States—History. | World music—History.
Classification: LCC ML1015.G9 T76 2016 | DDC 787.8709969—dc23
LC record available at http://lccn.loc.gov/2015041086

MIX
Paper from responsible sources
FSC® C008955

CONTENTS

Preface. B. B.'s Dreams *vii*

Introduction *1*

1 Guitar Culture in the Hawaiian Kingdom *10*

2 Joseph Kekuku's Steel Guitar and the Era of Overthrow *43*

3 American Debut: The Making of the Steel Guitar Craze *74*

4 Hawaiian Troubadours and the Global Reach of the Kīkā Kila *104*

5 Holly-Hawaiians, Electric Guitars, and Glass Ceilings *130*

6 The Disappearing of "Hawaiian" from American Music *153*

7 Banishment, and Return: Seeking the Steel Guitar in the Hawaiian Renaissance *200*

Epilogue. Remembrance and Kuleana *227*

Notes *235*

Bibliography *321*

Acknowledgments *345*

Index *347*

PREFACE *B. B.'s Dreams*

Riley "B. B." King was born on a cotton plantation near Indianola, Mississippi, in 1925. As a child in the Mississippi Delta, Jim Crow's ground zero, he labored as a sharecropper, as did nearly everyone he knew. King was restless, however, and soon the backbreaking labor that he and his family endured in those cotton fields, combined with the call of Memphis's bright lights, became too much for young B. B. to bear. Eventually, he found a way out, one built of six strings, wood, magnets, and wire; when he plugged it in, it burst with howls and despair that sounded far beyond his years. Eventually it, and the other guitars he would play for the rest of his life, would be named Lucille.

B. B. King was famous and loved, winning presidential honors and industry awards. But at his heart, he was a troubadour, always ready to travel with Lucille in hand. He lived for the music until it inevitably outlived his body. His vision, his life, teemed with the stuff of American history, the good and the bad, that shaped his twentieth-century world.

As a child, King sopped up the sounds around him like a sponge, twisting up all of these musical ideas in his head, and then cascading new sounds through his fingers as they worked the fretboard. His Mississippi Delta was not a land of isolation; he did not rehearse ancient field hollers from the days of slavery. And while he sang in the Baptist church, old time spirituals, ultimately, were not his game. He had radio. He could tune in the latest pop gems blanketing the countryside from New York City ballroom broadcasts; he could follow all the hit parades and keep up with the jazz kings and queens. Or, like he often did on Saturday nights, he could dial into the Grand Ole Opry on Nashville's WSM.

Yet through all of the sounds that competed for his imagination, one seemed to triumph above the rest. As he recounted it, it fundamentally shaped his sound as a bluesman. It was "*that* sound" of the Hawaiian steel guitar. "Well, I'd hear it on the radio," he told National Public Radio's Terry Gross in 1995. "I would hear the Hawaiian sound or the country music players play steel and slide guitars, if you will. And I hear that—to me a steel guitar is one of the sweetest sounds this side of heaven. I still like it, and that was one of the things that I tried to do so much, was to imitate that . . . that sound! I could never get it, I still have not been able to do it, [but] that was the beginning of the trill on my hand."[1] In his autobiography with David Ritz, he elaborated, "My technique of bending strings and trilling notes was giving me an approximation of that steel pedal sound that haunted my musical dreams. Lucille was singing the blues better than me."[2]

This book reveals the journey of the steel guitar, from its birth within the stunning guitar culture of late nineteenth-century Hawai'i, to its haunting the dreams of B. B. King and others, to its disappearance, and return, in its Hawaiian homelands. It places an instrument at the center of the story, and follows its travels and players around the world. It is a story of modern innovation and global proliferation, hidden and obscured over time. Above all, it is a story of how a Native Hawaiian instrument changed the sound of the world.

It is also a story close to my heart, as I have played the steel guitar for nearly half my life. During that time, I've played the instrument in some unusual places — from a dance hall in the middle of the Atchafalaya Swamp to grand English theatres; from a bowling alley in New Orleans to a film festival on the French Riviera. Once I played steel guitar at a comic book convention jammed inside a nondescript warehouse in Athens, Greece, surrounded by packs of roving dogs. The instrument seems unbounded by contexts; it creates a familiar sound in all of them.

The road stories that spring from such experiences are the stuff of life for working musicians. They eclipse the boredom imbedded in long days on the road, or in the hours of downtime between sound check and showtime. Musicians have told these stories ever since they first discovered that they could get paid to play. But what first led me to this book was my realization that a little-known indigenous technology centers in each of these stories, these gigs. A Kanaka Maoli — a Hawaiian — instrument.[3] Today the sound of the steel guitar is everywhere, it is practically impossible to avoid, no matter your musical preferences. So then why do this instrument and its origins seem so hidden from view? What can we learn from its travels, and where *did* it come from, anyway?

Though it has been called into the service of the blues, country, rock, and countless other genres, the steel guitar was originally built to better serve the melodies composed by Hawai'i's sovereigns. It fortified a Hawaiian culture then under attack by land-hungry hāole (foreigners) plotting to overthrow the kingdom. It soon spawned a yearning for Hawaiian music of unprecedented, global proportion, while it sparked musical revolutions in the United States. By the 1970s, however, it came to be shunned in some parts of the Islands, its sound equated with cultural loss rather than rebirth. It is an instrument with a heavy history. The instrument has endured a challenged and storied, yet remarkably adaptable existence. It has changed how we hear, and expect to hear, music throughout the world. The Hawaiian steel guitar demonstrates how the past is profoundly implicated in musical performance.

As I thought about writing this book, I wondered how I might stitch together the instrument's vast and unruly history. The instrument humbled me as I began to learn of its origins, and the many traditions that it has inspired. Likewise, the reach of the instrument is far more expansive than I originally imagined. As a consequence, the book took me on what became an eight-year research odyssey, from the Hawai'i State Archives to the British Library, from family reminiscences in Waimānalo to a luau under florescent lights inside a Holiday Inn in Joliet, Illinois. At each stop, a new history of modern music unfolded before me.

Along the way I encountered extraordinary communities of musicians and their relatives, enthusiasts, scholars, and community activists. Granted, some of them identify themselves in more than one of those categories, but this book represents my effort to place all of them in conversation with one another. The task is daunting, the results certainly imperfect. The challenge of holding the attention of audience members with such diverse interests is one that any musician can identify with. Some scrutinize your instrument of choice. Some are interested in the sound of the band. Some are only listening for the lyrics. Some just want to dance. And then there are those who are much more interested in conversations tangential to the performance—they are talking to one another by the bar, at the back of the hall, occasionally raising their voices in order to overpower the wattage rating on your PA. While perhaps frustrating at first, they are the individuals that ultimately you might fixate on from the stage. "Why aren't they listening? How can I get their attention?" you ask yourself. Or, perhaps, "What are they talking about? What am I missing?" This book is written in part for those of us in the front, who already are passionate about the historical force of music, but it is also written for those in the back, who are less willing to make assumptions—who remain less certain of the importance of music in understanding our collective past. Their healthy skepticism is what fueled this eight-year quest, and I can't thank them enough for it. My hope is that everyone in the audience will use this book to generate a conversation that, like musical performance, is inherently greater than the sum of its parts—a conversation that will not compete with the PA or with the talkers in the back but will allow all of its parts to find concert, just like the sounds that haunted B. B.'s dreams.

Kīkā Kila

INTRODUCTION

A few years ago, while wading through some unidentified films from the 1910s, I was surprised to encounter a familiar face. For the duration of the silent fifty-six-second clip, she sits in a chair in the middle of a room, surrounded by wounded American doughboys convalescing in a medical facility in England. She is singing to them a refrain we cannot hear.

Her name is Tsianina Redfeather Blackstone, a Muskogee singer about whom I have written in other places. By 1918, when the film was made, she had already enjoyed several years of success as a mezzo-soprano. But in this film, she wears beaded buckskin stage regalia and holds in her lap a Hawaiian steel guitar. Her left hand glides the steel bar gracefully across the fretboard, as she uses metal picks on her right thumb and middle finger to expertly strum wide chords or pluck dancing staccato melodies on the top string.

I marveled at the footage; it is, as far as I know, the earliest surviving film of *anyone* playing a Hawaiian steel guitar. Kanaka, or Hawaiian, guitarists had introduced the instrument to North Americans perhaps only twenty years prior to this moment; they were part a wave of Hawaiians who left home following the overthrow of their kingdom by Americans whose families had recently settled in the Islands.[1] The guitarists left for a variety of reasons, but most sought work and autonomy. Plantation labor for haole (meaning foreign, typically American) bosses did not appeal to them, and neither did taking clerical jobs within an American governmental bureaucracy that they did not support.

While the U.S. Provisional Government (PG) prohibited the teaching of the Hawaiian language in schools, the musicians' performance of Hawaiian mele, or songs, perpetuated, even proliferated its practice.[2] Such Hawaiian musicians and dancers labored intensely at their occupations, perfecting their craft while traveling the world in the years that followed. As a result, by the time that U.S. forces sailed to Europe during the Great War, Kanaka steel guitarists were well on their way toward revolutionizing how people throughout the Pacific Rim, North America, and Europe approached their music.[3] Indeed, by that time,

Hawaiian guitar music had become one of the most popular music genres in the United States. The steel guitar had already reached deeply into the world, touching hearts in almost every context imaginable: in this earliest surviving film of the steel guitar, for example, we find a Muskogee woman, born in Indian Territory and educated in Indian boarding schools, having survived a U-boat attack on her own vessel while en route to Europe, performing for wounded soldiers in England, on a Hawaiian instrument. Both the instrument and the singer were far from their homes. Yet, as we watch the soldiers in the film, their faces not only reveal a warm comfort with Blackstone and her steel guitar, but some of the men sing along, perhaps to one of the pop hits of the day, which, at that time, may well have been a Hawaiian song.[4]

Perhaps Blackstone was drawn to the instrument because of its indigenous origin, as were the Māori of New Zealand, who following its introduction to their lands immediately adopted the Hawaiian guitar. Or perhaps she merely gravitated to the instrument as so many did, Natives and non-Natives alike, during its first wave of international popularity. The silent song she sings in the film might have originated from a mele composer in Hawaiʻi, or from a closet-sized office on West 28th Street in New York City, along the famous Tin Pan Alley. What we do know is that, by the 1910s, people throughout the world had begun to discover in the steel guitar an exciting and unabashedly modern instrument of untapped musical and performative possibility.

This book traces how a Native Hawaiian technology generated the modern sounds of American (and indeed, other) popular music, sounds that remain familiar and vital in the twenty-first century. It upends current understandings of the most significant U.S. musical genealogies, understandings marred by a tendency to erase Native people from their central roles in not just American music but the nation's history writ large. When we look, we find steel guitarists reimagining the possibilities of Hawaiian music as they defend their imperiled sovereigns from imperial American designs. We find them inspiring the development of the most significant guitar innovations of the twentieth century. We see their broad cultural influence extend far beyond anyone's expectation, yet we also witness the instrument's near extinction in its homelands, divorced from its Native Hawaiian origins just as its sound became ubiquitous throughout the rest of the world.

To begin, we must acknowledge the Hawaiian Islands as one of the most significant crossroads of the nineteenth-century world. The archipelago represents but one region within the massive "sea of Islands" that Pacific Islanders have navigated, visited, or inhabited for thousands of years.[5] Ali'i, or people of chiefly status, maintained local governance throughout the Islands for hundreds of years, though Kamehameha I in 1810 consolidated his rule as mō'ī, or sovereign, over the entirety of the archipelago. By that time, foreign visitors such as the British captain James Cook and his crew had begun to appear with increasing frequency in the Islands. In the decades that followed, more sailors, whalers, merchants, missionaries, entrepreneurs, and laborers from distant lands routinely arrived in and departed from Honolulu harbor. They came from regions all over the Pacific and throughout the world. Since 1820, many of them had arrived with the blessing of the ali'i, and international relations and trade for the Hawaiian Kingdom vastly expanded during this period. Despite these good graces, as American missionaries and businessmen increasingly sought souls for salvation and lands for plantation, Hawaiians from the ali'i and kāhuna (priests) to the maka'āinana (nonelite residents, or the "producer" class) grappled with increasingly challenging and unforeseen circumstances. By the 1860s, it became clear that some of the American hāole—most often the entrepreneurial sons of the original missionaries—believed they were not merely guests of the Hawaiian sovereigns but rather were entitled to govern, exploit, and own the entirety of the archipelago. During the 1880s and 1890s, American conspirators worked to dismantle the cultural autonomy and enfranchisement of the Hawaiians and wrest the political authority of the Islands from the mō'ī, resulting in the illegal and internationally condemned overthrow of Lili'uokalani, her eventual imprisonment in 'Iolani Palace, and the "annexation" of the Islands by the United States in 1898.[6]

The impact of the foreign visitors and occupiers in the nineteenth century was immediate and complex. The Native population, estimated to range anywhere from 250,000 to 1 million people prior to Captain James Cook's arrival in 1778, plummeted to fewer than 40,000 by the 1890s, as Kānaka suffered casualties from diseases introduced by the vast numbers of foreigners visiting the Islands.[7] Foreigners inspired a wide array of cultural responses within the Islands, however. While some Kānaka may have shunned the hāole outright, most others embraced what ideas made sense to them. For example, adapting new tools introduced by the missionaries, Hawaiians quickly learned to read and write in Hawaiian as well as in English. During the mid- and late 1800s, in turn, they comprised one of the most literate populations in the world.[8] They also adopted foreign yet appealing singing traditions into their own, ever-changing repertoires. In addition, foreigners brought to the Islands a variety of trade goods—including, most significant for this story, Spanish guitars.[9]

Up to that point Kānaka had maintained a powerful, centuries-old complex of mele oli and mele hula that defined their musical culture and formally articulated their histories and genealogies, among many other social and sacred functions.[10] Mele oli are chants with no instrumental accompaniment, while mele hula can incorporate dances and instrumentation. Mele hula, like mele oli, comprise many genres of performance; through the mid-nineteenth century, repertoires were learned orally.[11] While catastrophic population declines challenged the oral tradition, and American missionaries attempted to outlaw hula dance outright, hula and oli proved incredibly robust throughout the nineteenth century.[12]

Before guitars arrived, mele hula were accompanied by a number of percussion and other instruments. The percussion instruments included the pahu, a drum typically crafted with a hollowed log and a shark skin drumhead; the puniu, made from a coconut shell; the ipu, a drum which joins two gourds together; and the ʻuliʻuli, a gourd rattle. Pūʻili, a split bamboo rattle, created a shimmering effect when struck. Along with these percussion instruments, Hawaiians during that time also played the bamboo hano or ʻohe-hano-ihu nose flute, which enabled players to produce three notes to accompany a chant, and the ʻūkēkē, a three-stringed bow, which was the only stringed instrument in the Islands prior to the arrival of Europeans. The player holds the bow of the ʻūkēkē against the mouth, which acts as a resonator, and alternates the three tones in combination.[13]

Eventually Hawaiians began to experiment with and incorporate foreign instruments and musical styles into their mele hula repertoire, which seemed to easily accommodate new musical technologies. No new instrument, however, made a greater impact in their musical life during the nineteenth century than the Spanish, or "standard," guitar.[14] Beginning around the 1840s, these guitars gained such a quick acceptance, circulation, and powerful role in mele hula and other newly developing musical practices in Hawaiʻi, that it is perhaps best to consider this phenomenon as the rise of a Native Hawaiian "guitar culture."[15]

This guitar culture embraced a variety of instruments within the guitar family. While guitars arrived in the hands of visitors from many distant ports, Portuguese and Madeiran laborers in the late 1870s and 1880s introduced a number of variations of the guitar that were eventually transformed in the

Islands into distinctively "Hawaiian" instruments such as the ʻukulele and taro-patch fiddle.[16] As well, during the late 1880s and 1890s, Hawaiian musicians developed a new guitar technology that became known, among other names, as the Hawaiian guitar.

The Hawaiian guitar. In Hawaiian, some identify the instrument as the kīkā kila.[17] Elsewhere you find it referred to as ʻkikala Hawaiʻi; ʻkikala maoliʻ; ʻkikala anuʻunuʻuʻ; ʻwiola anuʻunuʻuʻ; or kikala paheʻe.[18] Hawaiian newspapers in the 1910s and 1920s referred to the practice of playing the Hawaiian guitar as "hoʻokani pila me ke kila."[19] This book will refer to the instrument alternately as the kīkā kila, the Hawaiian steel guitar, the steel guitar, the steel, or the Hawaiian guitar, as it was perhaps most commonly referred to during its infancy. But we can link other instruments and playing styles to the Hawaiian steel guitar as well: Dobros, resonator guitars, National guitars, Weissenborns, electric steel guitars, pedal steel guitars, non–pedal steel guitars, and, as this book argues, slide guitars, all directly descended from one common ancestor: the acoustic Hawaiian steel guitar.

While the Hawaiian steel guitar remains an incredibly well *heard* instrument in all of these iterations, it is an instrument poorly understood and remarkably unacknowledged today, both in popular culture and in scholarly circles.[20] When I play the instrument onstage, I am often asked to explain the odd contraption in front of me—I have heard it called a keyboard more times than I can count, or a "table top guitar," or even a xylophone on a recent occasion. Its name derives from the small steel bar that a player glides along the top of strings that are suspended high above the fretboard. The earliest practitioners of the style, in fact, transformed standard, Spanish guitars into steel guitars by fabricating a "raised nut" that they inserted behind the first fret, where the strings transition from the neck to the headstock of the instrument, in order to ensure that the steel bar never touched the fretboard. It can produce a wide variety of effects, depending on the techniques deployed, including glissando sweeps reminiscent of the human voice, or perhaps waves rising and falling. It functions as a lead melodic instrument and can also generate a wide array of chords, depending on its tuning, of which there are dozens. Chords (as well as two-string combinations, known as dyads or double stops) are produced by placing the bar on the strings, either perpendicular to them or slanted forward or backward across them. Other steel guitar modifications that took place in the Islands in the late nineteenth century, beyond the fabrication of steel bars of various shapes and sizes, included the cutting of metal finger picks to produce greater volume from the instrument.[21] Hawaiians also built the guitars out of local koa wood, and they may have developed hollow-necked instruments by the early twentieth century.

The instrument's earliest origins remain both murky in some ways and surprisingly well documented in others. While a number of competing stories place the instrument's conceptual genesis in the hands of a few different individuals living in the Islands in the late nineteenth century, during the 1890s a young man from Lāʻie, Oʻahu, Joseph Kekuku, seems clearly to have transformed the idea of the steel guitar from an experiment to a translatable, disciplined practice of instrument making and playing—a modern technique and accompanying technology that could adapt readily to a variety of musical genres and to the hands of onlookers. This book acknowledges many musical practices around the world of unique origin that are similar in concept to, and that at times predate, that of the steel guitar. People have run objects along strings for millennia. Yet as we will see, the specific modifications to the modern guitar, the application of the steel bar and metal picks to the strings, and the highly melodic technique, steeped in long-standing mele hula traditions that Kekuku and his fellow Hawaiian practitioners carried forth from the archipelago, generated a clear break in how peoples in North America, Europe, East Asia, Oceania, India, other regions understood the guitar in relation to their own musical world. In certain ways, I argue, their modern vernacular musical traditions, and the sonic contours of their popular music industries, became contingent on the journeys of an indigenous instrument. Born from the tumult of an imperial design that threatened to silence Native voices, the instrument transformed into a Hawaiian technology that instead defied the empire.

The story grew more complicated as the steel guitar took on a life of its own. Kekuku's career, like that of several other Hawaiian musicians featured here, reveals the challenges, the promise, and the peril that entertainers of color faced in the early twentieth century.[22] With the instrument in the center of our view, however, we can move nimbly across space and time, cresting the waves of the instrument's greatest prominence in several cultural landscapes and moments, while contemplating its disappearance in the breaks elsewhere.[23] We can follow arguably its greatest player as a stowaway on a steamer bound from Honolulu to San Francisco. We can hear the instrument in Jimmie Rodgers and Son House recordings, or on the silver screen, accompanying Bing Crosby. For a while we see it in the hands of thousands of lei-bedecked haole boys and girls in places like Cleveland, Chicago, or Detroit. We hear it in Bollywood scores, even at the beginning of Warner Brothers cartoons. And though the instrument fell out of favor in the Islands for some time, perhaps for some of these very reasons, in the twenty-first century we find it slowly returning to the hands of young Hawaiian musicians. By placing a musical instrument at the center of our historical journey, we encounter all of these moments as we consider the deeply resonant politics and history of the Hawaiian guitar.

The book first explores the origins of the guitar culture in the Islands in the mid- to late nineteenth century, when Hawaiians incorporated string bands that featured the guitar, and often fiddles and banjos, into the kingdom's royal ceremonies as well as into luaus and other informal gatherings. As it became a fixture of "traditional" Hawaiian music, in fact, the guitar came to signify a challenge to foreign encroachment, even if it arrived just a few decades earlier in the hands of sailors, vaqueros from California, New England whalers and missionaries, Madeiran plantation laborers, and even blackface minstrels.[24] The rise in popularity of the guitar in the Islands took place just as the political turmoil generated by haole residents increased to a fever pitch in the 1880s. A vocal opponent of the overthrow and later "annexation" of the Islands by the United States, Joseph Kekuku played the most prominent role in physically modifying the guitar and inventing the modern steel guitar style and technique in the midst of this political upheaval. The book then follows Kekuku and many other Native musicians and dancers as they left the Islands and confronted the American vaudeville circuit.

By the time the Great War concluded and Tsianina Blackstone returned to the United States from England, Hawaiian troubadours were continuing to extend the reach of the instrument. The book pursues a number of itinerant steel guitarists who traveled the world in the interwar years and beyond, leaving a deep imprint in their wake. Meanwhile, musicians began to envisage new possibilities for the Hawaiian guitar. In the 1920s a new generation of Hawaiian steel guitarists pushed the boundaries of technique and technology, while non-Hawaiians incorporated the instrument into a variety of new contexts. Both Hawaiian and non-Hawaiian players performed hapa haole, a genre that blended English lyrics with Hawaiian words and sonic cues, and both began to build the steel into the music industry's infant genres of jazz, hillbilly, and the blues. Indeed, the instrument's impact was especially profound in the U.S. South, as the musical tastes of white southerners and southerners of color were irrevocably transformed by the Hawaiian guitar. Industry executives, meanwhile, ascribed the Hawaiian sounds of the southern steel guitar in strictly black or white tones. They believed southern music markets and consumer interest were as segregated and strictly biracial as the Jim Crow laws that blanketed the South. Popular understandings of southern music soon followed suit, obscuring the fundamental role of Hawaiians in shaping the sounds of American southern music.[25]

In California, meanwhile, second-generation Hawaiian guitarists such as Sol Hoʻopiʻi pushed the boundaries of the available technology with their virtuosic performances, and demanded more. The excitement they provoked during this vibrant era of guitar music led to promotional collaborations with guitar builders in the Los Angeles area. The builders amplified steel guitars first mechanically and then electrically. In consequence, and through the efforts of Hawaiians to showcase these instruments, the first mass-produced electric steel guitar quickly became the most popular electric guitar of any sort in the United States. At the same time, Hollywood's film and radio industry began attracting top talent from the Islands; Sol and his fellow troubadours filled the film studios by day and scored the glamorous social scene by night. From the movies and these musicians' live and recorded music, their influence continued to climb. Hawaiian guitar schools cropped up throughout the United States during the Great Depression, enrolling hundreds of thousands of boys and girls eager to demonstrate their talents at Hawaiian guitar conventions. Beyond the United States, Hawaiian steel guitarists inspired the imaginations of people from South Africa and India to Japan and the Philippines. The musical world of the twentieth century was forever changed by the Hawaiian steel guitar revolution.

Yet, just as quickly as Native Hawaiians transformed the global soundscape, they seemed to disappear from its memories and histories. By the 1960s, as this book reveals, non-Hawaiians only vaguely identified the steel guitar as a Hawaiian instrument. Even more telling, it was nearly abandoned by the next generation of Hawaiians in the Islands, in part because they associated the instrument with hapa haole or American cowboy music and haole tourism.[26] During the Hawaiian Renaissance movement of the 1970s, the steel guitar seemed to retreat to background music in a handful of Waikīkī hotels, while the kī hōʻalu, or slack key guitar, triumphantly emerged as the new musical embodiment of a Native Hawaiian nationalist movement.[27] Yet, as we will see, if one listened carefully, even to the most celebrated voices of the new generation, one could still hear the distinctive wail of the steel guitar.

You can hear the Hawaiian steel guitar in one of its many iterations every day, on virtually any radio station or media site that streams popular music. Yet few of us recognize the sound of it, let alone its Hawaiian origins. It is time for us, once again, to listen for it. This book considers the history of an indigenous instrument born in the cultural bedlam of colonialism, from its curious and occasionally mysterious origins, to its rise to near-global ubiquity, and then, invisibility, as an instrument heard but no longer "seen," less than 100 years later. The instrument's journey reveals a dynamic and sustaining musical culture in the Islands during a period of crisis and change; it bares the fundamental role of Kanaka guitarists in crafting the sonic palette of modernity in the United States and beyond; and, finally, it exposes the erasure of its indigeneity by a music industry defined in black and white, and by a sentiment born in the origins of the modern Hawaiian nationalist movement that came to associate the instrument with colonial oppression. The journey takes us from the docks of Honolulu harbor to the 1915 Panama Pacific International Exposition in San Francisco; from the stage of the Grand Ole Opry in Nashville, Tennessee, to a Japanese prison camp in the Philippines; from Hitler's limousine parading through the streets of Berlin, to tent shows and crossroads in Clarksdale, Mississippi. The journey ends, however, where it begins, in the hands of musicians strolling on roads and by streams along the windward and leeward coastlines of the Hawaiian Islands.

1 *Guitar Culture in the Hawaiian Kingdom*

By 1939, Curtis Piehu Iaukea had observed events of a royal hue and magnitude that few in the Hawaiian archipelago, let alone in the world, could imagine. Born in 1855 in Waimea, on the island of Hawai'i, Iaukea was raised in Honolulu by his maternal uncle, an attendant of Kamehameha IV. Gaining the favor of the ali'i nui, or high chiefs, as he came of age, Iaukea eventually came also to serve the Hawaiian sovereigns, from Kamehameha V and Kalākaua to Lili'uokalani. In 1880 he was appointed the kingdom's chief secretary of foreign affairs. In this capacity he served as an envoy at state functions throughout the world while he forged diplomatic alliances for his country. In January 1893, however, his world, like that of all Kānaka he represented abroad, collapsed into political chaos: American capitalists, with the backing of U.S. Marines, forced Lili'uokalani to abdicate her throne. Over the next several years Hawaiians campaigned relentlessly to restore Native rule to the Islands, to no immediate avail. Iaukea continued his service to his people despite the U.S. territorial annexation of the Islands; he served as their territorial senator, yet also stood by Lili'uokalani as one of her most trusted advocates and confidants. By the end of his career he had held over forty appointed and elected positions in the service of Hawaiian people.[1]

As an elder statesman, then, Iaukea retained many poignant, personal memories of the most significant political events to take place in the Islands during his lifetime. Writing for a Honolulu newspaper in 1939, however, he recalled a moment not situated in the grandeur of Kalākaua's court, or in his decorations of service by the governments of France, Venezuela, Sweden, or Serbia, but, rather, a moment steeped in technocultural genesis.

> Another noteworthy incident of my school days was the arrival of a number of Portuguese to work on the Pioneer Sugar Plantation owned by Harry Turton and James Campbell. These laborers were said to be some of the shipwrecked crews of the Whaling fleet which ran afoul of the Confederate Cruiser "Shenandoah," up North during the Civil War then raging

> at the time (1865). Husky fellows they were; dark complexioned; and natives of the Azores, I've heard it said. They brought their steel-stringed guitars with them, the first of the kind we had seen. At night-fall when the day's work was o'er, they would gather at one of their camps and entertain the crowd that had gathered to enjoy the music and see how these steeled guitars were played. Needless to say, it took like wildfire. Even the dance halls which flourished in Lahaina at the time, caught the fever by hiring the Portuguese musicians to supply the music.[2]

This was not the first time that Hawaiians had seen guitars in the Islands. Guitars had arrived decades earlier, carried over gangplanks from ships docking in Honolulu's busy harbor. What differentiated these particular instruments was that they were strung with steel, not the gut typical for the standard, Spanish guitars built in the nineteenth century.[3] Though string composition could seem easily a forgettable detail, it stood out in Iaukea's memory, nearly seventy-five years after Confederate cannons splintered the wooden bowels of the whaling vessel that brought the first steel strings to the Islands.

Why were steel strings so integral to this late recollection of whaling incidents in the Islands, a year before his death? And what were these guitar-driven dances and commercial dance halls that "flourished in Lāhainā" and other Hawaiian towns in the 1860s? How, furthermore, did guitars take like "wildfire" in such seemingly remote Islands, where Hawaiians had only very recently established sustained contact with those who brought fretted instruments from afar?

Guitars have evoked powerful local and global feeling, particularly since they came of age in the nineteenth century. Their resonant hollow bodies generated significant volume in a world without electronic amplification, almost (but never quite) matching that of brass and reed instruments. As an accompanying instrument, they well suited the balladry popular in Western Europe and in Mexico, and featured a tonal range of nearly four octaves. Most important, however, they were portable, built of light woods; sailors could easily stow the instrument below decks, just as workers laboring in fields could carry them on their backs or rest them in the shade. By the mid-nineteenth century they were relatively inexpensive to build and, for all of these reasons, had become one of the favored instruments of traveling minstrels in Europe, Latin America, and the United States. The instrument, along with the banjo and fiddle, freed musicians from the encumbrance of heavy pianos; blackface minstrels dispersed them throughout the United States as minstrelsy quickly became the most popular form of American entertainment in their century, while sailors introduced guitars to harbors throughout the world. Rough-necked laborers favored guitars for their boisterousness and portability just as the affluent assigned the instrument a domesticating respectability in their parlors. Ever portable, increasingly affordable, and constitutive of different meanings across class lines, then, guitars seemed innately suited to a world of accelerated transience, reified difference, and burgeoning democracy—characteristics and contradictions that in many corners defined the modern world of the nineteenth century.

Guitars seemed perfectly positioned to illuminate the cultural politics springing from this emergent modernity in nineteenth-century Hawaiʻi, including its most menacing attributes. Guitars, this chapter will suggest, could represent many things. Upon their arrival in the hands of sailors and merchants in the first half of the century, guitars signified the increasing web of long-distance trade that further linked the Islands and continents. In the hands of disembarking Congregationalists from New England, guitars embodied the proselytization enterprise that enveloped the Islands beginning in 1820, as missionaries hoped to increase their flocks while thousands of Kānaka died of devastating continental diseases. Guitars, in the hands of Hawaiian musicians, also resonated in many of the same diplomatic moments and formal spaces of sovereignty that Curtis Iaukea personally inhabited within the Islands. Guitars, as we will see, also came to denote innovation within Hawaiians' expressive culture as powerfully as they signified steadfast tradition. Guitars could culturally embody a politically tragic invasion of the Islands, just as they could exemplify a rejection of that turn, as an incisive instrument of resistance. This chapter will demonstrate the dynamism in the Hawaiian Islands that prefigured the eventual development of the Hawaiian steel guitar in the 1880s and 1890s, and it will contextualize the emerging Hawaiian "guitar culture," then, that aliʻi nui and other Kānaka deployed to resist haole efforts to undermine the kingdom.

The guitar culture that came to reverberate throughout the archipelago during the mid- to late nineteenth century was wrought by the abrupt ascendance of Honolulu as the most significant crossroads in the Pacific. The natural harbor offered the only haven for deep-draft vessels in the central northern Pacific, but this characteristic meant little to Kānaka prior to the nineteenth century, as their shallow-draft boats routinely navigated the archipelago and traversed great distances to reach foreign islands with no need for such shelter.[4] In fact, according to a foreign observer, Honolulu comprised "not more than half a dozen" residences in 1803, and only grew when Kamehameha I established a temporary residency on the inner harbor from 1810 to 1812.[5] By 1820 at least one foreign vessel visited the harbor each week, however, and by the 1830s, as more and more ships entered the kingdom's waters, the harbor's waterfront population grew to nearly 9,000 residents.[6] The migration to the new urban trading center was fast; once the prevailing kapu, or social rules, were broken, Kānaka built their thatch houses in Honolulu, according to Gavan Daws, "with no real attempt at segregation by race, class, or caste."[7] The recently arrived makaʻāinana, or nonelite, producer-class Kānaka, often became immediate neighbors to aliʻi as well as foreign residents.[8]

Most of the foreign ships that filled the harbor in the early nineteenth century were those of British or American merchants, often on their way to or from China. However, Russian, French, and Spanish crews also docked in Honolulu harbor and, to a far lesser extent, in the ports of Lāhainā on Maui and Kealakekua Bay on Hawaiʻi.[9] Though his father had soon abandoned the "dingy noisy port" as a residence in 1812, ʻIolani Liholiho, or Kamehameha II, was eventually persuaded to reestablish the sovereign's residency in the town in 1821.[10] By 1825, Honolulu hosted four general stores with a combined annual trade of $100,000, as well as "two public houses for the accommodations of strangers."[11] "Greasy-food booths" and well over a dozen grog shops in Honolulu catered primarily to sailors by the 1820s, while aliʻi and makaʻāinana alike increasingly traded for tools and utensils as well as luxury goods.[12]

Work and trade with foreigners in Honolulu attracted many Kānaka from elsewhere on Oʻahu or from the other Islands, but foreign intrusions came at a staggering cost. Hawaiians migrated in increasing numbers to Honolulu at the same time that their overall population diminished at a catastrophic rate, primarily because of recently introduced diseases. According to one foreigner who visited the Islands in 1870, "I met an old man who told me he had lived at Kealakekua forty-five years, and that he himself remembered when there was a city of sixty-thousand inhabitants where to-day there are not one thousand."[13] Another remarked a few years later, "The empty seats in the Honolulu native churches give you notice of the great decrease in population since these were built."[14] Whether or not this observer was correct that disease rather than lack of interest explained the locals' absence from the pews, the devastation wrought by the 1853 Honolulu smallpox epidemic and others was agonizingly clear to the people who survived.[15] Yet Honolulu drew Kānaka in increasing numbers, as many adapted their skills to suit the harbor's trade economy. While the Hawaiian population throughout the Islands plunged from 100,000 to just over 50,000 between 1840 and 1872, their number in Honolulu rose during that time from 10,000 to 12,000.[16]

It is clear that the interest in one Honolulu trade good—Spanish guitars—blossomed quite quickly. What is less clear, however, despite an abundance of theories, is precisely when that interest began. In the 1830s American Indian and mestizo vaqueros arrived in Hawai'i from the Mexican state of California; hired by Kamehameha III, they worked to control the archipelago's cattle herds, which had overrun the island of Hawai'i in the years following 1793, when British naval explorer George Vancouver presented them as a gift to Kamehameha I.[17] A 1888 feature in the promotional periodical *Paradise of the Pacific* suggested that the guitar first arrived in the hands of these vaqueros, who then shared their knowledge of the instrument, along with that of cattle handling, to paniolos (the Hawaiian word for cowboys).[18] A paniolo tradition remains celebrated and strong in the Islands, as does a tradition of paniolo songs; yet whether or not vaqueros introduced guitars to the Islands remains speculation.[19]

Of course, it is also possible that Hawaiians discovered guitars even earlier; in 1818, eighty or so Hawaiians reportedly traveled to Monterey, California, at the behest of Kamehameha I, to support the navy of Rio de la Plata (Argentina). They could easily have encountered guitars in California, where guitars had been introduced by 1792 and quickly become popular.[20] Guitars likewise were not uncommon in New England in the early nineteenth century, so it is also possible that whaling crews or missionaries brought the instrument to the Islands by the 1820s.[21] Evidence can be found to support each of these scenarios, particularly within local oral tradition, while merchants provide us with the earliest written evidence of guitars. On June 6, 1840, Henry Paty and Company ran an advertisement in an island newspaper, the *Polynesian*, offering for sale not guitars but guitar *strings*, along with sets for the bass viol and violin.[22] Presumably these strings were made of gut, not the steel introduced, if Iaukea was correct, by waterlogged Portuguese who washed onto a Maui beach. Nevertheless, gut strings certainly did not foreclose the interests of the many who became entranced by their sound.

The guitar soon featured prominently in the sacred and secular spaces of wealth and status that served ali'i and hāole alike. Guitar performances in homes and in new, mission-organized schools for ali'i children grew with increasing frequency, and at times, renown.[23] Guitars, harps, accordions, and pianofortes populated the parlors of elite Honolulu homes by the 1850s.[24] Honolulu merchants soon offered guitars and lessons for sale. An 1872 edition of *Ka Nupepa Kuokoa*, a Hawaiian-language newspaper, featured an advertisement for buke hīmeni (hymnals) that included *Guitar without a Master*, a popular instructional manual for the instrument, first published in Boston in 1850, which included "fifty pieces of popular music."[25] By 1868, guitars were featured in Kawaiahaʻo Church, a congregation composed almost entirely of the most influential and powerful aliʻi in the Islands.[26]

The arrival of the guitar to Kawaiahaʻo offered a physical demonstration of an extraordinary reimagining of musical expressivity long under way in the Islands. Many Hawaiian mele composed in the mid- to late nineteenth century, for example, borrowed the compositional form and harmonic intervals of hīmeni, or hymns either translated or written in Hawaiian. Established in the 1830s, and soon the most prominent Native-member church on Oʻahu, Kawaiahaʻo became renowned for its choral groups and services in the Hawaiian language. While Hawaiians may have developed multiple-part singing before the arrival of Europeans, by the 1880s Hawaiian singing groups featured three- or four-part harmony vocals, akin to congregational singing; falsetto singing also increased in popularity among Hawaiians during this period.[27]

Compositional methods and practice also changed during this time. Many aliʻi nui were by the 1870s transcribing their musical compositions in European musical notation and their lyrics in Hawaiian. Transcriptions were not merely a royal affair, however; Kānaka were then among the most literate populations in the world, and it seems evident that not only aliʻi but also makaʻāinana transcribed mele lyrics, if not music, on their own. The practice of maintaining family books of mele was quite old and well established, for example, by the 1920s.[28] Mele lyrics were also routinely reproduced in Hawaiian-language newspapers in the second half of the nineteenth century, as editors used recently introduced printing presses to further distribute musical compositions.

Hawaiians also associated the guitar with foreign troubadours. The latter frequented Honolulu in increasing numbers, plying their trade in the town's new theaters, dance halls, and grog shops. Foreign entertainments became as commonplace as the foreign masts in Honolulu's harbor. According to one observer around 1857, "the charm shops and the dance houses are open every night, and the lights and sounds of revelry are incessant."[29] The town began to take shape in response to the entertainment district along the waterfront, while leisure hotels very slowly appeared in the Waikīkī district. In a demonstration of the increasing influence of haole missionaries and merchants in local affairs, the waterfront district's increasing draw for Hawaiians and foreign laborers prompted the passage of an 1848 ordinance banning the issuing of liquor licenses beyond the confines of its already busy streets.[30] Eventually the wealthier haole residents signaled surrender in this, one of their many "respectability" campaigns in the Islands, by moving to the outskirts of town. Although the waterfront catered to foreign sailors, Hawaiian men and women frequented the entertainment district as workers or patrons, and there they directly experienced guitar-driven hit parades of new songs and styles from the Pacific Rim and beyond.

The influence of these new musics grew so apparent that when Mark Twain visited the Islands in the 1860s, he derided the popularity among Hawaiians of U.S. hits such as "While We Were Marching through Georgia": "And now," he protested, "here at dead of night, at the very outpost and fag-end of the world, on a little rock in the middle of a limitless ocean, a pack of dark-skinned savages are trampling down the street singing it with a vim and an energy that makes my hair rise!—singing it in their own barbarous tongue!"[31] Twain's despair at Native peoples' multicultural fluency and *opinions* on American music paralleled a similar repugnance expressed by Calvinist missionaries for hula dances and the foreign "vices" introduced in Honolulu, including secular music, dances, theaters, and circuses. In these efforts, however, the missionaries were truly outmatched. Though they rightly recognized that secular entertainment could challenge their authority, they vastly underestimated its power.

Yet, how could the missionaries' influence have waned so quickly? After all, by the 1860s, nearly the entire surviving population of Hawaiians had affiliated with one denomination or another, whether Calvinist Protestant, Catholic, Mormon, or Anglican. During that decade, the American Board of Commissioners for Foreign Missions in Boston removed the funding of missions in the Islands from its priorities, essentially declaring that the missions' work in the Islands was "complete," a rousing "success."[32] Many missionaries thus had only recently believed that secular entertainments and other foreign immoralities could never make significant headway in the Islands.

However, as Lilikalā Kameʻeleihiwa, Jonathan Kay Kamakawiwoʻole Osorio, Hokulani K. Aikau, and other scholars have demonstrated, Hawaiian people affiliated with congregations in the early and mid-nineteenth century for a wide variety of reasons, most profoundly, perhaps, in reaction to witnessing thousands of people dying around them to previously unknown diseases, deaths they found themselves unable to stop or even slow. This mortality destabilized pono, a "a state of balance between numerous dualities" that otherwise organized life and made sense of the spiritual and material relationships between the ali'i and the makā'ainana.[33] "The great dying," wrote Osorio, "disrupted the faith that had held Hawaiian society together for centuries."[34] Perhaps, some believed, a new, Christian god could halt the dying; in the meantime, missionaries could at least provide them with supplies and medicines during a particularly horrific half-century of radical demographic, social, and familial change.[35] Christianity also seemed to thrive in the Islands in this period because it aligned in significant ways with long-standing Hawaiian practices. As Osorio reflected on Kame'eleihiwa's work, he wrote that Christianity was incorporated by the ali'i nui "into their own rule and into Native society at large through the institution of new kapu."[36] Kapu were guidelines, rules that established "the sacred distinctions between chiefs and people, and men and women."[37] Christian behavioral prohibitions, especially those of Calvinist theology, could represent a new set of kapu for people to interpret. Finally, many agreed to "affiliate" with a missionary simply to halt the unrelenting entreaties by competing missionaries to "convert."

In other words, Christian "conversion" for Hawaiians could mean just about anything, and although some began to echo the Calvinists' moral condemnations of hula and foreign entertainments, such protests typically fell on deaf ears.[38] The Calvinists' failure to control expressive culture in the Islands was amplified when they fell out of favor with the ali'i nui, such as Alexander Liholiho, crowned in 1854 as Kamehameha IV, who showed much antipathy for the Calvinist cause.[39] Liholiho and his wife, Queen Emma, instead affiliated with the Anglican Church, a political move that acknowledged both their diplomatic alignment with Great Britain and the relative Anglican tolerance of secular entertainments.[40] Indeed, it seems that Anglican, Mormon, and missionaries of other denominations exploited the widespread resentment of Calvinist moral dictates to their advantage in recruiting congregants, as they recognized the futility of efforts to quell Hawaiian expressive culture. Other ali'i nui such as Kamehameha V (Alexander Liholiho's brother) were inspired by the condescension they endured from Calvinist missionaries to lump all Americans together in their critique.[41]

As Hawaiians incorporated more and more elements from foreign secular entertainments into their daily lives, they eroded further the strength of the Calvinists in the Islands. In this, they often found allies among other hāole, who likewise had little interest in subscribing to Calvinist moral ideals. Foreign sailors in Hawai'i, in fact, had violated Calvinist moral dictates since before the missionaries arrived, distilling the rum locally known as ʻŌkolehao, or "iron bottom," since the turn of the nineteenth century. The liquor's damage among Kānaka and hāole alike was "incalculable," according to one contemporary, but numerous grog shops opened in the next two decades, with seventeen in Honolulu alone by 1822.[42] The taverns often doubled as or sat alongside dance halls that attracted male and female Hawaiians alike, whose "humbler orders," according to one foreign observer, amazed the hāole with their "grace and elegance." By the 1850s, he remarked, they had mastered "the most intricate quadrilles, foreign waltzes, mazurkas, [and] redowas."[43] Dance of all origins irritated missionaries to no end, but they never fully succeeded in banning either these dances or the hula, which in some forms even moved to the dance halls as a paid, secular entertainment for a foreign clientele.[44]

The success of many Hawaiian and foreign dance hall and tavern operators in pushing back against the Calvinists' moral directives cleared more room for the expansion, not only of public hula performances, albeit in a newly commodified form, but also of Euro-American theatrical performances in the Islands. Many early nineteenth-century aliʻi nui took great interest in Euro-American theater; in 1809, the first such theater in Honolulu, in fact, was constructed by James Beattie, a skilled Scottish sailor employed by Kamehameha I.[45] From that point forward, theaters in Honolulu featured integrated seating to accommodate both foreign and Hawaiian audiences. The successful run of the "Oahu Amateur Theatre," which opened in 1834, inspired both the creation of a thespian association in Honolulu, and also the efforts by Calvinists to condemn the theaters as "hale diablo," or the "devil's playhouse."[46] Such efforts notwithstanding, according to Gavan Daws, "by the [eighteen] sixties, all but the most intransigent in the mission community had conceded defeat on the question of the theater."[47] Kamehameha III turned theaters into royal tradition when he initiated the sovereigns' long-lasting patronage of musical and theatrical organizations.[48] He financed the creation of the Royal Hawaiian Band and in 1851 rechristened the Hawaiian Theatre as the Royal Hawaiian Theatre — a space that soon showcased all kinds of guitars.[49]

Indeed, guitar sounds filled the air in Honolulu theaters by the 1850s. Guitars were entrenched already in continental American entertainments through the rise in popularity of blackface minstrel troupes, but the instrument's portability helped make it a favorite among sailors and entertainers traveling abroad as well. The Gold Rush first attracted such East Coast entertainers to California as they sought to make their own riches from the legendary fortunes quickly accruing beyond the Rockies. However, as they saturated the enter-

FIGURE 1. *By the 1870s masts crowded the horizon over Honolulu Harbor. Spanish guitars and other stringed instruments brought to town by merchants, sailors, and imported labor were quickly embraced in the Islands. Courtesy of Hawaiian Historical Society.*

tainment market around San Francisco, some troupes searched for new, less competitive, yet accessible markets to exploit their talents. As Matthew Wittmann demonstrates, a Pacific entertainment circuit developed in response to these concerns, thus bringing the most popular U.S. entertainments to ports of call all over the Pacific, including Honolulu.[50] Guitars regularly featured in a wide variety of such fare: in 1879, for example, even a Royal Hawaiian Theatre performance that included Moses Keumi, "the Greatest Iron Jaw Man," holding a "trapeze and actors suspended from his mouth," featured songs with guitar accompaniment.[51] Likewise blackface minstrel troupes, sailing the world with guitars, banjos, mandolins, fiddles, and bones, entertained diasporic audiences of American and British sailors, merchants, and laborers in Cuba, Nigeria, Ghana, India, China, Indonesia, and Australia, as well as in Hawai'i. While scant evidence exists of Hawaiians donning blackface, their appropriation of minstrelsy instruments was immediate and profound.[52]

Just as guitars came to structure the new sounds of Hawaiian sacred and secular expressive culture in the mid-nineteenth century, they physically adapted to the unique preferences of Islander guitarists. Local guitar builders had experimented with native woods such as koa since at least the 1870s.[53] By

1893, C. L. Brito's guitar and repair shop on Nu'uanu Street was selling "guitars of all sizes," "made of Hawaiian woods."[54] Likewise, steel strings came to immediately shape the guitar's sounds and possibilities in the Islands, apparently well before they caught on in North America.[55] Not until the 1920s, in fact, did continental luthiers begin in earnest to construct guitars suited to handle the increased tension of steel strings.[56]

In the Islands, however, guitarists early embraced the new possibilities that steel strings offered. In 1883, for example, an unnamed guitarist in Honolulu's Symphony Club performed "beautiful bell-like tones" with steel strings tuned to an open E chord.[57] Betraying the club's elitism, the presumably haole observer lamented, "It did not however, seem to everyone that the music of the Future will meet with much success in Honolulu. . . . The audience was very small[,] which we think shows lack of sympathy with the Club . . . on the part of the public that is highly reprehensible."[58] If bell-tone harmonics and open tunings alone constituted the "music of the Future" in the Islands, however, then the club members would have nothing to fear. Hawaiians not only embraced these innovations, but they led the charge: harmonics and open tunings came to play integral roles in both kī hō'alu (slack key) and the kīkā kila.[59] Indeed, steel strings became essential to guitarists of all ranks in the Hawaiian Islands.

Guitars, then, were sold through merchants and demonstrated in multiple social contexts in the Islands from at least the 1840s, and their sounds soon reverberated in the parlors of ali'i, the halls of Honolulu churches, and the theaters, dance halls, and grog shops along the waterfront.[60] During the 1870s guitars proliferated dramatically in the archipelago, when scores of Madeirans, transported to the Islands by haole plantation owners seeking field labor, brought with them even more guitars and other Portuguese stringed instruments. Such instruments included the rajao and machete—instruments that would soon influence the creation of uniquely Hawaiian instruments such as the 'ukulele and taro-patch fiddle.[61] Madeiran luthiers, former field workers, opened their own cabinet and instrument shops in Honolulu's Chinatown district to cater to the increased trade in these instruments. By 1899, guitars sold in Honolulu for as little as $3.50, and for some time had been within the economic reach of laborers and, more easily, that of Hawaiian clerical workers and others in Honolulu's burgeoning professional class.[62] Hawaiian music was changing drastically as a result.

Guitars soon traveled beyond Honolulu and the plantation fields and into the most remote Island valleys. Eddie Kamae, a legendary 'ukulele player, enjoyed extensive conversations with Sam Liʻa Kalainaina, a fiddler who was born in Nāpōʻopoʻo on Hawaiʻi in 1881 and who grew up in the island's Waipiʻo Valley. As Kamae recalled, Kalainaina told him that when he was eight, around 1889,

> a band of roaming musicians came to Nāpōʻopoʻo, the way they used to do, riding down into the valley on horseback, going from place to place to serenade the country folks. There would be a uke, one or two guitars, with a fiddle usually playing lead. . . . So one of these serenading bands played outside Sam's house. When they started to ride away, he begged his father to ask them to stay and play a few more songs. The next day Sam went out into the forest and cut some bamboo and made himself a kind of fiddle so he could start playing. When I asked him what he used for strings, he told me No. 10 thread, with mango wax.[63]

Far from the harbors and labor camps, both homemade and store-bought guitars and other stringed instruments soon excited the senses of rural Hawaiians.

Similar to how men and women performed hula in the pre- and early European contact periods, both men and women, boys and girls, participated in the quickly thriving guitar culture. In fact, collections in the Hawaiʻi State Archives suggest that during the late nineteenth century, Native women were the most photographed guitarists in the Islands. Instruments chorded and firmly in hand, the women's assertiveness gleams through the paper. For example, two studio images in the collections prominently feature Emalia Kaihumua holding a guitar, while other women surround her with a taro-patch fiddle, ʻukulele, and drums (fig. 2). A price tag hangs from the headstock of Kaihumua's guitar, revealing it to be borrowed from a local merchant. With her left hand she frets what appear to be, if the guitar is in standard tuning, F (or perhaps C) and A7 chords.[64] "Sweet Emalia," as her friends and admirers often referred to her, also composed popular mele and was well known as a hula dancer, as she danced in Mōʻī Kālakaua's court.[65] These images, then, demonstrate the fluency of mele composers and hula dancers with guitars and other stringed instruments.

Another image features five women, a young child, and an older man. The man looks at an ipu gourd drum, while the child holds another drum on the ground (fig. 3). The woman in the center wears a grass skirt. Two women on each side flank her. They wear dresses that appear to be sewn from flags. Their skirts feature the stripes, presumably, of the Ka Hae Hawaiʻi, or Royal Hawaiian flag, while their blouses feature stars akin to those found on the U.S. flag.

FIGURE 2. *The celebrated composer, dancer, and instrumentalist "Sweet" Emalia Kaihumua is featured in the center with a guitar. Courtesy of Hawai'i State Archives.*

The meaning behind the convergence of national symbols is lost. Is it a celebration of union? Does it simply reflect the use of vibrant, repurposed fabrics for making dresses? Or is it a subversive, unrepentant celebration of the kingdom, following the overthrow? The photo is undated, with no information provided, yet the use of the Hawaiian flag certainly parallels a tremendous movement following the overthrow, when "Hawaiian women busied themselves making flag-patterned bed quilts while men fashioned shields of koa wood, painting them with the Hawaiian coat of arms surmounted by crossed Hawaiian flags in order to keep their beloved emblem constantly before their eyes."[66] Given that the photograph was probably taken in the 1890s, it is likely that the women were subversively using the dresses to show support for the Hawaiian royalty. One woman holds a 'ukulele, while another holds a Spanish

FIGURE 3.
The guitar and ipu drums reveal the hula kuʻi instrumentation quite common in the 1880s or 1890s, when this photograph likely was made. Four of the women appear to have made skirts from the fabric of the Ka Hae Hawaiʻi, or Royal Hawaiian flag. Courtesy of Hawaiʻi State Archives.

guitar and positions in her left hand a chord (a D7?), while her right hand rests in position to strum the strings. Her eyes fiercely address the camera's lens.[67]

The image reflects significant change occurring in the Islands. The drums and clothing suggest that the individuals are involved in hula, an activity disdained by the invasive Calvinist missionaries and, by the 1860s, legally banned. The hula never ceased, however. As we will see, members of the aliʻi nui, most famously David Kalākaua, encouraged the dance to counter American influence in the Islands. But the photograph suggests the complexities that greeted hula practitioners as well. We can only guess what to make of the four women's flag dresses. If the donning of the Ka Hae Hawaiʻi during this period of political instability, the 1880s and 1890s when the photograph was likely taken, suggests the women's resistance to U.S. intervention in Native Hawaiian self-rule, the stars on their blouses present another challenge. What should we make of the dresses that combine American stars with Hawaiian bars? Regardless of any political intent in the use of the flags, all of the women's clothing—their holokū and even the grass skirt—reflects the floor-length, conservative vestmental demands of the era's missionaries. The drums, however, suggest outright resistance to another missionary demand, the hula ban; the photographer, clearly aware of the controversy surrounding the hula, knowingly exploited in this photograph what had become a *defiant* practice.

Meanwhile, the stringed instruments—guitar and ʻukulele—demonstrate that the nature of hula itself changed in this period as well. Most likely, given the instrumentation and dress, these individuals performed hula kuʻi, a new hula genre, birthed in the 1880s, and defined specifically by its incorporation of Western stringed instruments into the accompaniment of Hawaiian mele. *Kuʻi* translates as "to join, stitch, sew," and in it women, here making their dresses by literally stitching together a symbolic convergence of Hawaiian and foreign flags, took a leading role in folding guitars into hula traditions, traditions that expanded at the same time that many hāole worked to destroy them.[68]

The emergence of a distinctive Hawaiian guitar culture was thus fully realized and palpable in all parts of the Islands by the 1880s, and this culture engaged men and women alike, in Honolulu and beyond. We can begin to see the outlines of the guitar culture's relationship to the vast political upheavals that also characterized the decade. During this period, foreign travelers nearly without fail remarked on the Hawaiian guitar-driven ensembles—string bands—that seemed to appear at every turn. We have seen how Kānaka quickly adopted the guitar, along with other foreign instruments, and immediately began to reimagine the sounds of their expressive culture. They selectively embraced some foreign songs, genres, and instruments while rejecting others; they developed particular tastes for the physical aspects of the instruments; and they found unique uses for guitar music in urban and rural, sacred and secular settings. But what, exactly, did Hawaiian guitar music sound like at this time? What made these string bands sound Hawaiian? And how did these sounds relate to the period's political turmoil, and to the monarchy's efforts to defend its sovereignty? Recordings do not exist, unfortunately, so in attempting to sketch answers to these questions we can rely on only a handful of written sources. In them we find the guitar figuring in a number of often competing cultural and political agendas. For the remainder of the chapter, we will consider these guitar sounds and associations in the years leading to the infamous 1887 "bayonet constitution," a pivotal moment in Hawaiian history that would set the stage for the illegal overthrow of the Hawaiian kingdom six years later.

Writing in 1886, European diplomat and musician Auguste Marques was intrigued by the development of a rather unique and localized style of playing the guitar:

> Hawaiians . . . are exceptionally fond of the guitar, and they play it as a solo instrument, with a tenderness, a softness which speaks well for the delicacy

FIGURE 4. *During the late nineteenth century women were photographed more frequently with guitars than men and seem to have quickly integrated the instrument into Hawai'i's rich musical culture. Courtesy of Hawai'i State Archives.*

of their feelings. They also extensively use the guitar to accompany their modern meles and even their hulas: of late they have taken to the banjo and to that hideous small Portuguese instrument now called taro patch fiddle. I suppose there are few native houses . . . in which a guitar of some kind cannot be found. They learn quickly to play on it, but generally restrain to six or eight chords or keys, and I believe they commonly adapt their melodies especially to an accompaniment in C major, in which they give important scope and display to the bass. Though not using much of the formerly unknown scale in upper voice parts, yet they seem to enjoy it to its full extent in the accompaniments. Thus, taking any of their simple melodies, and starting the guitar on the chord of C, after a bar or two, they run up the basses alone on C. D. E. F., and strike a few chords on that subdominant (or fourth, sixth, eighth); then run the scale back F. E. D. C., on which last

> they take a few chords of tonic, then the scale runs down C. B. A. G., this last bringing the dominant with its seventh, after which the bass returns in scale G. A. B. to the final tonic chord of C.[69]

Thanks to this intriguing and surprisingly detailed account, we can see that guitars saturated Native homes by 1886, and that guitarists were adapting mele melodies to these instruments with precision, if not ease. That it was possible for Marques to provide such a specific description in 1886 also indicates that the guitarists had already established widespread and recurrent motifs in their accompaniment, an accompaniment that seemed to support and abide by specific, though perhaps changing, rules related to mele. Finally, it is also useful to note that his description of bass run fingerpicking alludes to the development of the kī hōʻalu, or slack key, guitar style.

Guitars seemed quite versatile to Hawaiian musicians, who experimented with them in multiple contexts. Guitars inspired hula kuʻi, what Adria Imada describes as "literally a 'joined hula' of indigenous and Western performance vocabularies," and what early hula kuʻi dancer Kini Kapahukulaokamāmalu referred to simply as the "modern hula."[70] Hula kuʻi is characterized by its inclusion of stringed instruments, and both male and female hula kuʻi practitioners incorporated guitars with older instruments such as ipu or pahu in order to accompany their dance.[71] Guitars occasionally performed alongside nose flutes as well, and it seems possible that the guitar began to replace the pahu as the principal rhythmic instrument.[72]

Sonically, the rhythms of the chant tradition shaped the guitar techniques developed in the Islands. According to Elizabeth Tatar and John Berger, "Both the rhythms and the melody of slack key are distinctive because they clearly reflect traditional hula rhythms and the melodic ornamental and vocal qualities of the chanter."[73] In addition to producing rhythmic bass lines similar to that described by Marques, however, guitars became increasingly associated with melody as well. Hula kuʻi melodies, meanwhile, often combined older rhythms with newer, dominant-tonic harmonies easily accessible on the guitar and developed in tandem with the increased adoption of multiple-part harmonies in the Islands. While modern slack key guitarists often play the melody line throughout a verse, it seems that in the late nineteenth century, the guitarist played simple chords to accompany the singer's voice, then vamped short, "abbreviated motifs" of the melody at the end of verses.[74] Guitars, then, came to serve Hawaiian traditions of mele in quite a specific and deliberate manner.

Guitar innovations continued in the Islands, such as, presumably by the

1880s, Native Hawaiian experimentation with open guitar tunings. Typically this involved detuning or "slacking" the strings (hence the term "slack key") from the standard E-A-D-G-B-E tuning to one that formed open major triad chords. In particular, it seems that the earliest tunings involved a dominant-tonic relationship between the bass strings, such that a guitar player could form an animated rhythm between the I (tonic) and the V (dominant) note without fretting the bass strings. A popular example of this sort of tuning, from the biggest bass strings to the thinnest treble strings, was D-G-D-G-B-D, also called the "taro patch" tuning. By setting the guitar's open strings to produce a G major chord, this tuning would allow the player to create a bass rhythm by moving between the tonic (G) and the dominant (D) notes, and would free the player either to play the higher strings open, forming ornamental notes with the G major triad, or to fret these strings to tag the melody with ornamentals and vamps. It is unclear precisely how this open tuning method was established. It may have been developed independently, of course, but other likely scenarios exist. For example, it may have been influenced by the open banjo tunings, typically in G, that were popular among minstrel troupes. Or it may have been learned from foreign guitarists, or from the instruction manuals, featuring the tuning as an alternative, that often shipped with guitars or sold in music stores in the late nineteenth century. Finally, it may have been learned, as was common in the United States, as the "Spanish Fandango" tuning. Indeed, the D-G-D-G-B-D "Spanish Fandango" tuning was quite popular in the mid-nineteenth through early twentieth centuries in North America. Considered a novelty tuning, it was widely disseminated through sheet music to play the composition "Spanish Fandango," copyrighted in 1860 by an English-born guitar instructor living in Ohio named Henry Worrall.[75]

Regardless of the inspiration, guitarists soon began to create new open tunings, often guarding them within their ʻohana, or family, as a family secret.[76] As a result, while dozens and dozens of tunings have been documented over the last century, many more remain either protected from public knowledge or lost. As we will see, open tunings made the kīkā kila style possible, though it is unclear if the open tuning practice began first in the kī hōʻalu or in the kīkā kila tradition. Both kī hōʻalu and the kīkā kila depend on open tunings, however, and innovations wrought by Hawaiians in open guitar tunings contributed to the unique qualities of the styles in Hawaiian music as well as to the ascendancy of the guitar culture in the Islands.

In addition to introducing the guitar into mele hula, using it to help create hula kuʻi, and developing open tunings, musicians organized their string

FIGURE 5. *Students from the Kamehameha School for Girls, likely photographed in the mid-1890s. The image suggests the value of guitars as highly portable and appropriate for a wide variety of genres. Guitars seamlessly figured into practically every social occasion in the Islands. Photograph by Christian J. Hedemann, courtesy of Bishop Museum.*

bands into relatively small groups, facilitating travel. These ensembles of Native troubadours in guitar-driven string bands walked the streets and rural hillsides with their guitars in hand. Certainly influenced in whole or part by the nimble instrumentation of minstrel troupes, Portuguese bands, and the evolution of hula kuʻi instrumentation, this practice of "strolling" musicians, as it was known, reflected an Island tradition documented as far back as 1823.[77] In the 1890s one observer reported that "a large number of native Hawaiian organizations . . . go out in serenading parties. They play a combination of instruments, such as the guitar, mandolin, banjo, flute and violin. They play in parties of from five to ten."[78] Men and women, aliʻi and makaʻāinana, city dwellers and kuaʻāina (rural people), all seemed to revel in the guitar's accompaniment and portability. One observer reported in 1889, "I have seen women galloping along on horseback, riding astride, a guitar in their hands, and their gowns streaming in the wind like a banner."[79] Hawaiian towns bustled to the vibrations of steel strings, particularly Honolulu; as another observer put it, "You cannot pass along any street in Honolulu in the evening without hearing some musical instrument or music of some kind or another. . . . In fact there is music everywhere."[80] In 1885, Henri Berger surmised, "It is rather a hard task to write about music — hard to begin at the right place and hard to know where or when to stop. Music is music in Honolulu in so many different ways it is difficult to take a whole view."[81]

The musicians and the press often characterized such string bands, comprised of anywhere between four and twelve musicians, as either "glee clubs" or "orchestras." Glee clubs typically featured a chorus of voices with instrumental accompaniment and entertained both the aliʻi and the makaʻāinana. Prince Leleiōhoku, reported to be "an expert on the guitar," organized one of the earliest and most influential such guitar groups, the Kawaihau Glee Club, in 1876.[82] Leleiōhoku died the following year, but his brother, Mōʻī David Kalākaua, soon took up the directorship.[83]

The glee club tradition spread rapidly throughout the Islands. By 1888, for example, clubs performing regularly around Līhuʻe, Kauaʻi, included the Nawiliwili Club (featuring twelve members), Niumalu Club (ten members), Lihue Club (nine members) and Pualoke (a quartet club).[84] By the 1890s, Oʻahu residents were routinely entertained by variously named glee clubs, mandolin clubs, and zither and guitar clubs.[85] A resident recalled that during this period "Hawaii was the land of music. There was music in the valleys, on hillsides and everywhere. Glee clubs were organized all over the Islands."[86]

One the one hand, a haole observer could have read the appropriation of the guitar by Hawaiians as a clear example of the locals' enthusiasm for integrating foreign, Western customs into their cultural repertoire, a tendency that could be cited in support of the kingdom's overthrow and later "annexation" by the United States. In this interpretation, for example, haole elites would appreciate the guitar as an assimilative tool — and thus a victory — in their bringing of "civilization" to the Islands. Certainly such associations occurred, but interestingly, newspaper and literary accounts from the late nineteenth century rarely (if ever) painted them as instruments of assimilation; instead, they were cast as instruments demonstrating culturally unique, local, Native practices. In fact, such publications sometimes associated this indigenous guitar culture with

FIGURE 6. *This lineup of the Kamehameha Glee Club toured the Islands during the summer of 1897. Sam Nainoa sits in the center with a violin tucked under his arm. Nainoa's fiddle playing may have inspired his cousin Joseph Kekuku's development of the steel guitar. At least seven of the eleven students photographed here soon left the Islands to work in itinerant Hawaiian string bands. Used with permission from Kamehameha Schools.*

a perceived reluctance by Kānaka to give haole plantation owners the docile labor force they desired.

Docile labor, indeed, remained a primary concern for haole planters throughout the nineteenth century. In 1835—the beginning of haole sugarcane cultivation—William Hooper of Boston arranged to lease plantation lands on Kauaʻi from Kamehameha III.[87] Sugarcane cultivation required hard labor, and the first planters assumed that the makaʻāinana would cooperate in providing it. Makaʻāinana were long familiar with laboring for others, and even with paying taxes, as the preplantation economy rested on a system of tribute to their aliʻi. In the beginning, then, the plantation economy seemed to offer something to the maka'āinana, as Kamehameha III required that haole planters pay laborers fair wages as well as cover all of the taxes they owed their ali'i.[88] For his part, however, Hooper considered his plantation as not only a prime economic free-market venture but also an "entering wedge . . . [to] upset the whole system" of "chief labour," as he called it.[89] "Chief labour," he wrote in his diary, "if not broken up, will be an effectual preventative to the progress of civilization, industry and national prosperity."[90] Kānaka labor on his sugar plantations, he surmised, would ultimately "free" Hawaiians from the shackles of "savagery."

The argument, while most convenient and ubiquitous among Hooper's settler peers in colonial and slave society contexts throughout the world, of course remained mere self-justification for his abusive practices; indeed, paying men 12½ cents per day and women 6 cents per day, all in scrip for exchange at his plantation store, left the laborers quite unhappy, their demands for just treatment unanswered.[91] He soon resorted to referring to them derogatorily as children, "dull asses," and "Indians" in his diary.[92] His ill consideration of them only hardened after he observed their reluctance to slave in the fields under those conditions. According to Ronald Takaki, accounts from Hooper's diary in 1836 typically included lines such as, "The natives do but little when my back is turned," or "The native laborers need to be broken in [but] when that will be *I* can not tell."[93] As traveler James Jackson Jarves recounted of his visit to the plantation,

> With many the object is to work as little, and play as much, as they can. It is really amusing to a disinterested individual, to watch the shifts that they will make to deceive their employers. . . . If the overseer leaves for a moment, down they squat, out come the pipes, and the longest-winded fellow commences upon a yarn, a sort of improvisation, that keeps the others upon the broad grin. Their humor is indescribable, and, to ears polite, rather vulgar. Nothing escapes their attention; they will mimic the haole . . . and then as soon as he comes in sight, seize their spades, and commence laboring with an assiduity that baffles description, and perhaps all the while not strain a muscle.[94]

It seems as if Hawaiians learned to integrate colonial labor resistance strategies into their repertoire as easily and quickly as they did the guitar. The resistance to laboring for foreigners, along with massive mortality from disease, prompted hāole to import foreign labor in increasing numbers. This absence of willing local labor was only amplified when Hawaiians began to emigrate in search of more equitable working conditions than the Islands' increasingly dominant plantation economy afforded them. In 1850 Kamehameha III tried to stunt this exodus, and thus reduce the population decline, by banning emigration to California.[95] Haole planters, for their part, began recruiting staggered, ethnically defined waves of Chinese, Japanese, Portuguese, and Filipino workers to replace the diminishing Native labor force.

Despite the obvious reasons for the decline of the Native plantation labor force — disease, emigration, and dissatisfaction with plantation working conditions — haole elites often attributed the decline to what they considered the inherent laziness of the Hawaiian people. By the 1860s, haole newspapers consistently plied the stereotype of a Native penchant to idle his or her time away. An 1869 editorial in the *Pacific Commercial Advertiser*, for example, urged strict and immediate enforcement of vagrancy laws to control the Native labor force: "If only we could compel our idlers, loafers or vagrants . . . to work, for their own good, and for the good of the kingdom, we would at once have a supply of perhaps 5,000 able-bodied men and women."[96] Interestingly, haole newspaper editors and writers soon began to associate their anxieties regarding Native laziness with the rising popularity of the guitar.[97]

In 1899, for example, Professor Osmer Abbott, describing "the mental characteristics of the Hawaiian," said that "the most prominent mental and moral characteristics, or, at least, the one which first attracts the attention of the stranger, is laziness. . . . He is perfectly happy to lie on his back under a mango-tree and play on his guitar for days together. And this is not true of the youth only. The Hawaiian at every stage of life is able and perfectly willing to put in ten-tenths of his time resting."[98] Another observer in 1898 concurred: "The kanaka's energy reaches its climax in the evening when he strolls out in the moonlight with his guitar swung before him to serenade his dark-eyed beloved, dressed in a red holoku, as she leans from some balcony overhanging the street."[99]

Guitars were not the only targets for haole elites who wanted to keep Hawaiians in the fields. Hula dancing was banned, Noenoe Silva argues, for just this reason. She points out that hula was not actually prohibited in the Islands until 1859, after missionaries and their descendants had developed a discrete interest in the plantation economy.[100] By the 1850s, editorials in haole newspapers routinely decried the "worthless," "lazy" Hawaiian laborers, even after the 1850 "Act for the Government of Masters and Servants" authorized the arrest of anyone refusing to labor.[101] Concerned when the hula became "the resort of the idle and vicious," the editors of the *Pacific Commercial Advertiser* seemed tolerant of the dancing halls that entertained haole men on the waterfront, while they condemned the hālau hula (hula schools) that kept Hawaiian men and women, they believed, from laboring on plantations.[102] Meanwhile, a missionary association that petitioned Hawai'i's House of Representatives to ban the hula in 1858 principally argued not that the hula created sexual debauchery but that it caused Native people to neglect "all industrial and intellectual pursuits" and "lay waste their fields and gardens"; the hula, the petitioners wrote, "foster[ed] idleness, dissipation, and licentiousness."[103] Expressive culture, indeed, was firmly implicated in the politics of island labor, either, in the eyes of haole elites, as a cause of decreased profits, or as a means for Hawaiians to resist that very proletariatization of their communities into plantation labor forces.

Guitars, in fact, seemed rather quickly associated with young men disinterested in working in plantation fields, an association by no means limited to the Hawaiian Islands. During 1906 Senate hearings over the proposed Philippine Tariff Bill, George Bronson Rea complained that the Native laborer was in short supply in the Philippines, lamenting that "we have failed to budge him away from his guitar and his vino."[104] A 1904 editorial in the *Bonham (Texas) Herald* elaborates on the guitar and its association with a refusal to menially labor: titled, "A Lot of These Loafing Guitar Pickers Ought to Be Transformed into Active Cotton Pickers," the piece continues,

> Music not only hath charms to soothe the savage breast, but when it comes out of a guitar or mandolin it seems to soothe all desire for labor which the young negro who can pick these instruments may possibly have. The guitar comes from a lazy climate. In Spain, where they have never worked except in the olden time, and then only to conquer other countries and peoples, and in Mexico, where labor is a punishment, this particular musical instrument was ever in high favor. From its throbbing bosom come plaints and sobs of love. From it come no two-step, swinging march or jig. It is a lazy person's delight, and a bore to the man or woman of action. In the hands of a negro between 16 and 30, dressed in big-legged, striped pants, it lulls all desire to work. There is no law against the guitar. There is no law against the big-legged striped pants, and to say there should be would be going rather far. But when a man meets a negro of the age and dress mentioned, with a guitar swung across his shoulder, he need not tell him that he is giving a dollar a hundred to cotton pickers. For that trifling though interesting character is on his way to serenade a square meal from the pantry of the man whom his lady love is hired to cook or nurse for.[105]

Such associations of their instrument were nothing new for Hawaiians — much less to Filipino, Mexican, Portuguese, Spanish, or African American guitarists — and it seems that their critics were onto something, at least in the sense that these musicians were thrilled to escape the low wages and back-breaking, mundane work that otherwise awaited them. But to suggest a lack of enterprise by the guitarists was to grossly misread the significance of the instrument in their hands. The relationship between guitars and labor (including a resistance *from* agricultural labor) was quite strong, and it was never made clearer than when guitar players began to develop professional opportunities in the Islands. Native musicians, strolling from village to village as they advertised and profited from their talents, worked to enter the modern entertainment industry from the ground up.

In the 1880s, haole Honolulu boosters began to market Waikīkī in the tourist trades as the "Long Branch" or "Newport" of the Islands.[106] By the time the tourist economy began to generate revenue, the Islands' guitar culture was attracting hotel operators and tourists alike. While some musicians continued to serenade kuaʻāina in rural valleys for meals or supplemental income, or to busk on docks or in city streets, professional opportunities in hotels and restaurants generated an entirely new and independent economic path.[107] Hundreds of musicians and dancers in the Islands discovered in professional work an economic opportunity that did not bind them to overseers and to back-breaking labor. Nor did it require them to work for hāole.

Donning white pants and shirts, beautiful leis and red sashes and ties, singing a repertoire almost entirely in the Hawaiian language, Hawaiian string bands allured haole kamaʻāina, or Island residents, and tourists alike.[108] Certainly their exoticism in the eyes of hāole contributed to the glee clubs' ability to earn income, particularly from the earliest tourists to the Islands. The account of an 1887 performance at the Hawaiian Hotel provides a sense of the atmosphere:

> As usual, Mr. Bartlett, the manager of the Hawaiian Hotel, made every arrangement for the comfort and convenience of the guests and visitors . . . at the Quintette Club concert . . . last night. Chairs were provided on the balcony for those who preferred that position, and seats were arranged in the yard below for any who wished to remain there. The entire sitting accommodation was pretty well taken up soon after the music commenced. The walks had been sprinkled early in the evening, laying the dust and producing an agreeable coolness. . . . From the front of the Hotel, the view,

under the blaze of electricity, producing light and shade, was truly fairy-like. The shadows of the abundant foliage, particularly of the pepper tree leaves and of the cypress, with their sharp cut outlines, presented a stereoscopic effect, which was very remarkable and much admired. The Quintette Club, composed entirely of native Hawaiians, sang a variety of songs, principally Hawaiian, to guitar accompaniments, and the intervals between music were pleasantly devoted to social talk. Atmospheric conditions were favorable, and another of those delightful evenings such as can hardly be duplicated out of Honolulu was added to the experience of those present.[109]

The passage suggests that for hāole in the late 1880s, string bands had already seemed to melt into the environs of the lush hotels.

Given the pleasing atmosphere described in this account, it would seem incongruous that only three months later, haole elites would force David Kalākaua to sign a new constitution that stripped him of much of what remained of his authority, and disenfranchised the vast majority of Hawaiians. Yet this is exactly what happened, just as guitar music in the Islands reached new heights of popularity. Were these developments entirely independent of each other? If not, what sort of relationship existed between the emerging guitar culture and efforts to defend or destabilize Hawaiian sovereignty? We have already seen how guitars came to represent laziness in the eyes of some haole elites, or freedom from the plantation fields for Native guitarists, or tourist revenue from the perspective of hotel managers and guitarists alike. They came to represent something very different for the mōʻī, who faced increased assaults on their sovereignty, and who began to imagine a role for the guitar in defending Native rule.

The relationship between guitar music and the overthrow is best understood when we consider how the aliʻi nui experienced music in the nineteenth century. Beginning in 1839, many aliʻi nui, including future mōʻī and mōʻī wāhine—kings and queens, respectively—attended a missionary-operated boarding school in Honolulu, the Chiefs' Children's School, or Royal School, as it was known.[110] During the school's short existence, four future mōʻī and two future mōʻī wāhine—Alexander Liholiho, Lot Kapuāiwa, David Kalākaua, William Lunalilo, Emma Rooke, and Liliʻuokalani (then known as Lydia Liliʻu Loloku Walania Wewehi Kamakaʻeha)—attended the school, as did an heir to throne before he died from rheumatic fever, William Pitt Leleiōhoku.[111] They received a fairly extensive Western musical training at the Royal School, and many of them clearly applied this training to their mele compositions or guitar and other instrumental performances.[112] The students occasionally performed songs in public during the 1840s; in 1843, for example, they sang "The Restoration Anthem" after the kingdom was restored following the attempt of an "upstart" officer to claim it for the English crown.[113] Singing in English and Hawaiian, accompanying themselves on a variety of instruments, the young ali'i rapidly made music a central element in their lives.[114]

The archives do not indicate how and when guitars first came into the hands of the ali'i, though it seems that it quickly became a favored instrument. A notebook belonging to Kalākaua dated to 1860 features a song, presumably his own, that celebrates the sound of the instrument:

> Hone ana i ku'u Dreamings
> Ka leo o ke guitar
> Me ka sweet voice nahe-nahe.[115]

More glimpses of the guitar's popularity among the sovereigns surface in the 1870s: during a reception in Hilo in 1874, with the revelers in attendance singing throughout the evening, one observer reported that the newly crowned Kalākaua "brought out his guitar and sang a mele of his own composing, accompanied by the queen [Kapiolani] and his sister the princess Lydia [Lili'uokalani], who is a fine singer and a good performer on several musical instruments."[116] William Pitt Leleiōhoku developed great interest in the instrument before his early death.[117] George Kanahele speculated that "the ali'i could probably all play the guitar" by the 1870s or 1880s.[118]

In fact, according to a Mormon missionary, by 1875 twenty-year-old Leleiōhoku was an "expert on the guitar," demonstrated when he and the residents of the village of Lā'ie on O'ahu spent a Saturday night "in social conversation, singing, playing on musical instruments."[119] His expertise may have developed through competition with his siblings. Lili'uokalani wrote of the rivalry in her autobiography: "There were three separate clubs or musical circles engaged in friendly rivalry to outdo each other in poetry and song. These were the friends and associates of the prince regent [Leleiōhoku], those of the Princess Likelike, and my own friends and admirers. . . . The singing-club of the regent was far superior to any that we could organize; it consisted in a large degree of the very purest and sweetest male voices to be found amongst the native Hawaiians."[120] Of Leleiōhoku's glee club, Lili'uokalani recalled, "they were all fine singers; and these songs, in which our musical circles then excelled, are to be heard amongst our people to the present day."[121] Although her siblings also composed mele and hula ku'i, Lili'uokalani was the most prolific, publishing

FIGURE 7.
Well before she succeeded her brother David Kalākaua to the throne, Lili'uokalani developed a reputation as a fine mele composer, publishing over 100 of them during her lifetime. Sheet music for "Lili'uokalani's Prayer," circa 1895–1900. Photograph by Christine Takata, courtesy of Bishop Museum.

over 100 songs and writing perhaps several hundred more over the course of her lifetime.[122]

Indeed, their enduring musical legacy rested here, in their compositions, which would become standards, if not the majority of the performance repertoire, for Hawaiian guitarists over the coming years; these melodies would become anthems, the soundtrack for Native resistance to overthrow and annexation. For while glee clubs and orchestras occasionally performed imported English-language popular songs, or, more frequently, Hawaiian-language hīmeni, in the overthrow and annexation periods their programs typically, and often overwhelmingly, consisted of compositions crafted by mōʻī, mōʻī wāhine, and aliʻi nui, most of whom had attended the Royal School. Compositions by Kalākaua, Liliʻuokalani, Leleiōhoku, and Likelike became wildly popular; Hawaiian-language newspapers reprinted them and string bands performed them all over the Islands. Liliʻuokalani's compositions include the most famous of Hawaiian songs, "Aloha ʻOe" ("Farewell to Thee") and "He Mele Lāhui Hawaiʻi," the first anthem penned for the Hawaiian Kingdom. Popular favorites by Likelike include "Āinahau" and "Kuʻu Ipo I ka Heʻe Puʻe One," while Kalākaua penned the famous "Sweet Lei Lehua."[123] Their subject matter was vast, ranging from intimate love songs to exquisitely rendered descriptions of favorite places or geological features found in the Islands. Many of the songs featured hidden, or kaona, meanings, which eluded interpretation and defied literal translation but were known only to the composers and perhaps a few others.[124]

At times, however, they wrote much more overtly literal, formal political songs, such as Liliʻuokalani's first composition, "Onipaʻa" ("Stand Firm," 1864), a piece that urged support for Kamehameha V's new constitution, and the Hawaiian national anthem penned by Kalākaua, "Hawaiʻi Ponoi," which soon eclipsed an earlier anthem penned by Liliʻuokalani in popularity.[125] John Charlot and Elizabeth Buck have noted how, "in successive anthems by Lunalilo, Kalākaua, and Liliʻuokalani, increasing stress was placed on chief, land, and people."[126] Charlot notes that "Hawaiʻi Ponoi" asserts Hawaiian sovereignty in particularly significant ways:

> *Hawaiʻi Ponoi* expresses important themes of Kalākauaʻs thought and policy; a unified nation structured in descending ranks; an activist king in the Kamehameha I tradition; a racial emphasis. . . . Also discreet is the religious but non-Christian character of the anthem. All references to the Christian God are omitted. As a result, *Hawaiʻi Ponoi* seems completely nonreligious and entirely political. The politics of the anthem are, however, Hawaiian: based on traditional views of chiefs that cannot be separated from the indigenous religion. The original title of the anthem, *Hymn of Kamehameha I*, must be taken seriously. *Hawaiʻi Ponoi*, like so many post-contact works, seems designed to exploit the gap between Hawaiian and non-Hawaiian understanding.[127]

In addition to the royals' own compositions, mele inoa composed in their honor also circulated in ever greater numbers during this period, demonstrating a groundswell of support for the monarchy.

As the number and the popularity of such mele increased in the years leading up to the overthrow, the music became indubitably linked to the lives of the sovereigns and the love and welfare of the ʻāina (land) and lāhui, or citizens. Hawaiian sovereignty also became inseparable from the practice of Hawaiian music. The celebration of Hawaiian culture, in turn, came to coincide with public defenses of the Native Hawaiian aupuni, or government, and lāhui—which together translated into a defense of Hawaiian nationhood.[128] In this manner, the nation was conjured through compositions that often emanated from aliʻi nui who had become lovers of, if not experts on, the most popular of instruments in the Islands by the 1880s, the guitar. Perhaps in the right place at the right time, the instrument soon became the preferred messenger of these sovereign sounds. At no other point in the years before the overthrow was this more apparent than during Mōʻī David Kalākaua's reign.

David Kalākaua was crowned in 1874, after a contentious struggle with Emma Kalanikaumakaʻamano Kaleleonālani Naʻea Rooke to claim the throne. William Lunaliho had died of pulmonary tuberculosis in February of that year, just thirteen months after he had become mōʻī. He had assigned no heir to the throne.[129] He was the last mōʻī of the Kamehameha line, and his death prompted a struggle for the throne between Kalākaua and Queen Emma, as she was known, the widow of former mōʻī Alexander Liholiho. Kalākaua claimed victory, but at a cost—many of Queen Emma's supporters continued to question his legitimacy, and he had to rely on American guns and support to quell an uprising by her supporters after the legislature voted for his ascendancy.[130] In addition, although both had pledged not to cede any more ʻāina to hāole, Kalākaua signaled a willingness to sign a trade reciprocity treaty with the United States, which provided him with additional haole support during the election; he delivered on his promise in 1876, which merely fueled the fire of his Hawaiian antagonists. Partially as a result of the treaty, over the coming years Kalākaua faced dramatically escalating economic problems. The treaty gave U.S. interests and haole sugar planters an even greater share of power and profits in the Islands, such that by 1890 the U.S. market claimed 99 percent of Hawaiian exports and sugar production rose to a staggering near 250 million pounds per year. At the same time, the Hawaiian population continued to decline in number, while the haole and the Chinese, Japanese, and Portuguese laborer population continued to grow.[131] In 1876 the haole-owned *Pacific Commercial Advertiser* seemed to menacingly warn the Kānaka of what they had already begun to fear: "Should your people continue to decline, the consideration of Your Majesty as the chief of an independent tribe of people must in such event be so far diminished, that the present courtesy of foreign recognition will be withdrawn."[132]

With a significant portion of his constituency questioning his legitimacy as mōʻī and a haole population seeming to display daily contempt for Native rule, Kalākaua realized that he had to work diligently both to win over his detractors in the lāhui and to reaffirm to hāole the sovereignty of his people and the crown. Kalākaua responded on multiple fronts; he constructed the ʻIolani Palace to glorify the throne, and he organized the Board of Genealogy to establish his aliʻi nui bloodlines and demonstrate his legitimacy. But more significant, he celebrated Hawaiian performative traditions in a manner that had not been publicly witnessed since the 1820s. On February 12, 1883, he orchestrated his brilliant coronation ceremony, nine years after he ascended to the throne, with over 260 varieties of hula performances.[133] Opening the grounds of the palace to all Hawaiians, and relegating elite hāole to "less-favored seats," Kalākaua enabled a public celebration of a national Hawaiianness, of the lāhui, unlike anything seen before in the Islands.[134] The ceremony involved familiar combinations of Hawaiian and European traditions, hīmeni and symbols, while he also displayed powerful vestments that demarcated his sovereignty.[135] The string-laden sounds of hula kuʻi also reverberated through the palace grounds, in a coronation event that historian Jonathan Kay Kamakawiwoʻole Osorio argues affirmed for all "the *Hawaiianness* of this king."[136]

Indeed, by 1883, the guitars that accompanied hula kuʻi dancers had become as essential to Hawaiian music as ipu or pahi, performing music that advanced Hawaiian sovereignty. As Osorio puts it, "Hula was never just entertainment. It represented the very finest art of an ancient civilization and was itself political because many of the mele were praises of the aliʻi genealogies and their relationships to the akua. . . . As resistance it might not have had quite the thrill of a military engagement, but it would be difficult to find a more significant contribution by this king than the rehabilitation of the dance."[137] The ceremony assuaged most of the concerns of Hawaiians who had earlier voiced doubts about the mōʻī's legitimacy; soon after, Kalākaua had the "firm support" of the electorate and a "comfortable margin" in the legislature.[138] And the guitar, first introduced only a few decades before, riding a wave of foreign interventions in the Islands, had come full circle, taking its place as an instrument of Hawaiianness at a time of extreme political concern.

The coronation ceremony generated great enthusiasm among Hawaiians and tremendous uproar from many elite hāole, who considered Kalākaua's celebration of Hawaiian expressive culture, and the libidinous nature they associated with much, if not all of hula repertoire, as a direct threat to the previous sixty years of Calvinist missionary efforts. Haole resident William Castle filed charges for printing obscenity against the company that published the hula program in Hawaiian.[139] Among aspects identified as obscene were the hula kʻui performances.[140] The haole press used the opportunity to blast the sovereign. The *Saturday Press* warned, "We do but half disclose the awful blasphemy and the horrible filthiness of the actions and the language when we say that meles were sung deifying with rite of phallic worshiping in whose honor (?) these meles were composed, and glorifying him most of all by representations of vilest licentiousness."[141] Indeed, the hula performances, Osorio argues, "put the missionary families in their place."[142] In turn, the haole press lambasted Kalākaua for the ceremony, framing him as inept, barbaric, or both. Kalākaua certainly recognized the political volatility of the hula, particularly since, for decades, public hula performances had largely been circumscribed to secular entertainments for sailors along the wharf. While he clearly understood the repercussions of his ceremony—that the haole elite, according to Osorio, would come "away from the celebration with a renewed sense of opposition to Kalākaua and all of the Native traditions that he represented"—he seemed much more concerned, instead, with bolstering his support among Hawaiians.[143]

Kalākaua surrounded himself with guitars at the same time that haole elites stepped up their efforts to dilute his sovereign authority in the Islands. According to a 1909 report by ethnologist Nathaniel Emerson, in fact, hula kuʻi's "formal, public, appearance dates from the coronation ceremonies of the late King Kalākaua, 1883, when it filled an important place in the programme."[144] A dancer in Kalākaua's court, Kini Kapahu, actually claimed that he was the genre's inventor: she said that the king "took some steps out of the old-fashioned and put them into the modern [hula] with guitar. He was the first one to start this."[145] A traveling journalist reported in 1895 that it was Kalākaua who "encouraged the hula kuʻi," if not invented it.[146] Throughout his years as mōʻī, Kalākaua reveled in the guitar and ʻukulele, and maintained his own Hawaiian string band, his "singing boys," with whom he used to entertain foreign diplomats as well as his friends and fellow aliʻi. Robert Louis Stevenson and his family were close to Kalākaua in those years; Stevenson's stepdaughter Isobel Strong described the five-member group, ubiquitous performers for Kalākaua's social functions, as "the best singers and performers on the ukulele and guitar in the whole Islands."[147] The string band often accompanied female hula dancers, who, according to one witness, danced on these occasions "to the melody of murmuring guitars."[148] The band's instrumentation, comprised of guitars, accordion, a banjo, ʻukulele, fiddle, and bones, included instruments closely associated with the minstrel troupes that had performed in the Islands since the late 1840s. The band's repertoire, from what we can gather, consisted primarily of Hawaiian mele, and further buttressed the celebration of a discretely Hawaiian expressivity that had become integral to Kalākaua's political strategy and cultural investment.[149]

Meanwhile, beyond the confines of the palace and Healani—Kalākaua's beloved boathouse, where many such performances took place—hāole who had attained positions of governmental authority continued their efforts to suppress public hula performances, just as they worked to topple Native rule. As one scholar put it, "The 'anti-Hawaiian' forces . . . maintained an iron hand whenever possible when it came to the repression of the native culture."[150] One such "anti-Hawaiian" haole was Lorrin A. Thurston, the grandson of two of the first missionaries from the United States to proselytize in Hawaiʻi. In 1886, representing the "Missionary Party," Thurston joined the kingdom's legislature, where he could amplify his disdain for the monarchy and Kalākaua's efforts to assert Hawaiian sovereignty. In 1887, with the support of a haole paramilitary force and the most powerful haole business leaders in the Islands, he authored and forced Kalākaua to sign the infamous "bayonet constitution." The constitution stripped Kalākaua of much of his executive authority in the Islands, established extremely high poll taxes that disenfranchised most Hawaiians, and replaced Kalākaua's selected cabinet members with hāole sympathetic to Thurston's religious conservatism and goal of eventual U.S. annexation of the Islands. Accordingly, once he elevated himself to the cabinet position of Minister of the Interior, he immediately began to personally deny requests by Hawaiians to practice hula.[151] Thurston seemed particularly threatened by kuaʻāina hula practitioners because they challenged his political and cultural authority in the Islands; he expressed much less concern for the commercial hula performed for haole audiences in the harbor district. At this moment, however, Hawaiians throughout the Islands remained deeply invested in practicing their expressive traditions, both in support of their embattled mōʻī and in spite of the political chaos befalling them. One young guitarist in particular, living in Lāʻie, several miles to the north of the turmoil in Honolulu, was already developing an entirely new guitar technology. Building on the many innovations that already characterized Hawaiʻi's vibrant guitar culture, his technology would sound a new score for the coming political drama and eventually revolutionize the musics of Hawaiʻi, the United States, and beyond.

2 *Joseph Kekuku's Steel Guitar and the Era of Overthrow*

Fifteen-year-old Joseph Kekuku watched as his parents and four siblings waved goodbye from the steamer, which was slowly navigating its way out of Honolulu harbor. It was the spring of 1889, two years after David Kalākaua was forced to sign the "bayonet constitution," diminishing his political power, and less than four years before the overthrow of Native rule demanded by American entrepreneurs and enforced by U.S. Marines. On this day, however, Joseph's family was leaving him and their home in Lāʻie, Oʻahu, the village to which Mormon missionaries had dedicated their most fervent economic and proselytizing efforts in the Islands. It was never clearer to Joseph, as the ship inched its way through the dozens of masts and smokestacks of foreign vessels far from home, that the missionaries had succeeded to quite dramatic effect with his family: they were leaving him, and leaving the Hawaiian Kingdom, to begin a new life in their Zion of Salt Lake City.

When the church leadership called for Hawaiian Mormons to abandon Lāʻie for the glorious future that Utah promised them, Joseph's parents, Miliama Kaopua and Joseph Kekukuʻupenakanaʻiaupuniokamehameha Apuakehau, volunteered to make the initial voyage. They were assured, like all of the Kānaka in the congregation, that they would arrive in a utopia of little sickness, bountiful harvests, and good neighbors — Mormon neighbors — who would encourage their works of faith as they made Salt Lake City their home. Such fortune, however, eluded them. Upon their arrival they and their forty-five companions from Lāʻie instead faced intense discrimination by their Mormon brethren. The Utah Mormons repeatedly denied them service and employment opportunities, and otherwise made them feel intensely unwelcome. Sensing that the Hawaiians would never be accepted in the Mormon zenith, their missionary sponsors decided to lead them three days outside of town to a desolate desert landscape known by the whites as Skull Valley, and by Utah's Goshute Indians as occupied homelands. There, they built an ill-fated settlement, a Hawaiian town they would name Iosepa.

In leaving young Joe Kekuku behind, however, his family inadvertently facilitated the development of a guitar technology that in one generation would transform vernacular and popular music traditions not simply in the archipelago but throughout the globe. Building on the Islands' pulsating guitar culture, Kekuku's kīkā kila, or Hawaiian steel guitar, catalyzed Hawaiians to expand and disseminate their musical practices at a critical juncture, when the assaults of colonialism — including intensive missionary efforts, the separation of Hawaiians from their lands, and sweeping attacks on their culture, would rise to a crescendo during the overthrow of Native rule.

Chapter 1 provided a "prehistory" of the kīkā kila, the introduction of the six-string Spanish guitar to the Islands, and the meaningful ways musical practice, along with its social and political significance, changed in the decades preceding the kingdom's overthrow. Despite the effort to ban hula performances, and the rapid expansion of English literacy and haole missionary efforts in the Islands, most continued to express themselves musically through forms rooted in the Hawaiian language, and in the older Hawaiian chanting and singing structures of mele oli and mele hula. Yet by the late 1880s, this music also conjured an expansive, international variety of sounds and styles. Guitars assimilated into this music; hula ku'i in fact was specifically tailored to the guitar and related stringed instruments. Guitars, likewise, had come to play a celebrated and fundamental role in the orchestras, glee clubs, and other Native troupes that performed not only in hotels and dance halls along Honolulu harbor but also for events sponsored by Hawaiian ali'i nui, as well as for gatherings of maka'āinana throughout the countryside. The guitar gathered prominence in public Hawaiian gatherings just as elite hāole increased pressure for Kalākaua and his successor, Lili'uokalani, to relinquish their sovereign powers. As the political turmoil increased, so did the array of musical innovations in the Islands: in addition to the development of hula ku'i, falsetto yodeling — now considered a core element in Hawaiian music — also began to flourish. The 'ukulele became a favored instrument alongside the guitar at this time, as did the taro-patch fiddle. None of these developments changed musical practice around the world, however, like Kekuku's Hawaiian steel guitar.

This chapter will examine the relationship between the genesis of the kīkā kila, on the one hand, and the climate of political havoc in which it was created, on the other. We will follow Joseph Kekuku's 'ohana to Utah, as well as ponder his determination to remain on O'ahu. We will deliberate upon the many origin stories surrounding his development of the instrument and the disputes surrounding its inspiration. We will consider Kekuku's locally influential and politically active household, a strong royalist family that, like the vast majority of Hawaiians, protested the illegal overthrow of Lili'uokalani's rule in 1893. We will investigate how Kekuku and his fellow musicians used musical practice to respond to the overthrow and the cultural restrictions that it threatened to impose, and to the looming threat of U.S. annexation. In consequence, finally, we will watch Kekuku set sail for San Francisco with his steel guitar in hand—leaving the Islands, as it turns out, never to return. It is impossible to understand Joseph Kekuku's story, however, without first considering the relationship of his ʻohana to the land.[1]

Since before the arrival of haole influence in the Islands, Hawaiian cosmology considered both the kalo, or taro plant, and the ʻāina, or land, as the people's older siblings.[2] Kānaka were responsible for caring for these elders, who would in turn nourish them.[3] By the turn of the nineteenth century, in contrast to the concept of private landownership later introduced by hāole, Hawaiians recognized shared land use rights in the Islands. Though during this time the system varied from island to island, generally speaking the aliʻi nui had divided the lands into districts called moku, which then were subdivided into smaller sections called ahupuaʻa. Carlos Andrade wrote that "an ideal ahupuaʻa extended from the cool, moist uplands, down across the alluvial and coastal plains, out in to ocean waters, encompassing fringing reefs and sand-bordered bays. . . . Ahupuaʻa life was distinguished by shared use of land and resources, regulated jointly by konohiki (head administrators) and makaʻāinana. . . . The resulting system included kapu, unwritten rules governing the behavior of people."[4] The konohiki were appointed by the aliʻi and enjoyed the social prestige, but they also worked on behalf of the makaʻāinana to "create order, encourage peace, and support prosperity."[5]

Between 1845 and 1855, however, a series of legislative acts privatized and divided the ʻāina as hāole established land claims of their own. Specifically the Māhele, or division, of 1848 and the Kuleana Act of 1850 reformed land tenure by establishing a system in which Hawaiian lands were assigned in fee simple title.[6] As a result, the relationship of the aliʻi and the makaʻāinana to one another and to the ʻāina changed dramatically: the aliʻi assumed fee simple ownership of the ahupuaʻa, while the makaʻāinana were to claim use rights within the ahupuaʻa for kuleana, which in this usage meant homestead lots.[7] The Islands' remaining, "undeveloped" lands, then, were divided into three parts, with one-third going to the mōʻī, one-third to aliʻi nui to manage as "absentee landlords," and one-third to an administrative government crafted and now dominated by hāole.[8] Recent scholarship has supported the theory that Kauikeaouli (Kamehameha III, the mōʻī at the time of the Māhele) strategically facilitated the passage of the legislation because, after the arrival of the Americans, he considered it the best option for protecting the claims of all Kānaka to the ʻāina.[9] Unfortunately, however, most of the mōʻī and aliʻi nui eventually lost their lands through mortgages, typically to developers or speculators. The results for the lāhui were disastrous: by 1893, hāole claimed the legal ownership of roughly 90 percent of the ʻāina.[10]

So what does this "Great Māhele," as this loss of land became known, have to do with Joseph Kekuku? Despite the Māhele legislation's eventual extrication of Kānaka from the ʻāina, Robert Stauffer argues, not only did many Hawaiians maintain their kuleana over the generation following the Māhele, but they also devised sophisticated strategies to hold onto these homesteads for decades to follow.[11] In this regard, in the Kahana ahupuaʻa, Kekuku's family played a prominent role. His family's history speaks directly to the massive shifts in land use, land claims, and status that occurred during the ensuing development of the guitar culture and the kīkā kila, and their efforts likewise demonstrate their commitment to the lāhui.

Joseph Kekuku (1874–1932) was born on the windward side of Oʻahu, in the Kahana ahupuaʻa, which lies along the southern border of the kingdom's district of Koʻolau Loa.[12] Kahana is a classic ahupuaʻa, in that it begins at the edge of the Koʻolau Mountains and extends, along the deep Kahana River valley and its adjoining Kahana and Kawa streams, until it surrounds and nearly encloses Kahana Bay. The bay features the 400- to 600-year-old Huilua Fish Pond on its easternmost edge, and a beach that today is lined with ironwood trees. The ahupuaʻa lies about twenty-five miles by road from Honolulu, and ten miles south of Lāʻie.

Throughout the nineteenth century, the people of Kahana predominantly raised taro, but they also grew a variety of other foods, including ʻawa (kava, in the 1870s a cash crop used in multiple products, among them a mildly narcotic drink), beans, bananas, potatoes, oranges, and wauke (a paper mulberry plant used for making cloth called kapa), while others raised fish in their loʻi, or irrigated gardens.[13] While their harvests were diverse and bountiful, the people of Kahana had experienced horrific population decline, from about 700 inhabitants in 1778 to perhaps 125 by 1850.[14]

On August 27, 1850, as part of the Great Māhele, the high aliʻi Keohokālole gained title, as konohiki, to the over 5,000 acres of land that comprised Kahana.[15] In May 1857, she sold Kahana to AhSing, a Pākē (Chinese) merchant living in Honolulu.[16] A Pākē presence in Hawaiʻi was not unusual in the mid-nineteenth century, when large numbers of Chinese planters and merchants, but more often laborers, moved to the Islands to clear taro patches and replace them with rice fields. Both Pākē planters and immigrant laborers readily married wāhine (female Kānaka), and by 1882, nearly a quarter of the Hawaiian Kingdom's population was of Pākē descent.[17] Pākē planters and merchants like AhSing often employed Native laborers to work the rice fields, including the owners of the fields that the Pākē rented.[18] AhSing remained in Honolulu after the sale, however, and became the absentee landlord of Kahana, taking a similar role, in some ways, to that of konohiki, as did Ahchuck, the individual who purchased the title in 1868 from AhSing and his wife, Mele (who was presumably Hawaiian).[19] Four years later, the Kahana ahupua'a was sold to H. Ahmee, a successful Pākē rice planter who lived in Ko'olau Loa with his common-law wife, Miliama Kaopua (1857–1919).[20]

Miliama "Miriam" Kaopua was born on the island of Hawai'i in Pā'auhau, a community located along the Hāmākua Coast.[21] By the time she was fifteen or sixteen, however, she was living with Ahmee at Kahana, on O'ahu.[22] According to an oral testimony by Miriam, recorded in 1916, Ahmee was "the owner of the land then, a rice planter." She continued, "We lived at Kahana until the land of Kahana was sold . . . [in 1874 or 1875] because of the desire of my husband to return to China. . . . I was well acquainted with all the people . . . living at Kahana [at] that time, because my husband with whom I was living then[,] being Ahmi[,] was the master over the people."[23] Miriam's language in speaking of her husband suggests a common understanding of these Pākē landowners as maintaining a new sort of konohiki role. We know little about their union, but we do know that when Ahmee returned to China, Miriam and her family not only remained on O'ahu but helped facilitate the sale of his lands to the Kahana Hui, a collective of maka'āinana and ali'i determined to "buy back" the Kahana ahupua'a from foreign ownership, to restore the lands to their collective use.[24] Before Ahmee left the Islands, however, it seems that Miriam became pregnant; in December 1874 she bore a son, presumably the son of Ahmee. The child would become known as Joseph Kekuku, the principal architect of the Hawaiian steel guitar.

I say "presumably" and "would become" because the identity of Joseph's biological father remains somewhat unsettled. Most family histories and written sources seem to suggest, however, that Ahmee was Joseph's biological father, and that Miriam's second husband, Joseph Kekuku'upenakana'iaupuniokamehameha Apuakehau (1857–1936), adopted him as an infant.[25] The Apuakehau family was ali'i; Joseph K. Apuakehau's maternal grandfather was Peni Keliiwaiwaiole (1801–75), who, after graduating from the Lahainaluna

FIGURE 8. *Miliama Kaopua and Joseph Kekuku'upenakana'iaupuniokamehameha Apuakehau, Joseph Kekuku's mother and adoptive father, in Lā'ie. Courtesy of the Walter K. Wong 'Ohana.*

Protestant Seminary on Maui in the 1830s, went on to serve as district magistrate and konohiki of Lā'ie during the Great Māhele, for a total of thirty-seven years.[26] Keliiwaiwaiole's loyalty to the king, along with that of the other Lā'ie residents, led them to resist the entire process: they did not understand why they should file for individual claims to the king's land, when the king already provided "all they needed in house lots, taro, and potato patches, fish, other foods and material needs."[27] Only at the last minute did Keliiwaiwaiole submit a personal claim for land; because of his status as konohiki, he was awarded nearly five acres of Lā'ie, more than any other claimant.[28]

Joseph K. Apuakehau followed in his grandfather's footsteps by attending the Lahainaluna Seminary between 1873 and 1876; he likely married Miriam during this period or shortly after his return to Lā'ie in 1876.[29] According to family history, Apuakehau maintained his family's ali'i status in Lā'ie, where he was born. This is perhaps reflected in the 1900 U.S. Census, where he is identified as one of a handful of people in the district of Ko'olau Loa who owned a house that census takers considered substantial enough to note.[30] Apuakehau's work in the Koʻolau Loa district, however, suggests for us that after the overthrow, status could also translate into assuming important clerical and bureaucratic functions of the Americans' Provisional Government (PG) and, later, territorial government. Apuakehau, for example, served as the deputy tax assessor for the district of Koʻolau Loa, a function he performed for many years; he also granted marriage licenses in Lāʻie, a job that his daughter Violet assumed after he retired; in addition, he served as a luna, or foreman, at the Kahuku plantation, about five miles from Lāʻie.[31] He also planted taro for the duration of his life, maintaining his relationship to his kalo and ʻāina elders.[32] He and his family resided on the Apuakehau family kuleana in Lāʻie, where they and their descendants operated a store for over seventy years, and where five homes remain in the family today.[33] He outlived his wife, Miriam, by seventeen years and his (adopted) son Joseph Kekuku by four.[34]

Joseph Kekuku, then, came from families with strong ties to the ʻāina, and to aliʻi. At the same time, his family became deeply involved with the Church of Jesus Christ of Latter-Day Saints (LDS). The Apuakehau family, like most Hawaiians in Lāʻie, joined the church after it acquired 6,000 acres of the Lāʻie ahupuaʻa in 1865.[35] With Lāʻie, Mormon missionaries finally established a firm beachhead in the Islands.[36] Joseph Kekuku's mother came to Lāʻie after her first husband departed, and shortly after Joseph Kekuku was born. The family quickly became a fixture in the LDS congregation, with Miriam and her daughters regularly singing solos in the choir.[37] It is important for Kekuku's story to note, however, that the impact of the LDS presence at Lāʻie is complex, particularly in regard to the maintenance of cultural traditions. According to scholar Hokulani Aikau, "For Native Hawaiians, [Lāʻie] was a place of refuge in the aftermath of the political storm we now call the Māhele. . . . It . . . became a site where many Native Hawaiians could revive their cultural relationship to the land and to the sea."[38] Native Hawaiians found shelter at Lāʻie to maintain their taro patches and older, communal forms of social organization, just as the Māhele was privatizing and dismembering one ahupuaʻa after another.

For one thing, the LDS missionaries at Lāʻie seemed much less concerned with suppressing Native music, language, and other cultural traditions than were missionaries of other denominations.[39] Facing what they considered their own persecution in the United States, perhaps the missionaries were more cautious when addressing the local Hawaiian traditions.[40] Moreover, they certainly observed the hostility of many Hawaiians—potential converts—to Calvinist efforts to disrupt hula and other integral aspects of cultural life. The LDS in fact, would begin not only to support local traditions but also to exploit them for profit, as when the church opened the Polynesian Cultural Center at Lāʻie in 1963. The center, which showcases hula dances and hosts luaus for tourists bused in daily from Waikīkī, remains one of the largest tourist draws in the entire archipelago.[41]

Indeed, Calvinists in Honolulu were equally appalled by both the celebration of Hawaiian musical traditions in Lāʻie and the resultant inroads that tolerance created for the Mormon missionaries. The editor of the Protestant Hawaiian-language newspaper *Ka Nupepa Kuokoa* proclaimed in 1871, "There is no righteousness in that sect for one of the chief activities of the Mormons at Salt Lake City and in Lāʻie is dancing. . . . In the month of August they had a feast which was attended by a multitude and the main occupation all through the night was hula dancing. Great indeed are the mistakes and errors of the Mormons! Do they not know that the hula belongs to the Devil's choir?"[42] When Kalākaua was crowned in 1874, he found an unlikely ally in the Mormons, who seemed to embrace rather than shun mele hula and mele oli. The people of Lāʻie embraced the guitar as well, as when Prince Leleiōhoku regaled a crowd there with one in 1876, shortly after Joseph Kekuku was born.[43] By the 1890s, if not sooner, violins, mandolins, and guitars had become fixtures in Lāʻie, even in LDS functions.[44]

Residents valued their relative cultural autonomy at Lāʻie, including the opportunity for families to maintain traditional taro and ʻawa fields in the Lāʻie ahupuaʻa, particularly as sugar plantations increasingly displaced such fields elsewhere in the Islands.[45] In 1889, however, Joseph K. Apuakehau and Miriam were among the first to volunteer their family for a mass relocation of over forty Lāʻie and Kahana residents to Salt Lake City.[46] It is difficult to determine with certainty what prompted the migration, but Lāʻie and Iosepa scholar Matthew Kester speculates that the 1887 "bayonet constitution," signed under duress by Kalākaua, "was the spark that ignited the flood of emigrants from Hawaiʻi to Utah between 1888 and 1889."[47] The constitution eased emigration restrictions at the same time that it disenfranchised many Kanaka Mormons. A combination of those factors likely generated the exodus from their homelands. Apuakehau might have owned enough land to maintain his voting rights, but the experience of Hawaiians in the late 1880s would have made it easy to predict a future of increasing mortality rates, land loss, and erosion of their kingdom's sovereignty as hāole tightened their grip on the Islands' governing, social, and economic institutions.

While the specific motive remains unclear, in April 1889, the Apuakehau family, now most often referred to as the Kekukus—Joseph; Miriam (or Miliama); daughters Hattie, Ivy, and Viola; and son Edwin—left Lāʻie for Salt Lake City.[48] Their degree of eagerness to depart is unclear, as are their expectations, but what they encountered in Salt Lake City did not suit them.[49] Within weeks of their arrival, the Supreme Court of the Territory of Utah determined that based on their race as "Hawaiians," they were ineligible to become U.S. citizens.[50] By then, however, the court's decree would not have surprised the recent arrivals from Lāʻie, for everywhere they turned in Salt Lake City, they were met with discrimination. They were refused work or, when they found it, were relegated to "manual labor and seasonal unemployment."[51] According to an observer, the court decision rendering Hawaiians ineligible for U.S. citizenship also "greatly depreciate[d] their political value to the Mormons."[52] When the case was decided, neither Hawaiian nor haole Mormons in Utah saw any viable options that would allow them to remain as a community in Salt Lake City. A church committee instead decided, two months later, to march the Hawaiian Saints out of Salt Lake City, on the three-day trek to Skull Valley.[53]

Joseph Kekuku's father and his family tried their best to succeed at Iosepa. Miriam accepted the role as counselor for the town's Young Ladies Mutual Improvement Association, while Joseph toiled for the Iosepa Company for a promise of thirty dollars per month. The church created the Iosepa Company in order to organize the new town's labor force. According to the senior Kekuku, however, "he never received any money during all this time. He was charged $4.00 for 100 lbs. of flour, eight and ten cents per pound for beef, twelve and one-half cents for mutton, seventy-five cents per bushel for potatoes, $2.50 per pair for shoes and from $5.00 to $7.00 per pair for boots." After eight months of working in Iosepa for no pay, the family returned to Salt Lake City, where Joseph found a job mixing mortar for $2.75 per day.[54] There he reported to an observer that "he left Skull Valley because he could get no money, and as he said 'no like stay,' and is anxious to go back to the Islands."[55] In addition to the lack of jobs and the unethical prices at the company store, family oral history also holds that the Kekukus felt brutalized by the weather in Skull Valley, particularly the freezing winter.[56] Fortunately, they had not relinquished their kuleana in Lāʻie, so when they finally came home, most likely in early 1891, they could return to their homesteads.[57]

During this period their son Joseph Kekuku enrolled at the newly established Kamehameha School for Boys in Honolulu. The trustees of the estate of Bernice Pauahi Bishop, a great granddaughter of Kamehameha I, had established the school two years before to train "good and industrious young men" in trades or other avenues of manual and clerical work.[58] As Catherine Szego describes it, "the vocational, industrial form given to boys' education was, by 1888, also modestly cast in the image of militarism: in that year, students were organized into companies, officered, and uniformed. As explained in an 1894 announcement of the *Handicraft*, the school's first serial publication, 'the military system is in modified use embracing in its benefits personal responsibility of officers, inspection of room and person, punctuality, bearing, and conduct.'"[59] The school in many ways resembled federal Indian boarding schools in the United States: assuming that Native boys lacked discipline, bearing, and employability, the school's strict regimen was designed to develop these attributes for them.

Bishop had envisioned that the boys' and girls' schools would serve children of Hawaiian ancestry; she also directed that the school particularly support orphaned or indigent children.[60] It is unclear under what conditions Kekuku applied to enroll in the school, as a youth who had stayed behind when his parents and siblings emigrated to Utah, as the son of an ali'i family (through his adoptive father), or both. The school today continues to enjoy a reputation as an elite institution. However Kekuku presented his case to the administrators, his family's departure and his subsequent enrollment in the school, as we will see, became essential to the development of the Hawaiian steel guitar.

The concept of the kīkā kila involves both a physical alteration of the Spanish, or standard, guitar, and a significant modification in how one creates tones and adjusts string pitch. As the guitar is traditionally played, a player generates tones by plucking strings depressed behind the frets (unless he or she is playing open strings). As the player plucks different single strings or combinations of strings depressed at different locations on the fretboard, the guitar produces a variety of single notes or chords. In contrast, the kīkā kila player produces tones by running a steel object along the strings and over the frets, without touching the fretboard.

Of course, objects have been moved along strings to change their pitch on instruments around the world for centuries. In that sense, it might seem a fool's errand to attempt to pinpoint the first time that someone casually glided something over the strings of a guitar. What is interesting about the history of the Hawaiian steel guitar, however, is that over the years significant effort has been expended to determine precisely whose hands were responsible for that moment.

Soon after the Hawaiian steel guitar attracted global attention in the early 1900s, many began to ask—and answer—the question of who first developed the instrument. Throughout his career, Joseph Kekuku claimed to have invented the technique. His promotional advertisements celebrated his invention; musicologists corroborated it; fellow Hawaiian (and non-Hawaiian) musicians unfailingly venerated him because of it, leaving us with a variety of oral histories that attest to his work. His role as the principal developer of the Hawaiian steel guitar, in fact, was never in dispute during his lifetime, nor have any credible theories to the contrary emerged since then. The questions that remain center not on his role in developing and refining the technique's practical application on the guitar, a process that he estimated took seven years to perfect; instead, the questions center on his inspiration.

On this matter, accounts diverge wildly. One story, attributed to a musical peer of Kekuku's named Mekia Kealakaʻi, claims that German sailors, who sailed into Honolulu harbor in 1882, "made up a bass violin out of a cracker box and a bass drum from an empty salmon barrel, and a narrow long box strung with two steel wires and a metal belaying pin run up and down and the strings strummed with the thumb. This latter instrument is what the boys tried to imitate on the guitar, first with a pen knife and another tried a file and Mr. Kekuku was the first to try a file."[61] Another account, by a local fisherman named David M. Kupihea, was published in the *Honolulu Advertiser* one week after the newspaper ran Kekuku's obituary in 1932. Kupihea suggested that a man named James Hoa, who he claimed was the "first Hawaiian bandmaster," had in fact invented the technique in 1876.[62] Both stories are intriguing; I have found no evidence to corroborate Kealakaʻi's story, while Hawaiian music scholar George Kanahele has satisfactorily discredited the Hoa claim. However, the fisherman's mention of a second individual to inspire Kekuku warrants a closer look.[63]

Kupihea claimed that a boy named Gabriel Davion played the Hawaiian steel guitar at Kalākaua's 1886 Jubilee Celebration. No evidence corroborates the presence of a Gabriel Davion, or of the steel guitar, at the two-week festival, an event heavily covered by the Hawaiian and haole presses. However, during a radio broadcast on Honolulu's KHU station in the late 1930s, celebrated Hawaiian mele composer Charles E. King also suggested that Davion's ideas inspired Kekuku:

> In 1884 I was living at Waiheʻe, Maui, and there appeared in the village a group of musicians from Honolulu, one of whom was Gabriel Davion—a young man who was born in India, kidnapped by a sea-captain and finally brought to Honolulu. This Davion attracted a great deal of attention be-

> cause he had a new way of playing the guitar. With the pocket-knife common in those days[,] the IXL knife, he manipulated the strings. Of course there was great interest created and some players used a hair comb instead of the knife. All the playing was done on one string, and the strings were not elevated by a bar. In a short while, a lead-pencil was used[,] which later on was displaced by the use of a steel bar, as in modern days. Joe Kekuku learned the method of playing and left for the mainland. He was one of the first to commercialize the steel guitar playing and located in Los Angeles where he had a studio in one of the leading music stores.[64]

An Indian captive? "Kidnapped by a sea-captain"? Inspiring a teenage Kekuku to spread the technique around the world? How may we learn more of this tantalizing turn?

A search for Davion's name in Hawaiian newspapers reveals little beyond a trail of litigation and real estate deals on Oʻahu and Maui in the early twentieth century.[65] Honolulu city directories between 1911 and 1923, however, consistently list a Gabriel Davion in the occupation of "painter."[66] King confirmed as much in a second broadcast: "Many of the kāmaʻāina [Island residents] remember him as a painter."[67] The 1900 U.S. Census lists a thirty-year-old painter named Gabriel Davien residing in Honolulu, although it indicates that he was French, as were both of his parents.[68] The next U.S. Census, ten years later, identifies a fifty-three-year-old Gabriel Davion from South Africa, also laboring as a painter.[69] Beyond the doubtless absence of many residents in census records, such discrepancies of ancestry, age, and origin are chronic in census records from this period, particularly as census takers often misrepresented, intentionally or not, the ancestry and origins of residents of color. In addition, it is quite possible that the Davion who told the census taker in 1910 that he was from South Africa *was* in fact of Indian descent—by the mid-nineteenth century, the British had imported over 1 million Indian indentured servants to South Africa.[70] This certainly lends credence to the idea that a Gabriel Davion of Indian descent resided on Oʻahu, regardless of whether or not he introduced this style of playing guitar to the Islands. King took another opportunity to detail Davion's life story on a third broadcast, when he reported, "John Baker, a man who was popular with the reigning monarch[,] got acquainted with Gabriel. When the ship was about to leave Honolulu, Baker hid the young man in a large empty salmon barrel until the ship [that was to carry the captive Davion to his captain's next port of call] had departed. Just think! If it were not for John Baker's little bit of trickery, Hawaii would not have been the birth-place of the steel guitar."[71]

The intrigue only continues to mount when one considers that the musical tradition of two instruments from India, the gottuvadyam and the vichitra vina, incorporate a similar technique as the steel guitar, and that the technique is documented in Indian literature to extend back at least a thousand years. The gottuvadyam developed in India's southern peninsula, while the vichitra vina developed in the north; both incorporate the sliding of a glass ball or ebony rod over strings.[72] Perhaps Davion had developed an ability to play the instrument before he arrived in Hawai'i? Given the high level of international traffic in and out of Honolulu harbor in the mid-nineteenth century, it is more than plausible that Hindus, captive or not, made their way into the harbor. Certainly this could explain the introduction of the concept, which could then translate to its application and later development on the Spanish guitar.

Other evidence tends to diminish the possibility that Davion would have been influenced by the gottuvadyam and vichitra vina traditions, however, even if he was born in India. According to Adrien McNeil, an Australian scholar of Hindustani music traditions, "Although [the introduction of the steel guitar technique by Gabriel Davion] is an intriguing claim, there are reasons to suspect the practicality of such an event. This is so because from the name Gabriel Davion we can infer that this person was either a Christian or Anglo-Indian. At that time the gottuvadyam or vichitra vina were both classical instruments in limited circulation and unlikely to be heard outside of the circumscribed environments of the princely courts or the homes of very wealthy patrons. The fact that Davion ended up as a stowaway on a ship to Hawai'i [a contrary theory to King's claim that he was a captive] suggests a fairly low social status relative to the elite strata which cultivated classical music." "Hence," McNeil concludes, "the opportunity for him to hear the music played on the classical Indian instruments, let alone the technique, would presumably have been fairly remote."[73] If his family was indentured in South Africa, there is even less probability that Davion would have seen those instruments. Finally, even Charles King seems to have seen Kekuku as more important in the development of the Hawaiian steel guitar than Davion, whom he did not even mention in earlier interviews on the subject (interviews conducted while Kekuku was alive). In a 1925 interview, for example, he attributed the steel guitar's introduction solely to Joseph Kekuku: "Modern Hawaiian music started in the latter '80s when Joe Kekuku developed the idea of the steel guitar from the scheme of playing the guitar with the IXL knife, a flat steel knife which was quite common in those days. When Kekuku went to the mainland he took the idea and introduced the steel guitar to the mainland people."[74]

So what to make of these claims of an Indian inspiration for the Hawaiian steel guitar? Nothing suggests that Kekuku spent much time in Honolulu as a child, but if he did, it is possible that he observed someone such as Davion near the harbor, or perhaps Kekuku would have seen him in town after he enrolled at the Kamehameha School. And even if Davion had no knowledge of the gottuvadyam and vichitra vina, he could have concocted the idea independently. It is striking, as well, that King provided such detail in telling Davion's story. We must consider Davion as a quite possible source of inspiration for Kekuku's development of the technique. Yet the evidence seems to point toward other more likely sources. For example, Kupihea's claim that Davion performed at the 1886 Jubilee Celebration seems entirely far-fetched, given his, and the innovative guitar technique's, absence from the kingdom's vast documentary record surrounding the celebration. If Davion had run a penknife over the strings of a guitar in public performances, his influence seems extraordinarily limited and certainly uninteresting to the press, as we find no claims of others observing or reporting on his innovation or picking up on his technique. Many who witnessed Kekuku's earliest performances in the Islands, in contrast, remembered them as performances of innovation, of his own making. For a kingdom thoroughly entranced with guitars by the 1880s, if the steel guitar technique had developed prior to Kekuku, we would expect to see either in the Hawaiian press more such evidence or more public rebuttals to all the attributions of the technique to Kekuku. Indeed, our skepticism increases when we note that the first documented mention of Davion's inspirational role appears only after Kekuku died, after thirty years of local musicians (including Charles King), musicologists, and advertisements recognizing Kekuku as the creator of the instrument.

Kekuku never alluded to someone named Davion playing a role in the instrument's history, but plenty of other stories developed during Kekuku's lifetime and beyond that attribute his development of the instrument to a variety of other inspirations. According to his later student and friend from England, Ken Reece, for example, Kekuku was eleven in 1885 when, "whilst walking along the railroad strumming on a guitar of the regular type, he stopped to pick up a bolt, and somehow or other he slid this bolt on the strings of his guitar, thus producing, in embryo, the well known slur so characteristic of the Hawaiian guitar."[75] Reece continued, "The bolt was far from being a success, and Kekuku tried the back of a penknife and various other things, until he settled down to using the blade of an ordinary razor with the edge ground down. Mr. Kekuku told me that he tried to practice in secret, but it was not possible, and other natives began playing in the same manner. This created a spirit of friendly competition and made Kekuku more determined than ever to be the first to master this new style of playing. . . . It took him seven years to master the instrument."[76] The inspiration of the bolt (in other places described as a railroad spike) is likely apocryphal; an early steel guitar manufacturer, Eddie Alkire, claimed that it was fabricated after the fact by music publishers who, because they had no idea what originally inspired Kekuku to develop the instrument, decided to make something up.[77] Kekuku, however, confirmed at least part of this story in a leaflet he prepared as an instructor. He wrote that he "originated the Hawaiian Steel Guitar method of playing in the year 1885 at the age of 11 years. At the time I was living in . . . Lāʻie. It took me seven years to master the guitar as I had no teacher to show me and no books to refer to for information."[78]

Musician Johnny Noble recounted a different version of the story, as told him by Kekuku's brother Edwin, who reported that while Joseph was at the school in his dormitory room, opening a gift that contained a small knife, "the knife fell on the [guitar], which was on the bed, made the pleasing sound, and Joseph experimented by sliding the knife along the strings."[79] Ethnomusicologist Helen Roberts collected yet another version as she was researching her book, *Ancient Hawaiian Music*, in 1923 and 1924. According to her account, "the guitar was a popular instrument among the students who were constantly strumming it. Like school boys all over the world, probably, they were not unfamiliar with the possibilities of the [metal] comb as a musical instrument, and one day as he was playing the guitar the idea occurred to young Kekuku to try the effect of a comb placed on the strings."[80]

In 1934, professional singer and ʻukulele player Alex Hoapili provided his own understanding of the role of the comb in inspiring Kekuku's technique. In an interview he observed, "sometime, somewhere, someone conceived the idea of touching the strings directly at the bridge with a comb with the idea of producing a vibrato. I suppose this was due to knowledge of the tone produced by blowing a comb with a piece of paper over it. Anyway, the habit of one person playing the guitar while another sat and rubbed the strings at the bridge with a comb soon developed, and it was a common sight to see three people playing two guitars." He continued, "While attending the Kamehameha School for Boys . . . , Joseph Kekuku began experimenting with his guitar one day by trying the effect of a comb laid on the strings with the left hand instead of the customary method just described. Then he tried substituting a pocket knife and later began using a piece of flat steel. It is generally supposed that he practiced the steel guitar secretly at his home for several years before coming to America."[81] Early Hawaiian steel recording artist "King" Bennie Nawahi had also heard the knife story, as he recalled in an interview: "So [Kekuku] took this pocketknife and laid it on his lap and played with this knife on the strings and that's how the steel guitar was invented."[82]

Perhaps the most detailed recollection of the instrument's early development comes from a letter to the editor of the *Pacific Commercial Advertiser* by Kekuku's Kamehameha classmate Simeon Nawaa. He reported in 1944 that when Kekuku and his cousin Sam Nainoa arrived at the school from Lāʻie, they were already skilled on the guitar and violin, respectively. He recalled that the two boys from Lāʻie "were good entertainers, and to our astonishment, Joe, besides playing the guitar the ordinary way, would shift to running a hair comb or tumbler on the strings[,] producing a sweet sound, while Sam, the accompanist, followed him with his violin."[83] Nawaa reported that Kekuku and Nainoa told their classmates they had been working on the idea for some time in Lāʻie, and that Kekuku's inspiration for using a piece of steel to run up and down the strings was in fact "the violin his mate played."[84] In a letter in the BYU-Hawaiʻi archives, Kekuku's niece, Kehau Kawahigashi, added that at home in Lāʻie "Joe liked the violin sound and often used his comb or a glass tumbler on the strings instead of his fingers," and that after he had begun to refine the technique at Kamehameha, "he also discovered that wire strings vibrated longer than gut strings & so he changed to wire & was pleased with the sustained tones."[85]

One day, Kekuku's great niece Kaʻiwa Meyer passed on to me the oral history that she had learned from her grandmother Violet, who was Joseph's sister. "Okay, would you like to know the REAL story of how Joseph Kekuku came up with the steel guitar?" she asked over the phone from Maui, perhaps an hour into our conversation. "Umm, . . . YES!" I stammered, hardly containing myself. She continued, "Well, when you were in Lāʻie, did you stop by the Lāʻie Cash and Carry?" I had to pause and think about that. She revealed that, though the store had changed hands over the years, this was the site of the store originally owned by her family. It had been in operation in one form or another since the 1880s, and had served as a central gathering place in the town. One day when he was about eleven, Joseph and his cousin Sam were sitting on the cement walk in front of the store, playing music for the passersby. At one fateful moment, Joseph leaned over, and his metal comb fell out of his shirt pocket and onto the strings, producing the sound Kekuku would work to perfect for the remainder of his life.[86]

The details of Kekuku's inspiration, therefore, remain contested, although the preponderance of recorded testimony supports the idea that it initially came by accident, with Joseph wielding a comb (or perhaps a knife). It is likely that such stories will continue to emerge. Of course, as I noted earlier, the basic concept of running an object up and down a string to produce music is centuries old and found all over the world. Even if we cannot pinpoint his initial inspiration definitively, it is clear from the written record that Kekuku did something no predecessor in Hawai'i or elsewhere could accomplish: he was the first to display a competence, a *technique*, for producing melodic tones on a guitar with a metal object. The innovation lay not in running an object over a guitar string but in making something out of this, in devising a transferable technique enabling the musician to organize the sound, perform recognizable repertoire, and accompany other instruments—to make the technique actually sound *good*. This is what Kekuku was universally hailed by his peers for having accomplished: he developed the technique and the technological apparatus for the guitar revolution that will unfold in the remainder of this book.

Indeed, two other essential components of the Hawaiian steel guitar are key innovations by Kekuku: in addition to experimenting with open tunings (it remains unclear whether slack key or steel guitar open tunings came first) and identifying steel strings as essential to the sound, he also fabricated the tools necessary to create a consistency of tone and a reliable technique, and physically altered the guitar itself. Had Kekuku not enrolled in the Kamehameha School after his family left for Utah, he likely would not have had access to the machines necessary to make these parts. According to his classmate Nawaa, Kekuku "wanted to be a mechanic and went to the school machine shop. What was in his mind, no one knew. But, he was working on something that later appeared to be the first steel bar. He might have seen the 'gouge stone' sharpen in the wood turning shop, for he patterned this accordingly. Later, he produced the round bar, which is now played by practically all steel guitar players."[87] Indeed, the "steel bar," as the tool became known, assumed a variety of shapes and sizes in the instrument's early years, after Kekuku and others remedied the aural and practical shortcomings associated with metal combs or knives. In addition to devising the steel bar to run over the strings, then, he also crafted finger and thumb picks in order to better attack the strings with his right-hand fingers, as his new technique involved laying the guitar on his lap (see fig. 10).

As for the guitar itself, Kekuku resized the nut, raising the strings higher

FIGURE 9.
One of the earliest known photographs of Joseph Kekuku and his steel guitar. Courtesy of Ron Middlebrook/ Centerstream Publishing.

over the frets in order to provide more clearance for them to handle the weight of the steel bar gliding over them without bumping into the frets below.[88] The raised nut also added volume, important because, with the guitar now in his lap, the sound hole faced up rather than out to the audience. Each of Joe Kekuku's innovations remains a standard tool and technique for playing the steel guitar to the present day. Later we will explore the steel guitar innovations of subsequent builders, but even these developments — Knutsen's and Weissenborn's hollow-necked guitars and the National and Dobro metal resonator

FIRST HAWAIIAN CONSERVATORY OF MUSIC, INC.

LESSON I

Learn One Thing at a Time

HAWAIIAN GUITAR

When playing the Hawaiian Guitar please remember that the RIGHT HAND "PICKS" and "STROKES." The LEFT HAND holds the steel and "TIPS" and "BARS." Study how to make each move. Never mind the notes. Play by the numbers. The drawings below show exactly what each hand does.

Pick solo strong. If thumb is too strong, discard thumb pick. Stroke very lightly.

The "X" means to "stroke" the second, third and fourth strings lightly with FIRST finger by drawing the finger TOWARD you over the three strings.

When two notes appear, ONE ABOVE THE OTHER, YOU "PICK" first string and the fifth string together or at the same time, with one pick.

Push the thumb AWAY from you.

Pick the first and second fingers TOWARD you.

"PICKING" HAND

THE THUMB AND 2ND FINGER ALWAYS "PICK" THE 1ST STRING AND 5TH STRING TOGETHER.

THE THUMB "PICKS" THE 5TH STRING. THE 2ND FINGER "PICKS" THE 1ST STRING. } PICK THEM AT ONCE TOGETHER.

"BAR" MEANS TO PRESS THE PLAYING EDGE OF THE STEEL ON ALL THE STRINGS. ALLOW YOUR 3RD FINGER AND 4TH FINGER TO SLIDE ON THE STRINGS BEHIND THE STEEL.

PICK UP THE TWO STRINGS TOGETHER

BAR OR STEEL HAND

3RD FINGER

4TH FINGER

ALWAYS KEEP YOUR 3RD AND 4TH FINGERS ON THE STRINGS BEHIND THE STEEL.

WHEN BARRING DON'T PRESS THE STRINGS DOWN TO THE BOARD.

PICK

BAR

THE 1ST FINGER ALWAYS "STROKES" THE 2ND 3RD AND 4TH STRINGS ALL TOGETHER

PRONG

BANDS

FIRST FINGER

SECOND FINGER

THE CELLULOID PICK IS PLACED ON THE THUMB THUS

THE THUMB AND 2ND FINGER "PICK" THE 1ST AND 5TH STRINGS TOGETHER

PLACE THE METAL THIMBLES OR PICKS, ON THE 1ST AND 2ND FINGERS AS SHOWN ABOVE.

BEND THE PRONG OF THE FIRST FINGER PICK BACK OVER THE BALL OF THE 1ST FINGER.

IF THE PICKS ARE TOO LARGE, BEND THE BANDS TOGETHER TO FIT.

PICKS

Study Each Hand Separate

"STROKE" THE 2ND 3RD AND 4TH STRINGS ALL TOGETHER WITH THE 1ST FINGER. DO NOT MOVE THE HAND. BEND THE FINGER TOWARD THE PALM OF THE HAND WHEN "STROKING"

FIRST FINGER

4TH STRING

3RD STRING

2ND STRING

REST THE WRIST OR HEEL OF YOUR HAND ON THE BUTTONS OF THE BRIDGE.

STROKE

BEND THE WRIST UP SO THAT THE STEEL IS CLEAR OF THE 2ND STRING

"TIP" THE STEEL SO THAT IT TOUCHES THE FIRST STRING ONLY.

TIP

THE STEEL IS HELD BETWEEN THE 2ND FINGER AND THE THUMB WITH THE 1ST FINGER LAYING STRAIGHT ON TOP OF THE STEEL

1ST FINGER

2ND FINGER

THUMB

THE STRAIGHT EDGE IS THE PLAYING EDGE.

KEEP ALL FINGERS STRAIGHT.

HOW TO HOLD THE STEEL

First Learn The 4 Important Moves

THERE ARE ONLY FOUR IMPORTANT POINTS TO LEARN TO DO, to play successfully you must study them carefully. These are the FOUR POINTS you are to learn. Don't bother about notes, you can learn them later.

X 1st. PICK—When TWO notes appear one over the other you PICK the FIRST and FIFTH strings TOGETHER. Use the THUMB and SECOND finger (see "HOW TO PICK.") Practise this 10 times.

2nd. STROKE—When an X appears, STROKE the 2nd, 3rd and 4th strings ONCE for each X. STROKE must be made LIGHTLY (see "HOW TO STROKE.") Practise this 10 times.

3rd. TIP—TIP STEEL at the NUMBER OVER the note, touching only the FIRST STRING when marked TIP (see "HOW TO PLACE STEEL ON STRINGS") IF THE STRINGS RATTLE. Your steel is touching the second string, TIP HIGHER.

4th. BAR—BAR or LAY the STEEL on ALL the strings at the NUMBER OVER the note when marked BAR. (NOTES, ETC., will be taught as you progress, learn this well first). By keeping the 3rd and 4th fingers on the strings behind the steel (lightly) the bad tone or rattle is killed when raising the steel. When taking the steel OFF the strings, RAISE the steel FIRST, then the fingers. Keep your fingers straight.

Slide the steel from one POSITION to the next slowly, if the strings rattle when baring, the steel it not being held firm enough on the strings. Slide the steel from number to number. You must count aloud. Read the lesson 10 times.

PLAY A LITTLE EVERY DAY, PLAY SOFTLY, PRACTISE THE HARD PART UNTIL YOU CAN PLAY IT WELL.

The number over the note shows where to put the steel. Play by numbers only.

HOW TO HOLD THE HAWAIIAN GUITAR

Place the guitar flat on the lap, with the neck pointing to the left. The lower, or widest part of the guitar should be held close to the body. Place the neck on the left limb close to the knee.

Compare these positions with yours to see whether you are doing it correct. Practise these positions faithfully.

Refer to these illustrations for correct position of instrument—steel, right and left hand.

Copyright MCMXXIII by First Hawaiian Conservatory of Music, Inc

FIGURE 10. *These illustrations demonstrate the fundamentals of Kekuku's steel guitar technique. Hawaiian steel guitarist Walter Kolomoku created this visual aid in 1923 to serve as the first lesson mailed to each student enrolled in his Hawaiian Conservatory of Music correspondence course. Courtesy of the author.*

guitars — all followed Kekuku's template. The only real gain that these types of guitars brought to Kekuku's design, in fact, was volume, the thirst for which would only be quenched in the 1930s with the production of the first electric guitars, the most popular of which were Hawaiian guitars, designed to play Hawaiian music.

Hawaiian music, it is clear, was central to Kekuku's innovations. Central to the articulation of Hawaiian music at this time, meanwhile, was the political turmoil that had overtaken everyone's lives in the Islands. The Hawaiian guitar, as conceived by Kekuku, had everything to do with perpetuating specifically Hawaiian musical traditions. And at this moment, maintaining indigenous practice was of critical concern.

As we will see, the repertoire performed by Kekuku and the first generation of professional steel guitarists consisted, often exclusively, of mele and other songs composed in the Hawaiian language. And while Kekuku's innovations were quickly adapted into other vernacular musical traditions throughout the world, the Hawaiian guitar seems as if it was conceived specifically to overcome the standard guitar's limitations in rendering distinctive traditions of Hawaiian music making. With a bar in hand to glide over the frets, eliminating the strict half- and whole-step increments found on the fretboard, the instrument could produce infinite microtonal possibilities. Kekuku used the steel bar to create a glissando effect on the strings, to build a sweeping movement into guitar passages, akin to the human voice, the violin, or perhaps the crescendo of waves rising, cresting, and breaking onto the beach.

More specifically, as Helen Roberts argued in 1920, modern Hawaiian music was "coupled with a habit, which is to be definitely traced to ancient hula music, of gliding swiftly from a tone finished to one to be attacked, slightly in advance of its normal appearance."[89] Although she was describing modern Hawaiian singing, she may as well have been describing this defining glissando sweep of the Hawaiian steel guitar. It also seems that the "ornamental effects" exploited on the Hawaiian guitar — sliding the notes with the steel bar, damping the strings to imitate glottal stops, wavering the steel bar over a note to produce a vibrato, and chiming harmonics or "bells" on the strings, developed in very distinctive ways to imitate the vocals in older Hawaiian chants as well as the newer yodeling falsetto acrobatics that transformed Hawaiian music making at the turn of the century.[90] Early steel guitarist David Kanui (1892–1965) offered his own opinion to a newspaper reporter: the "Hawaiian guitar," he said, "was adopted universally because the inhabitants of the Islands readily recognized that their music could be played on it more nearly as they intended it to be than on their own instruments."[91]

Kekuku's new guitar technology and technique, then, yielded an instrument perfectly suited to accompany the blending of new and old traditions that characterized the modern Hawaiian music of the overthrow and early territorial eras. It seems that once Kekuku introduced the Hawaiian guitar and technique to his classmates and others in the Islands, Hawaiians immediately began developing competency on the instrument. Anecdotal information confirms the quick proliferation of the instrument, originally through his classmates. "By this time," Roberts writes, "his singular and beautiful playing had become the talk of the boys, who were all emulating him, and one of them, Tilton, who went to his home on Maui during a vacation, performed on his guitar with the aid of his knife for the benefit of his family. His sister-in-law, . . . from whom this account was obtained, . . . asked him where he learned to play in such a curious manner and he told her that Joseph Kekuku at school had been the first to think of it and had taught the others how to do it. She later met Joseph Kekuku, who verified the statement. According to [her], the fashion spread very rapidly after a concert which she attended and at which, if her memory serves her correctly, Kekuku himself played."[92] Roberts continued, "The audience was delighted, and, as [her informant] expressed it, 'it took the house,' as it has since taken the musical world."[93]

This account in Roberts's book *Ancient Hawaiian Music* reveals much about how the steel guitar traveled throughout the Islands in the early 1890s, but it ignores the period's overriding concern: at the moment of Kekuku's breakthrough, the Hawaiian world was on the cusp of falling apart. On January 17, 1893, a small coalition of haole conspirators, supported by armed U.S. Marines and other armed hāole, mounted a coup d'état that resulted in the overthrow of the Hawaiian constitutional monarchy. The conspirators included the wealthiest haole planters and entrepreneurs in the Islands and acted with neither the authorization, nor even the knowledge of the U.S. Congress or president. This haole oligarchy, many of whom were the descendants of the first missionaries to the Islands, represented the Islands' so-called Big Five firms that controlled the Island industries in sugar, banking, shipping, railways, and insurance.[94] After having eroded the power of the monarchy for several years, particularly after imposing the 1887 "bayonet constitution," these conspirators sought to consolidate their economic and political dominance and dismantle Native rule altogether, particularly after Liliʻuokalani made moves to reinstate monarchical powers and the right to vote for Hawaiians. Before her brother, David Kalākaua, died in San Francisco in 1891, he had gained the overwhelming trust and support of the lāhui, in no small part thanks to his rejuvenation of Hawaiian expressive culture, and his condemnation of the Calvinists who sought to destroy it. The people likewise adored his successor; they gave her their unwavering support in the months and years following the overthrow. Known as the "royalists," the queen's supporters refused to acknowledge the legality of the coup and waged a sophisticated campaign on her behalf, both in the Islands and abroad. The "annexationists," meanwhile, overwhelmingly haole, supported the PG and believed that annexation by the U.S. Congress would lead to territorial status and eventually U.S. statehood.[95]

Tensions continued to rise, and no one was sure what would happen next. U.S. president Grover Cleveland, for his part, commissioned a federal investigation of the overthrow. The ensuing "Blount Report" found the overthrow illegal and the involvement of U.S. troops abhorrent. Cleveland proposed to reinstate the queen, but she resisted what she considered his quite paternalistic terms. Meanwhile, the annexationists, led by Lorrin A. Thurston, dug in their heels.

In the years that followed, Hawaiians, including Joseph Kekuku, his family, friends, and fellow musicians, stood nearly unanimously with Liliʻuokalani and against the overthrow and the push by haole elites toward U.S. annexation. The overthrow caused great anxiety and despair in the Islands. Disenfranchised, losing their homelands to hāole at a furious pace, and facing diminishing economic prospects, Kekuku and other musicians sought relief by channeling the cultural and economic autonomy of the Islands' guitar-driven string bands.

During the turmoil of the 1890s, professional and semiprofessional string bands in their many incarnations—orchestras, glee clubs, guitar clubs, and more—multiplied in towns like Honolulu and Hilo, as well as in the countryside, a demonstration that the guitar culture carefully nurtured in the Islands could thrive under duress.[96] Guitars had become integral to life, regardless of the challenges life presented. During the 1900 burning of Chinatown, when controlled fires designed to quell bubonic plague flared out of control, witnesses reported Hawaiians fleeing their burning apartments with guitars in hand.[97] The Kamehameha Schools' mandolin and guitar clubs survived the political upheaval, while local organizations such as the Waiahole Zither and Guitar Club continued to perform on Oʻahu. Meanwhile, luthiers continued to build and sell great numbers of stringed instruments made from Hawaiian woods.[98]

With families facing disenfranchisement and uncertain economic futures under the colonial regime, however, many guitarists learned to profit from their increased demand in local hotels.[99] By 1905, Sam Nainoa, whose violin, as we have seen, may have helped inspire his cousin's kīkā kila, was managing the Kawaihau Glee Club, a string band and vocal group that performed regularly at the Hawaiian Hotel. They donned what became the standard outfit of hotel string bands in the Islands: white uniforms with red sashes and neckties. Their selection of apparel was deliberate, and perhaps coded. As one newspaper reporter noted, such outfits reminded kāma'āina of the "monarchy days."[100] Hawaiian guitar-driven string bands became so famously associated with hotels on O'ahu that in 1905 the Astor House Hotel of Shanghai requested through the front page of the *Advertiser* to secure a six-month contract for the "best quintette club in Honolulu. . . . The hotel, it is understood, will pay the transportation both ways, give board and lodging free and pay a tidy sum daily to the players who are expected to play both in the afternoon and evening, and every day in the week."[101]

A fundamental objective for many musicians in the wake of the overthrow, then, was economic stability. Predictably, as Hawaiian string bands became the most popular and most profitable music ensembles in the Islands, competition between the bands grew fierce. Even Henri Berger, the long-standing leader of the Royal Hawaiian Band, had to concede that glee clubs were outpacing his group in receipts. He had witnessed during a continental tour in 1905 that haole audiences flocked to the glee club that accompanied his military band. The next year, Berger capitulated to the guitar, as reported in a *Honolulu Star Bulletin* article titled "The Band Is Now a Big Glee Club": "The experience last year at the Portland exposition and elsewhere demonstrated the benefit of a glee club in connection with the band, as the singing features, and especially the native songs were the most taking features. . . . In the first place every member of the band, if he didn't already know how, had to be taught to play the guitar, ukulele, violin, 'Cello or bass viol—some instrument [that] would go properly in a glee club. . . . The songs and music were written, and rehearsals began. There were forty-five members of the band. Ten of them played violins, three played 'Cellos, two played bass viols, and the rest were evenly divided between guitars and 'ukuleles."[102] If the aging German military brass bandmaster was willing to transform his entire forty-five-member organization into a string band, it is safe to conclude that the ascendancy of stringed instruments in the Islands was now complete.

As the number of professional string bands increased in the Islands, however, female guitarists were excluded from the ranks. This is striking, given the photographic evidence we saw in chapter 1 of the long-standing associations between wāhine and guitars, particularly in hula kuʻi performances. It is also surprising, given that missionary-influenced educational institutions approved of the guitar as an appropriately feminine, domestic instrument for their female students. The Kamehameha School for Girls, for example, sponsored public performances of its guitar and mandolin clubs in the 1890s.[103] In addition, a number of women in hula troupes offered demonstrations of the ʻukulele or taro-patch fiddle during their professional appearances, particularly while abroad. However, it was kāne, or men, who dominated the wage-earning string bands as the tourist economy in Honolulu expanded.

In step with this gendered alignment of economic roles, female dancers quickly outnumbered males in professional hula troupes, until men, who in other contexts could play prominent roles as dancers, were virtually excluded from this professional role. It is unclear precisely what prompted this gender bifurcation in professionalized Hawaiian performances. However, this development did not necessarily contradict the long-standing association of kāne with what already were considered to be the "highest echelons of hula"—that is, their assumed roles as kumu hula (teachers), chanters, and musicians. Likewise, these gender roles were paralleled and likely influenced by the long-standing exclusion of women from all sorts of professional musical organizations in the United States, from brass bands to minstrel acts.[104] As the tourist economy provided entertainers with opportunity for wage work, musicians and dancers were forced to adapt to haole audiences, who demanded women on the dance floor and men behind the instruments.[105] Brass bands such as Berger's also bowed to audience demands, Hawaiian and haole alike; in the years following the overthrow, men's Hawaiian string bands came to provide the dominant and most sought-after island sounds.

It is typically male musicians such as Joseph Kekuku, as a result, who populate the archives and provide most of our insight into how professional musicians reacted to the overthrow.[106] Many, as we have seen, sought financial stability in the Islands' growing tourist economy. In addition, since so few Hawaiians owned land by the late nineteenth century, or wanted anything to do with the PG and those who orchestrated the overthrow, many preferred the independence provided by the musician's trade over laboring in plantation fields or toiling in Honolulu's burgeoning colonial bureaucracy. And while many gritted their teeth in the wake of the overthrow, others bared them.

The members of Berger's Royal Hawaiian Band perhaps most poignantly demonstrated the views of Kānaka musicians regarding the overthrow. Less than two weeks after Liliʻuokalani was forced to vacate ʻIolani Palace, Berger, acting under orders, demanded that all of his musicians sign an oath of allegiance to the PG. As one haole editorialist wrote hopefully, "one thing that, more than anything else, will appease the natives and bring them around will be the band; they are a people fond of music, and attend in large numbers all the band concerts. Seeing their boys taking the oath they will be influenced very much by their actions."[107] Instead of signing the oath, however, on February 1, 1893, all but five of the musicians quit in protest, leaving Berger to hire non-Hawaiian musicians to populate the new Royal Hawaiian Band. One journalist described the result as "a weird collection of alleged musicians of every nationality but Hawaiian."[108] Berger's former musicians then formed a new outfit, Ka Bana Lahui, or the Hawaiian National Band, a royalist group that also featured in their performances a quintet glee club, likely the same organization as the King's Singing Boys, formerly Kalākaua's string band.[109]

One of their first acts as a new band was to solicit lyrics for a song, arranged by their new director, that would protest the overthrow and treatment of the queen.[110] They approached the lyricist Eleanor Kekoaohiwaikalani Wright-Prendergast. Her daughter Eleanor described the encounter as her mother sat in her garden, "while her prized guitar lay close at hand": "[Her guests'] familiar faces proved to be the troubled ones of all but two members of the Royal Hawaiian Band on strike. 'We will not follow this new government,' they asserted. 'We will be loyal to Liliu. We will not sign the haole's paper, but will be satisfied with all that is left to us, the stones, the mystic food of our native land.' So they begged her to compose their song of rebellion."[111] The song became known as "Kaulana Nā Pua" (translated as "Famous Are the Flowers [Children]").[112] The transcribed lyrics are worthy of inclusion here:

Kaulana nā pua aʻo Hawaiʻi	Famous are the children of Hawaiʻi
Kūpaʻa mahope o ka ʻāina	Ever loyal to the land
Hiki mai ka ʻelele o ka loko ʻino	When the evil-hearted messenger comes
Palapala ʻānunu me ka pākaha.	With his greedy document of extortion.

Pane mai Hawaiʻi moku o Keawe.	Hawaiʻi, land of Keawe answers.
Kōkua nā Hono aʻo Piʻilani.	Piʻilani's bays help.
Kākoʻo mai Kauaʻi o Mano	Mano's Kauaʻi lends support
Paʻapū me ke one Kakuhihewa.	And so do the sands of Kakuhihewa.
ʻAʻole ʻaʻe kau i ka pūlima	No one will fix a signature
Maluna o ka pepa o ka ʻenemi	To the paper of the enemy
Hoʻohui ʻāina kūʻai hewa	With its sin of annexation
I ka pono sivila aʻo ke kanaka.	And sale of native civil rights.
ʻAʻole mākou aʻe minamina	We do not value
I ka puʻukālā a ke aupuni	The government's sums of money
Ua lawa mākou i ka pōhaku,	We are satisfied with the stones,
I ka ʻai kamahaʻo o ka ʻāina.	Astonishing food of the land.
Mahope mākou o Liliʻu-lani	We back Liliʻu-lani
A loaʻa ē ka pono a ka ʻāina.	Who has won the rights of the land.
(A kau hou ʻia e ke kalaunu)	(She will be crowned again)
Haʻina ʻia mai an aka puana	Tell the story
Ka poʻe i aloha i ka ʻāina.	Of the people who love their land.[113]

The musicians became famous for their declaration that they would rather eat the stones of their homeland than sign the document; the song remains popular, and the sentiment strong, among many Kanaka Maoli today. Their debut performance on the grounds of the Hawaiian Hotel on March 22, 1893, drew a "packed mass" of 5,000 people.[114] The performance also marked the debut of "Kaulana Nā Pua," listed in the program as "Aloha ʻĀina." One local English-language newspaper referred to it after the performance as a "black flag" song, while another observer recalled that "the song proved to be written in Hawaiian for the occasion, in which the missionaries and the P.G. were soundly rated. Its reception was unmistakably warm."[115] The message and content was not hidden, or kaona, but immediately clear and apparent to all who attended the event. Ka Bana Lahui toured the Islands for years, and much of the United States in 1895 and 1896, in vocal and unequivocal support of the queen's restoration.

Hundreds of royalist hula kuʻi compositions were published in Hawaiian-language newspapers in the 1890s. Nearly 100 were written after a single event, the failed effort to restore the monarchy on January 6, 1895.[116] Antiannexationist, Hawaiian nationalist songs in the guitar- and ʻukulele-centered hula kuʻi genre flourished in the years following the overthrow, the failed restoration, and the 1898 "annexation" by the United States.

Like Ka Bana Lahui, Hawaiian string bands and steel guitarists in the decades immediately following the overthrow increasingly featured in their performances these nationalist mele, as well as compositions written by or in tribute to members of the deposed royal family. The bands, then, served to publicly celebrate and pay tribute to the royal family during the same years that Liliʻuokalani and her supporters fought to restore the Islands to Native rule.[117] They could also perform explicitly royalist songs in front of mixed audiences of Hawaiians and the most tyrannical annexationist hāole. While some hāole knew Hawaiian and understood the significance of the songs, most would have no idea that the aesthetically pleasing music was in fact rousing nationalist sentiment among the people standing beside them.[118]

Beyond supporting the royal family through mele that explicitly or covertly honored them, however, Hawaiian string band repertoire also demonstrated a fidelity to both language and land. Indeed, in the 1890s and early 1900s string bands traveling the Islands and abroad performed songs nearly exclusively in ʻŌlelo Hawaiʻi (the Hawaiian language). This is particularly significant because soon after the overthrow, the PG officially banned the Hawaiian language as a "medium and basis of instruction" in public and private schools.[119] A haole minister revealed the motives for the prohibition six months before the law's passage: "Here is an element of power in many ways. With this knowledge of English will go into the young American republican and Christian ideas; and as this knowledge goes in, kahunaism, fetishism and heathenism generally will largely go out."[120] While in the 1880s 150 schools used Hawaiian as the medium of instruction, the number dropped to zero by 1902.[121] Hawaiian glee club and orchestra performances thus provided one of the only public arenas for not only the use of the Hawaiian language but also the celebration of it. In addition, in accordance with long-standing and vital mele traditions, the songs often focused on beloved geographic or marine features in the Islands—features that kept the musicians connected in spirit to their occupied homelands, even when they were performing, as many came to do, halfway around the world. Indeed, after the failed restoration of 1895, with U.S. annexation increasingly likely and more and more Kānaka disenfranchised or removed from their lands, many musicians responded by professionalizing and then leaving the Islands altogether.

In addition to providing an income generally greater than work in the sugarcane plantations offered—in the mid-1890s musicians could make almost twice what a plantation field laborer was paid—professional performances at home or abroad could also generate unprecedented upward social mobility.[122] Adria Imada notes that while, "with few exceptions, Hawaiian society was highly stratified, with birth determining commoner or chiefly rank," many of the women who danced in Kalākaua's court, for example, were makaʻāinana.[123] Their access to hula repertoire and instruction was uncommon for non-aliʻi women, and this training provided them with opportunities to travel and work professionally in the 1890s. Likewise, the males who populated Kalākaua's Royal Hawaiian Band, as well as his court's string band, were selected based not on their rank but their ability.[124] Fourteen-year-old Mekia Kealakaʻi (1867–1944), for example, was toiling in a reform school in 1882 when he was recruited by Henri Berger to play flute in the Royal Hawaiian Band.[125] After the overthrow, however, Kealakaʻi quit the band and toured the U.S. continent as a member of Ka Bana Lahui; at the 1901 Pan-American Exposition in Buffalo he demonstrated a "triple-tongue" technique so accomplished that John Philip Sousa called him the "greatest flutist" he had "ever heard."[126] Kealakaʻi played for twenty years afterward in string bands that toured the world before eventually returning home to take over the leadership of the Royal Hawaiian Band, complete with a glee club, largely, as he put it, "to help preserve Hawaiian music."[127] The musicians who came of age during the Kalākaua and Liliʻuokalani eras gained economic and social opportunity and mobility just as the overthrow and annexation generated vast upheaval.

After the overthrow, more Hawaiian musicians not only performed abroad but also used the opportunity to forward pro-restoration and other countercolonial cultural agendas through press interviews and song dedications. After Liliʻuokalani was imprisoned, the members of Ka Bana Lahui used their access to the U.S. press to, as one of them put it, "let the people of [the United States] judge whether the natives of the Islands are a barbarous, ignorant, uncivilized tribe . . . with cannibalistic tendencies, or an enlightened and educated race of people who have been deprived of their property, their liberty and their country by an intriguing lot of foreigners masquerading before the world in the virtuous garb of the missionaries."[128] On another occasion, cornetist Sam K. Kamakaia asked a San Francisco reporter, "Do you think we want to be regarded as a sort of Indian agency, and that we want to be referred to as wards of your nation, to be fought over by the Bryans and the McKinleys? Never, so long as there is Hawaiian blood in our veins."[129] In 1895, musicians and dancers performing on the U.S. continent learned of Liliʻuokalani's arrest and sentencing to five years of hard labor, which could only have deepened the conviction with which they performed her most famous composition, "Aloha ʻOe," and the many others by members of the royal family that had become mainstays in their repertoire. They had no shortage of mele that they could dedicate to the monarchy, as Liliʻuokalani composed approximately 165 songs during her imprisonment alone.[130]

Like many of the best-known Hawaiian musicians of this period, Joseph Kekuku emerged from a family and community characterized by strong royalist sentiment and activism.[131] A December 1896 issue of the royalist newspaper *Ka Makaʻainana* indicates, for example, that Joseph Kekuku was a member of the Ahahui Aloha ʻĀina, or the Hawaiian Patriotic League, a nationalist organization dedicated to restoring Native rule to the Islands.[132] It is unclear whether or not this referred to the guitarist or his father, but we do know that, like most of the Hawaiian population in the Islands, both men signed the 556-page Hui Aloha ʻĀina antiannexation petition of 1897–98, which demanded that the U.S. Congress not annex the Islands as a U.S. territory. The guitarist's fourteen- and sixteen-year-old sisters, Hattie and Ivy, also signed the petition.[133] All of them except for the younger Joseph, of course, had experienced life in the United States during their ill-fated migration to Utah, an experience that could hardly have warmed them to the prospect of annexation. Anticolonial politics ran deep on Joseph Kekuku's mother's side as well. When Miriam had helped organize and cooperatively purchase the rights of the Kahana ahupuaʻa from her first husband, Ahmee, before his departure for China, she had participated not only in a restoration of sorts of her people's pre-Māhele relationship with the land, including communal access to all of its resources, but also in the creation of new legal protections for Native control of those resources.[134]

Countercolonial and royalist sentiment also seems to have been prevalent in Joseph Kekuku's broader community of Lāʻie, also home to two other significant first-generation steel guitarists who left the Islands: Kekuku's cousin Sam Nainoa and Pale K. Lua. A search in the archival record on Lāʻie villagers' responses to the U.S. occupation reveals the testimony of Benjamin Cluff, a haole member of the LDS church who spent part of his childhood in Lāʻie, who spoke the language and considered residents of Lāʻie to be his "friends and neighbors."[135] In early 1898 he was asked by his senator to return to the Islands to determine "the attitude of the Hawaiian people toward the subject of annexation to the United States." That February the Mormon community of Lāʻie organized a meeting for Cluff with 200–300 people, whose leaders, in turn, "expressed the feelings of the great majority in attendance, on opposing annexation, on the grounds that they desired the queen restored to her throne. 'The United States,' they said, 'has been instrumental in the overthrow and it should be instrumental in the restoration of the queen.'" Cluff then asked what they would do if the United States refused, and they replied, "We will petition England for restoration." He asked what they would do if England would not aid them. They answered, "We will then petition other powers." Then he noted that "a young man, Kekuku by name," told him, "'I want primarily for the restoration of the queen.'"[136]

It is likely that the guitarist Joseph Kekuku made this comment, as he is the only "young" Kekuku male from Lā'ie at this time that I can identify, other than his brother Edwin, who was then only ten years old. In his report on the meeting in Lā'ie, Cluff also noted, "The belief is quite common that in case of annexation the natives would be driven to the mountains, and be treated like the Indians of the west, or rather as they have heard the Indians are treated; that their lands would be taken from them and their property confiscated; that they would be ostracized from society; and that there would be a great rush of tramps and beggars such as infest large cities like San Francisco. Some even think they would be enslaved like the negroes of the South."[137] Cluff said he met only one person who could not read or write in the Islands, and he acknowledged the depth of Hawaiians' understanding of the history of their Islands and of the United States.[138] He was told by one Lā'ie man that if annexed, "the natives would have to flee to the United States, as there would be no protection for them on the Islands."[139] This statement may seem ironic, even naive, at first glance, but emigration was a tactic particularly well suited to Hawai'i's highly mobile and highly skilled entertainers, especially kāne string band musicians and wāhine hula practitioners. Many men and women in the two decades following the overthrow used such talents to access foreign entertainment markets. Perhaps they felt that by touring the United States, they could, at least for a time, avoid the experience of occupation by Americans. Or perhaps they refused to labor in a colonial context. Such concerns compounded economic motives fueled by low-paying wage and clerical work in the Islands.[140] Certainly a lust for travel and adventure guided many of them as well. A combination of these sentiments doubtless fueled the wave of emigration by entertainers that carried Kekuku and the first generation of steel guitarists — royalists, every one — to, of all places, the United States.

We do not know which of these factors drove Kekuku from the Islands. He continued to refine his skills on the kīkā kila after leaving the Kamehameha

School around 1893 (he did not graduate). He may have already gained some independent financial footing, as one report suggests that while a minor he inherited some small property on O'ahu, perhaps from his biological father, Ahmee.[141] It appears that he married Jennie Keliimiola Kiilehua, from Lā'ie, in 1893.[142] He continued to share publicly his guitar technique, and by 1897 J. M. Webb's Golden Rule Bazaar was marketing "Hawaiian Guitars" as instruments distinct from those listed in the same advertisements as "Spanish guitars," "taro patch guitars," and "ukuleles."[143] He performed guitar recitals over the next few years, attracting the attention of the local press.[144] By 1900 Kekuku, separated and soon to be divorced from Kiilehua, was boarding at a house in Ko'olauloa, a few miles south of Lā'ie near his birthplace, and by 1901 he was living in Honolulu and working by day as a copyist.[145]

In the summer of 1904, Kekuku boarded a steamer for San Francisco. His employer claimed that he had written himself an extra paycheck before his departure.[146] News traveled quickly back to the Islands that after Kekuku's arrival in San Francisco, he was making "a precarious subsistence through his musical talents."[147] If Honolulu authorities indeed believed that he had broken the law, they knew where to find him in San Francisco, and they never acted on the information. Honolulu's *Evening Bulletin* reported that at 217 Leavenworth Street Kekuku was teaching students what he advertised as a "new method" of playing the guitar.[148]

3 *American Debut*

THE MAKING OF THE STEEL GUITAR CRAZE

It appears that the Hawaiian steel guitar's introduction to North American audiences preceded Joseph Kekuku's 1904 voyage to San Francisco. Although the evidence is fleeting and difficult to assess, George Kanahele reported that either July Paka or Tom Hennessey, both Hawaiians, recorded the steel guitar with a troupe in 1899 in San Francisco; letters from the musicians to their families suggest that they recorded on wax cylinders then for Peter Bacigalupi, the owner of the city's downtown Edison phonograph parlor.[1] However, only one cylinder from the session has surfaced, and it is too damaged to verify the use of a steel guitar; in fact, the vast majority of cylinders were likely destroyed in the city's great 1906 earthquake and fire.[2] Joseph Puni, who later became well known as a steel guitarist, performed with July Paka at the 1901 Pan-American Exposition in Buffalo and later that year led a Hawaiian troupe through Georgia, South Carolina, and Florida.[3] A guitarist from Mexico learned the technique while visiting Hawai'i and was giving lessons on the steel guitar in Pasadena, California, by 1902. One of his students, William Miles, had first heard the steel guitar in Hawai'i in 1899, played by a man named Keoki Akea. Shortly after beginning lessons with the Mexican guitarist, Miles introduced the technique as a member of a hotel orchestra in Winnipeg, Canada.[4] In addition, Frank Ferreira Jr. (aka Frank Ferera), born in Hawai'i of Portuguese descent, traveled to the continent in 1902 and eventually became the most prolific steel guitar recording artist of his generation.[5]

Although his instrument may have reached the continent before him, however, Kekuku was the first musician whose mastery of the steel guitar was recognized in the press, immediately after he began touring with professional Hawaiian bands. He found such work quickly, thanks to his embrace by a network of Hawaiian musicians who already had made their way to California after the overthrow. David Makuakane, a resident of Santa Cruz for several years already, hired Kekuku around July 1905 to join his Hawaiian Sextette, a glee club that also featured William Alohikea, William Kapu, J. Harrison, and J. Kalaina. In a glowing review that year, the *Santa Cruz Sentinel* described

FIGURE 11.
Photographed in Frederick Bushnell's San Francisco studio, Kekuku likely commissioned this portrait soon after he arrived in the city. He then mailed a copy home, and it has remained in the family. Courtesy of the Walter K. Wong ʻOhana.

Kekuku's playing "the guitar with a steel, on a system entirely his own."[6] This review, perhaps the first by a continental newspaper to acknowledge the steel guitar, was quickly followed by many more. California audiences loved Hawaiian music: two days before Makuakane's sextet left Santa Cruz to play San Francisco, the Royal Hawaiian Sextette rolled into town featuring another assemblage of Hawaiian musicians, including Sonny Cunha, the renowned composer of hapa haole songs; George Kia, who a few years later would begin teaching the steel guitar in Los Angeles; and John Ellis, known as "the best tenor of the Islands."[7] While Kekuku at first made his living on the continent teaching guitar, he, like the many Hawaiian musicians living in tightly knit communities along the West and East Coasts, quickly became an in-demand performer.

The Hawaiian steel guitar flooded the public consciousness in the United States over the next ten years; the rate and the depth of the instrument's diffusion throughout the country is nothing short of astonishing. Several factors help to explain this phenomenon, but they all ultimately hinged on the success of Hawaiian musicians in exploiting, indeed mastering, the new century's vaudeville, recording, and musical instrument industries. As this chapter will demonstrate, if their ability to do so was challenged by the racialized assumptions that underlay the vaudeville and recording industries, it was enhanced by the fact that the Hawaiian steel guitar was one of the most modern and cutting-edge instruments available to entertainers on the popular stage. The dissonance between the instrument's modernity and white audiences' assumptions of Hawaiian inferiority remained palpable, even if everyone who saw and heard this Kanaka technology recognized its revolutionary character.

A look at Kekuku's career, and that of his most well-known band, Toots Paka's Hawaiians, reveals the extensive Hawaiian entertainers' network that existed in the early twentieth-century United States, with hubs in Los Angeles and New York City. It also demonstrates American audiences' immediate fascination with Hawaiian music, and more specifically with the Hawaiian steel guitar. Kekuku and his friends spent their early careers on the stages of theaters linked on vaudeville circuits that traversed the country. Troupe personnel changed frequently, as did job prospects from one company to another. Ethnic novelty genres and minstrelsy heavily shaped employment opportunities, and they practically defined them for entertainers of color. The labor force was transient by design, and the work was relentless. Despite the challenges of road life and the constraints imposed by the industry, however, the work quite often excited the performers and even felt liberating compared to the oppressive anti-Hawaiian cultural policies deployed in the now "annexed" Islands.

This chapter will explore the opportunities and limits facing Hawaiian entertainers in the first two decades of the twentieth century, and the early rise of the Hawaiian steel guitar in the American consciousness. We will examine the vaudeville career of Kekuku and the Paka troupe, and consider also the significance of a variety of other entertainment mediums that circulated the instrument before American eyes and ears during this period. Wax cylinders enabled Kekuku to record, preserve, and sell his performances of Hawaiian mele through talking machines, for example, while large-scale musical productions such as Richard Tully's *Bird of Paradise* traveled with Hawaiian troupes even deeper into rural North America, where vaudeville theaters gave way to tent shows. Two of Kekuku's first students in the United States, and soon, many other practitioners of his technique, published instructional materials for the instrument; correspondence courses soon followed. A number of world's fairs, including the 1915 Panama Pacific International Exhibition in San Francisco, enabled Hawaiian steel guitarists to perform before hundreds of thousands, if not millions, of people from all over the country in a matter of months. Finally, the advent of 78 rpm shellac records, and the rapidly growing recorded music industry disseminated the sounds of the Hawaiian steel guitar to so many Americans that by 1916, Hawaiian guitar music was outselling every other genre of recorded music in the United States.[8] Indeed, just twelve years after Kekuku opened his music school at 217 Leavenworth Street in San Francisco, it was nearly impossible for an American to not have seen or heard the sounds of the Hawaiian steel guitar.

For the first few years, Kekuku worked his way up and down the West Coast, playing in a variety of Hawaiian ensembles. In March 1907, for example, he was billed in Bellingham, Washington, as "Kakuku—The Hawaiian—the World's Greatest Guitar Soloist."[9] One month later, the *San Jose Evening News* described his local performance: "He lays the guitar across his knees and plays it like a zither. He executed a medley of Hawaiian songs."[10] Although also being placed on the musician's lap, the steel guitar plays and sounds nothing like a zither, but this description conveys the novelty and foreignness of the instrument at that time. Like many musicians trying to make a living, Kekuku expanded his repertoire, to include in San Jose the popular hits dearest to his haole audiences, including "The Mocking Bird," "Lindy," and "Dearie" (the latter two featured piano accompaniment). He indeed met with great success as he learned to anticipate the desires of his audiences: "The Hawaiian and his guitar were kept on the stage quite awhile," reported the San Jose critic.[11] Critics took note of what one referred to as Kekuku's "more than usual cleverness" on the instrument.[12] Quite likely they had never heard the guitar played this way before. In fact, they probably had never encountered the guitar played in any guise as a soloist's instrument. Up to this point, the guitar in the United States was essentially limited to rhythm sections and to accompanying singers. Kekuku seemed to be singlehandedly reinventing its purpose.

As Kekuku's performances continued to gather attention along the West Coast, guitar builders quickly worked to exploit and better accommodate his technique in their designs. One of the earliest and most significant Hawaiian steel guitar builders was Chris J. Knutsen, an immigrant from Norway who, while living in Port Townsend, Washington, in the 1890s, had made a name for himself building harp guitars.[13] These guitars, first developed in Europe, incorporated the features of a standard six-string guitar with a wooden chamber that extended from the upper bout of the guitar above the fretboard to the headstock of the instrument (which typically houses its tuning pegs).[14] Along the extended chamber he strung an additional three to five harp strings tuned to lower bass notes. When plucked with the thumb, the open harp strings produced droning tones that could complement a simultaneous performance on the instrument's guitar neck. Knutsen later built a number of other instruments, including ʻukuleles and mandolins, but it seems that he became particularly enthralled with Kekuku's steel guitar performances in Seattle, after Knutsen moved his business there in 1906.[15] It appears that by this point, guitarists were traveling from the Islands with kīkā kilas built of koa wood and perhaps with hollow necks. With Kekuku teaching many Seattle students and more guitarists continuing to arrive from the Islands, Knutsen came to sense that there was a growing but untapped market for Hawaiian steel guitars.[16] He apparently came into contact with Kekuku during this period, and by 1909 he was building his first prototypes of hollow-necked Hawaiian steel guitars.[17]

Knutsen learned through Kekuku and his fellow practitioners some of the professional challenges facing the instrument: players needed greater volume to compete with the violins, flutes, ʻukuleles, and standard guitars that characterized Hawaiian string bands at that time. As well, the steel or wire strings that Kekuku and the other early steel guitarists required could bow or damage the necks of the standard Spanish acoustic guitars that they modified when specially built steel guitars were unavailable to them. Knutsen's hollow-necked guitars combined the body and neck into one resonant cavity rather than joined a body to a separate (and thus movable) neck, the design of standard guitars. The hollow-neck design, along with improved bracing adapted from Knutsen's experience with harp guitars, provided additional strength to handle the increased tension generated by the steel strings. Combining the strength and unique tonal qualities of koa wood with a body further amplified through a gracefully expanded upper bout and hollow neck, Knutsen's expertly crafted Hawaiian guitars became increasingly sought after by Hawaiian musicians.[18] Soon additional luthiers began to trade on the concept. In the midst of these technological innovations, Kekuku honed his work as a performing artist; in Toots Paka's Hawaiians, his audience expanded exponentially.

A brief examination of the Paka troupe's collective and individual histories reveals the precarious nature of work in the vaudeville industry in the early twentieth century. The Paka troupe centered on the marriage and professional partnership of July Paka and Hannah "Toots" Jones. Iolai "July" Kealoha Paka (1874–1943) was brought up in Kalākaua's court and left the Islands after the U.S. "annexation." He was the son of Juliana Walanika from Mānoa Valley, Oʻahu, a favorite singer and dear friend to Kalākaua and Liliʻuokalani.[19]

Walanika performed on Oʻahu throughout the 1880s and during Kalākaua's Jubilee festivities in 1886, and was known as "the Nightingale" for her vocal qualities.[20] Her son July developed a strong baritone singing voice and talents on the Spanish guitar, ʻukulele, the taro-patch fiddle, and, most famously, the Hawaiian steel guitar. By 1899, the year after the Islands' "annexation" by the United States, he had left Oʻahu for the U.S. West Coast and recorded for Edison in San Francisco.[21] Paka's Hawaiian Quintet performed regularly in San Francisco theaters, dances, galas, and parties over the next two years.[22] In 1900 he performed in the city for Liliʻuokalani.[23] By 1901, he had made his way with eighteen women and twenty-five men to perform at Buffalo's Pan-American Exposition. The roster featured a who's who of Hawaiian composers and musicians, including David Nape, Mekia Kealakaʻi, and William Alohikea.[24] Paka and his next band, the Hawaiian Glee Club, graced the 1902 sheet music cover for the first Hawaiian song both composed and published on the mainland, Kealakaʻi's still popular "Lei ʻAwapuhi."[25]

While Paka remained quite busy as he moved between the East and West Coasts, he eventually met a white dancer from the Midwest named Hannah Jones (1871–1942). Jones grew up on a "shantyboat" with eleven siblings on Lake Huron, where her father shipped lumber until his third and final boat sank in a storm.[26] She was off the boat and working as an actress in Port Huron, Michigan, by 1902, and around that time or soon after, she met July Paka, whom she married in Chicago the next year.[27] It is unclear exactly what happened next, but by May 1905 they were working with the Lemon Brothers Circus. In the circus she performed as "Tootsie Jones, Oriental Dancer," while Paka performed in a different act called the Hawaiian Glee Club.[28]

As their billings suggest, they had waded into an industry that continued to trade heavily on ethnic novelty. While the industry built new regional circuits and local theaters and standardized its formulas for the sentimental and humorous songs that wafted from the windows of Tin Pan Alley offices, it likewise modernized the well-worn racial and ethnic representations that had long circulated in blackface minstrelsy and medicine shows. Blackface minstrelsy, by the 1890s, had translated into vaudeville as popular blackface comedy troupes and "coon songs" sold through sheet music and wax cylinder recordings. Ironically, blackface at that time also was one of African Americans' only entry points into the culture industries, and some of the genre's biggest stars by the first decade of the twentieth century were people of color who had to wear burnt cork and assume sometimes grotesque personas in order to work on the popular stage. Likewise, professional American Indian singers typically

FIGURE 12. *John Wilson's troupe at the 1901 Pan-American Exposition in Buffalo, New York.* Back row, left to right: *Jack Heleluhe, Dick Reuter, and William McComber;* center row, left to right: *Anthony Zablan, James Kulolio, July Paka, and Charles Baker;* front row, left to right: *Mekia Kealaka'i, William Alohikea, and David Nape. This lineup featured some of the most accomplished Hawaiian composers and instrumentalists of the early twentieth century. July Paka would form Toots Paka's Hawaiians with Joseph Kekuku just a few years later. Photograph by Beach, courtesy of Bishop Museum.*

succeeded only when they inhabited the novelty personas of male "chiefs" or female "princesses." Because Jones's dances were considered inappropriate for white women to perform, even she had to take on an "oriental" persona. Hawaiian hula likewise was marketed as erotic rather than sacred, and vaudeville promoters sold Hawaiian musical performances as ancient, traditional, and heathen—all the antitheses of modernity. Vaudeville fostered a normativity of whiteness through its heavy circulation of and reliance on racialized, prescribed, one-dimensional, antimodern novelty roles, despite the mastery of modern technologies by performers of color and the sophisticated social navigation that such performances, and indeed, life on the road, required.

Road life was harrowing for a number of reasons; the Lemon Brothers show, for example, was rife with grifters, gamblers, and pickpockets. In 1905, after several men riding the Lemons' circus train engaged in a gunfight with authorities in Quebec, Hannah and July quit the Lemons and joined William Atherr's Dog and Pony Circus as one act: Toots Jones and Her Hawaiian Troupe.[29] By the end of 1906, July and Hannah were performing in Washington State as "July & Paka—Hawaiian Duo, Singers & Dancers."[30]

At this point, perhaps as many as 200 Native Hawaiian musicians were touring the continent in dozens of string bands, from Frank J. Vierra's Hawaiian Quintet to Sonny Cunha's Royal Hawaiian Band; from Lu Thompson Keouli's Honolulu Students to the Irene West Royal Hawaiians, the Ellis Brothers' Quartette and Glee Club, and dozens of generically named Hawaiian duos, trios, quartets, quintets, sextets, and orchestras.[31] The musicians, and the dancers who accompanied them, connected through a vast Hawaiian entertainers' network that had been woven throughout the continent over the previous decade. It is easy to surmise, then, that during their stint in the Pacific Northwest during the winter of 1906–7, July and Hannah found Joseph Kekuku.[32] By 1908 the three were working together, touring the West on a bill featuring acrobats and whistlers.[33]

Kekuku was already attracting a great deal of attention in the West; he could have joined any act, but he recognized the Pakas' talent. So did Pat Casey, one of the most powerful operators and agents in New York's vaudeville scene, who after "discovering" them sent them East, where they debuted that September at Manhattan's Fifth Avenue Theatre.[34] With both men playing guitar and singing, they were noted by New York critics primarily for Kekuku's method of holding "his guitar across his knees like a zither, and by some manner of manipulation [getting] a weird, plaintive sort of music out of it, utterly fascinating and unlike ordinary guitar playing."[35] Within months Kekuku's playing had captivated his New York and New England audiences. "Toots Paka's Hawaiians came into New York a little less than a year ago unknown and almost unannounced," reported *Variety* in May 1909. Their first engagement at the Fifth Avenue Theatre, *Variety* continued, "made the trio a recognized standard vaudeville number. . . . As a musical feature alone it is a striking entertainment. Two native Hawaiian musicians coax amazing harmonic effects from their guitars, a style of melody that has a curious resemblance to that of the violin in its sweetness."[36] Although other Hawaiian steel guitarists likely made it to New York before them, Toots Paka's Hawaiians was the first such group to garner reviews from vaudeville critics. The latter struggled to comprehend Kekuku's steel guitar technique and to describe his never-before-heard sounds. During a spectacular forty-week run with Casey's United Booking Office, Toots Paka's Hawaiians, and the steel guitar, truly arrived in New York City.[37]

Practically everything about their performances was innovative, from the steel guitar to the mele selections. American critics and journalists, however, more typically turned to minstrelsy—their only reference point for entertainers of color in this era—in order to explain the act. Indeed, with professional blackface performances beginning their slow decline in popularity during the 1910s and 1920s, increasingly popular and numerous Hawaiian troupes seemed to satisfy critics' and white audiences' desire to rejuvenate minstrelsy's racial paradigm. A Chicago correspondent for the *New York Telegraph*, for example, described Hannah's skin tone as "the color of café au lait," compared the rhythm of their "outlandish ditties" to "patting juba," and regarded Kekuku's "weird solo on his zither," in this case his "Hawaiian version" of the popular song "The Rosary," as "fine barbaric thrill": "it makes the harmonies of the plantation darky sound like the caterwauling of Sir Thomas on the back fence."[38]

Kekuku performed "The Rosary," penned in 1898 by a Pittsburgh composer, every night. Critics seemed awestruck by his interpretation, yet they struggled to assess the musical and racial significance of his execution of "their" song on this new, *Hawaiian* steel guitar.[39] A seasoned entertainer by the time he joined Paka's outfit, Kekuku clearly knew how to stack his repertoire: after first intriguing audiences with foreign yet alluring mele, he shocked their senses by rendering their own musical traditions through the voice of his instrument. Even with "The Rosary," however, Kekuku introduced significant technical dynamics derived in the Islands, for he performed the entire piece with natural and artificial harmonics, a steel guitar technique that originated in the Islands and had never before been witnessed in the United States.[40]

Kekuku "spell-bound" some critics with his "brilliant guitar playing," as one Los Angeles critic noted in 1912.[41] A critic for the *Brooklyn Daily Eagle* remarked in June 1909 that "the guitar playing of the two men is a revelation."[42] Yet critics generally remained uncomfortable, unable to abandon the interpretive allure of racial or colonial novelty. The Brooklyn critic referred to the troupe as "representatives of Uncle Sam's insular possessions."[43] Kekuku and July Paka certainly understood the complexity of their position: while the expectation of racial novelty that they traded on in the vaudeville circuit gave them immediate opportunity, it also threatened to limit their professional horizons, the respect they could garner from white audiences, and the credit they deserved for so dramatically reimagining the possibilities of the guitar, Hawaiian or otherwise.

On rare occasions, journalists would ask performers to explain the steel guitar technique, providing them with the opportunity to demonstrate the modernity of their music. Kekuku seems to have incorporated significant discussion of the instrument's innovations into his performances whenever possible, and eventually he was acknowledged in the press to have invented the instrument, even if the revelation remained couched in the terms of ethnic novelty. After Kekuku left the Pakas in New York City and relocated to Los Angeles, Paka took over as the group's steel guitarist. In 1916, an Atlanta-based journalist asked him if learning to play the steel guitar was easy. He wryly responded, "Sure, anybody can learn the Hawaiian style of playing—provided he has the ordinary fundamentals of a musical education and patience. All you've got to do is to set your instrument in the 'Spanish fandango' key, put on the Hawaiian steel finger pieces and practice four or five hours a day for ten years."[44] During an interview with another Hawaiian troupe at an El Paso theater in 1916, dancer Luana Kulainoheo confirmed Kekuku's origination of the instrument and then explained for the journalist his fundamental modifications of the instrument: "The bridge is slightly raised, and a steel piece is passed along the strings to give the slurring tone that is characteristic of Hawaiian music."[45] Kulainoheo took this opportunity, as well, to correct the insulting greeting offered by the journalist ("no princess, please!" she remarked during the interview), along with the assumption that her dance was not modern: she was "emphatic [in] her denial that the hula hula she is giving is antiquated."[46] "Our dance is the modern hula," she insisted, and, to remind the journalist of the colonial conditions now facing the Islands, added that the dance was "given before the consort of Queen Lil[i]uokalani before she was deposed by the revolutionists in the early '90s."[47]

Paka and Kekuku's desire for racially unencumbered professional respect in the industry was unlikely to be fulfilled. Critics seemed to cast their racial gaze at every turn. Wrote one in 1912, "Los Angeles has had so-called 'Hawaiian' music and musicians galore, of all sorts and grades, from imitation negroes up, but in this case, the Orpheum will offer the real article, for Toots Paka is herself a native of Hawai'i. . . . It is an offering of . . . the genuine, old-time diversions, uncorrupted by the influx of the whites, that she and her troupe will proffer."[48] While we can savor the irony of the critic's decision to incorrectly believe Hannah Jones's claim (on a vaudeville stage, no less) that she was Hawaiian, the statement otherwise is pregnant with intrigue: how extraordinary is it that Hawaiian music and musicians had overrun Los Angeles as early as 1912?[49] As another article in the *Los Angeles Times* reported the very next week, "Many players of stringed instruments after the Hawaiian fashion have been heard in Los Angeles, but Kekuku excels them all."[50] And to what extent were African American entertainers really "playing Hawaiian" onstage? We know of a few examples of this, such as the famous entertainer Bert Williams, who performed at the 1894 Midwinter Fair in San Francisco as a Hawaiian musician.[51] Was this a tactic that enabled racial passage in some cities, where perhaps, as "Hawaiians," they hoped to avoid inferior, segregated accommodations, or confuse (or defuse) white supremacists on the road? Or were they, like Hannah, merely trading on Hawaiian brownface at the height of the Hawaiian fad? Finally, how is such dissonance possible, that audiences at this time would hear modern music, on modern instruments, by entertainers donning suits and garments considered the most fashionable in Europe and the United States, on the most modern of stages, and truly believe that they were experiencing "old-time diversions" by uncivilized, inferior peoples, diversions "uncorrupted by the influx of the whites"?[52]

Kekuku's steel guitar was not immune to the gaze. As a Colorado reporter noted, "Mr. Kekuku is conceded to be the world's greatest solo guitarist. He is the genius of that seductive slurring of the notes as they softly swirl like an incense from the strings. Even after the notes have departed from the instrument with the taste and delicacy of a sweet thought, they form an echo chorus that seems to sing the racial poetry of the Hawaiians."[53] His rendition of "The Rosary" demonstrated the instrument's capacity to render sublime non-Hawaiian melodies, yet critics in this period entrenched the steel guitar in racial casting. Kekuku and the Pakas, however, do not seem to have had much interest in further exploiting the instrument's crossover appeal at this point, or in catering to the racial caricatures expected or demanded by white audiences. With few exceptions, they seemed particularly inclined to instead cut through the racial noise associated with their act by performing a quite specific, very modern, and nearly exclusive repertoire of mele hula from the Islands.

Indeed, despite the efforts of critics and audiences to circumscribe their performances as ahistorical ethnic novelty, the otherthrow of Liliʻuokalani seemed to remain a foremost concern for the Paka and other Hawaiian troupes, if their music and hula repertoire is any indication. Though record companies were less interested in capturing politically or culturally significant mele than in marketing commercial ethnic novelty recordings, the Pakas found ways to take advantage of the situation. July and Hannah Paka, Joseph Kekuku, and the newest member of their lineup, stringed instrumentalist John K. Paʻaluhi, gathered at the Edison studios in New York City for their first recording session on the morning of October 23, 1909. Because the Edison staff had such limited knowledge of Hawaiian music, the Pakas established tremendous latitude in determining what would become the foundational, recorded Hawaiian repertoire.[54]

From this first session forward, their recorded repertoire represented almost exclusively the most modern and popular Hawaiian compositions in the Islands, most of them written within the previous twenty or thirty years. The recorded sides included "Kawaihau Waltz," by David Nape (this side was credited to Joseph Kekuku and John Paʻaluhi as a guitar duet); "Kamawae" (Kapualu), "Ninipo" (Kaleikoa); "Koleo" and "Akahi Hoi" (King Kalākaua); and "Moani Ke Ala" (Prince Leleiōhoku).[55] Members of the deposed monarchy composed a third of the songs cut in their first session. During the session, the Pakas, Kekuku, and Paʻaluhi also recorded Sonny Cunha's "Honolulu Tom Boy."[56] Cunha, like Nape, had traveled the U.S. continent in Hawaiian troupes and was a primary developer of a new genre known in the Islands as "hapa haole." The genre mixed Hawaiian and haole song traditions much more explicitly, in that he wrote lyrics that combined Hawaiian- and English-language phrases.[57] This genre would facilitate the Hawaiian music booms that seemed to recur cyclically in American popular culture during the teens, twenties, thirties, and forties.

As hapa haole recordings sold in greater numbers, and as Tin Pan Alley songsmiths began to cash in on the phenomenon by producing their own, often offensive, pseudo-Hawaiian songs, the Paka troupe continued to focus, nearly exclusively, on recordings in the Hawaiian language. Perhaps their focus on Hawaiian-language repertoire stemmed from their royalist political stance, or from their resistance to the suppression of the Hawaiian language in the Islands.[58] Regardless, their recorded titles (issued and unissued) following the first 1909 session through their 1915 session reflect this near-total emphasis on Hawaiian-language recordings.[59] What is also clear is that their recordings were making it back to the Islands as well as throughout the diaspora.[60] Hawaiian musicians and singers, then, found tremendous possibility in the early recorded music industry. While their language was under attack in the Islands, they found new opportunity in the modern technologies of the period, not only to celebrate the songs of the deposed monarchy but also to use the industry's distribution channels to reach an expanding Hawaiian audience.

Their emphasis on modern Hawaiian repertoire was also reflected in Hannah's dance selections. Hannah and July visited Oʻahu regularly, purchasing a home in Mānoa Valley where they would spend several months at a time with his mother.[61] While Hannah could hardly have received more than a modicum of the training required to fully comprehend and appropriately articulate the dances, she spent as much time in the Islands as they could afford, seemingly for the express purpose of gaining what training she could.[62] While newspaper coverage rarely differentiated her dances, in one interview she was granted the opportunity to name the several genres of hula that she performed onstage, including those of hula kuʻi, pūʻili, and kālaʻau.[63] Also included in her list, however, was the sacred hula ālaʻapapa, a genre that seems particularly inappropriate for performance in commercial venues.[64] It is unclear whether she had witnessed a precedent of such a performance in a commercial dance hall on Oʻahu, and given the reviews by critics who were incapable of (and otherwise uninterested in) providing an informed assessment of her dances, it is impossible to ascertain the degree by which she sought to perfect the dances by the standards she witnessed during her residencies in Mānoa Valley. Yet, it is important to note that commercial venues provided a rare space for Hawaiians in the diaspora to perform publicly any sort of mele or hula. Also noteworthy is that she lived with, traveled with, and otherwise spent all of her time around Hawaiian musicians, all trained or practiced in the Islands, who likely had much to say about which dances she should perform, and how she should go about learning them. A number of Hawaiian musicians working in New York in 1913, for example, commented informally to a visitor from the Islands that Hannah Paka had "learned the dance quite well."[65] Indeed, even while working overseas and beyond, Hawaiian troupes faced critical assessments of their performances by peers from the Islands who, as we will see, provided deeply embedded social obligations to one another and formed a large, tight, yet fluid and mobile diasporic community of musicians and dancers. While during the 1910s Kekuku and July Paka achieved significant success on the vaudeville stage, they were part of a much larger community of Hawaiians in New York, and part of a much bigger story.

By then, of course, New York had already begun to serve as the heart of the country's music industry. There, aspiring songsmiths and vaudeville entertainers from around the world struggled to break into an already overcrowded scene, in an unfamiliar and often overwhelming maze of buildings and bright

FIGURE 13. *By 1910, Toots Paka's Hawaiians had become one of the most popular acts in vaudeville. After Joseph Kekuku left in 1912, July Paka (seen here on the right) became the troupe's principal steel guitarist. Courtesy of the author.*

lights. It also served as a global crossroads for Hawaiian entertainers, one that harbored a large, dynamic, and, because of the nature of their labor, a quite transient Hawaiian community of hundreds and hundreds of performers and their families. By word of mouth, however, all Hawaiian musicians arriving for the first time knew they could find safe harbor and a warm bed at Alexander's, a short- and long-term hotel that catered to traveling artists at 209 East Fourteenth Street, two blocks east of Union Square Park.[66] While the residents shared small double rooms upstairs, the large living room featured comfortable furniture, a piano, a Victrola, and walls of photographs autographed by entertainers to the owner, known to them as "Mrs. Alexander."[67] There, Mrs. Alexander and her guests provided a clearinghouse of information, news and gossip for everyone arriving for a local contract or returning from tours in the United States and abroad.

A visitor to Alexander's in mid-August 1912, for example, received a quite thorough update on the goings on from David Kaleikoa, his spouse, and their troupe members W. K. Bohling, Alfred K. Jones, and John K. Pa'aluhi (by this time a former member of the Paka troupe), who were then taking up residence at the hotel.[68] The group had just returned from several months in England, France, and Germany, and was preparing to begin a thirty-week tour of the central United States. When asked by the visitor where other Hawaiian troupes were performing, they quickly reeled off the locations of some of their friends: Hilo musician George Vierra and his partner Henry K. Kenona's troupe, they reported, was hitting Atlantic City and other nearby seaside resorts, while Joe Puni's outfit was wrapping up a run in New England. That summer, David N. Manaku's troupe was traveling the western vaudeville circuit operated by the colorful "Big Tim" Sullivan and John Considine, while steel guitarist William K. Alohikea and his spouse, along with Joe Keliiaihue, were basing their operations out of Boston, spending that month "swinging around the circle" in Canada.[69] Another steel guitarist, Lui Thompson, along with his spouse, Jack Kumalae and his spouse, and John K. Polihale were at that time "playing one night stands in the Southern States," and planned to remain there through the winter. Steel guitar and ʻukulele player George Kia was playing Santa Cruz, California, while Solomon Moki was winning over audiences at the time in Los Angeles. The reporting went on and on. Finally, the visitor learned, while Duke Kahanamoku was giving surfing exhibitions in Atlantic City, July and Hannah Paka, Dick Reuter, and Joseph Kekuku presently were blowing the roof off the Orpheum in Manhattan.[70]

Less than six months later, another visitor to New York from the Islands began inquiring as to which Hawaiian entertainers were in town or otherwise on the continent. The network again revealed itself. In New York, he learned, "the Hawaiians were the rage." He described Hawaiians Willie and Jack Ellis as "the king-pins in New York City" — Willie was working as an orchestra leader, while Jack was "one of the very best lad singers in the metropolis." With two companies at work in the "leading cafes," they were about to place a third into East Houston Street's "Little Hungary," "one of the biggest show places of New York City. Anybody 'seeing New York' always goes there. It is Bohemia of the Bohemians and is the most unique restaurant in the United States." The musicians on their roster included John Paʻaluhi, David Kaleikoa (referred to as "fully as good" a steel player as Kekuku), Kalama Bohling, Joseph Keliiaihue, Alfred Jones, and William Kanui. George Vierra was working in the city, as were fellow Native musicians Henry Smith, J. A. C. Peterson, and George Kalaluhi. An adolescent boy from Honolulu named Moke Kaiawe was generating a great deal of attention as a hula dancer, while Ben Waiwaiole and steel guitarist Walter Kolomoku were touring in the *Bird of Paradise* theatrical production. Dick Reuter, the former star pitcher of the "old Kam baseball team," had left the Paka troupe and was working in Los Gatos, California.[71] The visitor reported that eighteen men had recently performed at a reception, and that Joseph Kekuku had formed a new company with George Nahaolelua and Miranda Kalaluhi and "commands a big salary." Meanwhile, in Seattle, Solomon Hiram, steel guitarist Frank Ferreira, Willie Kinney, David Nape, and James Kulolia were securing steady work. Mekia Kealaka'i and Joseph Kulolio were working in Los Angeles; David Makuakane and Robert Nawahine were in Portland, Oregon; John Padigon was working in Sacramento while Joseph Pa, John Paoakalani, and Joseph Kalaina were performing in San Francisco. Jimmy Hicks and Henry Manu were working in Omaha, while William Holoua was performing in Boston, and Joe Puni was building a new act in Philadelphia, along with Henry Kamakani, Bill Kahea, Sol Kahananui, and steel guitarist William Alohikea. Finally, the visitor was told that Philip Kanoho was working as the orchestra and bandleader for Admiral Hugo Osterhaus, commander of the U.S. Atlantic Fleet.[72]

While excerpting such lengthy lists here might seem excessive, it exposes a piece of a quite extensive Hawaiian musicians' network operating on the continent by the 1910s. Clearly, as these two kama'āina visitors to New York quickly learned, not only were Hawaiian entertainers well dispersed throughout the United States and other countries by 1912, but they knew where to find each other. With nearly all of them now demonstrating Kekuku's technology, they continued to find lucrative job opportunities that lured them from the Islands. On tours that extended throughout the world, they could generate wages that far surpassed those offered by the unskilled labor and menial trades available to them in a homeland annexed in defiance of their wishes, with prohibitions that stymied their language and traditions. And though the American music industry assimilated Hawaiian music into its category of ethnic novelty, it likewise provided physical and aural space for Hawaiians to expand those traditions, and enough job opportunities to relocate and support large, fluid, but familiar communities of performers.

These communities fostered their language and traditions, and produced regular feasts of poi (cuisine prepared from taro root) and the sharing of important family moments with one another, as when July Paka served as the priest during the naming ceremony for a fellow Hawaiian musician's daughter on the stage of Maxine Elliott's theater, following an afternoon performance.[73] Indeed, they often traveled with spouses, if not entire families. And they shared joy in each other's accomplishments in the diaspora. News traveled fast along the culture industry network, a network that facilitated the labor of Hawaiian entertainers but also reinforced the bonds between them throughout the diaspora. The diaspora flourished in this period, and the industry, wittingly or not, nourished the Hawaiian language, their indigenous guitar technology, and a variety of modern hula and mele genres.

The Hawaiian touring community and the steel guitar flourished in the years that followed, in large part thanks to the dozens of theater companies that traveled throughout the United States and Europe to stage *Bird of Paradise*, a new play by Richard Walton Tully. The plot did not diverge from a then-common formula for American plays featuring Native roles, in that it suggested the ultimate impossibility of interracial unions through the doomed relationship of a white American man and a Hawaiian woman.[74] Similar to the racial logic found in vaudeville and Tin Pan Alley, Tully sought to theatricalize the supremacy and modernity of the white race partially through assigning Native Hawaiians an antimodern role. As he put it, *Bird of Paradise* was a dramatization "of the well-known fact that though we dress, educate, and polish the members of a lower race to the superficial religious and social equality with the Caucasians, at heart he is still the fetish-worshipping savage who will become atavistic in every moment of stress."[75] Tully first workshopped the production with the Los Angeles Belasco Theater's stock company in 1911.[76] In January 1912, it debuted in New York City.[77]

Two aspects of the production seemed to attract the greatest interest, if not praise, since overall the reviews remained mixed. The first was the staging: during the climax of the production, the "chief's" daughter hurls herself into an erupting stagecraft volcano in an effort to appease the volcano god and to resolve the tension created by her interracial relationship with the white protagonist. However, the second main attraction of *Bird of Paradise*, and the source of its lasting cultural impact, was the music. While staging them as poor, maka'āinana "cane-cutters," Tully hired a top-shelf Hawaiian string band to delight the audience in their renditions of several Hawaiian mele. Pivotal to their sound was the prowess of another first-generation steel guitarist and vocalist, Walter Keaumakalani Kolomoku. Born in Honolulu in 1889, Kolomoku was living there with his father, working as a machinist, and developing exceptional skills on the steel guitar when it seems that he was recruited to perform in Tully's New York production.[78] It is unclear whether the rest of the band was in Honolulu at the time or already in New York, but by January Kolomoku was playing the steel alongside Benjamin Waiwaiole (vocals, guitar), S. M. Kaiawe (vocals, 'ukulele, tenor guitar), A. Kiwala (vocals, 'ukulele), and W. B. Aeko (vocals, banjo ʻukulele).[79] It is likely that the band presented repertoire selections to Tully and not the other way around, as there is no indication that he had any understanding of Hawaiian music (or culture, for that matter). They selected, interestingly enough, a number of mele written by royalty, including Kalākaua's "Hawaiʻi Ponoi" and Liliʻuokalani's "Aloha ʻOe." In addition, they performed a number of other modern numbers, including "Waiʻalae," "Ua Like No a Like," "Pua Mohala," "Ahi Wela," "Kuʻu Home," and "Tomi Tomi," along with new hapa haole selections from Cunha and others.[80] Critics raved of the music by day, while by night, Kolomoku and his crew consistently brought the house down.

Victor Records saw great promise in recording the group and signed them in 1913. As for the performers' reaction to Tully's white-supremacist themes, the musicians "severely criticized" Tully's production, at least in private, for not being "fair to the native Hawaiian."[81] Nonetheless, they found professional opportunity in the otherwise offensive production, where they could at least challenge the antimodern roles offered them by playing a modern mele repertoire that demonstrated technical mastery of the steel guitar and ʻukulele—instruments that, indeed, were likely the most modern to be found at that time on Broadway.

The company had staged 112 performances by the time it closed on April 13, 1912.[82] The records of Kolomoku's Hawaiian Quintette circulated beyond the confines of the five boroughs, as did Kolomoku's *Bird of Paradise* troupe, which performed along the East Coast. However, the play's true impact on American music was felt through the countless continental tours of the production by a shifting cast of Hawaiian troupes in the years that followed. Through these tours, and the relentless traveling of Paka's troupe and others, the steel guitar continued to very rapidly seep into the vision, the imagination, the musical palette—the consciousness—of the American populace.

While Kolomoku's troupe performed the production in large cities, a survey of newspapers in the period 1912–19 is striking in their demonstration of the play's widespread popularity.[83] By 1913 *Bird* productions were moving throughout the West, playing in towns of all sizes, from Anaconda, Montana, to Reno, Nevada.[84] Other troupes were meanwhile working their way through the Midwest; Xenia, Ohio's *Daily Gazette*, for example, reported the return of one *Bird of Paradise* troupe in 1915, reminding its readers that the company had already played to "large and interested audiences" the year before.[85] By 1916 the Des Moines, Iowa, society page was blaming the *Bird of Paradise* production for Hawaiian songs' having "taken such a hold on us."[86] A 1918 performance in Greenville, Mississippi, was "greeted by one of the largest and most representative audiences ever gathered in the Grand Theatre here to see a play."[87] When a troupe featuring a Kanaka steel guitarist presented the production in Anniston, Alabama, that same year, the local newspaper billed it as "The Play That Made Hawaiian Music Popular."[88] Its influence and wide exposure is also recorded in the wake of the performances, when the mention of *Bird of Paradise* had become shorthand, as it was in a 1918 Hartford, Kentucky, newspaper, for the impression that "Hawaiʻi is a land where Americans go and just naturally forget how to work, lie down beneath a shady, spread tree and listen to the thrum of the Hawaiian guitars until they're lulled into a sleep from which they seldom are aroused."[89] By the mid-1910s, vast audiences in every region of the United States, in small towns and large, had heard and witnessed the Hawaiian steel guitar firsthand. This must have dumbfounded Joseph Kekuku, who could recall fabricating the first steel bar at Kamehameha School's machine shop, while under Liliʻuokalani's rule, just twenty years before. Now his instrument had found a direct audience that conservatively figured into the hundreds of thousands, with millions more soon to come.

In fact, 19 million people gained the chance to see and hear the steel guitar firsthand in 1915, during San Francisco's seven-month-long Panama-Pacific International Exposition.[90] Celebrating the opening of the Panama Canal, U.S. state and territorial legislatures expended millions of dollars on their individual buildings and displays to promote trade for their constituencies. Because of the close economic and travel ties between Honolulu and San Francisco, and sensing an opportunity to expand the territorial economy through tourism and trade, the territorial legislature dedicated $100,000 to the construction and occupancy of the "Hawaiian Pavilion."[91] While visitors were initially drawn to the pavilion's massive aquariums, endlessly replenished with (rapidly dying) fish, it was Hawaiian string band music, performed daily on a bandstand in the center of the building, which enraptured the visitors.[92] And the visitors were plentiful; on a good day, 34,000 visitors from all over the country entered the pavilion and listened to the band.[93]

Musicians living in the Islands understood the stakes as clearly as did the legislature. Securing a seven-month contract to play in the pavilion could do wonders for their reputations and marketability, particularly as Hawaiian guitar music, thanks to the Pakas, Kekuku, and the *Bird of Paradise* troupes, was among the most requested music on the continent. In addition, unlike the vast majority of Hawaiian musicians, they would not have to stow away or shovel coal on merchant or cruise ships in order to secure their passage to new mar-

FIGURE 14.
Keoki "George" Awai (seated) and his Royal Hawaiian Quartette were one of the most popular acts to perform during the 1915 Panama-Pacific International Exhibition in San Francisco. Courtesy of the author.

kets across the Pacific.[94] For that reason, Hawaiian string bands in Honolulu fiercely competed for the contract, which by November 1914 had yielded two leading contenders: Ernest Ka'ai's Glee Club and Jonah Kumalae's Glee Club. Eventually a third group emerged, organized by upstart songwriter Henry Kailimai. Kailimai's string band won the contract to play daily at the pavilion's bandstand, which led to massive sales in the United States of his hapa haole composition "On the Beach at Waikiki." Meanwhile, Jonah Kumalae won a concession to sell his guitars, ukuleles, and taro-patch fiddles in a pavilion booth. He brought his glee club, featuring steel guitarist Keoki "George" Awai, to demonstrate his instruments.[95] While a young boy in Waialua, O'ahu, Awai was introduced to Kekuku, and practiced Kekuku's method by fabricating his own wooden nut adapter and metal picks.[96] By 1915, just over ten years later, he was performing the instrument before the largest audiences he and his friends had ever seen.

Although the Pakas, Kekuku, and the many *Bird of Paradise* productions crisscrossing the country had already laid the groundwork, the steel guitar gained extraordinary exposure at the fair. While it had been familiar to San Francisco residents for over ten years, visitors to the fair from all over the country seemed to find the instrument wherever they turned. Other Hawaiian guitarists performed throughout the fairgrounds at locations such as the Horticultural Palace and the California Building, while some three dozen Hawaiian musicians performed at the opening ceremony for the Hawaiian building alone.[97] Others performed in nightclubs near the fairgrounds.[98] Visitors did not simply wish to see and hear the instrument, however; they wished to play it as well.

Many of the first-generation Hawaiian steel guitarists began offering instruction on the instrument, as did Kekuku when he first arrived in San Francisco in 1904. Awai remained in San Francisco to locally publish one of the first instructional manuals for the steel guitar, *The Superior Collection of Steel Guitar Solos*.[99] Using an open "A" tuning and the Peterson method of tablature to render the instruction more accessible to those who could not read music, the first selection in the book was Kalākaua's "Hawaiʻi Ponoi."[100] As early as 1914, Hawaiian musician George Kia was teaching the steel method at the George J. Birkel Co. music store in Los Angeles.[101] In 1915 William K. Alohikea published the *"Hawaiian Method" of Playing Guitar Self Taught*.[102] That same year, one of Kekuku's former students, Myrtle Stumpf, published her own *Original Hawaiian Method for the Steel Guitar* through the Southern California Music Company in Los Angeles, purportedly selling 7,000 copies by the summer of 1917.[103] Around the same time, another Kekuku student in Los Angeles, C. S. DeLano, opened a steel guitar conservatory.[104] Kekuku's cousin from Lāʻie, Sam Nainoa, whose fiddle perhaps served as Kekuku's inspiration for the steel guitar, opened the "Sam K. Nainoa Foundation of Hawaiian Music" in Los Angeles a few years later in order to teach the steel guitar.[105] After Walter Kolomoku left the *Bird of Paradise* productions, he founded the First Hawaiian Conservatory of Music in New York City's Woolworth Building and developed steel guitar instructional materials for a popular correspondence course.[106]

The vaudeville tours, the *Bird of Paradise* productions, the conservatories and instructional manuals, the correspondence courses, and world's fairs such as the 1915 Panama-Pacific International Exposition provided unprecedented

FIGURE 15.
Myrtle Stumpf produced one of the earliest method books for the steel guitar in 1915. She had studied with Joseph Kekuku when he lived in San Francisco. By her count she sold 7,000 copies of the book within two years. Courtesy of the author.

opportunity for Hawaiian steel guitarists to transform musical culture in the United States. Wax cylinder and 78 rpm recordings increased their influence even further, with Hawaiian guitar recordings outselling every other genre of music marketed in the United States in 1916. But this begs important questions: Exactly what did American audiences make of the music, particularly when it was recorded, and not performed, in front of their eyes? And why were Hawaiian guitar cylinders and records so popular in the 1910s?

These are not easy questions to answer, but we can begin to address them by considering the state of the music industry in its infancy and early adolescence, from the 1880s through the 1910s. Perhaps most striking about this period are the powerful roles of globalization and ethnic representation in shaping the industry and its genres. As Karl Hagstrom Miller explains, "American music is a product of globalization. Global markets were a major concern of the industry practically from the start, and global experiences were intimately intertwined with the conception and development of music markets in the United States."[107] Through the 1910s, the dominant recorded music companies in the United States—Victor Talking Machine Company, Edison's National Phonograph Company, and Columbia—found their greatest initial success in selling "foreign" recordings in international markets, as well as in selling racial or ethnic novelty recordings made in the United States and its territories. Both phenomena imply a fixation with otherness: blackface minstrelsy, "coon song," and other ethnic novelty songs (songs with themes or lyrics that purported to represent American Indians, Irish immigrants, Jewish immigrants, etc.) had demonstrated long-standing success in the vaudeville and Tin Pan Alley sheet music businesses, and this success translated fairly easily to the recorded music industry. Such songs catered both to multiethnic, urban, working-class audiences and to members of the middle class who were attracted to working-class entertainments. However, record companies quickly ascertained that "ethnic" or "foreign" recordings, made by artists abroad and originally marketed to foreign audiences, attracted American consumers in even greater numbers. By 1910, in fact, the "foreign" or "ethnic" records and wax cylinders sold in the United States "outnumbered domestic releases by a significant margin."[108] From the very beginning, then, aural ethnicity triggered remarkable sales of recorded sound in the United States.

Eventually the music industry adopted a variety of marketing strategies to increase the sales of domestic releases, from marketing Western art music recordings in the name of "cultural uplift" to selling "foreign" recordings to corresponding diasporic immigrant populations. From the latter effort emerged, by the 1920s, the development of a new local market strategy: all of the major companies soon launched "hillbilly" record lists of southern white string bands marketed to southern white audiences (as well as to those southern whites migrating north for factory work). They additionally produced "race" lists that featured African American string bands and other black vocalists and ensembles to target African American consumers. Indeed, it seemed that all of the recorded music industry's marketing strategies were profoundly informed by supremacist views on race, civilization, and primitivism, and infused with concerns over how best to profit from them.[109]

Of course, audiences brought a variety of interpretations to the recordings that they purchased in furniture and talking machine shops, and Hawaiian guitar music was no exception. The recordings were marketed and sold in the Islands, and they circulated among the diasporic population as well. Yet in the United States the Hawaiian guitar records sold in much greater numbers to non-Hawaiian consumers, to whom the recordings would have indeed sounded quite foreign: nearly all of the recorded mele were sung in Hawaiian, and the instruments, as the previously cited critics' remarks attest, sounded unlike anything the record purchasers had ever heard before. Hawaiian guitar music recordings, then, found a quite unique footing in the U.S. market, as their sales exceeded those of most other genres in the mid-1910s.

The sales are explained at least partially through the music's allure of ethnic novelty. The music, often explicitly marketed and associated with female hula dancers, had long entranced non-Hawaiians as exotica, if not erotica. Knowledge of Calvinist prohibitions of the hula dance in the Islands only provoked the interest of many non-Hawaiians, who yearned to experience what these social conservatives had expressly forbidden. A haole from the Islands who saw the Pakas perform in San Francisco put it thusly: "You can see much racier Toots Pakas in Honolulu anytime, or could not long ago, and when our friends from the Coast came ashore with a knowing leer and said 'I want to see it,' if we boys couldn't stir up a better show than 'Toots' gives we'd feel ashamed of the Bohemian atmosphere we tried to throw over the day's visit of the steamer 'stopovers.'"[110] He continued by noting that "Toots was assisted by a trio of *brown enough* Hawaiians," and he lamented that "she's a headliner not for what she does evidently as what she represents in the minds of the average citizen east of the Sierra Nevada mountains. . . . Nobody would go to see a motley crew of Filipinos, but crowds will swarm to see a group of Filipino 'headhunters' and go away with a very definite idea of what life was like in the Philippines."[111]

For such consumers, Hawaiian guitar recordings, as well as live performances, conjured images that reinforced white supremacy while tapping into a voyeuristic, sexual desire for women of color. In addition, the popularity of blackface minstrelsy and "coon songs," while still quite strong in the 1910s, seemed to lose their footing in this period, just as white Americans began attending Hawaiian performances, listening to Hawaiian records, taking up the ʻukulele and steel guitar, and, slowly but surely, donning their own leis and grass skirts. Kekuku and July Paka, the "brown enough" Hawaiians in that San Francisco performance, certainly seemed to fit the writer's racial expectations, akin to those assigned to blackface minstrels.

The reasons for audience attraction to Hawaiian guitar music could vary dramatically, however. For some, the recordings conveyed antimodern primitivism, notwithstanding the fact that steel guitars were among the newest, most cutting-edge instruments available. Others developed an interest in the music from their curiosity about the Islands, enhanced by their recent "annexation" by the United States and the territorial government's marketing campaigns to develop tourism. Still others, as we have seen, became mesmerized by the sound of the music, in particular that produced by the steel guitar, and the new skill set required to conjure those sounds. With consumers driven by each of these interests and more, sales of Hawaiian guitar records broke the mold of prior marketing strategies by combining them in a new focus on the archipelago and its music.

In the 1910s, however, even while non-Hawaiians slowly began to cash in on the Hawaiian "craze" through the creation of pseudo-Hawaiian songs and bands, commercial Hawaiian guitar recordings remained dominated by Kanaka musicians, who seemed to maintain significant control over the repertoire. It is likely, given the mele selections recorded by the Paka troupe, that no industry representative would have understood the songs' lyrics and meanings, or realized that the monarchs had written many of them, or that their language had been banned from many elements of life in Hawai'i.[112] The industry personnel likely would not have cared about such things, as long as the records could sell. And they did. This disinterest gave Hawaiian recording artists extraordinary leeway in determining the nature of the genre itself. And during this period, steel guitarists, the most prominently featured musicians in the Hawaiian music genre, produced hundreds of recordings by the end of World War I, and thousands by the end of the 1920s.

A double-columned Hawaiian records advertisement in a 1917 Gulfport, Mississippi, newspaper demonstrates the immense reach and popularity of recorded Hawaiian guitar music and also identifies the most popular steel guitarists of the period and their recorded repertoire. Thirty-three of the sides advertised are either steel guitar instrumentals or songs performed on the steel and sung in Hawaiian, while the remaining three, written by Sonny Cunha and Sylvester Kalama, incorporate English and Hawaiian lyrics and represent the emergence of the hapa haole genre. In addition to Kalākaua's "Hawai'i Ponoi" and multiple songs by Lili'uokalani, the list includes popular recordings by the

FIGURE 16.
Pale K. Lua was one of the most gifted steel guitarists of his generation. He recorded several top-selling sides with David Kaili in the 1910s, spurring Hawaiian guitar music to outsell all other genres in the United States in 1916. Like Joseph Kekuku, he was born in Lāʻie. Courtesy of Les Cook.

Paka troupe and Kolomoku's Hawaiian Quintette. The ad also announces the arrival of new steel guitarists to the States.

The new arrivals, who had recorded most of the songs represented in the advertisement two to three years before, included Pale Kealakuhilima Lua and David Kaili, who recorded sides both as a duo (Lua and Kaili) and with the Irene West Royal Hawaiians (aka the Royal Hawaiian Sextet). Lua and Kaili had both arrived in New York around 1913. Lua was born in 1895 in Lāʻie,

Kekuku's home, and while he became known in O'ahu for his skill on the violin, he may have learned the steel while a very young boy from Kekuku.[113] By early 1914 he and Kaili had joined with Irene West (1882–1966), a white dancer from Dallas who had earlier toured on vaudeville circuits.[114] With West now their manager and booking agent, Lua and Kaili's instrumental recordings in 1914 and 1915 included "Kohala March," "The Rosary" (earlier made famous as a steel guitar instrumental by Kekuku's performances), "Ua Like No a Like," "Kilima March," and "Wailana Waltz."[115]

The stunning clarity of Lua's playing is not heard in previous steel guitar recordings. A new group of Kanaka guitarists, only a few years younger than Kekuku and Paka, seems to have greatly advanced the technique. Most of their work must have taken place before they left the Islands, for Lua had only lived on the continent for a short time before his talent was noticed and recorded in the Camden, New Jersey, Victor studios.[116] West certainly recognized it, as she took Lua and Kaili on tours throughout the United States, London, and perhaps South America before his untimely death.[117]

The final act mentioned in the Gulfport, Mississippi, advertisement was a steel guitarist from Hawai'i who came to dominate Hawaiian guitar recordings for nearly twenty years. The first recordings by Frank "Palakiko" Ferreira (Ferera) were released in 1915; by the time his recording career wound down in 1933, he had recorded thousands of sides with dozens of Hawaiian and non-Hawaiian groups, and he had produced perhaps an eighth of all the Hawaiian guitar recordings made during that period, often hailed as the "golden era" of the Hawaiian steel guitar.[118] While other guitarists combined extensive work on the road with their recording careers, Ferreira seems to have toured very little once he moved to New York City. As Hawaiian music discographer Malcolm Rockwell put it, "Musicians like Ferreira practically lived in the recording studios in New York City, and would play for any company who asked them and had the money to hire them."[119] He recorded in bands whose names ran practically all the way through the alphabet, from the Aloha Hawaiian Orchestra to the Waikiki Serenaders. Yet despite his ubiquity on the era's recordings, we know surprisingly little about his life.

We do know that Ferreira was born in Honolulu on June 12, 1885, and that he was not Hawaiian. His parents were Portuguese; both arrived in the Islands sometime before he was born.[120] At least for a time after the guitarist had left for the U.S. continent, his father worked as Honolulu's assistant hack (taxi) inspector.[121] It is not clear when he began to play the steel guitar, but his daughter recalls very clearly Ferreira stating that his father "was not a kind man" and

FIGURE 17. *Frank Ferreira recorded thousands of sides over the course of his career—likely more than any other steel guitarist in history. This image features Ferreira (seated with the steel guitar) recording with Anthony Franchini (Spanish guitar) and the Crescent Trio singers in an acoustic recording studio in New York City. Together they recorded predominantly Hawaiian songs during at least four sessions held between November 1920 and June 1921. Courtesy of the Library of Congress.*

strongly disapproved of his interest in the instrument. As a result, she says, he stole away into Oʻahu's Koʻolau Mountains to practice.[122] Perhaps owing to his difficulties with his father, shortly after completing the eighth grade Ferreira left the Islands for the U.S. continent, around 1900.[123] He began performing on the vaudeville circuit soon after he arrived.[124] By 1913 he had established himself as a steel guitarist in Seattle, where he likely met his second wife, Helen Louise.[125] The two of them began recording together as "Louise and Ferera" in 1915 and from the beginning combined Hawaiian music with hapa haole and non-Hawaiian hits from Tin Pan Alley. They recorded on Columbia, Victor, Edison, Gennett, Pathé, Imperial—practically every major label.[126] They attracted a great deal of attention and cultivated their career as a guitar duo, bolstering the already burgeoning Hawaiian guitar record genre.

Louise's fortune changed quickly toward the end of 1918, when the couple relocated to Honolulu and spent several months there "for her health." After a brief return to New York for studio work in mid-1919, they traveled west once more, to San Francisco and Los Angeles. In December of that year, the couple took a steamship from Los Angeles to Seattle. According to Frank Ferreira, she left their stateroom around four in the morning and never returned; Louise was considered "lost at sea."[127]

Frank Ferreira had begun recording with guitarist Anthony Franchini in the months before Louise died, and he recorded a few sides in the months that followed with David Kaili, Pale K. Lua's former partner.[128] For Ferera and Franchini, as well as their other groups—the Hawaiian Trio, the Hawaiian Quartet, the Hawaiian Dance Orchestra, the Ferera Waikiki Sextette, the Hawaiian Entertainers, Ferera's Hawaiian Serenaders, and many others—the next five years were a period of staggering recorded output, during which they cut hundreds and hundreds of sides.[129] Ferreira would record thousands more before he effectively retired in 1933.[130] Bailing out of a business hard hit by the Great Depression (in 1933, records sales dropped to 10 million, from 110 million sold in 1921), he then dedicated his full attention to a delicatessen he had previously opened in Queens.[131] Though playing occasionally for parties at his friend Thomas Edison's house, or in his kitchen with the family, Ferreira never again recorded or publicly performed on the steel guitar.[132] His stature as the world's most recorded steel guitarist was unrivaled, however, for decades to come.[133] As a non-Hawaiian guitarist, his willingness to apply the steel guitar to practically every musical genre lay the groundwork for a vast expansion of the instrument's application beyond the repertoire first established by Kekuku, Kolomoku, and other early Hawaiian masters.

From the mid-1920s until his retirement, Ferreira partnered with John Pa'aluhi, one of Joseph Kekuku's earliest performing partners on the East Coast.[134] Pa'aluhi's accompaniment bridged the work of the most prolific steel guitarist of the 1920s and early 1930s with that of the originator of the steel guitar technique and technology. Such interesting connections only increased as Hawaiian musicians expanded their vast diasporic network, tethered together through the wild popularity of steel guitar music in the entertainment markets of the United States.[135]

Kekuku eventually broke with the Paka troupe to refocus his work under his own name. After returning to Los Angeles in 1913, he taught lessons and led a number of Hawaiian troupes, including Kekuku's Hawaiian Quintet, a highly successful group that often headlined on Chautauqua circuits throughout the country. In June 1919, however, soon after the conclusion of the Great

FIGURE 18. *After leaving Toots Paka's Hawaiians in 1912, Joseph Kekuku continued to tour the United States in acts such as Kekuku's Hawaiian Quintet until he sailed for Europe in 1919. Courtesy of the University of Iowa Libraries, Iowa City, Iowa.*

War, he sailed for Europe with fellow musicians Mekia Kealakaʻi and William Kamoku.[136]

Kekuku's relocation to Europe, while emblematic of the global success of his invention, was also quite routine by this point for Hawaiian musicians, many of whom had already played in the theaters of France and England, if not for European royalty. Between military service during the war, and the rising popularity of the steel guitar overseas, the pull to Europe was strong and sustaining for many young Hawaiians throughout the next two decades. However, other guitarists began venturing elsewhere, to India, New Zealand, China, and beyond. The steel guitar, as we will see in the next chapter, came to link commercial and vernacular musics throughout the world to a very specific guitar tradition, of Hawaiian origins.

4 *Hawaiian Troubadours and the Global Reach of the Kīkā Kila*

Museums, universities, and municipal buildings in Hawai'i protect vast collections of documents produced by Hawaiians over the last two centuries. Their nature and provenance sometimes reveals tortured, imperial histories: Lili'uokalani's diaries, for example, stolen from 'Iolani Palace in the days following the overthrow and occupation, are now kept in the vaults of the Hawai'i State Archives. So are the deeds of foreclosure that alienated incredulous and bereft taro planters from their lands surrounding Kahana Bay—Joseph Kekuku's birthplace—in the early twentieth century. Yet the indigenous archives in the Islands, manifold and vast, conserve a profound literary record of Hawaiian knowledge and experience.

During one trip to the Bishop Museum Library and Archives, I studied the facsimiles of photographs of Hawaiian musicians that fill cabinets along the walls of the reading room. Wonderful photographs taken in the 1880s and 1890s feature young male and female guitarists, including Kalākaua's famed Singing Boys, posing in 1890 with a guitar, fiddle, banjo, 'ukulele, and accordion.[1] Steel guitars are everywhere in the photographs, but two images, in particular, made me pause: one features several Hawaiian musicians in white outfits with leis and sashes, gleefully posing with a familiar-looking steel guitarist. The other includes some of the same musicians, this time in traveling clothes aboard a steamer, destination unknown. The photographs are located in different folders, yet their six-digit catalog numbers are nearly identical. Curious, I asked the archivist if he could provide me with the sources of the original images. It took him a while, but eventually he produced a box that contained two dusty scrapbooks, marked on the covers, "Queenie Kaili and Her Vaudeville Troupe, 1924–5."[2]

It is extremely rare to come upon such an intimate view of life on the road. The inside cover of the first scrapbook holds an 8″ × 10″ of a young woman's shining face signed, "To Queenie and Dave. The Incomparable Duo. Aloha Nui, Goldie Kolomoku." The snapshots that follow document the troupe's ambitious travels over two years in Australia and New Zealand. Some feature

FIGURE 19. *Queenie Kaili (left) with friends at the Christchurch, New Zealand, Opera House. The billboard advertises their show as "Queenie and David Kaili, Monarchs of the Steel Guitar." Courtesy of Bishop Museum.*

their swims in Byron Bay. Others show them visiting monuments and local museums. In another, two gentlemen donning leis hold beautiful hollow-necked guitars above a caption that reads, "Home-made Steel Guitar." Some photographs are labeled, others are not, while many feature zany poses with jagged edges cut into them, pasted at playful, wacky angles in the scrapbook. Favorite pets are immortalized in some images, while another finds the musicians on the SS *Aorangi* bound for New Zealand. Some feature fellow Hawaiian musicians such as steel guitarist (indeed instrumentalist extraordinaire) Henry Bishaw, and Goldie's husband, steel guitarist Walter Kolomoku. In a photo with friends taken by the stage door of the opera house in Christchurch, New Zealand, we see a large promotional poster that reads, "Queenie & David Kaili, Monarchs of the Steel Guitar." And, finally, the scrapbook confirms the identity of the steel guitarist who first attracted my attention—the subject of two snapshots with friends—as none other than Pale K. Lua, the brilliant musician from Lāʻie.

FIGURE 20. *From David and Queenie Kaili's scrapbook, this image features Pale K. Lua on the steel guitar and his old partner David Kaili on the standard guitar, along with several unidentified individuals. Given Kaili and Lua's pairing, this image was likely taken in the mid-1910s. Courtesy of Bishop Museum.*

Surely similar scrapbooks by Hawaiian performers from this period survive today as family heirlooms. It is unclear how Mary Louise "Queenie" Kaili's scrapbooks left her hands and fell into those of the rare-book appraiser who donated them to the Bishop in 1978.[3] Mystery surrounds the scrapbooks' journey, as well as the identity of many of the friends and family inside them. Yet Queenie Kaili's scrapbooks are also instructive. For here we can gain a semblance of the perspective of Hawaiian troubadours as the world unfolded before them, as musicians, ambassadors, entrepreneurs, tourists, friends, lovers, family. Of course, Kānaka had traveled for centuries throughout the Pacific Ocean and beyond. When the Kailis left the Islands to embark on their own journeys, their experiences followed such tradition, yet it ended in tragedy, a

FIGURE 21. *Another image from David and Queenie Kaili's scrapbooks, this image features a music shop owned by their friend from Hawai'i, Henry Bishaw. Bishaw set up several shops in Australia and New Zealand during the 1920s. This one featured a range of instruments for sale, including a steel guitar, hanging in the upper right side of the frame. Courtesy of Bishop Museum.*

consequence of the ravages of war. Their brushes with adventure, awe, success, and struggle along the way, however, reflected those of their fellow Hawaiian troubadours who traveled the world during the interwar years, in a vastly expanding diaspora.[4]

North American markets attracted some of the most significant Hawaiian guitarists following the overthrow and, as we will see later, the sounds of the continent changed dramatically as a result. Yet many of those same guitarists, including Kekuku, also labored far beyond the Pacific world, far beyond North America. Their itinerant travel exposes the channels, markets, and mediums that globalized the modern culture industries, in which the United States played an ever-increasing role. For this reason, this chapter's foray beyond the Islands during the interwar period, and beyond the United States, explores the arc and the breadth of the Hawaiian steel guitar's influence, while also providing us with an intimate view of life on the road.

Relying principally on letters, scrapbooks, interviews, and other personal recollections, this chapter illuminates the experiences of a few steel guitarists and fellow musicians laboring in Europe and Asia during the early to mid-twentieth century. Their stories, while often quite personal and unique, speak to common themes encountered by performers navigating interpersonal relationships as well as broader, geopolitical forces during this period. Letters home from a steel guitarist in London reveal the joys and curiosities of encountering new lands and new peoples, as well as new communities of Hawaiians already abroad. The recollections of steel guitarist Tau Moe and his daughter Dorian, meanwhile, demonstrate not only the challenges encountered by foreign audience dynamics and expectations but also a stunning tale of intrigue behind enemy lines in Nazi Germany. Equally remarkable is the influence of Tau Moe's steel guitar in India, which flourished deep into the twentieth century. Indeed, the stories that unfold in the following pages collectively demonstrate how a handful of Pacific Islander steel guitarists navigated challenges and opportunities in unique and remarkable ways as they created a world that became fascinated by the Hawaiian steel guitar.

Soon after steel guitarists embarked on tours of the United States, they began to capitalize on Europeans' interest in Hawaiian music. Visits by aliʻi nui in the nineteenth century, vaudeville tours, and campaigns by the recorded music industry sparked interest within burgeoning European entertainments markets. By the conclusion of World War I, several Hawaiian musicians had already established successful careers throughout Europe. Steel guitarist Kiwini Panui's letters from London to his mother in 1920, published while he was abroad in the Hawaiian-language newspaper *Ka Nupepa Kuokoa*, open a window into the world of musicians and their loved ones traveling the British Isles in the aftermath of World War I.[5] Such letters expressed their love and affection for their families, but when published in Hawaiian newspapers, they also served as important news sources. Panui and others who left home detailed the whereabouts and welfare of fellow Hawaiian musicians they encountered abroad.

Panui encountered over a dozen Hawaiian entertainers working in London when he arrived in 1920, including Joseph Kekuku.[6] Other entertainers had already left London after squandering their money, as Panui put it, or losing their contracts; they had to work on ships, some "pouring oil into the engine," in order to return to the States, where the work was more plentiful. Panui's troupe had secured consistent work, however, most recently at the restaurant in London's Selfridge store, which claimed to accommodate 5,000 diners; many "bought" seats near the stage for the duration of Panui's residency. Mekia Kealaka'i's troupe also performed regularly at the department store, where patrons eagerly requested such mele as "Pua Carnation" ("all of London knows the song"). For those under contracts, Panui wrote, the money was good and the hours were short. This gave them ample time to explore their new surroundings.[7]

Explore they did. Panui described London's architecture as "like the houses you see in Fairy Tale books," though he preferred the vistas and beauty of the skyscrapers in New York. The city still exhibited destruction unleashed by German zeppelin raids during the war, but he was awed by the size of the Palace of Westminster and the Abbey. The zoo also delighted him: "Its size is maybe the same as the town of Honolulu," and it was filled with "monkeys, elephants, giraffes, rhinoceroses, hippopotamuses, all sorts of birds, eagles, tigers, llamas[,] . . . snakes," and more. He enjoyed the "huge" market at Piccadilly, watched a world championship bantam boxing match, and thrilled at his group's first performance before a motion picture camera. He and his bandmates took in the city's famous fog, quite literally, when it invaded not only their performance hall but also their throats as they sang. "It is as if you had no voice," he complained. Panui and his friends were quite taken by the habits of Londoners, from their unusual expressions to their drinking rum at any occasion, such as "when the British see that there is a lot of fog," to drinking tea . . . all the time: "I believe that the British are the most fanatical behind the Chinese and the Japanese. You wake up in the morning at 7 A.M., and drink tea; at 9 A.M., drink tea again; at 12 noon, you drink tea; at 4:30 P.M., you of course drink tea; at 6 P.M., you have tea while you dine."[8]

Of course, Panui also missed home. He expressed how he missed his family and how he enjoyed receiving his mother's letters and newspapers from home ("I was delighted to read the news of my beloved land"). In particular, he missed poi, noting that while his mother was certainly enjoying pig with poi at the celebration of the New Year, he was stuck in London, "having chicken on this side of the world." Fortunately, his troupe eventually found a chance to eat poi palaoa (made with flour and water) with stew and raw mackerel ("like opelu") when fellow Hawaiian musician John Moa invited them to his London flat. Panui wrote that he planned to return to the Islands soon and added,

"If I accumulate a sufficient sum, I am coming home for good."[9] Indeed, he returned to Honolulu with the others on June 1.[10]

Beyond providing a first-person window into the leisure activities of musicians on the road, Panui's letters reveal the expansive travels of Hawaiian musicians during this period, as well as the interconnectedness of the diaspora. This window also enables us to reconstruct the travels of the many Hawaiians he encountered in England. Several of those mentioned in his letters, for example, were on tour under the leadership of troupe manager and steel guitarist Joe Puni. Born in Honolulu in 1868, Puni by 1901 was managing various Hawaiian troupes as they performed in New England and the southeastern United States.[11] After playing for eight years at Coney Island, Puni sailed for Paris in 1913 with fellow steel guitarist William Kulii Kanui on a three-month contract.[12] Though modest, this engagement sparked for Puni a twenty-six-year run of tours that spanned four continents.[13]

When Panui met him, however, Puni was in London to accompany a Hawaiian ensemble for the first British production of *Bird of Paradise*, which debuted at the West End's Lyric Theatre in September 1919.[14] Puni was accompanied by a married couple, John and Lily Moa, brothers William and John Kamoku (William was assigned to play the steel guitar in this production), and Diamond Kekona, who years before had married an Englishwoman and enlisted in the British army during the war.[15] Puni was for a time married to a Frenchwoman from La Fère (in the Picardy region) named Lucia, though it is unclear if she had accompanied him for the London contract.[16] This *Bird of Paradise* production, postponed by the war but soon after introduced to the London stage with great fanfare, ran for 310 performances before closing in June 1920. Long before the end of the first run, however, Richard Walton Tully had organized and deployed yet another *Bird of Paradise* company—his twenty-ninth such company, in fact—to take the show to Portsmouth and other towns in the British Isles.[17] With Hawaiian guitarists traveling throughout the United Kingdom to perform in the show in the years that followed, the production was revived once more in London at the Garrick Theatre in 1922.[18]

Although these *Bird of Paradise* productions, like those in the United States, perhaps should receive the most credit for so early and so quickly introducing the steel guitar to residents of small towns throughout the British Isles, many British and other European audiences had already had some familiarity with Hawaiian culture. A long list of aliʻi nui had visited and conducted diplomatic missions to England, from Kamehameha and Kamāmalu's journey in 1824, to the visits of Kalākaua and Liliʻuokalani, to Princess Kaʻiulani's abrupt depar-

FIGURE 22. *Richard Tully's dozens of roving* Bird of Paradise *productions likely introduced more American and English audiences to Hawaiian steel guitarists than any other phenomenon. This company included John Moa and Diamond Kekona on ʻukulele, Joseph Puni and Gabriel Papaia on Spanish guitar, and William Kamoku on steel guitar (second from left). They debuted at London's Lyric Theatre in 1919. Courtesy of the author.*

ture following the overthrow, so the British court had considerable exposure to Hawaiian sovereigns and their mele.[19] Makaʻāinana had visited as well, however: soon after the overthrow, a hula troupe that had trained in Kalākaua's court toured Europe. A charm bracelet that once belonged to dancer Kini Kapahu and made its way in the 1980s into the hands of a Honolulu stamp and coin dealer gives us a sense of the places they visited: stamped into the bracelet are charms from Hamburg, dated April 28, 1894; Munich, May 10, 1894; Chemnitz, June 6, 1894; and Berlin, June 6, 1894.[20] Yet we know that Kapahu's troupe also performed in Paris and toured England for two months before sailing for the U.S. continent.[21] Doubtless more Hawaiian entertainers soon followed; a 1912 letter to the Hawaiian newspaper *Kuokoa Home Rula* indicates that several musicians from the Islands had performed in England, Germany, and France in recent years.[22] The steel guitar quickly followed, if it had not arrived before: Pale K. Lua seems to have performed in London with David Kaili and the rest of Irene West's Royal Hawaiians in 1914.[23] Finally, steel guitarist Louis Thompson, a Kamehameha School graduate from the class of 1900, relocated to Europe in 1914 and performed and recorded regularly in England and France over the next several years, using a colorful series of aliases along the way.[24] By 1919 he had performed with his steel guitar in Sweden, Norway, Denmark, Holland, Germany, and several other European countries. By early 1920, at least, London music stores were responding to customer demands by stocking steel guitars with "Kamiki Method" instructional materials.[25]

Joseph Kekuku, for his part, arrived in London in 1919, alongside Mekia Kealakaʻi and William Kamoku, and at the behest of Joe Puni, to fulfill a contract at the prestigious Savoy Hotel.[26] Soon after their arrival, however, Kamoku signed onto the first English *Bird of Paradise* production, while Kealakaʻi returned the next year to Honolulu to head the Royal Hawaiian Band by the request of the Honolulu mayor, Johnny Wilson. Wilson, interestingly enough, had managed Louis Thompson, Mekia Kealakaʻi, and July Paka on their 1901 U.S. continental tour and performances at the Buffalo exposition, and was the husband of Kini Kapahu, the dancer from Kalākaua's court whose charm bracelet had ended up years later behind the counter of Hawaiian Islands Stamp and Coin. The network continued to unfurl across the continent. Kekuku seems to have performed in at least one European *Bird of Paradise* production, but he remained in Europe for eight years; assuming residences in Paris and London, he performed during this period in Spain, Switzerland, Belgium, Italy, Germany, Portugal, Sweden, and Denmark.[27] Consistently referred to in the British press as the "originator of the Hawaiian steel guitar," he taught the instrument in England, performed in a number of stage productions, and eventually developed a successful vaudeville routine before returning to North America.[28] The work of Kekuku, Panui, and their compatriots generated a passionate following in the British Isles for the Hawaiian guitar. In turn, for Hawaiians traveling in Europe and beyond, the steel guitar seemed to create boundless opportunity.

Sitting in her kitchen in Lāʻie on an afternoon in 2013, as a summer rain drizzled on her roof, Dorian Moe insisted that for foreign audiences "steel is the first. Steel would be the key. That would be the main draw."[29] Born while her family was "on the road" in Calcutta during World War II, she had spent her first four decades living in Europe and India, performing in the Aloha Four, her family's Hawaiian music and dance troupe. Her parents, Tau and Rose Moe, had worked on the road since they left Hawaiʻi in 1928. Though

Rose also played steel guitar, Tau became famous for his virtuosity. Together, they embarked on a steel-guitar odyssey that led them around the world and did not end until they returned permanently to Lā'ie in 1982. Their recollections provide tremendous insight into the assumptions of their audiences, their professional strategies as entertainers, and the far-reaching resonance and cultural reverberations that the steel generated in the twentieth century. At the same time, their navigation of quite harrowing geopolitical forces demonstrates the cultural and linguistic fluencies required of itinerant musicians working global circuits during this period.

Dorian's mother, Rose Ka'ohu (1907–98), was from Kohala on the island of Hawai'i but moved to Honolulu at some point before 1928. Living with her brother, a policeman, she worked in a laundry while developing a potent combination of singing, dancing, and other musical skills.[30] Tau Moe (1909–2004) was the son of Savea Aupiu Moe and Talalupelele Lupe Tuitogama'atoe, Samoans from Pago Pago and Pue Mutiatele, respectively, who had converted to Mormonism and moved with their children to Lā'ie in 1918, when Tau was ten years old.[31] Though encouraged by the missionary opportunities that the Mormon church in Lā'ie presented them, it is likely that their move to Hawai'i during the same year that the influenza epidemic decimated Samoa was no coincidence. Tau Moe recalled a death rate of 90 percent in his village shortly before they left, with British soldiers disposing of hundreds of corpses in mass burials.[32] He could also recall, in the 1980s, hearing the wails of ghosts haunting their final nights in his deserted village.[33] Perhaps with the memories of his homeland obscured by such horror, he rather quickly embraced his new life in Lā'ie, learning Hawaiian, working in the nearby taro patches, and taking up the steel guitar in its birthplace.[34]

Tau Moe's family was quite musical; his father was a chorister in the church, where Tau learned to read music. He learned to play his friend's five-string banjo, and when he became enthralled with Hawaiian guitar records — the first being a wax cylinder recording of Joseph Kekuku that he heard soon after he arrived — his sister saved the money she earned from a Chinese laundry to order him a guitar from a Montgomery Ward catalog.[35] He quickly converted the standard guitar to a kīkā kila by installing a raised nut; he filed the ridges off of a metal file to serve as a bar. Recognizing the additional need for fingerpicks, he used his mother's hairpins to craft his own.[36] Tau quickly developed his own style; while tuning his guitar to the popular steel guitar open A chord, and playing the lead melody on the top strings, he simultaneously picked combinations of the open bass strings, in kī hō'alu fashion.[37]

Tau thus learned to play the steel guitar by combining several different approaches, likely paralleling the paths of many who took to the instrument. Most often, he attended luaus, parties, and other gatherings with string bands where people would gather in order to watch the steel players. He vividly recalled seeing one of his favorite steel guitar recording artists, Sol Hoʻopiʻi, perform in Honolulu in 1928. After moving there and landing a job with the telephone company, he enrolled in guitar lessons with M. K. Moke.[38] Moe learned any way he could, however. He recalled, "M. K. Moke gave us lessons in a room over a music store called 'Hawaiian Sales.' They had all the latest Victrolas and records. I didn't have any money to buy a record but I wanted to learn the music you know. So they would demonstrate the records there in the store, and me and my friends stand outside and listen to it. Try and remember it and go home to copy it. We had to learn the hard way (laughs)."[39]

The records of Pale K. Lua, Frank Ferreira, and Sol Hoʻopiʻi made the greatest impressions on Tau, who would rush home after hearing them and "practice, practice, practice!"[40] Other popular records in the Islands from 1928 included "Hilo Hanakahi" and "On the Beach at Waikiki" by the Waikiki Stone-Wall Boys, featuring Joseph Kawehi Punahele on steel. Tau recalled, "I took his recording and arrangement for Rose to dance when we left Hawaii on December that year, it was . . . the hit recording of the time," as was, a few months later, he remembered, Moke's "Moana Chimes."[41] Moe met Rose Kaʻohu when he walked in on her own steel guitar lesson with Moke. She was playing "Hula Blues," and he was quite taken with her.[42]

Their futures became further entwined through the efforts of a French educator and entertainment entrepreneur, Madame Claude Rivière (1883–1972).[43] After Rivière's husband died during World War I, she moved first to the United States, teaching French at Bryn Mawr College, and eventually relocated to Tahiti in 1923 to study the economy at the behest of the French government. There, she became absorbed with local music and met Tau Moe's young uncle, Tauivi Moe, who played ʻukulele for her in Samoa.[44] By 1926, she was teaching French at the University of Hawaiʻi at Mānoa and had converted three or four rooms of her house into a theater in order to stage a "Polynesian show."[45] Rivière met tourists as they disembarked from their ships and lured them to her home; in consequence, the shows became quite successful and provided part-time income for several entertainers.

Tau's half uncles, Tauvivi, Fuifui, and Pulu, had recently relocated from Samoa to Honolulu, and all three soon joined Rivière's show, with Tau Moe joining on Spanish guitar on the weekends for two dollars per day.[46] In an interesting precursor to the shows later developed at the LDS-operated Polynesian Cultural Center in Lāʻie, the Moe Brothers, as they were billed, not only played music but performed tree-climbing and basketry demonstrations as well as Samoan knife and other dances.[47] Yet Rivière had also grown fascinated with Hawaiian string band music and hired Frank Jonah Keiki to play steel on the weekends.[48]

Eventually Rivière determined to take the string band on an Asian tour and begged Tau to join. Moe recalled, "Madame Riviere was looking for a guitar player for her show. Well, I did not want to join because I already made arrangements to stay here to go to school. Then in the end she keep forcing me. She offer everybody $20, but she offered me $30," he recalled, out of desperation for his talents as a guitarist.[49] Eventually Rivière offered Tau forty dollars per week, plus transportation, an offer he could not refuse. Rose also joined the troupe after entering a competition held by Rivière to attract a female performer. According to her daughter Dorian, "out of a hundred and something women they picked my mom for the simple reason that she could dance and she could sing. Most of the other girls could do either one or the other, you understand. She could do both . . . plus she could also play."[50] The new troupe performed a week of "farewell shows" at the Oʻahu Theater.[51] Then, with the cautious blessings of the Moe and Kaʻohu families and a Martin guitar given to Tau by M. K. Moke, the troupe set sail for Manila on December 27, 1928. Rose and Tau married soon after.[52]

Their farewell performance at the Oʻahu preceded five years of nonstop touring with Rivière. In 1929 alone, the group—billed variously as the Royal Samoan Dancers, the Samoan Troupe, and Madame Riviere's Hawaiians,—performed for audiences in Manila, Hong Kong, Shanghai, Beijing, and Hankow, as well as several cities in Japan.[53] Frank Jonah Keiki left the group in Tokyo, where he was hired by fellow Hawaiian Dan Pokipala to join his large band.[54] At that point Tau Moe took over the steel guitar duties; the group cut thirteen sides in a Tokyo studio before moving on to perform in Singapore, Kuala Lumpur, and Burma, as well as Calcutta, Delhi, and many other cities and towns in India, where they continued to work through 1933. After performances in Karachi and Manila, where they ran into Queenie and David Kaili, Rose and Tau eventually embarked on a career as a duo, all the while training their young son, Lani, who was born in Kyoto, to join the act.[55]

In those first years, however, the troupe toured under Rivière's aegis. Her shows were very particular—she lent them an "educational" bent by attempting to demonstrate Samoan and Hawaiian lifeways both before and after their

FIGURE 23. *Tau Moe on steel guitar with his half uncles (left to right), Fuifui, Pulu, and Tauvivi Moe. This photograph was likely taken just before or at the beginning of their 1929–34 tour of Asia. Courtesy of Ron Middlebrook/Centerstream Publishing.*

contact with "civilization." Such a trope was not original to Rivière; it had been common in Wild West shows and other entertainments featuring indigenous peoples.[56] Tau Moe described how Rivière instructed them to provide a "before and after" presentation in quite stark terms: "Madame Riviere had us wear our hair all bushed out to look li[k]e savages, you know. We couldn't speak English or wear jewelry. I had to take my watch off. . . . At the opening of the show, I had to climb up a big tree onstage and go up, way up, to pick a coconut. . . . The second part of the show was Occidental—Hawai'i today. Here we dressed modern and I played tunes like 'Show Me the Way to Go Home,' and 'Yes Sir, That's My Baby' while Rose danced."[57] Tau intimated that while Rivière succeeded in keeping the troupe booked for nearly five years—no easy feat—she ultimately treated the troupe members as children, unable to take care of themselves.[58] The steel guitar figured prominently in both halves of Rivière's program, as programs from Tau and Rose Moe's scrapbooks attest.[59]

News of their act preceded them throughout South Asia as their bookings multiplied. Tau delightfully recalled that in 1932 "it was because of my steel guitar that we met Mahatma Gandhi," with whom he engaged in long conversation.[60] Such attention paid to Tau's steel playing was one source of tension with his uncles, who, after playing in Bombay one night in 1933, suddenly quit the Rivière troupe and signed a contract with Hawaiian music impresario Ernest Ka'ai.[61] Tau, Rose, four-year-old Lani, and Rivière formed the Royal Hawaiian Entertainers and over the next year and a half began working their way through contracts in Singapore, Shanghai, Kuala Lumpur, Penang, Bangkok, Manila, and Bombay. Tau, who recalled that by 1935 they "had already played every town in India," was at that point celebrated by name in playbills as "the Kreisler of the Steel Guitar."[62] Yet by the end of that year, after Rivière was swindled out of the group's entire savings by a carnival operator, the trio—now featuring six-year-old "Baby Lani"—for the first time found themselves broke and without contracts. Taking a chance they sailed, without Rivière, and without contracts, to Port Said, Egypt.[63]

The Moe family scrapbooks featured clippings that documented their travel over the next two years.[64] After quickly finding work in Alexandria, by January 1936 they were playing the Continental Cabaret in Cairo with the already famous American blues singer Alberta Hunter.[65] Tau Moe's recollections of Egypt indicate that Hawaiian guitar records were by that point selling well all over the world: "We were the first Hawaiian act ever to come to Egypt. When they heard the steel guitar music they came to our hotel and wanted to see how I played it. They took my fingers in their hands to see the picks. *Of course*, they all had Sol Ho'opi'i recordings and they were crazy about Hawaiian music and the steel guitar. They kept on taking us to the radio station and our picture was always in the newspapers. They even booked us to appear at the Folks Theater where only Egyptian culture was allowed, just to let the Egyptian people hear the Hawaiian steel guitar music. The same thing happened in Turkey, Bulgaria, and Greece, where I also gave steel guitar lessons."[66] After several successful months in Cairo, they moved on to Abu Qir, Egypt; then Istanbul; Greece; and Belgrade, Yugoslavia. They introduced their steel guitar trio to new audiences in Albania, Bulgaria, and elsewhere in Eastern Europe, then moved on to Denmark and Sweden. In 1938, after tours in western Russia and Poland, they settled into a significant run in Germany.[67] The breadth of their travels in the 1930s, and the notoriety that the Hawaiian steel guitar had already achieved in so many of those locales, demonstrates the degree to which the instrument had infiltrated Asia, the Middle East, and Eastern Europe.

The arrival of the Moe's steel guitar shows in Poland and Germany in 1938 could scarcely have come at a worse time, however, given the circumstances of Adolf Hitler's consolidation of power. Once in Germany, the Moes began to comprehend Nazi efforts to terrorize Jews and others, particularly as they befriended more and more people in the entertainment world who had been targeted. With contracts in Germany, they found themselves in a peculiar and difficult circumstance: for as they fulfilled their contracts, many members of the Nazi elite became quite fond of them, including Hitler himself.

Although the Moes tried to avoid Hitler and the Nazis whenever possible, they failed repeatedly to do so. Tau remembered their first close encounter with him: "In Munich there was a special house that Hitler used [around 1938]. He was there at the time, with the S.S. troops stationed outside. We worked in a theater nearby. Someone directed us to the restaurant down the street. We misunderstood and walked right into the house where Hitler was staying."[68] The guards promptly escorted them out. They continued to attract his attention as they collected donations for German orphans through the Winterhilfswerk (Winter Help) organization. Tau Moe recalled that because the Moe's troupe collected the most money, "Hitler sent for us to come and meet him."[69] Lani had become the face of their fundraising campaign; to his parents' horror, when Hitler met the family and asked Lani if he could do anything to thank him, the nine-year-old asked to see his Mercedes-Benz limousine.[70] Lani was then placed in Hitler's car during the campaign's parade. Following an accompanying Berlin performance, Hitler, Goebbels, and Goering enthusiastically praised and greeted them.[71] According to his daughter Dorian, when Tau met Hitler he was absolutely terrified.[72]

It is interesting to ponder how a Samoan-Hawaiian family became celebrities in Hitler's Germany. A German newspaper described their "exotic revue" thusly: "These three artists move us with their Hawaiian folk music, with their dances and Hawaiian guitars in a South Sea–like atmosphere. The couple and their seven-year-old son come from Honolulu. They surprise through their particular skill on Hawaiians guitars, in a variety of speeds, and through the genuineness with which such people bring us joy and dreaminess."[73] Tau put it this way: "We always worked as a Hawaiian family." By that, he suggested that their music and appearance worked to mask their U.S. citizenship, whether from Nazis in Germany or anti-American rioters in Turkey.[74] Likewise, the steel guitar, just as it seemed to affect the English, the French, and the haole Americans, seemed to produce of a sense of exotic escape for the Nazis rather than serve as a demonstration of a technology built by people of color. The innocence that the instrument seemed to evoke, however, stood in great contrast with the way the Moe family would deploy it in war.

Into the fall of 1938, the signs grew worse: from their apartment windows, the Moes witnessed the beginnings of Kristallnacht—the arrests of Jews and the smashing of storefronts. While walking the streets, they saw books seized in synagogues and burned.[75] They became acutely aware that the situation had rapidly deteriorated, but their good standing with Hitler also gave them opportunity.[76] The Moes were granted German passports that enabled them to travel in and out of Germany with relative ease.[77] Although Jews were not prohibited from leaving Germany until October 1941, the Nazis already had made it extremely difficult for them to do so and had begun confiscating Jewish property. In 1938 through the spring of 1940, when the Moes were advised by the American consulate to leave the country, they worked to assist Jewish friends who had earlier fled without their property. According to Dorian Moe,

> My father used to smuggle things out for Jewish people. . . . It wasn't smuggling, he was taking their possessions and things like that they had to leave behind because in those days when they told you to get out, you just dropped everything and took whatever you had in your hand and you were out. And a lot of my dad's friends were well-to-do people that he knew either from managing, [as] director[s] for the company you work for, things like that, and my dad, he did, he had a good friend that became a film producer here in America, but when they left they needed their money and things and my dad did take it out for them. . . . As . . . you get through the [border], people would ask, "Are these your things?" and my dad would say "Yes," you know. And they'd think, "Oh you crazy people, you're from capitalist countries like America," and my father would say, "No, we're from Hawai'i and we're cold!" My mom smuggled this rich lady's three fur coats! She put one on top of the other, and the guy at the [border] thought she was totally off her head, and she said, "No, in Hawai'i it is very very warm, and this is very very cold!" (laughs).[78]

In this case, the furs belonged to the wife of an entertainment agent named Hans Lederer. The Moes in fact recalled transporting fifteen trunks to Paris on behalf of the Lederers. When Tau contacted Lederer in 1947 at his office in New York, however, Lederer feigned ignorance as to who the Moes were. It was not until 1977, when Tau contacted him again, that Lederer emotionally confided that in 1947 he was still terrified that the Germans would locate him.[79] In other cases, the Moes experienced emotional reunions as they delivered unopened envelopes of jewelry to their owners in the years following the war.[80]

The Moes transported not only property out of Germany but also their friends. As Dorian recalled, "Even those that couldn't get out would go with [the family.] I wasn't born at the time but my dad told me that they would just get all their stuff and go with them."[81] Disguising their friends as performers or stagehands, or even hiding them in the trunk, they reportedly evacuated as many as 150 people out of Germany.[82] While remembering Tau's stories, his daughter Dorian, who was born in Calcutta in 1945, said that two photographs in the possession of the Moes provided them extra credibility when border agents questioned them. According to her, in addition to a photograph of her brother Lani riding in the parade with Hitler, they also had a promotional photograph of Hitler that he had signed for them. At least on one occasion, according to Dorian, "they got stopped on the border but . . . [their Jewish friends] were in the car, they were dressed [in the troupe's costumes]. . . . When they asked, 'who are these people?' my father [said], 'that's part of my show,' you know, the rest of the performers. They were not, of course, but they were all sitting in the back with the instruments. He had this folder with a couple of pictures, [including] the one of my brother sitting in [Hitler's] car and then [the guards] happened to see the one that was signed [by Hitler] and then . . . they let them *go*! But my father said he was totally . . . you know how nervous you can be, because at that time, they'd just take you out and shoot you right there."[83] The situation in Berlin became increasingly tenuous, and in 1940 the family finally fled. According to Tau Moe, the American consul told them, "I'm getting a bus, to leave for Baghdad tomorrow morning. You can expect four days and nights on the desert. Don't take any luggage."[84] After arriving in Baghdad in a sandstorm, they eventually made their way through Greece and Turkey, and on to Beirut.[85] After Italy declared war on Lebanon, however, they had to relocate to Baghdad, then to Basra, and then to Bombay; on the first night at sea, with battleships escorting them and lights blacked out, they rammed into an Italian submarine by accident. Moe recalled, "The Italian sailors had come out on deck naked, and were lying about in the fresh air. When we rammed them, their sub went down and we took them all aboa[r]d our ship in their bare skins. They surrendered."[86]

Although the Moes had planned to sail from Bombay to Honolulu, they had to cancel this plan when the Japanese bombed Pearl Harbor.[87] They thus remained in India for the duration of the war, where, in Calcutta, their daughter Dorian was born. While the Moes were there, a number of their Jewish friends ended up as refugees in nearby relocation camps. Seeing an opportunity, Tau persuaded local hotel operators to hire musicians from the camps to perform in their establishments. In turn, the musicians and their families were fed and given care for the remainder of the war.[88] Though she was not born until after her family's experience in Germany, Dorian recalled their later tours in Israel, where "we met a lot of friends my dad had helped, and they still remembered. They survived the Holocaust, so they still remembered."[89]

The Moe's wartime odyssey staggers the imagination. The steel guitar troupe's exotic allure and success in the German market secured the good graces of the Nazi Party, which seemed taken by the family's act as innocent, naive Natives bumbling their way through Central Europe. Yet the Moes, like other Hawaiian entertainers, had long refined their ability to turn the ignorance of their audiences to their advantage on some occasions, and to engage and correct their ignorance on others.

Dorian Moe also remembered how, later, when she joined her parents as a performer, they handled the challenging expectations of their foreign audiences. She recalled her father working in a German studio in the 1950s, when the producer asked him, at the end of each song, to strum all the strings and then rapidly slide the bar up a full octave, creating a cartoonish (or, for the German, an ostensibly "Hawaiian") resolution. She continued, "So my father said, 'But you know, I don't know what your concept is of Hawaiian music, but we don't end every song with' . . . [Dorian sounded out a "swoosh!" and laughed]. . . . So we finally convinced this producer that that's not how the music goes, that's not how the steel guitar goes, and he understood." In other instances, audiences seemed to have no concept of "Hawai'i" at all; Dorian recalled that some Japanese, hearing they were from "the Islands," asked if that meant they were from Hong Kong, while they were more than once introduced as coming from Christmas Island. Her father used humor with his family to deal with the constant misconceptions they encountered. The Moes continued to turn such misconceptions to their advantage. Just as they traversed the German borders wearing the fur coats of their friends, feigning for the guards an inability to acclimate to cold weather, Dorian, though fluent in five languages (her family spoke eight or nine between them), would often quite intentionally speak to the audience using poor grammar and heightened hesitation.[90] As she put it, "As far as narrating the show I always did it in the language of the country . . . a little broken, but in the language of the country. . . . Not too perfect, because then they'd think I'm a stuck up person! [laughs] See John, it's a gimmick! [laughs] You've got to keep them to a certain level — humble yourself." If such gimmicks endeared the family to its foreign audiences, they also made the audience members more comfortable in their fantasy of the troupe as docile, Native entertainers from an exotic, yet nonthreatening world. The Moes' remarkable language skills, along with the assumption by their European and Asian audiences that such fluency was impossible for them to attain, enabled them to understand what others said about them in their presence. Their Hawaiian fluency also protected them, as they could speak ʻŌlelo Hawaiʻi to each other and be certain that no one around them could understand. They certainly found ways to profit from their fluency in so many languages, a skill necessitated by their labor as modern entertainers, working circuits with such an expansive geographical reach.[91]

While the Moes learned to play into some stereotypes, however, they challenged others. Presentation was very important to them: Tau and Lani made a point to wear nice, flowered tuxedo jackets at their performances, and not Aloha shirts, while Rose and Dorian wore evening dresses — "We were very particular on that," Dorian recalled. As people of color, they also had to grapple with discrimination. Around 1950, for example, while the family was working (once more) in Germany, the neighborhood children began to tease Dorian as "the little Indian." She recalled, "I was a little kid, I didn't really care, but then the parents started saying something, oh you know, 'the little black girl is playing with our kids' . . . so they started getting together and stopping the kids from coming to play with me." Eventually the controversy made it into the local newspapers. To resolve the matter, her parents decided to invite the entire block of families to their afternoon show. She continued, "We took all the kids, forty-eight or fifty kids. . . . ALL the kids came, and then we found out it was only these two ladies that were a little bit particular. . . . They just didn't like dark people I guess, you know. The day was really good, we had a wonderful day, the kids all came, the parents came too. It ran in the papers again, and then they all brought me the biggest doll that you could find — the *blondest* doll you could find [laughs]. And they put it in the papers, and here I am with this big humongous blonde doll, taking a picture, and I say, 'Okay, okay.'" Conscious of their outsider status while abroad, the Moes developed an array of strategies to handle the challenges that it generated, from concealing their linguistic abilities, to devoting great attention to their presentation, to coping, as Dorian routinely demonstrated in her stories, through a bountiful supply of humor.[92]

Music, meanwhile, remained at the forefront of the act, with the steel guitar as its focal point, and members of the Moe troupe took pride in exercising their sophisticated talent. Tau intentionally played complex chords and refused to attend to what he considered the simplistic conventions demanded by the German producer and others. Dorian said, "The steel was the key, and the music was our first priority. . . . My father was always very particular, and he always said, 'Remember your culture, remember your country, don't embarrass.' [It] was kind of upsetting, you know, when people said, 'Oh, you're from Hawaiʻi, huh, you play that chalangalang music,' you know. But my father always wanted to show the good part of Hawaiian music, which is the steel guitar." In addition, when in a new country, Dorian would always perform "espionage," as she jokingly called it, by learning what sort of music was preferred in the country, and then, what songs were currently the most popular. The Moes would identify one of the songs, and then ask local musicians about the lyrics—what the song meant—and whether or not it would be appropriate to play at their venue, in their own style. Tau exhibited tremendous agility on the steel guitar in their shows, taking the audience through a cavalcade of Hawaiian songs as well as numbers from their host country's hit parade. He even recorded with the Austrian Philharmonic, reading his part and responding to the conductor as well. As Dorian Moe, a consummate professional musician, put it, "You gotta be versatile." But their performances were not merely versatile, they were transcendent: they challenged their audiences by shaking their hosts' musical assumptions and demonstrating an adaptability of the steel guitar that perhaps no one, not even Joseph Kekuku, could have anticipated.[93]

The Moe family continued to tour the world for another thirty years. For the duration, their reach extended well beyond the affluent audiences who encountered them in the early days of ritzy hotel contracts in Kuala Lumpur and Bombay. According to Dorian, Tau spent much of his "off-time" jamming with locals. Tau Moe recalled having returned to Athens two years after they had last resided there, when he had given local residents steel guitar lessons during the day. During his return, however, "we happened to hear the sound of a steel guitar and four voices singing in beautiful harmony. The song was 'Imi Au Iā 'Oe,' the same one I had taught two years before. They sang it so beautifully, except the words were not pronounced clearly. Then they found out we were there; they nearly mobbed us and we had to get out fast. . . . Even in the islands of the Mediterranean, Malta, Cyprus, Gibraltar, . . . Portugal[,] and Spain they loved Hawaiian music. . . . We played in Spain about 20 times, also Beirut Lebanon, Baghdad, also Iran where I taught music to fourteen boys. . . .

In Israel . . . it was a 'must' for me to play 'Maui Chimes' and 'Aloha No Au I Kou Maka.'"[94] Italians demanded he record "O sole mio" and "Santa Lucia" on the steel guitar, and in Berlin and Vienna he recorded with their symphony orchestras.[95]

Of the dozens of countries in which Tau Moe performed on the steel guitar, however, he may have had the most influence on the music of India. Indian audiences had been familiar with his family's music since the 1930s, when the Moes performed there in Rivière's troupe. Even earlier, Ernest Ka'ai and perhaps Queenie and David Kaili had toured the country.[96] In addition, as we saw in chapter 2, parallels already existed in technique between the Indian gottuvadyam and vichitra vina and the steel guitar. However, Tau Moe's increased exposure to Indians in the 1940s and 1950s—particularly through the popularity of his locally recorded music, his lessons to both paying and indigent children, and Moe's routine radio broadcasts—clearly launched a revolution in the country's vernacular musics. Indian musicians, enamored by the steel guitar's sound and versatility, began adapting the instrument to their ragas.[97]

Tau Moe's lasting influence as the source of inspiration for modern Indian guitar music began with his star student, Garney Nyss, who later recorded Hawaiian and other songs in India with a group of Anglo-Indian and Goan musicians who called themselves the Aloha Boys.[98] Like Tau Moe's radio broadcasts and records produced in India, Nyss's output became well known throughout the country, not simply in Calcutta, where Moe's family lived for many years. Modern-day Indian steel guitarist Kay Das emphasizes the impact of both Moe and Nyss when recalling his initial interest in the instrument. Das's parents developed a passion for Hawaiian music beginning when he was about ten, in the mid-1950s. His mother bought an acoustic steel guitar and took lessons in Secunderabad from an Indian woman, one of two people teaching steel guitar in that town, before she eventually passed the instrument along to him. When I asked how he learned to play the instrument, Das responded, "Okay, you must know of Tau Moe? Tau Moe started a school in India, in Calcutta. And one of his students was a guy named Garney Nyss. . . . My mom would come home occasionally, [having bought] one of these shellac 78s, and one time she had Garney Nyss's steel guitar 78 and it had 'Moana Chimes' on one side, and 'St. Louis Blues' on the other, and I must have played that record, over three or four years, I must have worn it thin. I still have it! . . . . It never got out of my ear. I still hear it. . . . And he was a student of Tau Moe."[99] By the 1960s, the Hawaiian steel guitar had created what one Indian music scholar called a "craze" for Hawaiian music in Northern India.[100]

This craze translated into a significant growth of steel players and teachers in the country, who in turn began to reshape a number of its genres. Garney Nyss taught Sri Brij Bhushan Kabra, who later recorded a breakthrough album, not of Hawaiian music, but of Indian classical music ("shastriya sangit") adapted to the steel guitar.[101] His 1967 album *Call of the Valley* featured his steel, modified with a drone string, alongside traditional Indian instruments.[102] Illuminating the possibilities of the Hawaiian steel in Indian music, Vishwa Mohan Bhatt further modified his Hawaiian guitar to create a new instrument, the mohan veena, that, in addition to melody strings played with a steel bar, incorporated four chikari drone strings and twelve tarab sympathetic strings to create the buzzing sound of the sitar.[103] Another prodigy, Barun Kumar Pal, had mastered the sitar under the instruction of Ravi Shankar and Nikhil Banerjee; yet the Hawaiian guitar was his first love, and in 1973 he applied their instruction to a steel guitar that he modified in similar fashion to Bhatt's.[104] Van Shipley, a major figure in Bollywood soundtracks, recorded many steel guitar albums in the 1950s and 1960s, while other Indian steel guitarists recording filmi, Tagore, and Nazrul songs during this period included Batuk Nandy, Kazi Aniruddha, Nalin Mazumdar, Mohon Bhattacharya, Robin Paul, Hazara Singh, Sujit Nath, and Sunil Ganguly.[105] One of the greatest contemporary Indian steel guitarists is Debashish Bhattacharya, one of Kabra's students, who during one of his tours stopped into Lā'ie to thank Tau Moe, who had recently retired from the road. Tau remained sought out by Indian guitar royalty to the end of his life because, quite simply, they all understand his significance: he created a steel guitar culture during the 1940s that has profoundly shaped the sounds of modern Indian music and film today.[106]

While Tau and Rose Moe spent over fifty years circumnavigating the globe before they and their children retired to their homes in Lā'ie, most other steel guitarists' travels abroad were far less extensive. Some decided to return to the Islands after only one or two seasons of foreign tours. Some left the Islands and never returned, either taking their families with them or creating new families abroad. Several died on the road.[107]

So many Hawaiians traveled the world during the first half of the twentieth century, continuing a long-standing tradition of vast exploration into uncharted territory. In the process, they engaged sprawling new entertainment circuits that seemed to stitch together a global, cultural economy, town by town. Our information on their fates is uneven, and at times scant. Yet we know, for instance, that Joseph Kekuku eventually married an Englishwoman with whom he relocated to Chicago in 1926, and eventually to Dover, New

FIGURE 24. *Today Pandit Debashish Bhattacharya carries on the steel guitar tradition that Tau Moe inspired. Bhattacharya has designed several steel guitars with additional tarab and chikari strings in order to better serve the aesthetics of raga music. Courtesy of Debashish Bhattacharya.*

Jersey, where he died from a cerebral hemorrhage in 1932. Joe Puni, who was touring North America by 1901, and Europe by the 1910s, continued to tour for decades afterward. After surviving World War I in Paris and London, he and his Hawaiian troupe made their way through Europe, North Africa, Asia Minor, and South America, picking up, like the Moes, several languages along the way. He did not return to the Hawaiian Islands for forty years, until the end of 1940, at seventy-three years of age, when he was evacuated along with 800 other American refugees from German-occupied France.[108]

But what of Queenie and David Kaili, whose lingering scrapbooks at the Bishop Museum so lovingly document their adventures in Australia and New Zealand? David Luela Kaili, born at Joseph Kekuku's birthplace of Kahana, O'ahu, in 1890, had achieved early fame through a series of records that he had made in the 1910s with steel guitarist Pale K. Lua. Lua and Kaili, as part of Irene West's Royal Hawaiians, toured the United States and Great Britain together and recorded over twenty of the best-selling 78 rpm Hawaiian records of all time, all cut between 1914 and 1916.[109] Sometime later, perhaps as a result of Lua's untimely death in the 1920s, Kaili began to record as a steel guitarist in his own right. He married a singer and guitarist named Mary Louise, or "Queenie." Together, as their scrapbooks document, they joined Ernest Ka'ai for a tour of Singapore, Australia, and New Zealand that began in 1923 and ran for several more years.[110]

During the first half of their shows, the Kailis would perform a set of mostly instrumental pieces, followed by a second half in which the troupe would sing and perform hapa haole and more jazz-oriented popular songs.[111] Queenie, a "high class vocal star" according to a 1930 Perth newspaper review, sang, played instruments, and danced, while audiences regaled in the Kailis' sense of humor.[112] David's performances on an acoustic, hollow-necked steel guitar commanded frequent encores and were captured in a series of popular recordings made by the Kailis in Australia in the late 1920s that also featured Hawaiian chants.[113] A critic in Perth remarked after a 1928 performance that "the undiminished popularity of the Hawaiians, Queenie and David Kaili, was reflected in the sustained applause they received, especially from the gallery."[114] Their reputations began to precede them: by 1930, one Australian critic long familiar with the Kailis noted, "David's wizardry on the steel guitar has always been a source of delight to audiences everywhere."[115]

The Kailis continued to travel together, circling the globe three times, by Queenie's count. By 1933, however, they decided to establish their home in Manila, where they opened a club, the Bali Grill.[116] There they continued to perform until the Japanese invasion of the Philippines became imminent: "We had planned to go home," she recalled, "but before we knew it hell broke loose." The Japanese troops "came rolling into Manila on their motorcycles by the thousands." David and Queenie burned all of their documents and attempted to "pass" as Filipinos, but one day Japanese soldiers "burst in on me and started beating me with bamboo sticks." Queenie was transported to Fort Santiago, where Japanese soldiers tortured her relentlessly and demanded that she confess her true nationality.[117] Eventually they released her, but they then picked up her husband, whose experience was even worse; soon after, he succumbed from his injuries.[118] After David's death, she continued to struggle in Japanese-occupied Manila for the duration of the war, until the city was liberated and she was transported, first to San Francisco and finally to Honolulu.

Queenie returned to Honolulu in a devastated state; her sorrow and her gruesome recollection of their treatment in Manila was reported on the front page of the *Honolulu Advertiser*. Joyful memories remained intact in her scrapbooks, however. I wonder how many albums she had filled before the soldiers arrived. Over the course of their two-decade career together, she and David had embarked on seemingly endless adventures through the global embrace of their Hawaiian steel guitar.

At the end of the couple's run, it seemed as if you could find the kīkā kila anywhere: by the early 1940s, according to one observer, "the night clubs of Shanghai were packed to capacity every night. The Chinese patrons demanded at least one session of Hawaiian music before the night was over."[119] After Tau Moe first performed on Athens radio in the mid-1930s, "just about every Greek record . . . through the late '30s ha[d] a Hawaiian guitar on it."[120] Likewise, although Hawaiian music was banned in Japan during World War II, its popularity there grew afterward to the point that today Hawaiian music is probably better loved in Japan than in any other part of the world outside of Hawai'i. The instrument sparked imaginations throughout Africa as well; a Griqua guitarist from South Africa known as Kimo Koa learned the technique directly from Joseph Kekuku when the two toured Europe together.[121] In Zimbabwe, Malawi, and Zambia, according to African music scholar Gerhard Kubik, a "Hawaiian guitar craze" led guitarists to seek ways to "reproduce the glissando effect of Hawaiian guitar music."[122] They named the technique and its accompanying open tuning "Hauyani[,] . . . an adaption of the English word 'Hawaiian' in the languages of South-east Africa, such as Cinyanja/Chicewa. . . . 'Hawaiian guitar' playing was extremely popular in Malawi during the late 1940s and the 1950s," made famous by a number of players, including

Ndiche Mwarare and Daniel and Donald Kachamba.[123] And by the 1970s in Nigeria, juju music legend King Sunny Adé was featuring the sounds of Demola Adepoju's steel guitar as a fundamental component of his music.[124] In a few decades, the Hawaiian steel guitar revolution had seemed to reverberate in nearly every corner of the world. In the United States, meanwhile, Hawaiian guitarists labored to reshape the modern sounds and technologies of the country's popular culture from the ground up.

5 *Holly-Hawaiians, Electric Guitars, and Glass Ceilings*

While Hawaiian steel guitarists fanned throughout the globe during the first half of the twentieth century, their influence continued to flourish in the United States. The second generation of professional players, including Sol Hoʻopiʻi, Dick McIntire, and Eddie Bush, shared a number of biographical traits. All were young men, leading all-male trios, quartets, and quintets, often performing onstage or in films with female hula dancers. Although born after the overthrow, they had witnessed the economic dependence and the loss of homelands that accelerated quickly in its aftermath.[1] Some steel players retained control of their labor by performing independently for tourist audiences at Waikīkī Beach or on the Moana pier. Others by the 1920s had joined professional groups such as the Johnny Noble and Dude Miller orchestras that maintained residencies at the Moana, Royal Hawaiian, and other hotels as they opened in Waikīkī.[2] As we have already seen, many young musicians left the Islands in their search for work, and the numbers of émigrés only increased in the 1920s. Some made their way to the burgeoning markets in California by working below decks on merchant or passenger vessels, joining the U.S. Navy, or stowing away. It seemed that for many of them California promised steady work, on their own terms, performing Hawaiian music. Certainly the letters from successful musicians printed in Hawaiian newspapers contributed to the exodus. No less enticing to many musicians, however, was the glory they could obtain as artists and innovators, particularly in the new entertainment industry hub of Hollywood.

During the interwar years musicians and dancers forged a strong Pacific Islander community in Southern California, one that fostered a sense of camaraderie and belonging, and enabled them to work in the motion picture studios and nightclubs that increasingly sought their labor. Hawaiian guitarists thrived in Hollywood during this period, although they continued to face significant challenges. While they expanded the American public's interest in the steel guitar, particularly through the new mediums of radio and motion pictures, they continued to face an industry unwilling to acknowledge their talent and strong work ethic and uninterested in distinguishing their music from the offensive, pseudo-Hawaiian songs peddled by non-Hawaiian songwriters. This chapter will explore each of these developments while examining the careers of a number of the era's most significant Hawaiian guitarists working in the United States. The promise of Hollywood was never truly realized for any of them, despite the social overtures paid them by many of Hollywood's elite. However, in addition to developing higher profiles than ever before through radio and film, this generation of Hawaiian steel players inspired and promoted some of the most important guitar design innovations of the twentieth century. The Hawaiian steel guitar came to feature prominently in the landscape of American popular culture and became fundamental to the making of American popular music.

Hawaiian musicians and dancers had been making their way to California for quite some time already, as had Joseph Kekuku in 1904. San Francisco served as California's primary port of destination from Honolulu, and it provided some of the earliest opportunities for Hawaiian musicians. The 1906 earthquake, however, dispersed most musicians to other markets—first to the Pacific Northwest, and then to Los Angeles. The population of Southern California grew fivefold between 1910 and 1930, creating unprecedented opportunity for entertainers on the West Coast.[3] Kekuku briefly made his home there in 1913 after he quit touring with Toots and July Paka, but the local Hawaiian entertainers' community did not take off until a few years later, when Hollywood became the filmmaking capital of the country.

Solomon Hoʻopiʻi Kaʻaiʻai was one of the earliest and most innovative and influential steel guitarists from Hawaiʻi to take advantage of the new opportunities in Los Angeles. He was born in Honolulu in 1902, one of twenty siblings. His father took several jobs in the city, from preaching for a small congregation in the neighborhood of Kakaʻako, to working as a turnkey at the Honolulu Jail, to serving as a city rat catcher.[4] Playing the ʻukulele since the age of three, and the guitar since the age of four, Hoʻopiʻi became an uninvited star attraction at the Royal Hawaiian Band's weekly Sunday performances in Kapiʻolani Park.[5] One of his friends, Bill Tapia, recalled nearly eighty years later, "When the band took a break, we would sit on the grass and play. And we would draw a bigger crowd than the Royal Hawaiian Band. The tips were good! Sol was the best."[6] Others also recognized his talent, and he soon found work in Johnny Noble's orchestra, one of the leading bands in Honolulu.[7]

In 1919, at the age of seventeen, Hoʻopiʻi stowed away onboard the SS *Sonoma* as it departed Honolulu for San Francisco.[8] Taking the professional name of Sol Hoʻopiʻi (typically printed in the California press as Sol Hoopii), he found little work in San Francisco, save for some professional boxing matches in the Bay Area.[9] Making his way a few months later to the new entertainment markets in Los Angeles, however, he joined Decker's Hawaiian Serenaders and was quickly recognized in the press as a "steel guitar virtuoso."[10] After working as a musician in downtown Chinese restaurants and marrying dancer and ʻukulele player Georgia Stiffler in 1921, he formed Mackie's Queen's Hawaiians in 1922, with fellow Hawaiian Lani McIntire on standard guitar, and began transmitting regular broadcasts on KHJ and KFWB, two of the city's earliest radio stations.[11] The Queen's Hawaiians were hailed by the *Los Angeles Times* in 1923 as "one of the most popular organizations in broadcast."[12] Hoʻopiʻi and McIntire relentlessly honed their act, performing seven nights a week at the Dragon Café by 1923.[13] Hoʻopiʻi soon performed regularly with many Hawaiian musicians who relocated in increasing numbers to Los Angeles in the coming years, including Lani McIntire's brothers Dick and Al, and Buddy Kalani, Tommy Ainahau, and Bob Vierra.[14] By 1924 his namesake group was performing in theaters and restaurants throughout the city.[15]

Sol Hoʻopiʻi's broadcasts and club performances generated widespread interest for the steel guitar in Southern California, and through his work there in the radio, film, and recorded music industries, he nurtured what would become his key innovation on the steel guitar: its adaptability to jazz. Although first-generation players such as July Paka had dabbled in southern African American genres, Sol seemed to devour these styles, delivering syncopated and fluid jazz-inspired guitar solos on his very first recording sessions in mid-1925. Multiple takes survive from the sessions, demonstrating his mastery of improvisation.[16] According to Tony Todaro, "Sol developed his clean, sharp tones by listening to clarinet players every chance he had. After memorizing the runs of clarinet musicians, Sol would practice at home until he perfected the style."[17] It is clear that his fingers measured the pulse of the most groundbreaking (and often obscure) recordings in the genre: his trio's take on Bix Beiderbecke's landmark composition "Singing the Blues," for example, followed the original recording by only six months, yet fewer than 2,000 people owned a copy of the Beiderbecke record at the time.[18] It is difficult to pinpoint the origins of his penchant for improvisation; before the crystallization of a jazz genre, improvisation was already deeply rooted in the Hawaiian genre of hula kuʻi, as the genre's melodies, ever since its guitar-inspired origins in the 1880s, were not fixed. Likewise, Kanaka guitarists had long embellished melodies and vamps.[19] Perhaps the emphasis on improvisation in both genres inspired Ho'opi'i and other early steel guitarists to recognize and exploit a parallel tradition. Whatever the case, the results were explosive: his attack on popular jazz tunes was not merely novel, it was thrilling to his audiences. By recording mele like "Nā Lei O Hawai'i," "Akaka Falls," and "Hilo March" alongside "Yes Sir, That's My Baby" and "Moonlight and Roses," juxtaposed with hapa haole numbers such as "Hula Blues" and "My Little Grass Shack in Kealakekua Hawaii," Ho'opi'i demonstrated an extraordinary fluency in multiple genres at the same time that he introduced a variety of audiences to an entirely new understanding of the guitar's capabilities.[20]

After Ho'opi'i signed with Columbia Records in 1926, the records of "Sol Hoopii and His Novelty Trio" won legions of fans for this new Hawaiian/jazz/hapa haole music. Beginning with his March 1928 sessions, however, he channeled this fusion into a focus on recording songs performed in the Hawaiian language; this trend continued through 1938, when he concluded his contract with Brunswick.[21] Significantly, while most foreign-language recordings were issued by the major labels in smaller, niche catalogs, Ho'opi'i's recordings, and those of his peers such as Sam Ku, Sol K. Bright, Mike Hanapi, Bob Matsu, and Andy Iona, were featured in their labels' much more expansive "popular" catalogs. According to one music researcher of this period, "no other foreign language material was ever as prominently featured in the mainstream catalogs of the major record companies as that of the favored Hawaiian artists."[22] Perhaps for this reason, records traveled fast throughout the Islands as well as the continental United States. Ho'opi'i's 1928 return to Honolulu was nothing short of triumphant. The *Los Angeles Times* noted him as a "prominent" passenger on the Lassco liner *City of Los Angeles* as it embarked for Honolulu, and his wife, Georgia, recalled that upon their arrival throngs of fans and friends blockaded him on the harbor dock for three hours.[23] Honolulu newspapers reported his every move, from his performances in movie houses and clubs to private parties.[24]

Ho'opi'i's popularity at the head of this second generation of Hawaiian guitarists led to a new wave of excitement for the Hawaiian steel guitar in the Islands as well as on the continent and beyond. Ho'opi'i, in particular, commanded the attention of his fans as well as luthiers, who asked for his input in guitar design. As a result, his endorsements led to the widespread adoption of new, cutting-edge Hawaiian guitar technologies, nearly all of which through the mid-1930s were developed by guitar companies in Los Angeles.

This relationship between artist and design began with Kekuku's creations at the Kamehameha School and grew significantly in California, beginning with the hollow-necked guitars that Hoʻopiʻi showcased in his first years in the clubs of Los Angeles.[25] In the days before mechanical and electric amplification, only the resonance of guitar bodies could amplify the strings. Hoʻopiʻi and other Hawaiian guitarists competed with other instruments, particularly while playing in large or noisy venues. Hollow necks generated greater volume, and they were complemented by a stronger, reinforced bracing to support the tension of the steel strings that were necessary for a steel bar to create resonance. Nearly all guitars built in the 1800s (and most through the early 1920s) could only withstand the tension of gut strings; steel strings would bend their necks upward, often making them difficult if not impossible to tune or play.[26] Hawaiian guitarists needed instruments with stable, immobile necks. Hollow necks seemed to solve multiple design problems, and it appears that luthiers had begun to build them in the Islands. Experts on this period of guitar design suggest that Hawaiians introduced hollow-necked guitars to the United States around 1905–7, or that at the very least they inspired Seattle's Chris Knutsen to adapt his harp guitar designs to suit their needs.[27] In the years that followed, the popularity of these guitars expanded primarily through the combined efforts of several players, builders, and instructors in Los Angeles.

Knutsen moved to Los Angeles in late 1914 after he learned that his guitars had inspired a local piano repairman to copy the design and build hollow-necked instruments for sale to a growing body of steel guitar students.[28] The repairman, a German immigrant named Hermann Weissenborn, had only recently learned of Knutsen's design, when his live-in housekeeper, a Mexican immigrant named Concepción Ybarra, brought home a loaner guitar from her steel guitar class.[29] The teacher of her class was Charles S. DeLano, a former student of Kekuku who seems to have shipped some Knutsen steel guitars to Los Angeles when he opened a steel guitar teaching studio downtown.[30] Knutsen and Weissenborn worked blocks apart in the years that followed, and often closely with steel guitar instructors DeLano and Myrtle Stumpf (another former Kekuku student), as well as Hawaiian steel guitarist George Kia and even Kekuku himself, who was teaching in the city by 1913.[31] DeLano sold students his own line of guitars, which were in fact built by both Knutsen and Weissenborn under the Kona brand. With this influx of Hawaiian guitarists, builders, and instructors into a city soon flush with recording and film studios and eventually, radio outlets, Los Angeles played a leading role in the rapid expansion of the Hawaiian guitar craze in the years that followed.

Sol Hoʻopiʻi took full advantage of the fertile conditions for Hawaiian music in Los Angeles and continued to push for instrument innovation that would sate his thirst for volume and tone. Leading Hawaiian guitar manufacturers routinely offered Hoʻopiʻi prototypes to test in hopes of winning his valued endorsement and adoption of their instruments. In 1926, however, three men approached him with the wildest, most otherworldly looking guitar that anyone had ever seen. The idea for the design took root in the shop of John and Rudy Dopyera, two brothers who had emigrated from Slovakia a few years before.[32] They eventually established a musical instrument business in Los Angeles that specialized in banjos when the third man, a haole steel guitarist named George Beauchamp, sought their help in creating a louder instrument to better compete with his raucous vaudeville orchestra. Their collaboration led, after a great deal of trial and error, to the development of a Hawaiian hollow-necked guitar built almost entirely out of German nickel and featuring three mechanical, aluminum conical resonators bolted inside the body to amplify the volume of the strings.[33] The result sounded as amazing as it looked—superbly modern—accentuated with a stunning Art Deco design cut into the shimmering metal body.[34] In order to raise money to build a line of them for public sale, they determined that Sol Hoʻopiʻi, the hottest guitarist in town, was the perfect candidate to demonstrate the potential of their prototype, built at their newly formed National String Instrument Company. Hoʻopiʻi obliged the Dopyeras and Beauchamp by accepting the extraordinary sum of $500 to perform with the instrument during a three-day party hosted by millionaire Ted E. Kleinmeyer.[35] The National, or "tricone," guitar, as it was variously known, mesmerized the wealthy partygoers; Kleinmeyer wrote a $12,500 check on the spot and came to serve as the new corporation's president.[36] Completely taken by the exciting new instrument, Hoʻopiʻi went on to record most of his catalog with National guitars. He continued to serve as the leading endorser for the company, and after having personally debuted the instrument at industry conventions in 1927, Sol, along with Sam Ku and several other Hawaiian guitarists, became prominently featured in National's promotional materials and advertisements for the next several years.[37] By the end of the decade, it seemed that nearly every professional steel guitarist was performing with Nationals. Thanks largely to the efforts of Sol Hoʻopiʻi, Nationals quickly became the most sought-after Hawaiian guitar in the industry.[38]

Sol Hoʻopiʻi's association with the most significant innovations in guitar design did not cease with National. While the Dopyeras eventually formed the Dobro Manufacturing Company in Los Angeles, George Beauchamp in 1931

FIGURE 25. *Sol Ho'opi'i (standing in the front row) promoted the cutting-edge National tricone steel guitars at instrument conventions. This photograph may have been taken at the 1927 Western Music Trades Convention in San Francisco and features a stage full of National instruments. Courtesy of Lani Ellen McIntire.*

formed the Ro-Pat-In Company (soon to be called the Electro String Instrument Corporation), also in Los Angeles, with Swiss immigrant Adolph Rickenbacker.[39] Despite the increased volume that Nationals and Dobros generated for their players, Beauchamp and Rickenbacker were interested in moving beyond mechanical amplification to electricity. They experimented by winding magnetically charged coils to pick up the vibrations caused by plucked strings, and in 1931 they produced their first prototype "electric" guitar. This prototype translated by 1932 into the "electro string"—the first production-line electric steel guitar ever built, nicknamed the "frying pan" because of its small cast circular aluminum body and long neck.[40]

Beauchamp and Rickenbacker did not file for patent protection on the instrument until a couple of years after they began operations. When they eventually filed, the U.S. Patent Office had no idea what the invention was; patent officials certainly did not think it could generate sound. In order to convince them that their invention actually worked, Beauchamp and Rickenbacker hired Sol Hoʻopiʻi to travel to Washington, DC, and demonstrate the instrument at the Patent Office.[41] Hoʻopiʻi soon abandoned his National for electric instruments.

In twenty short years, then, the guitar had undergone revolutionary innovations. It had been ushered into American popular music as a lead, melodic instrument by Hawaiian musicians, whose demands and demonstrations continued to blaze the path as the instrument gained even greater ascendancy. Kekuku and other Hawaiian guitarists inspired Knutsen, Weissenborn, and other early builders to manufacture hollow-necked guitars. The National company visually and sonically transformed the instrument through radical design concepts advanced by the endorsement and demonstrations of Sol Hoʻopiʻi, who also helped secure the patent registration for Rickenbacker and Beauchamp's frying pan, the world's first successful production-line electric guitar.[42] Some of the most important guitar innovations of the century, and indeed the crafting of the modern sounds of popular music in the United States, took place, then, through the extensive collaborative relationships of Hawaiian musicians and European immigrant luthiers in Los Angeles.

Hoʻopiʻi's success in L.A. ushered in a new Hawaiian music movement in the local entertainment scene. Polynesian-themed nightclubs and restaurants opened from L.A. to Tijuana, but they centered in Hollywood, where, in the words of one observer, a "Holly-Hawaiian club" scene flourished.[43] The nightclubs catered principally to affluent whites, and particularly to the film industry's biggest stars, directors, and producers. Most of the dancers and musicians were from Hawaiʻi, with others from Samoa and Tahiti, and together they developed an extensive Pacific Islander community in Los Angeles that was built on new labor opportunities in Hollywood.

While the scene that Hoʻopiʻi fostered grew quickly in the 1920s, an upstart teenager named Eddie Bush quickly became one of the most recognized and sought after steel guitarists in the city. Bush was born in Milwaukee in 1911, the son of Kanaka musicians then touring the United States with a troupe called "Lei's Hawaiians." Soon after the family relocated to Los Angeles in 1924, fourteen-year-old Eddie Bush joined a trio and began rehearsing six days a week, for up to twelve hours per day.[44] The group perfected their harmonies and began inverting them, as one peer recalled, "changing the traditional placement of the voices in unique ways, shifting the melody from one voice to the next, never allowing one voice to carry the melody throughout. The effect was marvelous and in its day it was new and unique and ahead of its time."[45] By 1927, when they were hired to play at the Biltmore Hotel as the Biltmore Hotel Trio, their repertoire extended to over 150 songs with full vocal harmonies, from Hawaiian mele and hapa haole songs to the latest pop songs from Tin Pan Alley. Their timing, given the burgeoning Hollywood social scene, was perfect, and their impact on Hollywood was staggering.

Louella Parsons, the leading movie columnist of the day, placed their influence in context: "The Biltmore Trio has entertained more film stars, to say nothing of Los Angeles society debutantes, than any triumvirate that has ever descended upon Hollywood."[46] Their fan base quickly included the biggest stars in town, from Charlie Chaplin, Douglas Fairbanks, and Joan Crawford to Claire Windsor and Clara Bow.[47] Leaving their early struggles behind, when they would spend their last nickels on bus fare to get to a gig, they soon were performing two-and-a-half-hour radio network broadcasts from the hotel, six nights a week. In 1928 they began to work in films and soon became the first vocal group of any kind to be featured in major "talkies." They performed and acted in dozens of films, including, in 1929 alone, *Broadway Melody* (MGM), *Hollywood Revue of 1929* (MGM), *Footlights and Fools* (First National), *Party Girl* (Tiffany), and *The Great Gabbo* (Sono-Art-Worldwide).[48] The group's vocal stylings attracted a great deal of attention, but steel guitarist Eddie Bush was the star.[49]

Hawaiian musicians flocked to Los Angeles as Polynesian clubs opened around Hollywood and catered to industry actors, directors, moguls, and everyone who wished to associate with them. In 1937 the *Los Angeles Times* suggested several such sites as the most likely venues in which to "see the stars," including the Cocoanut Grove, the Seven Seas, the Hula Hut, the Hawaiian Village, the Hawaiian Paradise, Beachcombers, Bali, Club Hawaii, the Tropics, and the Luana.[50] Sol Hoʻopiʻi long maintained a residency at yet another club, the Waikīkī at La Brea and Beverly, where one could eat "Native Hawaiian" dinners and sometimes see famous Hawaiian vocalist and mele composer Lena Machado perform with Hoʻopiʻi's orchestra.[51]

Each club provided opportunities for musicians and dancers both to secure steady, short-and long-term contracts, and to network for recording and acting jobs on films. As Lani Ellen McIntire recalled, by "working at the Seven Seas, they knew all the producers, and directors, and main actors and actresses." McIntire, the daughter of Kanaka bassist Al McIntire and niece of his steel

FIGURE 26. *Eddie Bush (center with steel guitar) entertaining at a Hollywood party. Courtesy of Jay C. Munns.*

guitarist and bandleader brothers, Dick and Lani, was literally born into the Hollywood scene: her father and uncles had endeared themselves to film director John Ford and his wife Mary, who paid for Lani Ellen's delivery at Queen of Angels Hospital in 1934 and even asked to be her godmother.[52] Today in her apartment in the Hawaiian homestead community of Waimānalo, framed photographs line the shelves: her father and uncles pose with Bing Crosby in one; on another, country music legend Jimmie Rodgers penned a note to her father, who had performed with him. She reminisces about spending time with family friends such as Louis Prima, Gene Autry, and Jimmy Doolittle, going on a double date with Marlon Brando, and working on major film productions with many other stars of the day. She remembers Cecil B. DeMille as her father's "drinking buddy," recalls finding John Wayne's missing young son once during a shoot on Catalina Island, and even jokes about the unique challenges of teaching Annette Funicello to dance. She grew up quickly in the clubs; first hired to hula dance at Catalina Island's Avalon Ballroom for bandleader Harry Owens at the age of twelve, by the age of fourteen she had married another entertainer, the originator of the Samoan fire knife dance and part-time actor and stuntman Freddie Letuli.[53]

As her reminiscences attest, Hawaiian musicians not only socialized with the Hollywood elite, but they often worked closely with them as well. Sol Hoʻopiʻi would oblige the requests of film star Mary Pickford to perform for her off camera, right before the film rolled, in order to inspire her tears.[54] In fact, during his early days in Hollywood, after Western movie star Hoot Gibson befriended and played in a band with him, Hoʻopiʻi worked in several movies as an actor and a musician.[55] With a filmography extending from films like *Those Who Dance* (1924) and *His Jazz Bride* (1926), through bigger productions such as *Bird of Paradise* (1932) and the Bing Crosby film *Waikiki Wedding* (1937), Hoʻopiʻi not only provided music for soundtracks but often appeared in the films as well. Typically, the editor would cut to brief shots of him performing on a club stage. In other instances such as *Hawaiian Nights* (1939), however, Hoʻopiʻi and his band prominently featured in plot points.[56] Even when the screen time for Hoʻopiʻi and other steel players was short, however, Hollywood film studios vastly expanded U.S. audiences' exposure to Hawaiian steel guitar music.[57] At the same time, the cameos by Hawaiian musicians and their performance of Hawaiian-language repertoire on the silver screen excited Hawaiians who filled the theaters in the Islands. Such performances apparently excited industry censors as well, as the Motion Picture Association of America (MPAA) production code staff routinely screened lyrics and required English translations of songs performed in Hawaiian or other languages from the Pacific. Thus, during the filming of *Song of the Islands* (1942), for example, Hoʻopiʻi had to provide the MPAA with lyrics in both Hawaiian and English for his adaptation of "Home on the Range" and his own composition, "Huʻi Mai."[58]

FIGURE 27. *Hawaiian musicians often worked closely with Hollywood's most famous celebrities. In 1937 Lani McIntire and His Hawaiians recorded "Sweet Leilani" and "Blue Hawaii" with Bing Crosby. Hawaiian guitarist Bob Nichols is seated with his National tricone steel.* Standing left to right*: George Kainapau, Al McIntire, Bing Crosby, and Lani McIntire. Courtesy of Lani Ellen McIntire and HLC Properties, Ltd.*

FIGURE 28. *During the 1930s Hollywood's community of Hawaiian musicians was both versatile and tightknit. This series from a photography session features Al McIntire, Harry Baty, Sol K. Bright, and Alan Kila. In the right image Al (holding the bass) is cracking up while looking at the maracas stuffed under his strings. Sol K. Bright, likely the maraca culprit, is holding a Rickenbacker "frying pan," the first electric steel guitar ever manufactured. Courtesy of Lani Ellen McIntire.*

Thanks to their industry connections, Hawaiians worked both as featured musicians and as extras in many Hollywood films during the 1930s and 1940s. Of the steel guitarists working in Hollywood, for example, Sol K. Bright performed in *South Sea Rose* (1929), *Charlie Chan's Greatest Case* (1933), and *The Flirtation Walk* (1934); Andy Aiona Long (aka Andy Iona) played steel in *Honolulu* (1938) and *Moonlight in Hawaii* (1941); Freddie Taveres performed in *Coconut Grove* (1938) and *Song of the Islands* (1942); and Sam Koki's guitar work featured in *The Hurricane* (1937), *Waikiki Wedding* (1937), and *Paradise Isle* (1939), among others.[59] In addition to working and acting as musicians, Hawaiians also were hired to play other people of color in film. Lani Ellen McIntire carried her youngest child on her back while working as an extra in *The Ten Commandments*, recalling, "They wanted anyone with dark eyes." Paniolo experience was also highly valued: Hawaiians who rode horses secured a good deal of work as American Indians.[60]

It was the quality and consistency of labor opportunities that drew Hawaiians to Hollywood over anything else. When Lani Ellen McIntire was sixteen, for example, she danced for a time at both the Beachcomber and the Waikiki

FIGURE 29. Left to right: *"Little Joe" Kekauoha, Al Ceballos, Archie Kahanu on electric steel guitar, and Lani Ellen McIntire. McIntire's father, Al, and uncles Dick and Lani were core members of the early Hollywood Hawaiian entertainers community. She followed in their footsteps and chronicled their community in dozens of photo albums. Courtesy of Lani Ellen McIntire.*

Tavern in Waikīkī, Oʻahu, earning five dollars per night. "Going to Los Angeles," she remembered, "I got fifty dollars for the same gig." As early as 1930, in fact, musicians in Los Angeles were earning an aggregate salary estimated at around $137,000 per week. With "about the highest quota per capita in the country," according to *Variety*, Los Angeles musicians professionally operated over 100 bands and orchestras in the city at that time.[61] According to McIntire, her family found abundant work ("Dad was never without a job"), even during the worst years of the Great Depression. Lani Ellen McIntire was a member of several Hollywood unions, including the Screen Actors Guild, the American Guild of Variety Artists, and the Screen Extras Guild. When she used puʻili sticks, she had to join the musician's union as well.[62] Her union memberships demonstrate the variety of work that she, her father and uncles, and other Hawaiians found in Hollywood. Eddie Bush was by the age of sixteen earning an impressive $95 per week in the Biltmore Hotel Trio, but even this pay was not union scale. Immediately after a court nullified his Biltmore Hotel contract in 1930 because he had signed it as a minor, at the age of nineteen he signed a new one with the Biltmore Hotel's biggest rival, the Ambassador, where his pay increased to $225 per week.[63]

The draw to Hollywood was not simply one of economics, however; for many Hawaiians, Southern California also provided them with community, social prestige, and excitement. "During the time I was a little girl in Los Angeles," Lani Ellen McIntire laughed, "we had more Hawaiian musicians in L.A. than I think we had back home here!"[64] She remembered feeling dazzled by the clubs in which the Hawaiian musicians and dancers performed nightly. Recalling the Seven Seas nightclub on Hollywood Boulevard, she exclaimed, "They had rain on the roof. . . . I remember . . . I was really little . . . but you walk in and you think you're on an island, and there's the stage. . . . The owner . . . had those velvet paintings of island women. . . . To your left is this beautiful bar, and behind the bar is bamboo and palm trees, and then the bartender would press a button, and it would *rain*!"[65] In similar fashion, the Hawaiian Paradise, billed as "Hollywood's most popular café and night club," opened on Melrose Avenue in 1937 and featured steel guitarist Sol K. Bright's orchestra alongside a trio led by Eddie Bush. Soon after opening, the owners installed an "all-glass roof for year-round starlight dancing."[66] Some Hawaiians owned their own nightclubs on the West Coast. Lani Ellen's uncle Dick owned a club in Tijuana, and her father operated a club in the 1940s on Catalina Island.[67]

Many of the musicians and dancers maintained apartments or homes near each other in the city. Lani Ellen recalled festive times when her father, uncles, and their friends would continue to jam long after their gigs ended at one or two in the morning, or when they would gather in their backyards, particularly Dick McIntire's, to unwind and converse in Hawaiian or pidgin. More formally, Hawaiian musicians organized the Polynesian Society and met regularly in the afternoons, during their "off time," to talk story. The members gathered during the day at a small Hollywood club called Whistlin's Hawaii and later expanded the membership to include dancers and other Pacific Islander performers. Lani Ellen met her husband Freddie Letuli at the very first Polynesian Society luau, held at White's Point in 1947.

While the opportunities seemed vast, however, Hollywood's glass ceilings were not limited to those above the starlit dance floors of Polynesian clubs. Hawaiian entertainers in Hollywood faced significant professional challenges in an industry that tended to entrench rather than transcend white supremacy.

FIGURE 30. *Hollywood's Hawaiian entertainers gathered together regularly. This photograph, taken at a social function in the 1930s, features four professional steel guitarists: Dick McIntire, Sam Koki, Sol Ho'opi'i, and Buddy Silva. Courtesy of Lani Ellen McIntire.*

Hawaiian musicians forged close social ties with Hollywood's elite actors and directors. Yet producers and studio executives hesitated to assign them much value beyond their utility to represent racial "types" of Pacific Islanders or other people of color onscreen.

In a revealing example, in 1941 20th Century Fox's director of publicity, Harry Brand, developed an exegesis on the Hollywood Hawaiian community in the form of a press release to promote Fox's upcoming musical comedy with Betty Grable, *Song of the Islands*.[68] The idea seems to have come to him while wandering the studio's Stage 14 during the production of the film, when on any given day, ten Hawaiian musicians and several Hawaiian extras milled about between takes and set changes. At first, the press release seemed intended to dispel stereotypes of Native people:

> Scattered throughout [the studio stage] are virtually all the Polynesians of Hollywood. . . . You spot a little group of these simple, happy islanders, intent upon something in their center, their arms shuttling in and out. Weaving tapa cloth, probably, you think, unless you take the trouble to look more closely: then you see that they're playing gin rummy. Another little group listens raptly to the tale unfolded by a grey-haired elder. Ah, you think, tribal legends. You move a little nearer and you can hear what he is saying. . . . "So then, when the finance man came to repossess the car . . ." You move along to where a group of simple native musicians are strumming dreamily at guitars and ʻukuleles. They pause as you step up. "There's nothing like island music, is there?" you murmur to the leader. "Well," he says, "it's not exactly eight-to-the-bar but people like it." . . . Hawaiian music has been popular, in one degree or another, for more than 20 years, and many are musicians and dancers in cafes and floor-shows. They work periodically in pictures enjoying a small boom when there is a flurry of South Sea productions, such as now.[69]

Brand's condescension becomes clearer when he notes that Hawaiians were also "hilariously doubling for American Indians and Orientals if the need arises." Indeed, if there was ever any notion that studio executives took the Hollywood Hawaiian community seriously as actors or even as musicians, his press release shattered it:

> You talk to a few of the veterans of the Hollywood Polynesian colony and you realize that it is their very light-hearted simplicity that has made them adapt themselves completely to Occidental life. They are an incurably happy people, and there is in the Polynesian colony here none of the painful nostalgia found in other alien groups. . . . Their language has no word for 'enemy,' and the concept of social caste is one that they cannot learn to understand. They rear their children with a minimum of dogma, to become brown-skinned versions of American urchins. Some of the elders tell the children the old island legends, like the story of Pele, the volcano goddess (illustrated by a reference to some neighboring factory chimney belching smoke), but this is more for entertainment than from any self-conscious wish to retain a native culture. . . . About the only time the work situation becomes unsatisfactory is when it is too steady. Hardly an employer of Hawaiian musicians

> can keep the same personnel for three weeks running, and in all other work the commitments are brief and erratic. This is because the one island trait they stubbornly retain is a belief that one works only when it is strictly necessary. . . . That, of course, is because they remain, under a thin lacquer of mainland sophistication, a simple island people, and they can't be expected to understand right away the civilized doctrine of working oneself into a premature grave.[70]

Convincing himself that music came naturally to Hawaiians, Brand seemed willfully ignorant of the relentless work that generated virtuosity, and the intense, seven-nights-per-week schedule that Hoʻopiʻi and indeed all musicians who sought to earn a living in Los Angeles had to endure in order to establish themselves.

A few days after the press release was mailed to markets throughout the country, the Japanese bombed Pearl Harbor, generating an altogether different image of the Islands in the press.[71] Nonetheless, the studio released the film successfully just three months later, with a score that included performances and compositions by Sol Hoʻopiʻi and the Harry Owens orchestra. Even the bombing could not shatter the insistent, ironclad impression of Pacific Islanders in popular culture, encapsulated in Brand's press release: indigenous traditions ultimately were unimportant and should be willfully disregarded. Pleasant as their "tribal legends" and "island music" might be, Hawaiians ultimately revealed little interest "to retain a Native culture." In addition, Hawaiians could not transcend the bonds of their race; they were doomed, as "simple [and lazy] island people," to never absorb anything more than a "thin lacquer of mainland sophistication."

Of course, Hawaiian musicians encountered the constraints of their employers' imaginations in workspaces far beyond the Hollywood studios. Polynesian clubs were known as such for a reason—developing in cities all over the United States, highly stylized and racialized, generic Pacific Islander themes became quite easily predictable, and comfortable, from the perspective of the patrons, whose expectations typically reflected Brand's. It was in these venues, however, that Hawaiian musicians and dancers found relatively stable work. Eventually Dick McIntire left his brothers in Los Angeles to seek new opportunities in New York City's emerging Polynesian club scene. When Lani Ellen's father joined Dick, the family moved into an apartment near Broadway, at 110 West 49th Street. She recalled New York City's audacious Polynesian club, the Hurricane, where Eddie Bush and later her uncle Lani's band performed their sets on one-half of a revolving stage, with a Latin band set up on the other half, awaiting its turn from behind the curtain.[72] Bands and dancers, differentiated and branded by ethnicity, labored nightly on the Polynesian club scene to fulfill contracts that required them to play specific roles in the racial calculus of interwar and postwar entertainments that rarely gave opportunities for escape.[73] As Adria Imada put it, the Hawaiian- and Polynesian-themed clubs that popped up in the 1930s and 1940s throughout Manhattan and the United States offered a "feminine, sensual, and uncomplicated Hawai'i" to its patrons, at least 80 percent of whom, in New York, at least, were not simply non-Hawaiian, but white.[74] Imada continues, "offering white middle-class American audiences easily digestible hula and Hawaiian music, the [Lexington Hotel's] Hawaiian Room catered to a growing market for consumer culture and cultural commodities after the Depression and World War II. During this period, white spectators eagerly consumed other exotic performances at jazz, Cuban-themed, and 'Spanish' nightclubs in New York City."[75]

Escape from these audience-assigned roles was also constrained by the influence of hapa haole music on haole songwriters. By the 1930s hapa haole had existed as a significant genre in the Islands for decades, as its earliest composers were Hawaiian. Albert R. "Sonny" Cunha (1879–1933), for example, became famous for his penchant to combine Hawaiian and American musical and lyrical elements. Published locally in Honolulu, his earliest compositions, such as "Waikiki Mermaid" (1903) and "My Honolulu Tomboy" (1905), combined structural and melodic elements from hula ku'i with clever combinations of Hawaiian- and English-language lyrics.[76] Hawaiian troupes quickly adopted his genre, which they began to perform, alongside more standard hula ku'i fare, in the Islands and beyond. Such a combination was not particularly novel; Hawaiians had been appropriating and repurposing musical ideas and lyrical themes from other peoples for decades. Most of that work involving haole music had been rooted in the Christian himeni tradition, however. By contrast, Cunha's hapa haole genre was unambiguously secular, with Cunha going to great lengths in some of his compositions to describe the physical attributes of alluring wāhine.[77] The genre became even more popular after Cunha's protégé, Johnny Noble, assumed the leadership of the Moana Hotel Orchestra in 1920 and in the same year composed his smash hapa haole hit "Hula Blues," with words by Cunha. Noble had studied hula ku'i music and attempted, like Cunha, to write hapa haole songs in a manner respectful of Hawaiian music traditions, and most Hawaiian musicians saw little or no problem performing hapa haole compositions by Native composers.[78]

FIGURE 31. *By the mid-1930s, a number of Hawaiian entertainers had left Los Angeles for new opportunities in Polynesian-themed clubs in New York City and other cities in the Midwest and East. In 1937 the Hawaiian Room opened at the Hotel Lexington in New York City. This image features a number of entertainers working with Lani McIntire, the orchestra leader standing at the center front of the stage. Courtesy of Lani Ellen McIntire.*

Tin Pan Alley songsmiths had begun to apply their own sensibilities to the hapa haole genre, however, resulting in songs that much more closely resembled disparaging ethnic novelty genres of the day.[79] Typically rendered as comedic or nostalgic, romantic fare through their exploitation of racial and hypersexualized stereotypes, songs such as "Oh, How She Could Yacki Hacki Wicki Wacki Woo (That's Love in Honolu)" could sound simultaneously ephemeral and absurd, while neatly buttressing in their belittling thematic and lyrical content the laws and social mores that fueled colonialism and white supremacy. Some songs included gibberish lyrics such as "She had a Hula, Hula, Hicki, Boola, Boola in her walk / She had a Ukalele Wicki Wicki Waili in her talk" — lyrics that were offensive enough to Hawaiian entertainers who had to field requests for such songs from their haole audiences — while other songs about "my little brown Hawaiian maid" or "brown skin babies" were even more provocative.[80] Such racial mockery was an American musical theme nearly a century old by this point, given the origins of blackface minstrelsy, and the use of suggestive lyrics regarding women of color was likewise a long-standing trope; yet both found new life in pseudo-Hawaiian music.

Like other people of color who sought opportunity for autonomy in the entertainment industries, Hawaiians often faced immense pressure to incorporate ethnic novelty hits in their repertoire. The demand by white audiences could be overpowering, particularly in Polynesian clubs. Their set lists, drawing from an immense catalog of songs by Hawaiian and non-Hawaiian composers, demonstrate that they struck a line between what they considered to be respectable hapa haole music and degrading ethnic novelty; musicians and dancers insured that their selections remained dignified. As hula dancer Betty Puanani Makia recalled of her days working in the Lexington Hotel's Hawaiian Room, "We did mostly hapa haole songs. If we did one ancient number, it was an ʻōlapa, and that was 'Kawiki' or 'A Kona Hema' [hula ʻōlapa in honor of King Kalākaua]. But most of it was hapa haole, because we had to introduce Hawaiian songs and dances to the hāole there. If we did it all in Hawaiian, they wouldn't understand you. So we had to do hapa haole, and that went great. We did 'Hula Hands,' '[Little] Brown Gal,' 'Grass Shack,' those old day songs."[81] Even while dancing to suggestive songs such as "Little Brown Gal," however, Makia noted an important distinction in their interpretation of them, declaring, "We didn't do hootch cootch. We did good Hawaiian dance. [They] might be hapa haole, but they were modern dance[s]."[82]

The musicians and dancers working in Hawaiian- or Polynesian-themed clubs also segmented their public performative lives as entertainers from their private lives. Imada makes this point in her discussion of entertainer and orchestra leader Ray Kinney: "As a form of protest, Ray Kinney's mother refused to speak English after the U.S. overthrow of the Hawaiian monarchy in 1893, so Ray and his siblings grew up speaking fluent Hawaiian. Ray spoke to his hula troupe largely in Hawaiian, especially when giving the dancers directions for their performances. The troupe played hapa haole, English-language music for white tourists, but when they got together as a family and community, they performed a variety of their favorite music, including hapa haole mele and Hawaiian-language mele from the nineteenth century. His children said, 'Some people criticized Dad for being too haole in his song choices. But he had to. It was his profession, and he had to cater to people on the mainland. But when he was at home, he sang Hawaiian songs.'"[83] Even the backstage was segmented from the front, and carefully protected; there, Imada notes, they could visit with friends from home, speak Hawaiian or pidgin, and reinforce a sense of community.[84] As Betty Makia recalled, the "Hawaiian Room [was] like home . . . you know, the Eastern Outpost? It was really where you would meet the people from Hawai'i. And you get homesick but when you see someone from Hawai'i, you become Native again."[85]

Native Hawaiian guitarists working during the interwar period generated critical mass for the immersion of Hawaiian guitars in American entertainment culture. By 1920 Los Angeles had become the focal point for Hawaiian guitar music in the United States. Many of the best Hawaiian steel guitarists lived, loved, recorded, played, and acted there. Their likenesses began to precede them in movie theaters throughout the country. The technological innovations they advanced changed the face of American guitars, and the success of their steel guitars inspired their electrification. As the beginning of the next chapter attests, they generated legions of haole fans and educated them in modern genres of Hawaiian-language as well as hapa haole music. Their impact in the entertainment industries seemed to know no bounds.

At the same time, Hawaiian musicians faced challenges over the control of Hawaiian music representations in popular culture, and they struggled to gain acknowledgment of their influence and due respect as artists in the music and film industries. Many Americans began to receive Hawaiian music differently during this period. Despite the interest of Sol Ho'opi'i and others guitarists in recording and singing mostly Hawaiian-language songs through the 1930s, Tin Pan Alley and other haole songsmiths now working for Hollywood pushed back, circulating hit pseudo-Hawaiian songs much closer in form to blackface minstrelsy than Hawaiian mele. Polynesian clubs sheltered Pacific

FIGURE 32. *Dick McIntire and Sol Hoʻopiʻi both played significant roles in promoting the latest innovations in Hawaiian guitar technology. This advertisement for Dickerson electric steel guitars dates from 1938. Courtesy of the Sousa Archives and Center for American Music, the University of Illinois at Urbana-Champaign.*

Islanders and generated good jobs during the Depression years in major cities throughout the country, but audience members came to expect that musicians would perform the demeaning numbers. In addition, producers and studio executives hired Hawaiians to fulfill a racial "type" with heavily circumscribed, antimodern roles, even when plot points revolved around Hawaiʻi or Hawaiian music. They seemed incapable of associating Hawaiian artists with innovation, modernity, and progress. Such a perspective obscured the strong work ethic and substantial professional goals of Hawaiian artists in Hollywood, and all but ignored their agency in crafting some of the most modern and most popular music in the world. These forces eventually combined in popular understandings of the steel guitar, as we'll see, to divorce Hawaiians from its history. Just as the kīkā kila began to fashion a new American musical landscape, its cultural associations with Hawaiians began to slowly wash away.

6 The Disappearing of "Hawaiian" from American Music

In 1933 the members of the Oahu Serenaders began to appreciate the extent to which radio's ability to compress time and space had redefined the music industry. At the very moment that the global depression crested and the production of records had all but ceased, the Serenaders found themselves buried each week in a sea of fan letters from all over the country, sent by listeners deeply engaged in each week's fifteen-minute program. In a decade that seemed to bring unceasing bad news, their Hawaiian steel guitar radio programs, sailing through the air via a continent of transmitters and antennae, seemed to ignite the imaginations of millions of people.

For some listeners, of course, the Serenaders' Hawaiian mele enabled momentary escape from their material and emotional conditions. Bjorn Johnsen wrote from Brooklyn, "I have never been to Hawai'i but someday I will go, when I listen to your music, I just have to close my eyes and imagine that I am there, your playing makes one forget the care's worries of the day and makes one want to forget the humdrum existence of the city for the dreamy shores of a white beach where the sun always shines. Please don't think I am foolish when I write a letter like this but I mean every line of it and hope you will continue."[1] Helen Ward from Akron, Ohio, agreed: "I must say, I for one am a lover of Hawaiian music, it is my favorite music. Especially, when tired, nervous, and, overtaxed, from worry. It is so resting[,] so comforting, when, all, alone, and Blue, and, thinking, of *home* and *mother* and Kiddies."[2] According to "Nashville Listener," "I must say the quarter hour you play on Mondays holds me spell bound. I didn't have any idea a human being could make such music. I am lost for words to express."[3] From Milwaukee, a listener wrote that her "entire family stops work long enough to sit by and listen to your very short time on the air. Hawaiian music is [the] most beautiful of all."[4] A Cherry Valley, Massachusetts, listener explained, "Hawaiian music has been my favorite since I was a little girl, as it seems to give me a different idea on life."[5]

While the Hawaiian music of the Oahu Serenaders provided an escapist salve to some, however, their fan mail reveals in many cases a quite active audience, one that bucked the pseudo-Hawaiian music trend increasingly apparent in movies or radio, and one that in fact seemed quite well-versed in Hawaiian-language and hapa haole compositions. Mrs. J. O. Holbrook from Red Bank, New Jersey, requested "Sweet Lei Lehua," "Ua Like No a Like," and "Hilo March," for example, while Bill Winston from Shreveport, Louisiana, reported that "the madame and I never miss a program. Yours is the best on the air but *please* don't play those Haole jazz pieces, the Hawaiian guitar and ʻukulele was never meant for such junk. Please play *and sing* Hanohano Hanalei, Kuʻu Lei Pikak[e], [Ka] Wiliwili Wai and Mai Poina ʻOe Iaʻu."[6] Two sisters from Manitowoc, Wisconsin, wrote a fifteen-page letter expressing their love of "sweet Hawaiian mele," and provided a detailed schedule of well over a dozen Hawaiian music programs they tuned into each week from stations broadcasting from all over the country. In addition to subscribing to the recently introduced *Hawaiian Guitarist* magazine and writing their own hapa haole compositions (some of which they included with their letter), they maintained a favorite repertoire, requesting no less than seventeen Hawaiian songs for the band to play, then adding, "We've done our part by writing you boys a line. That's the only way the Radio Entertainers have a way of finding out how people like their programs. We're right there when it comes to letter writing, especially [while listening] to Real Mele."[7] The Serenaders' program, broadcast and relayed from Cleveland, even reached Hawaiʻi twice a week; Rose Kua from Līhuʻe, Kauaʻi, wrote that "your programs . . . have been enjoyed immensely by the whole family," adding, "Imagine tuning in to Cleveland, Ohio, for some Hawaiian music."[8]

Many listeners seemed to hang on every note that rang through the steel player's guitar. One wrote, for example, that "we've been playing Hawaiian guitars for about five years, and when we hear good Hawaiian music we know it. In fact every time I hear your Hawaiian guitarist, when your program is over, I get the sudden impulse to place my Hawaiian guitar in the center of the floor and jump . . . on it, or a thousand other destructive ideas."[9] The radio provided an unprecedented platform for steel guitarists to reach every living room in the country and inspire other musicians to strike out on their own. But who was this guitarist who attracted such adoration for the Oahu Serenaders? He was not from Oʻahu, or the Islands, or even the Hawaiian diaspora: Eddie Alkire (1907–81) was a white guitarist who had come of age working in the coal mines near Flemington, West Virginia.[10]

Indeed, as we have already seen, by the 1930s non-Hawaiians from all over the world had come to embrace and adopt the Hawaiian steel guitar. Like Eddie Alkire, they grew up listening to Hawaiian troupes that played in their towns, or on the silver screen, or on wax cylinders and 78 rpm records. The fan letters to Alkire suggest that Americans throughout the country had developed intense relationships with Hawaiian music, regardless of whether or not they ever picked up a Hawaiian guitar. They cultivated a fluency in classic kingdom-era hula kuʻi and hapa haole music. They judged the ability of troupes they encountered on the radio to faithfully render "Real Mele" and to avoid "Haole Jazz." Some of them, like Alkire, enrolled in conservatories owned by Hawaiian musicians or even developed the skill necessary to collaborate with them on the professional stage.[11] Alkire sits at one end of the spectrum, in that he was so absorbed by the steel guitar that eventually he launched his own Hawaiian guitar correspondence courses and conservatories, and designed a very successful line of Hawaiian guitars. Such devoted audiences and practitioners understood the Hawaiian guitar as a Kanaka technology, designed to perform mele; that relationship to Hawaiian music is what drew them to the instrument in the first place.

Others grew perhaps more enamored with the Hawaiian guitar than with Hawaiian music, often through those same encounters—of seeing a Hawaiian troupe performing in their town, of catching a Hawaiian guitarist in a Hollywood movie, or hearing the otherworldly playing of Pale K. Lua or Sol Hoʻopiʻi on 78 rpm records. They, too, often enrolled in correspondence courses with Kanaka guitarists, collaborated with them professionally, and found any way that they could to emulate the sounds of the Hawaiian guitar in their own performative context. The reach of Hawaiian guitarists into the heart of local music-making in the United States cannot be overestimated, and is demonstrated by the ways Americans assimilated and adapted the instrument to redefine the sonic contours of their own vernacular traditions, much as Hawaiians had adapted the Spanish guitar into their own. By the 1920s, the Hawaiian guitar had generated a profound impact on the sounds of local music making in the country as well as on the production of commercial recordings in a variety of new industry genres. Kanaka guitarists were deeply implicated in these developments from the beginning.

Their role in American music making became increasingly obscured, however, for a variety of reasons, including the increased competition for steel guitar students by non-Hawaiian-owned franchises. Observing the success of Hawaiian-operated conservatories in the 1920s and seeking a piece of the action, two brothers launched the Honolulu Conservatory of Music empire from a storefront in Cleveland. They had no knowledge of the Hawaiian guitar or any interest in Hawaiian music, but by actively soliciting graduates of their correspondence courses to open their own schools, the brother who stayed in the business eventually oversaw an extraordinary 1,200 Hawaiian guitar school franchises throughout the country. Rather than serving as arbiters of Hawaiian music, the schools provided students with lessons from the American songbook, arranged for the steel guitar. In these schools, Hawaiian music, and Kanaka guitarists, faded quickly from view.

Likewise, as musicologists, folklorists, and popular music enthusiasts became enraptured with the sounds of southern American music, it seems that most came to ignore or downplay the influence of modern, "foreign," Hawaiian innovations and musicians in the region. Following the lead of the music industry in segregating the recordings of white southerners into the consumer category of "hillbilly" music, and that of southerners of color into the category of "race" music, these musicologists, folklorists, and aficionados came to affirm a bipartite racial view of southern music. This view of southern music created, even romanticized, a complementary cultural infrastructure for the Jim Crow South—one that associated the "blues" exclusively with an essential, segregated, timeless southern black experience, and "country" music as the exclusive domain of impoverished rural whites. Together, as this chapter will demonstrate, all of these developments worked by the 1950s to significantly mask both the multicultural origins of the blues and country music genres, and, more broadly, the Hawaiian origins of the steel guitar.

We can begin with the South. Eddie Alkire grew up on its fringe and began to excel on the steel guitar in the 1920s. We do not know how he was first exposed to the Hawaiian guitar. However, we do know that by that time, whether in the coal-mining camps of West Virginia, or in the most rural pockets of the Deep South, Kanaka steel guitarists were familiar sights. In southern Victrola shops, their recorded music was heavily advertised and routinely played. In movie theaters, parades, vaudeville houses, and tent shows, regardless of segregation, southerners of all colors experienced firsthand the Hawaiian technology of the steel guitar. Later on, by the 1930s, some African American guitarists such as Robert Johnson were recording songs for niche "race" and "blues" labels while using a technique that departed only slightly from that of Hawaiian guitarists: in contrast to the well-known "Hawaiian style" of laying the instrument across their laps, they held their instruments in the standard fashion and used glass or brass tubes rather than steel bars to express string pitch. They called it the "slide guitar." During that same period, meanwhile, most steel guitarists recording for niche "hillbilly" or "old time" labels continued to hold the instrument as did their Hawaiian contemporaries—on its back in their laps, with a steel bar held between their fingers. The "slide guitar" would come to powerfully shape the sounds of Mississippi Delta and Chicago blues in the coming decades, while the "steel guitar" eventually replaced the fiddle as the most prominent instrumental voice of the country music genre. But what, exactly, was the relationship between these genre's architects, and the Kanaka guitarists who preceded them or continued to perform in the South? What role did Hawaiian guitarists play in influencing the development of two of America's most influential, enduring, and racially bifurcated music traditions? And why did Hawaiian musicians disappear from the histories of those traditions in the process?[12]

Indeed, the "blackness" of the blues and the "whiteness" of country music were not simply associations asserted through music industry marketing strategies to attract southern black and white consumers. They also came to resonate with folklorists, musicologists, and fans.[13] The blues genre, in particular, came to attract ever increasing numbers of white enthusiasts by the 1960s, many of whom felt that the music provided them intimate, romantic access to what they contended was an authentic black experience, unencumbered by the taint of white (or other) influences. For them, the "blues" came not just from the South but from southern blacks. It came from slavery. It came from the Middle Passage. It, and even the ancestor of the "slide" guitar, came from Africa.[14] It led white blues enthusiasts, often born into suburban enclaves, far from the South, on door-to-door scavenger hunts in the most poverty-stricken districts of Mississippi. They sought the rarest recordings of the country blues masters, and more often than not the masters at the top of their lists played slide guitar.

What is missing from popular, and in many cases, scholarly understandings of southern music, however, is its cultural messiness. Just as the nineteenth-century Hawaiian Islands continued to develop into an increasingly diverse cultural crossroads, so too did the American South. Recent scholars have demonstrated that the South in the early twentieth century was much more colorful than previous historians and folklorists imagined.[15] Yet through the present day, it seems impossible for many blues and country scholars to remove the biracial lens through which they have viewed southern music. The South, for them, is essentially a land of only two cultural ancestries, with black music coming from Africa, and white music coming from ancient English or Scottish ballad traditions. The dozens of vibrant southern American Indian communities are excluded from this strictly black-and-white mosaic, as are people rooted more intimately in the Caribbean world, or migrants from Nova Scotia, Eastern Europe, Latin America, Asia, or, of course, Hawaiian troubadours.

No scholars had previously searched for a presence of Hawaiians in the South during this period, so when I began to look for them, what I found was breathtaking. Hawaiian guitarists generated a tremendous amount of publicity in the southern press during the early twentieth century that detailed the wonder of their steel guitar technique and the sounds it produced—sounds that the astounded reporters and music critics said they had never encountered before. It suggested to me the role that Hawaiian guitarists played, at the very least, in disseminating the technique early on; whereas others may have experimented with the concept here and there, Hawaiian guitarists instantly demonstrated the viability and beauty of it to southerners, to an unprecedented degree. The same press is silent on demonstrations of a similar technique by any white, African American, or other non-Hawaiian vaudeville or tent show troupes.[16] The press's embrace of *Hawaiian* guitarists, meanwhile, is profound.

The prevalence of Hawaiians in the early twentieth-century southern press indeed reminds me of why the South *was* so fundamental to the making of modern music genres in the United States. It after all was a land of exploited labor and bruised souls, a land that fiercely incubated fire and brimstone evangelicalism, a land of demolished infrastructure and unspeakable violence most prominently realized in the unyielding terrors of white supremacy. At the same time, it was a land of spectacular cultural diversity and entanglement, a multilingual region with Gullah speakers at one end, French Creoles at the other, and a multitude of indigenous languages in between. It was a land of transience—of survivors fleeing the white terror or the sharecropper fields for the bright lights and big cities to the North, or for textile mills in the Piedmont. It was a land of traveling minstrels, tent shows, and foreign entertainers working their way through the region town by town to seek their livelihood. A place like no other—and highly combustible—it had by the early 1900s become very familiar to innumerable tours of Hawaiian troubadours.

Hawaiians had exploited the burgeoning southern entertainment markets long before 1916, the year that recorded Hawaiian guitar music outsold every other genre of music in the country. Indeed, by that time, two generations of southerners had become familiar with Hawaiian music. The Royal Hawaiian Band introduced Hawaiian music to the South as early as 1884, when the lyrics to "Aloha 'Oe," penned by the future Queen Lili'uokalani, were displayed at the New Orleans World's Fair. Other Hawaiian troupes traveled the southern states as early as 1893, as hula dancer Kini Kapahu noted in an interview decades later. In 1896, she and a fellow dancer posed for photographs at the Howell photography studio in Louisville, Kentucky.[17] After touring the country heavily for several months, we also know that the royalist band Ka Bana Lahui performed at the Texas State Fair in Dallas.[18] The 1900 tour diary of Hawaiian troupe manager John Wilson includes the routing for a southern tour featuring July Paka. The route included Kansas City, New Orleans, Birmingham, Memphis, Atlanta, and Louisville.[19] Paka would later make the first major commercial Hawaiian guitar recording with Joseph Kekuku in 1909, only a few months after he and Kekuku toured the South together. At the conclusion of the Buffalo Exposition in 1901, several musicians under the management of Joseph Puni toured Georgia, Florida, South Carolina, and Virginia.[20] And they kept coming: in 1912 the *Hawaiian Gazette* reported that the troupe of Kanaka steel guitarist Louis Thompson (who, like Puni, performed considerably in Europe) was "playing one night stands in the Southern States, and expect[ed] to stay in the South all winter."[21] By then, the sight of Native Hawaiian musicians making their way through southern towns and countryside must have seemed almost commonplace to many southerners.[22]

Tracing the footprint of Hawaiian guitarists in Louisiana alone can reveal their frequent access to the South and their influence on local musicians and vice versa. New Orleans served as a major destination point for Hawaiian vaudeville tours. In 1912, three years after the release of Paka and Kekuku's first hot-selling steel guitar recordings with the Edison label, their troupe with Toots Paka booked into the city through the Orpheum circuit. The Paka troupe in fact booked several tours through the state. Newspaper advertisements for Hawaiian guitar music frequented the *Times-Picayune* in those years, featuring recordings by the most significant first-generation steel guitarists to leave the Islands: July Paka, Joseph Kekuku, Pale K. Lua, David Kaili, and Frank "Palakiko" Ferreira. A few of the Hawaiian acts traveling through New Orleans at the time included the Comet Royal Hawaiian Serenaders, who visited in 1917, and the Big Kawa'a Hawaiian Troupe, which traveled along a vaudeville circuit in 1921 to the Louisiana Theatre. Kuleella's Hawaiian Troupe followed them in the theater six months later.[23] Louisiana residents were hardly passive recipients of these new sounds; perhaps lured by the novelty or exoticism, they succumbed to the Hawaiian guitar craze like the rest of the country. By 1918, the LSU Men's Glee Club had included its own steel guitar performances on tours through the state, and just a few years later in New Orleans, students who enrolled in the Hanley Brothers' guitar classes received free Hawaiian guitars.[24] And, just as Louis Armstrong, Joe "King" Oliver, the Dixie Jazz Hounds (featuring Sophie Tucker), and a few other New Orleans jazz combos recorded hapa haole and pseudo-Hawaiian songs in the 1920s through the 1940s, Hawaiian guitarists also showed up on jazz recordings.[25] New Orleans jazz singer and pianist Walter "Fats" Pichon, for example, hired Kanaka steel guitarist Bennie Nawahi to play on "Dad Blame Blues," "Black Boy Blues," "Wiggle Yo Toes," and "I've Seen My Baby (And It Won't Be Long Now)" in 1929, and Louis Armstrong featured a Hawaiian steel guitar on his 1930 recording of "I'm in the Market for You."[26]

Of course, New Orleans jazz and the blues tunes that W. C. Handy and others made famous in the 1910s deeply inspired Hawaiian guitarists as well. Referring to July Paka by name, the *Atlanta Constitution* observed in 1916, "No one yet has been known to get enough of his rendition of the 'Memphis' and 'Hesitation Blues.'"[27] When a troupe called the Waikiki Players and Singers toured Georgia in 1917, the *Columbus Ledger* remarked, "But it remained for Mr. Paaluhi with his magic guitar to win the audience. True it is that this man can produce music of all kinds from the instrument. Wailing and crying, the appealing Hawaiian melodies seemed to pour from the instrument through the great building. The audience sat silent throughout, and when the artist branched from the music of the island [to] the rag music of today, playing 'The Memphis Blues' with more runs and 'rags' than the writer ever heard before, he brought down the house." A couple of years later, Joseph Pa'aluhi (perhaps the same individual as the above-mentioned "Mr. Paaluhi") was giving Hawaiian guitar lessons at a music shop on New Orleans's Canal Street.[28] The relationship of the steel guitar to jazz may have run even deeper: a provocative and pithy article published in a 1923 music journal blamed the popularity of the Hawaiian steel guitar for the "glissando effects" adopted by jazz trombonists that had "wrested" the instrument from its otherwise "sublimely dignified position" in classical orchestras.[29] Regardless of the veracity of this claim, the bonds between jazz and the Hawaiian guitar continued to tighten. As we saw in chapter 5, by the mid-1920s Sol Ho'opi'i had become obsessed with jazz music and the spirit of improvisation and acrobatic virtuosity that inspired it, forever changing how the steel guitar was approached by all who followed him.

Hawaiian guitarists found all sorts of opportunities to play in the South, however, not only in the musical wellspring of New Orleans. In 1922, during the same period that African American guitarist and singer Blind Lemon Jefferson was busking on the downtown Dallas streets, for example, the *Fort*

Worth Star-Telegram reported that one Hawaiian troupe's "Haunting Hawaiian melodies . . . will be included on the program of free entertainment which will be provided for visitors to the Southwestern Exposition and Fat Stock Show," featuring David Kaleipua Munson on steel guitar. Several troupes traveled through Mississippi, including the Royal Hawaiian Players, who booked three days in Hattiesburg's Strand Theatre in 1919, and the Sanine Hawaiian Troubadours, who performed with the "ukulele, steel guitar and taropatch" in Biloxi less than two months later. In April 1918, Vierra's Royal Hawaiian Singers and Players closed the Lyceum season in Fayetteville, Arkansas. Born in Hilo to a Kanaka mother and a Portuguese father, Joseph, Albert, and Frank Vierra left the Islands around 1910 and organized several Hawaiian troupes that toured for many years, always with steel guitarists.[30] They played all over the country, but they frequented rural and southern venues from Hattiesburg, Mississippi, to Lumberton, North Carolina, in the late 1910s.[31] A photograph of a Vierra troupe with one of several steel guitarists that the brothers employed over the years graced the pages of the *Clarksdale (Mississippi) Daily Register* in May 1917, along with an announcement of the troupe's local performances that week (see fig. 33).[32]

This was likely not the first and certainly not the last visit by the Vierra brothers' troupes to the Deep South, however. The surviving financial records of their Chautauqua tours illuminate the extent to which Hawaiian troupes became familiar with the South, and to which southerners could become accustomed to witnessing Kanaka steel guitarists firsthand: in Mississippi alone during one tour in 1923, Vierra's Hawaiians performed in Biloxi, Gulfport, Laurel, Hattiesburg, Brookhaven, McComb, Jackson, Canton, Vicksburg, Winona, Indianola, Greenwood, Charleston, Water Valley, Holly Springs, New Albany, Aberdeen, West Point, Okolona, Tupelo, Amory, and Corinth.[33] This particular tour, one of many in the Deep South, included an equally impressive number of stops in Louisiana, Florida, Alabama, and Georgia—the group visited over 100 towns before it was over. Tour receipts and Hawaiian musicians' oft-reported appearances in small-town southern newspapers reveal not only that many markets existed for Hawaiian steel guitarists at this time in the South but also that these musicians were working every small town, nook, and holler along the way.

Hawaiian guitarists also found plenty of opportunities to be heard in between their tours. The 1917 Gulfport, Mississippi, advertisement described in chapter 3 reveals the accessibility and interest of recorded Hawaiian music in the South: even those who could not afford a Victrola could hear the latest

FIGURE 33. *Vierra's Hawaiian Singers and Players, like so many other Hawaiian troupes in the early twentieth century, traveled all over the U.S. continent. This image of the group was featured in a promotional advertisement for an upcoming local appearance in Clarksdale, Mississippi. It appeared in the city's newspaper, the* Daily Register, *in 1917, but the troupe posed for it in a Great Falls, Montana, studio in 1912. Courtesy of Hawai'i State Archives.*

Lua, Kaili, and Paka Hawaiian guitar records played in front of George Northrup's Gulfport shop as he blasted the latest hits to lure in potential customers. By the early 1920s, Hawaiian guitarists also played regularly on radio stations heard throughout the South, such as WFAA in Dallas, WBAP in Fort Worth, and WLS in Chicago. By 1923, eighty-nine radio stations were in operation in the South alone, and many offered live Hawaiian guitar performances throughout the day and evening.[34]

Other shows and entertainment circuits further contributed to the deep reach of Hawaiian steel guitarists in the South. Tully's *Bird of Paradise*, the theatrical production that premiered on Broadway in 1912, perhaps became best known for the songs and interludes performed by Hawaiian steel guitarists (and for the large erupting "volcano" on its set). The initial Broadway run lasted for less than four months, but the production's true impact would be felt when numerous traveling troupes staged it throughout the country in the years following. The *Columbus (Georgia) Ledger*, reviewing one of many traveling productions of the play in 1918, reported that "the Kanaka musicians are exceptionally proficient guitarists, and they obtain from their instruments musical effects never achieved by American players."[35] When that same year a troupe featuring a Kanaka guitarist presented the production in Anniston, Alabama, and Greenville, Mississippi, the local papers billed it as "The Play That Made Hawaiian Music Popular." If Hawaiian steel guitar music was renowned in Anniston and Greenville by this time, it clearly was well established throughout the Deep South.[36]

Despite Jim Crow segregation, southerners of color could see, hear, and interact with these guitarists. In order to advertise their local theater bookings, for example, recently arrived vaudeville groups would often march through town during the day, offering a view of their musical performance for everyone in town to behold. In this manner musicians of color presented a great deal of music from other parts of the country and the world to southern audiences. W. C. Handy, for example, recalled parading through the streets with Mahara's Colored Minstrels before selling tickets for the evening shows in the 1890s; they would play anything from Tin Pan Alley numbers to Sousa marches, introducing the locals to the latest hits emanating from the big cities.[37] When Harvard archaeologist Charles Peabody spent the summers of 1901 and 1902 in the Mississippi Delta, he reported the frequency of Tin Pan Alley hits such as "The Bully Song," sung with glee by the local African American men laboring for him on excavations. "Undoubtedly picked up from passing theatrical troupes," he wrote, "the 'ragtime' sung for us quite inverted the supposed theory of its origin." Although Peabody referred to their guitar playing as "limited" in repertoire and "lacking" in spontaneity and did not seem to observe any guitarists playing with a bottleneck, steel, or knife, certainly if local African Americans sung several of the latest hits from New York City, they would have seen Hawaiian guitarists when they traveled through town and countryside.[38] African Americans, in fact, had access to these performances both in the street and on the stage. As historians John S. Otto and Augustus M. Burns astutely noted in 1974, "most [southern] states did not pass legislation segregating public amusements: this task was left to local authorities or to custom. Only in Louisiana and South Carolina, did the state legislatures consider segregation of amusements, and there they segregated only the ticket offices and entrances for tent shows. . . . Therefore, once inside southern amusement shows, whites and blacks could listen to the same lectures or to performances by Hawaiian guitarists, Tyrolean yodelers, ministrels, vaudevillians, or cabaret blues singers."[39]

Jim Crow laws actually may have created some opportunities for African Americans and Hawaiians to interact at the time, as Hawaiians would likely have taken up lodging with African American families or in boardinghouses reserved for African Americans and other people of color as they toured the segregated South. This phenomenon extended at least into the 1940s; Lani Ellen McIntire recalled to me her traumatic childhood experiences in 1939–40 of being twice spit on by white men (offended, she believes, by her walking with her haole mother and Hawaiian father) while touring with her family's Hawaiian troupe in Mississippi and Tennessee. She spoke of the embarrassment of being refused lodging in white-only hotels, including those that her family entertained in, just as she gleefully remembered the camaraderie of boarding with African Americans, American Indians, Latinos, and other itinerant entertainers of color.[40] Presumably her experiences in the Jim Crow South reflected those of Hawaiians who traveled the same roads before her. Indeed, we do know that the Ka Bana Lahui, or Hawaiian National Band, decided to speak publicly only in the Hawaiian language when south of the Mason-Dixon Line in the 1890s, both to confuse white supremacists and to avoid their wrath.[41] As late as 1959, a Hawaiian entertainer reported exiting a Montgomery, Alabama, cafeteria only to face its owner and a police officer, who told her never to return.[42] Jim Crow laws and the terrors of racial violence in the South created a complex series of hazards on the road that Hawaiian musicians, like African Americans, had to navigate with great care. At the same time, their shared experiences of segregation certainly created opportunities for musical collaboration.

Hawaiian guitarists also played the earliest black segregated "chitlin circuit," the Theatre Owners Booking Association. Lizzie Wallace, an African American entertainer who was part of Black Patti's show in the 1910s, gained firsthand experience with Hawaiian music when she performed in the Islands as part of Hen Wise's Bronze Review. According to the *Chicago Defender*, in 1917, when she returned to the continent, she brought with her six Hawaiian musicians: David Burrows, George Sam Ku, Walter Ho, Sam Clement,

Johnnie Kasihue, and Zachary Pali. Adopting a Hawaiian persona and naming her outfit Princess Pauhi and Her Hawaiian Song Birds, she led her troupe, featuring the steel guitar, on tours through the Midwest. Although we don't know if Her Hawaiian Song Birds toured the South, it does seem clear that in the early twentieth-century South, Kanaka steel guitarists were playing everywhere, for everybody.[43]

Of course, it is possible that southerners were themselves experimenting with similar guitar techniques, independent of the influence of Hawaiian guitarists. Some blues scholars claim that one-stringed zithers of African origins, commonly known as "diddley bows," preceded guitars to the South and required a similar practice of running an object up and down a string, and that furthermore, they inspired the development of the blues slide guitar style in the South. But as Gerhard Kubik, one of the leading proponents of this hypothesis admits, such instruments do not appear in the Delta's historical record until the 1930s, decades after the Hawaiian steel guitar began to saturate the South. Even then, one-stringed zithers seemed more of a children's instrument than one that engendered technique, refinement, and use as a social instrument.[44]

Meanwhile, the guitar culture that had transformed the musical and social landscape of Hawai'i during the 1870s and 1880s was not as immediately replicated in the American South. That began to change by the 1890s when guitars, diminishing in price and made more easily accessible through mail order catalogs, became increasingly common. Steel-string guitars with reinforced bracing, however — those best suited for steels and slides — remained quite rare for some time to come.[45] By the time Hawaiian guitarists began touring the region, the South's guitar culture was in its adolescence, but it soon grew with a vengeance.

To date, only four recollections or documented examples have been located in the written record that suggest southerners experimenting with steel or other objects on guitars prior to the 1920s. We may find more in the future, which might alter our understanding of this period. Of these four descriptions, however, two of the players were described by the observers as playing in the "Hawaiian" manner, which challenges our ability to tease apart the Hawaiian influence from the non-Hawaiian origins of the playing, and a third player did not seem to develop a strong technique until he received personal instruction in 1922 from one of the most prolific steel guitarists to leave the Islands.

One of the earliest examples appears as a recollection, forty years after the fact. W. C. Handy (1873–1958), a native of Florence, Alabama, who popularized the new genre of "blues" songs on a national level, described the scene in his 1941 autobiography. In 1903 at the train station in Tutwiler, Mississippi, he saw a "lean, loose-jointed Negro" press a knife on the strings of his guitar, "in a manner," he wrote, "popularized by Hawaiian guitarists who used steel bars."[46]

Meanwhile, white guitarist Jimmie Tarlton (1892–1979), born near Cheraw, South Carolina, claimed to have developed a steel method on his own, sometime in the early 1900s.[47] It is not clear whether or not he was proficient in this style and played it publicly, or whether he was merely experimenting with steel objects on the strings. Around 1922, however, he met Frank Ferreira at a hotel in Los Angeles. Ferreira taught Tarlton how to use a steel bar, rather than the knife that he had earlier experimented with, and introduced him to an additional array of Hawaiian guitar techniques.[48]

I am aware of one final observation and one recollection. In 1907, sociologist Howard W. Odum observed some African American guitarists passing through Lafayette County, Mississippi, who found occasion to use a knife on their guitar.[49] Likewise, banjo player Gus Cannon said that he saw an African American playing guitar with a steel or slide-type device around 1900, though he referred to the episode as "the first guy I heard playing on a Hawaiian guitar."[50]

These four documented recollections or instances of non-Hawaiians playing in this style in the South before the 1920s came close on the heels of the Hawaiian guitar's introduction in the States, and we likely will never know whether these guitarists developed their techniques independently or, if they were indeed independent, to what stage they had gained proficiency in their techniques. Kekuku, we must recall, spent seven years developing the necessary competency and tools to adapt the technique to modern songs and to make it comprehensible to audiences. By the mid-1890s, however, steel guitarists in the Islands had mastered the technique to the degree that they were attracting a good deal of attention by onlookers, sailors, and other visitors, enough to prompt some observers to return to the continent and diffuse the technique before Kekuku even arrived in San Francisco.[51] The body of evidence in favor of the Hawaiian introduction of the technique to the South is not conclusive. It is tantalizing, however, and more supported by the documentary record than any other explanation. As we have already seen, Native Hawaiian guitarists canvassed the rural and urban South during the first two decades of the century, and by the early 1920s documentation of the Hawaiian guitar's influence in southern vernacular and commercial music practices picks up dramatically.

At that point, southern steel guitarists slowly began to establish a recording legacy on the instrument. Their recorded output, however, defied simple categorization. Having grown up in Florida and Georgia, for example, vaudeville entertainer Sam Moore (1887–1959) perhaps made the earliest steel guitar recording by a guitarist born outside of the Islands. Moore recorded his "Laughing Rag" in 1921 with an "Octa-Chord," an eight-string acoustic Hawaiian guitar developed by a company in Chicago.[52] An upbeat and nimble instrumental, "Laughing Rag" was described by Richard "Dick" Spottswood as "aggressive mainland verve . . . which stands halfway between Hawaiian and the 1920s country guitar rags of Sam McGee, Blind Blake, Roy Harvey, and Sylvester Weaver," two out of four of whom were African American.[53] Moore recorded several sides in the years that followed, including a number of hapa haole songs with his Octa-Chord.[54]

Moore was a white southerner, however, and while most southern music from the period could claim provenance as culturally complex as his, industry leaders ignored such diversity of origin in their marketing strategies. Within a few years, the industry would locate the music of most white southern musicians within their one-dimensional "hillbilly" catalogs. The word "hillbilly" was not yet in vogue when Moore recorded, not that it would ever have properly characterized his or his fellow southerners' multicultural influences. It was only first assigned by the record industry to the music of rural white southerners in January 1925. During a session that month, Okeh Records' talent scout Ralph Peer had to come up with a name on the spot for a North Carolina group he was recording in New York. Without thinking too much about it, he branded them the Hill Billies.[55] Soon after, they returned to New York to repeat their success, this time with a North Carolina–born, haole steel guitarist in tow.[56] The name of the outfit stuck, and Okeh and other labels soon began to market the "hillbilly" or "old-time" record list to southern white consumers, just as they marketed their "race record" lists to African American consumers.

Like Moore's songs on the Octa-Chord, however, the music recorded by southerners during this period defied the racial categorization insisted on by the industry one way or the other.[57] White West Virginia steel guitarist Frank Hutchison recorded thirty-nine sides for Okeh Records' "old-time" list from 1926 to 1929, but he evoked a style that combined the Hawaiian method of playing with the repertory influence of a local African American musician.[58] Between 1930 and 1932, Oscar "Buddy" Woods, an African American steel guitarist from Shreveport who took up the instrument after seeing a traveling Hawaiian troupe perform in town, recorded several sides (many of which were risqué) with white singer Jimmie Davis.[59] Davis later came to record a hapa haole song with Lani McIntire and His Hawaiians, scored a huge hit with "You Are My Sunshine," and then traded on his celebrity to serve the state of Louisiana as a prosegregation governor.[60] Cutting sides in New York City, with whites like Hutchison recording blues-titled songs and African Americans like Woods recording with segregationist whites in the Jim Crow South, and with all of them inspired by Hawaiian musicians, it was difficult to see how the racially bifurcated industry genres could stick.

They did, and they didn't. But one thing is for sure: Hawaiians directly influenced musicians featured in the contrived genres of both "race" and "hillbilly," particularly as they brought their guitar techniques to the South. African Americans no doubt developed their own techniques on the instrument by the 1930s, when we find the first descriptions of them playing with a "slide" rather than a "steel" and holding their guitars not in their laps like the Hawaiians but in the conventional fashion. But the documentary record much more substantively supports this as a recent adaptation of the Hawaiian guitar technique rather than as an adaptation of a now distant, one-stringed African instrument. African Americans developed their guitar techniques with no documented connection to such African retentions, and they did so in the wake of Hawaiian guitarists working their way deeply through the southern entertainment circuits.

In New York City in late 1923, for example, African American guitarist Sylvester Weaver cut four sides accompanying blues and vaudeville singer Sara Martin. Weaver had arrived in the city from his home near Louisville, Kentucky, where he worked as a day laborer and a jug band guitarist at night. Weaver was an incredibly agile guitarist, commanding a variety of the most modern music styles of the day. After hearing him play, it is no wonder that Sara Martin would bring his talents all the way to her sessions in New York.[61] However, during their second session, on November 2, 1923, he recorded his own "Guitar Blues" and "Guitar Rag," the two sides blues scholars suggest comprise the first blues "slide" guitar recordings ever made.

I have found no evidence that links Weaver's recordings to an indigenous southern slide guitar tradition or a connection to African musical traditions, but one does find, in the years preceding Weaver's landmark recordings, Kentuckians treated routinely to the sounds of Kanaka guitarists. In 1906, the Royal Hawaiian Band performed in Louisville; in 1909, July Paka and Joseph Kekuku performed in Lexington and likely other nearby towns.[62] By 1916, Louisville's Krausgill Piano Company was stocking koa wood 'ukuleles, Mekia

Kealaka'i's method books, as well as Hawaiian steel guitars that for ten dollars included fingerpicks and steel bars.[63] In August 1918, the *Hartford (Kentucky) Republican* reported that a *Bird of Paradise* production had recently passed through town; the next year a Hawaiian troupe featuring a steel guitarist performed in Middlesboro, Kentucky. That year, the *Mt. Sterling (Kentucky) Advocate* listed an advertisement for Paka's records. In 1922, a year before Weaver's recording debut, the Royal Serenaders, yet another Hawaiian troupe, performed at the opera house in Paris, Kentucky. Further examples abound.[64] As a resident of Louisville, Sylvester Weaver lived and worked in a town that served as a major crossroads for musical troupes that paraded their novelty through the daytime streets, segregated or not, so that *everyone* in the community could watch. Weaver was among the best and most versatile guitarists of his day in the South, and certainly when new players came through town, he would ensure that he had a front seat, either on the streets or in the balconies of the town's segregated theaters. In fact, for these first recordings Weaver most likely played his guitar with a steel or a knife and when doing so, held the guitar in his lap, "Hawaiian style."[65]

Indeed, when we take a comprehensive look, many of the most significant, earliest-documented "slide" guitarists actually played "Hawaiian style" by laying the guitar across their laps and using steel bars or knives. These players included Weaver, Huddie Ledbetter (aka Lead Belly), and likely Charley Patton and perhaps Blind Lemon Jefferson as well. W. C. Handy, we can recall, referred to that player at the Tutwiler, Mississippi, train depot as playing with a knife, "in a manner popularized by Hawaiian guitarists." Music scholar Samuel Charters also suggested that Blind Willie Johnson learned to play in the "Hawaiian style." East Texas guitarist B. K. Turner (aka "Black Ace") also performed in the "Hawaiian" lap style, as did Louisiana-born guitarist Sam Collins, Georgia-born guitarist James "Kokomo" Arnold, Oscar "Buddy" Woods, and Eddie Schaffer from the Ark-La-Tex region.[66]

Evidence suggests, furthermore, that African American guitarists were familiar not only with Hawaiian guitars but with Hawaiian music as well. Arkansas-born African American guitarist Casey Bill Weldon, who recorded as "Casey Bill, the Hawaiian Guitar Wizard," played "Hawaiian style" and became quite popular among African American consumers in the 1930s.[67] Working in St. Louis in 1927, Lonnie Johnson, perhaps *the* most influential black guitarist of his day, recorded several intriguing Hawaiian guitar sides with Henry Johnson and His Boys, including "Blue Hawaii" and "Hawaiian Harmony Blues." In addition, one of the first stars in the blues idiom, Ma Rainey,

FIGURE 34. *Charley Patton is one of the preeminent figures in blues history. When playing with a knife or steel, he likely played his instrument on his lap, "Hawaiian style." Courtesy of Jon Tefteller/Blues Images.*

featured the Hawaiian-style work of Milas Pruitt in two of her early recordings from March 1924. African Americans indeed took up not only Hawaiian guitars but also ʻukuleles: commercial recordings from the mid-1920s by groups such as the Two of Spades, Ukulele Bob Williams, Danny Small & Ukulele Mays, and the Pebbles attest to this broad familiarity with Hawaiian instruments.[68]

Southerners remained captivated by the virtual Technicolor of musical sounds that surrounded them, with roots stretching to the Hawaiian Islands, the Caribbean, Nova Scotia, or beyond. Yet by the 1920s, the recorded music industry increasingly worked to fit the output of their southern secular artists into the much simpler, racially defined marketing categories of "hillbilly" and "race" music. The artists continued to pull their influences from all directions, however, regardless of their origin. For example, one of the earliest stars in the "hillbilly" genre, Vernon Dalhart (1883–1948) was the first to generate national, even international interest in the recorded commercial hillbilly genre.[69] Dalhart broke open the floodgates for the genre when his mid-1920s recordings of the "The Wreck of the Old 97" and "The Prisoner's Song" sold up to 25 million copies over a period of two decades.[70] He was by all counts one of the genre's first "superstars."[71] Yet while Dalhart was born on the fringes of the South, in northeastern Texas, his background reflected a far more cosmopolitan background than what the prevailing myths of the origins of country music prepare us for.

As Karl Hagstrom Miller argues, musicians such as Dalhart were highly mobile, and many had to leave the South in order to attain success. They "were in search not of American tradition but of access to the modern American theater, music publishing and phonograph industries centered in New York. . . . [There] they encountered a musical world that traded on stereotypes of rural and southern music, from hillbilly comedy records to the minstrel stage."[72] Dalhart learned to exploit southern stereotypes, but only after he tried to succeed in many other genres, first light opera stage productions and recordings, then dialect minstrel performances, and, right before his success in the hillbilly genre, Hawaiian music. From Liliʻuokalani's "Aloha ʻOe" to hapa haole songs like "Aloma," "Hawaiian Rainbow," and "Lalawana Lullaby," Dalhart began to engage Hawaiian repertoire in the early 1920s and recorded with the most prolific Hawaiian guitarist of the period, Frank Ferreira (aka "Ferera"). In addition to recording such repertoire under his own name, however, he also recorded hapa haole songs as a member of Ferera's Hawaiian Instrumental Quartet, the Hawaiian Entertainers, the Hawaiian Serenaders, the Hawaiian Duet, the Hilo Hawaiian Orchestra, the Hilo Serenaders, Palakiko Pala's Hawaiian Serenaders, the Waikiki Hawaiian Orchestra, and in several other incarnations with Ferreira and John Pa'aluhi.[73] Dalhart developed his career in New York at the time that Hawaiian guitarists began to pack the city's stages and recording studios and Ferreira became one of the most recorded studio artists in the industry's history. Dalhart finally struck his own gold in 1924, soon after he hired his friend Ferreira to play standard guitar on his first recording in the hillbilly or "old-time" genre, "Wreck of the Old 97."[74]

Meanwhile, new ingredients were added to the South's cultural stew. Nearly all southerners seemed to become entranced by the Western pulp or film genres, and cowboy songs figured in the repertoires of black and white southern musicians. John Lomax collected a performance of "Home on the Range" and "Git along Little Dogies" by an African American who had worked as a camp cook on Texas cattle trails. African American guitarist Muddy Waters was proudly performing at least seven Gene Autry hit songs in venues around his Clarksdale, Mississippi, home in the early 1940s, including "Deep in the Heart of Texas" and "Take Me Back to My Boots and Saddle." Another African American Delta musician of the time, performing on a weekly cowboy radio show, reported, "You have to play all the Western tunes for the colored these days."[75]

Even those Western tunes, however, broadcast on movie screens or by radio throughout the southern countryside, had been long infused with Hawaiian steel guitars. One pivotal figure in early Westerns was Edmund R. "Hoot" Gibson (1892–1962), a seminal actor in the genre, second only to Tom Mix, from the silent era through the 1940s. Gibson worked in Hollywood at the same time that Hawaiian guitarists such as Sol Ho'opi'i and Eddie Bush were defining the sounds of the town's celebrity set. He also got to know Lani McIntire in the early 1920s, when Lani worked for about four years providing "atmospheric music" for Gibson and other actors on film sets.[76] Gibson became entranced by Hawaiian music and in the 1920s formed Hoot Gibson's Hawaiian Foursome, an act made up of largely unidentified musicians, although it is likely that Lani McIntire played with Gibson at this time, as did, according to Hawaiian guitarist Ralph Kolsiana, Sol Ho'opi'i. Kolsiana (1912–2002) recalled, "Not many people know that Hoot Gibson, the famous cowboy movie star, brought Sol out here to Los Angeles to play with his western group. That's how the western guys got into using the steel guitar. I don't think anybody's ever covered that story. This was way, way, back as I recall, in the early 20's."[77] Whether or not Gibson had any role in bringing Ho'opi'i to Hollywood from

FIGURE 35. *After Lani McIntire (holding the standard guitar at the center of the frame) arrived in Los Angeles, he spent about four years providing "atmospheric music" on film sets for "Hoot" Gibson and other cowboy stars. That is perhaps how Gibson (at left with the steel guitar) took such an interest in the instrument. Courtesy of Lani Ellen McIntire.*

San Francisco, his Hawaiian Foursome recorded ten Hawaiian-language and hapa haole mele in 1928, and a compelling early photograph in one of Lani Ellen McIntire's many scrapbooks illuminates the relationship of Gibson, and the early film industry, to the Hawaiian guitar.[78] Another Western star, Roy Rogers, also became fascinated with Hawaiian music and early in his career joined steel guitarist Bennie Nawahi's troupe, the International Cowboys.[79]

As we continue to examine the formative musicians of the hillbilly or old-time genre and the related "western swing "and "country" industry categories that soon followed, the direct influence of steel guitarists from the Islands becomes indisputable. To begin with, it is impossible to underestimate the influence of Frank Ferreira in the 1920s; as a session steel guitarist in New York City, he produced thousands of records under dozens of band names during this period, and they were bought and sold all over the country. His recorded music spoke to southerners, as it did to legions of record buyers elsewhere, and it certainly inspired southern musicians.[80] Maybelle Carter of country music's famed Carter Family, for example, was impressed enough by Ferreira's work that she took up the steel guitar and recorded it on two Carter Family sides in 1928.[81] As we have seen, Jimmie Tarlton was trained by Ferreira in 1922 to play the Hawaiian guitar. When Tarlton returned to the Piedmont in 1927, he had mastered what Ferreira taught him and went on to record eighty "hillbilly" sides for various record companies over the next six years in the group Darby and Tarlton. Darby and Tarlton's biggest hit in Columbia's hillbilly catalog, "Birmingham Jail," with the B-side "Columbus Stockade Blues," sold an impressive 200,000 copies.[82]

Many of the most significant steel players in the "hillbilly" and later "country" catalogs of the 1920s through the 1950s recalled being directly and dramatically influenced by Hawaiian musicians as they forged their own sound. Steel guitarist Cliff Carlisle, born in Tennessee and raised in the hills of Kentucky, was asked by one interviewer when country music first "impressed" him. He responded, "Well, I always liked music. I had an old broken-down phonograph, or graphonola, or whatever you want to call it back in those days; they call them by a different name today. . . . I had quite a few Hawaiian records, and this is how I got interested, I suppose, in the Hawaiian guitar. I thought it was the most beautiful music I'd ever heard."[83] Some directly incorporated Hawaiian melodies into their own compositions. In 1929 and 1930 Darby and Tarlton, and Cajun French music duo Cléoma Breaux and Joe Falcon, for example, each released commercially successful sides that incorporated the melodic refrain from Liliʻuokalani's "Aloha ʻOe," while Cliff Carlisle put his own spin on it by both strumming and *yodeling* the refrain on his 1930 recording "Never No Mo' Blues."[84] One southern observer even recalls discovering the steel guitar at an evangelical tent meeting in 1928, when the Hawaiian steel guitarist traveling with the preacher broke up the gospel songs with a stunning rendition of "Hilo March," a composition written by Joseph Kapeaeau Aeʻa in 1881. "Well, Brother, that 'done it,'" the observer recalled, "I dreamed of that sound for days."[85]

Beecher "Bashful Brother" Oswald (1911–2002) grew up in the Smoky Mountains of Tennessee and was surrounded by a musical family; so much so that he even carried his father's moonshine in a guitar case to distribute to their neighbors before moving to Flint, Michigan, like so many other southerners, to work at an auto plant. There he played music at clubs and restaurants for extra pay, and one night he met Hawaiian guitarist Rudy Waikuiki at a party. The chance encounter changed his life: "That was when I first heard someone play something like my style. He was a real Hawaiian boy, from over in the Islands, and he was playing this way and I loved it. I'd go to them parties just to watch him play. Then I'd go home and get my guitar and try to do the same thing. I was just playing a straight guitar and I had to raise the strings up, put a nut under the strings."[86] After one café owner told him that he would be out of a job if he didn't learn Hawaiian music (a not uncommon demand by venue owners in the 1920s and 1930s), Oswald learned quickly.[87] Waikuiki put the year around 1932. He recalled, "Yeah, I remember him. He followed me around all over the place. Every time I turned around he was there listening. Well, I didn't mind. He was welcome any time. I was glad to help him."[88] When Waikuiki upgraded to a Dobro resonator guitar, Oswald ordered one as well.[89] He took that instrument to work for country singer Roy Acuff in 1939. For the next fifty-three years, Oswald's Dobro was broadcast nationally, nearly every Saturday night, on WSM's Grand Ole Opry radio program. Opry announcer Hairl Hensley said that Oswald, revered as Acuff's "right-hand man," was "the glue that held the Roy Acuff show together."[90] Oswald's Dobro, and particularly the "trilling" technique that Waikuiki taught him — the sound that trademarked Acuff's songs — elevated the steel guitar to unprecedented associations with country music.[91]

The beginnings of the modern genre of country music seem by all accounts to crystallize around the foundational recorded work and celebrity of Jimmie Rodgers, yet, like all of the other musicians described in this chapter, his influences ran the gamut of the incredibly diverse musical practices and traditions accessible to southerners. Born just north of Meridian, Mississippi, in 1897, Rodgers engaged all of the sounds of the South: as a waterboy for the railroad he listened to its construction crews, comprised of people of color, as they sang while they labored. At the age of thirteen he joined a medicine show. At twenty-two he was playing pop standards at fairs and political rallies. For a time he toured the Midwest as a blackface minstrel. He later toured the southern vaudeville circuits, and soon joined the Hollywood Follies show in Louisiana and Texas, where he performed nightly with "an Irish comedian, a Hawaiian group, and a blues singer." He later toured in his own "Hawaiian" troupe, but he became famous for his yodels and his blues, recording one of his most enduring songs, "Blue Yodel No. 9," with Louie Armstrong on trumpet and Armstrong's spouse, Lil, on piano.[92] He also recorded with ten different steel guitarists during his six-year recording career, including Cliff Carlisle and four Kanaka guitarists: Joseph Kaipo, David S. Kanui, Charles Kama, and Lani McIntire's unidentified steel accompanist.[93] Universally regarded by country music scholars as "perhaps the most influential country singer of all time,"

Rodgers worked directly with Kanaka musicians, demonstrating Hawaiian music's particularly intimate bond with the burgeoning genre that he came to dominate before his early death to tuberculosis in 1933.[94]

Rodgers also recorded with non-Hawaiian steel guitarists, of course, but even these owed a direct debt to Kanaka guitarists. Cliff Carlisle identified Sol Hoʻopiʻi as the first Hawaiian guitarist he listened to, while Ferreira's recordings also played a large role in Carlisle's musical education.[95] After Carlisle began to learn the instrument, he soon formed his own "Hawaiian" troupe in Kentucky. Eventually he and his brother adapted their sound to replicate the swagger of Jimmie Rodgers and his blue yodels. Years later Carlisle told an interviewer that he never had played in a blues style before Rodgers exposed him to it, but he then corrected himself: "Oh, no—yeah—I'll take that back. I believe that Sol Hoʻopiʻi done 'St. Louis Blues,' (sings) and I copied him on the steel guitar before I started in any yodel or anything."[96] Through remarkable convergences, then, we find Carlisle, a white southerner, learning to play by emulating steel guitarists from Hawaiʻi, then forming his own Hawaiian troupe in Kentucky, and then learning the *blues* aesthetic from Sol Hoʻopiʻi, who was by then intrigued with the music most associated with African American southerners. From this sea of connections, Carlisle would then record his steel guitar with Rodgers, the "Father of Country Music."

It is around this time in the 1930s that we find African American guitarists beginning to record with their instruments held in the conventional fashion (instead of in their laps), using a glass or metal "slide" rather than a steel bar. Their unique style generated a bright and occasionally shrill sound. More African American musicians soon adopted the style, as photographs and recordings attest. However, even these guitarists often acknowledged the Hawaiian style of playing as a foundational reference point for their technique in interviews conducted during the blues revival period. Tampa Red (born Hudson Woodbridge), for example, one of the most popular black guitarists to record and perform in the 1920s and 1930s, explained to Jim O'Neal, "I used two, three, maybe four strings sometime. It's got a Hawaiian effect. I couldn't play as many strings as a fella playin' a regular Hawaiian guitar, but I got the same effect. I was the champ of that style with the bottleneck on my finger." In 1965, Mark Levine, Barry Hansen, and John Fahey interviewed the legendary early slide player Eddie James "Son" House; they spent much time teasing out details of early twentieth-century Mississippi Delta guitar culture. Son House quickly shut down the notion that such a guitar culture, and certainly not a slide guitar culture, existed before the 1910s. He instead told his interviewers that his father and uncle mostly played tuba and trombone and only later picked up the guitar. When pressed about the interest around Clarksdale in guitar music, he said, "Long back in that time, they didn't care nothing 'bout guitar much." Son House reported that he didn't see his father play guitar until he was about ten years old (ca. 1912), and then, his father (and all the other guitarists he recalled) used a standard tuning, not an open tuning necessary for a slide or Hawaiian guitar style. In fact, "none of the old guys," he said, played in open tunings, and he did not recall anyone from that period playing with a bottleneck or knife. He made no mention of diddley bows. When asked how he came about the slide guitar and open tunings, he thought for a while and responded, "The first guy I paid attention to . . . was a guy by the name of Rubin Lacy. . . . And he's the first guy, him and this guy [James McCoy], . . . that I see play the slide — the *Hawaiian* way." Even after diligent urging by his interviewers to deliver the goods on the ancient origins of the Delta blues slide guitar, Son House characterized it as a new style, learned by him and his peers, as the "Hawaiian way" of playing.[97] Still, by the mid- to late 1930s, while some African American southern guitarists continued to play in the "Hawaiian way," others like Son House and Robert Johnson began their mastery of their slide guitar style, and the Hawaiian influence on their sound and technique became increasingly opaque to audiences and blues scholars alike.

However, later recordings by famous southern African American guitarists suggest that the Hawaiian repertoire remained more than familiar to them. Take, for example, an informal recording session from 1968 at the Memphis apartment of Furry Lewis. Lewis, born in the 1890s in Greenwood, Mississippi, played in jug bands around Memphis in the 1910s and 1920s, traveled in medicine shows, and was invited to play with numerous legendary performers from that period, including Bessie Smith, Blind Lemon Jefferson, Gus Cannon, and W. C. Handy. In his apartment, among friends, Lewis sang a bluesy number he called "Farewell to Thee" and played a guitar solo that replicated the melody to Liliʻuokalani's "Aloha ʻOe" (which means, in Hawaiian, "Farewell to Thee").[98]

One of the most curious traces of Hawaiian repertoire derives from a recording of Huddie Ledbetter, himself a Hawaiian-style knife player, performing at a private party in 1948. By the time Ledbetter was "discovered" in the Angola prison farm by John and Alan Lomax in 1933, he had already spent a great deal of his life as a musician, having worked the streets of Dallas with Blind Lemon Jefferson in the late 1900s and 1910s. It was at this time that he learned how to play the Hawaiian guitar. Though the Lomaxes presented

FIGURE 36.
Huddie "Lead Belly" Ledbetter was born in Mooringsport, Louisiana in 1888 or 1889. In his twenties he began performing professionally. As seen here, he sometimes played his guitar with fingerpicks and a knife or other object for a slide, "Hawaiian style." Courtesy of House of Lead Belly, LLC.

him as a "folk" singer, his early repertoire was loaded with commercial Tin Pan Alley material. One of Ledbetter's early chroniclers, Frederick Ramsey, remarked, "Travelling in the South even singing for Negro audiences you would get requests . . . , people who could know about the current popular songs even though they [were] Broadway and white inspired or Tin Pan Alley songs, and [Ledbetter] had quite a few of them in his repertoire." Ledbetter was a consummate professional, so he knew that in order to get paid, whether on street corners or in the finest theaters, you had to know how to play whatever your audience expected or demanded. At this 1948 party, in one of his last recorded performances, Ledbetter sang what he called the "Hawaiian Song." The last time that this song, otherwise known as "My Hula Hula Love," was recorded by any artist was when Hawaiian guitarists Pale K. Lua and David Kaili cut it with the Irene West Royal Hawaiians for Victor Records in 1916. Prior to that, according to Edison publicity materials, it had been "introduced to metropolitan audiences by Toots Paka" and, of course, her bandmates, Hawaiian guitarists July Paka and Joseph Kekuku.[99] Ledbetter, then, conjured a song from deep in the past, from the days of his street work with Blind Lemon Jefferson, in the days when Hawaiian guitar music was among the most popular, if not *the* most popular, music in the United States.[100] Hawaiian influences remained engrained in the repertoire and techniques of southern African American guitarists for decades to come.

Meanwhile, for southern steel guitarists performing in what they gradually came to embrace as "hillbilly" or "country" music, 1933 marked a sea change. During the years that followed, the sound of the electric steel "frying pan" guitars played by Sol Hoʻopiʻi and other Hawaiians in Los Angeles came to transform the aesthetics of these genres, along with those of the jazz-infused "western swing" that began flowing from the musical wells of Texas and Oklahoma. Among the players most responsible for the electric revolution in these contexts were Bob Dunn, Leon McAuliffe, and Jerry Byrd, but they followed in the footsteps of Hoʻopiʻi and other Kanaka steel guitarists. The first commercial record ever produced with an electric guitar was cut by the Noelani Hawaiian Orchestra in February 1933; the next musicians or acts to use the electric "frying pan" guitar during the year that followed were Eddie Bush, Andy Iona's Islanders (featuring Danny Kalauawa Stewart on steel), and Dick McIntire's Harmony Hawaiians.[101] In January 1935, however, white Oklahoman Bob Dunn became the first non-Hawaiian to record electric steel, when his Fort Worth–based band, Milton Brown and His Musical Brownies, cut thirty-six sides in two days at a Chicago studio. [102] By that point Dunn had developed his own style of playing that seemed to replicate a horn more than anything else, but the style perfectly suited boisterous western swing. As Bill Malone writes, "It is no accident that electrification made its first inroads among the southwestern string bands which played in honky-tonks and in large dance halls and ballrooms."[103] For the first time, the steel guitar could compete not only with the other instruments in the band, but also with the newfangled public address systems that bands trucked around to dance halls to amplify their vocalists' voices. Dancers and fans immediately took to the instrument, and the musicians never looked back.

Like so many other vanguard steel players in the country genre, Dunn was first inspired by, and learned from, Hawaiians. He discovered the instrument when he saw a Hawaiian troupe perform in Kusa, Oklahoma, in 1917. Eventually he enrolled in a correspondence course with Walter Kolomoku, and by 1927 he was playing professionally. Kolomoku, a member of the original cast of musicians who toured the United States and Europe in a *Bird of Paradise* production in 1912, had developed an intricate array of weekly teaching correspondence materials for students all over the country.[104] The schools, discussed at the end of this chapter, allowed rural Americans to develop their own skills on the exotic instrument that Hawaiian troupes had introduced to them in itinerant tent and stage productions.

Jerry Byrd (1920–2005), like Dunn, also experienced his first Hawaiian music at a tent show, this time near his hometown of Lima, Ohio.[105] As he recalled, "They had tent shows that traveled all over areas, one or two, three states maybe. They were known as Chautauquas. . . . So, anyhow, we went and it was a troupe of Hawaiians. Over on the left — there was about eight of them, as I remember, and they had the beautiful painting, you know, the backdrop, the volcano erupting and all of that exotic stuff, you know, the palm trees and stuff that was far remote from me. This guy [was] sitting over on the left hand with his instrument on his lap, and it was all shiny, like a mirror. I found out later that it was a National, made before the electric guitars were made. This was about 1930 — '29 or '30."[106] Captivated by this first encounter, he devoured every bit of Hawaiian music he could find: "I would sit through — all of these Hawaiian movies, I would sit through all day Saturday. It would be double feature, so you had to sit through the other movie, which you didn't want to see, to get the seat. Some guy [would] play a chorus on steel guitar that lasted fifteen seconds (Laughter)." Byrd also tuned into the Hawaiian music radio broadcasts of "Jim and Bob," a duo that featured the magnificent playing of Hawaiian guitarist Bob Pauole.[107] Byrd religiously followed the best players as he taught himself to play: "[Hawaiian players] were blazing the trail for steel guitar. . . . Dick McIntyre, Sol Ho'opi'i, Sam Koki and a lot of those guys, they were creative, prolific, coming out with new tunings for steel guitar. They led the way, the Hawaiians."[108] Byrd turned professional and, while not from the South, he played with the biggest country stars of the 1940s and 1950s, including Patsy Cline, Ernest Tubb, Hank Williams, and Red Foley. His influence in the genre was such that Bill Malone remarked, "in the playing of Jerry Byrd one could hear the sound of country music's future."[109] It was a future steeped in the technique, style, and sounds of his Hawaiian predecessors: "I played really a kind of Hawaiian style in country music. Steel guitar's always been in

The earliest surviving example of a hollow-necked Hawaiian steel guitar, this instrument was built in 1909 by Chris J. Knutsen in Seattle during the city's Alaska-Yukon-Pacific Exposition. Joseph Kekuku likely inspired Knutsen to build the guitar, which features Hawaiian koa back and sides. Hawaiʻi's territorial government provided a supply of koa for sale at the exposition. Courtesy of Tom Noe.

Left: *Knutsen Convertible Harp Hawaiian Guitar, ca. 1914–20s. Beginning in 1914, Knutsen added harp strings to some of his Hawaiian guitars. This guitar features four harp bass strings and six treble strings. The guitarist would pluck these strings and allow them to resonate while playing steel guitar on the main neck.* Right: *Weissenborn Style 3. A piano repairman named Hermann Weissenborn began building and selling copies of Knutsen's hollow-necked steel guitars in Los Angeles in 1914. Southern California's thriving market for steel guitars prompted Knutsen to relocate to downtown Los Angeles later that year. Offering four models, Weissenborn's Style 3 featured koa wood and rope marquetry binding around the body, the fingerboard, and the sound hole. Courtesy of Ben Elder.*

Built in 1927, one of the earliest surviving examples of a National Tricone Style 1 square-neck steel guitar. It looked and sounded like nothing that preceded it. Sol Hoʻopiʻi played the prototype of this nickel-plated guitar at a three-day party in order to win investors for the National String Instrument Company. The grille work is hand soldered; by peering inside the screen surrounding the bridge one can see the outlines of the three cones that mechanically amplify the instrument. Courtesy of Ben Elder.

National's Triolian model was set up as a standard guitar. However, the company traded on the popularity of Hawaiian guitar music by featuring a range of mostly Hawaiian-themed decals on the instruments. This 1928–29 wood-bodied Triolian features the most popular design offered, the "Hula Girl." Far from the climes of Hawai'i, the original owner wore the paint off of this instrument by playing in a Salvation Army Band in Minneapolis. Courtesy of Ben Elder.

In 1929 the Dopyera brothers left the National String Instrument Company to build their own line of guitars with mechanical amplification under the Dobro brand. This ca. 1931 Dobro Model 55 is set up for Hawaiian playing and features a single inverted resonator cone to generate the expansive sustain that Dobro guitars are known for. Courtesy of Ben Elder.

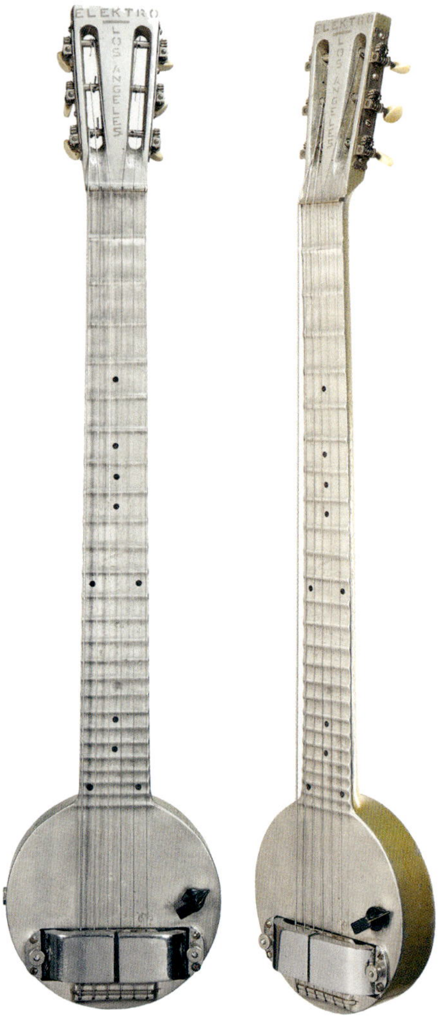

Left*: One of the very first production line Rickenbacker Electric Hawaiian (EH) guitars, this instrument shipped in September or early October 1932. The body was made of cast aluminum and featured a revolutionary horseshoe-styled electromagnetic pickup; the shape of the instrument quickly earned it the nickname "frying pan."* Right*: Alvino Rey (shown with his guitar in the inset) received an EH model in the fall of 1932 and was likely the first musician to broadcast the electric guitar to a national radio audience. The guitar was so unusual in shape and sound that Rey grew tired of people coming up and asking him what it was. As a result, he soon cut up an old acoustic Columbia guitar body in his backyard shop and placed the Rickenbacker inside it. Courtesy of Lynn Wheelwright.*

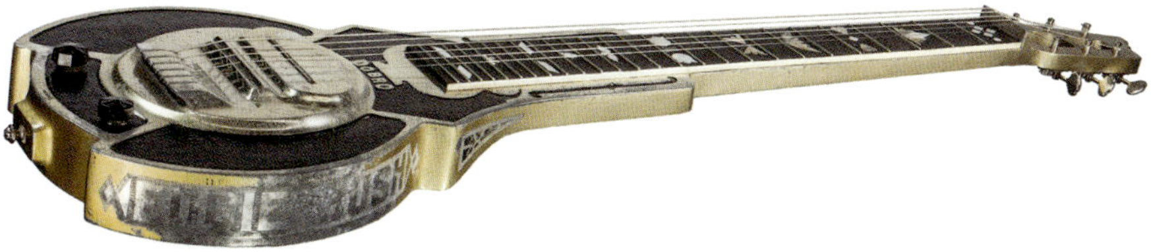

Top: *The Dopyera brothers entered the electric guitar market soon after the Rickenbacker company demonstrated such quick success with the "frying pan" model. In 1936 the Dopyera brothers built for Eddie Bush, one of the most celebrated guitarists in Hollywood, this quite ornate custom steel guitar.* Bottom left: *1936 Rickenbacker Model B6. With a body made of Bakelite, this instrument was known to warp if placed too close to warm stage lights. Nonetheless, it was a very popular design that produced spectacular sound.* Bottom right: *Given the popularity of Hawaiian music throughout the world, individuals and companies outside of the United States quickly began producing their own steel guitars. This guitar, manufacturer unknown, was built in China in the late 1930s. It was closely modeled after the Rickenbacker B6 to its left. Courtesy of Lynn Wheelwright.*

Soon after the release of the "frying pan," Rickenbacker, along with several other companies, began manufacturing a variety of models with metal, wood, and Bakelite bodies to keep up with consumer demand. Soon Hawaiian guitar conservatories and publishing companies began licensing their own guitars and amplifiers. Top*: 1939 Rickenbacker "Silver Hawaiian" NS100. This model featured a nickel-plated body stamped from sheet metal. Courtesy of Pascal Mesnier.* Bottom*: 1940s Oahu electric steel and amplifier. By the late 1930s, Harry Stanley's Oahu Publishing Company was marketing Oahu-brand electric guitars and amplifiers. Though not of great quality, matching instruments and amplifiers with vibrantly colored plastic covers attracted their sizable student clientele. Courtesy of Ron Middlebrook/Centerstream Publishing.*

country music, but it was kept Hawaiian pretty much. I played a lot of Hawaiian songs solo, but they went together back then."[110]

Of course, players in the country and western swing genres evolved their styles, as did the Hawaiians and the guitarists of color in the blues market. Not all of the foundational country steel players, however, were as open about their influences. The story of the electric steel guitar's first instrumental hit record once again reveals the cultural entanglements that nurtured the dominant genres of southern music. Leon McAuliffe (1917–88) is considered as essential as Byrd and Dunn to giving the electric steel guitar its prominent role in modern country music. Born in Houston, McAuliffe grew up learning Hawaiian tunes and began playing on Houston station KRPC when he was only sixteen years old. That year he joined the Light Crust Doughboys, a dance hall band that featured future western swing legends Bob Wills and Milton Brown. In 1935 Bob Wills left the Doughboys and asked Leon to join his new band, the Texas Playboys. Wills bought McAuliffe an electric steel after he heard Dunn's recordings with Brown, and McAuliffe soon earned a lead role in what would become the Playboys' seminal lineup.[111]

McAuliffe is best known for his work with the Playboys, a tenure that lasted until he enlisted in the military during World War II. His most lasting contribution to the history of the instrument, however, was his recording of "Steel Guitar Rag" with the Playboys, cut in Chicago in 1936. Beyond the attention that the title of the tune brought the instrument, the simple but melodic steel lines leaped out of the speaker and put the electric guitar on the map. As Malone put it, the recording "probably did the most to popularize the electric guitar among a national audience."[112] Years later McAuliffe recalled the origin of the tune thus: "I had messed around and made up a little tune. It was the first tune I played on the Doughboys program, and the first tune I played on Bob's program. Now whenever you make up a song and it sounds good to you, you don't know whether it's going to sound good to anybody else or not. I played it, and all the musicians liked it and then I played it with Bob, and that night we went and played a dance and Bob liked it. He called it 'Steel Guitar Rag.' Well, Bob could see the reaction from the people, and he knew that we had a good song on our hands, so I played it every night."[113]

The problem with McAuliffe's account of his composition, however, was that he didn't write it. The song was a verbatim copy of "Guitar Rag," the first steel song ever recorded by an African American, Sylvester Weaver, who cut it thirteen years earlier.[114] McAuliffe never owned up to origins of the song

FIGURE 37. *Leon McAuliffe, seated at left with the electric steel guitar, played a fundamental role in establishing the steel as the iconic sound of country and western swing. Bob Wills is pictured front and center with the fiddle, and Gene Autry, wearing a cowboy hat, stands to his left. Texarkana, Texas, 1937. © Michael Ochs/Corbis.*

and instead claimed its copyright, thereby depriving Weaver of his due royalties, a common occurrence that musicians of color endured for decades to come. McAuliffe's theft also revealed the open channels of musical appropriation that fed into the wellspring of prewar southern music. McAuliffe grew up on Hawaiian steel guitar music, applied its fundamentals to his Texas dance hall bands, and struck gold with a song composed and recorded by an African American player from Kentucky who had cultivated his own style on the Hawaiian steel. Between traveling tent and stage shows, radio broadcasts, and the circulation of records, southern musicians developed a fluency in multiple genres that eluded the racial marketing schemes of the industry and spoke to the cultural fluidity that permeated the region.

This brings us back to Eddie Alkire's fan mail, to those letters expressing such a sincere and deep fondness for Hawaiian music, from every region in the country. Although the industry's southern music genres came to increasingly shape the country's midcentury pop music sounds, distinctly Hawaiian music traditions continued to resonate greatly in other outlets and markets throughout the United States during the interwar years. When Eddie Alkire broadcast his Oahu Serenaders radio show out of Cleveland in the 1920s and 1930s, his fan mail attests that he was tapping into a deep national passion for Hawaiian music, even if the listeners' passion was infused with a desire for escape from economic hardship or steeped in colonial nostalgia, or colored by their passion for racial mimicry. Indeed, while some non-Hawaiian musicians adapted the steel guitar to shape newly developing music genres, particularly in the South, many other Americans played the steel guitar to more fully inhabit their understanding, however misguided, of Hawaiianness.

Captivated by the new sounds and the exotic imagery that Hawaiian music generated in their minds, some of these musicians, like Alkire, formed professional bands that performed hapa haole music, while hundreds of thousands of amateur musicians hung artificial leis around their necks and plucked steel guitars and ʻukuleles at parties, or donned grass skirts and parodied the hula. As Jane Desmond described the advent of hula instructional manuals and dance classes, "such a coexistence of a simulation and its potential parody would lighten the import of the dance further, emphasizing its playful, unthreatening quality of otherness. In the same mode of play, Caucasian women could experiment with exotic styles noted in magazines, trying them on as one might a dress, shading themselves with a dose of the primitive for a limited time, provocative yet protected from any real danger of their difference."[115] As a white hula instructor put it in *Dance Lover's Magazine*, "When you do a 'South Sea Dance,' a 'Hula-Hula' dance, a 'Voodoo dance,' or any kind of an Oriental dance, one of the most important things for you to remember is that you are not Mary Smith or Jones or whatever your name may be. While you work you have another personality, you have left commonplace America behind and you are out on the white sands of a desert island. . . . You are this girl, Hawaiian, Indian, or whatever she may be."[116] Emerging from such tendencies, scores of white Hawaiian bands by the 1920s show up in photographs from parties, picnics, and other gatherings in every part of the country. Taking

FIGURE 38. *As blackface minstrelsy began a slow retreat from the national stage, non-Hawaiians thrilled at "playing Hawaiian" in the 1930s. This group, featuring a guitarist with a National tricone steel, called itself the Luka Kamiki Hawaiians. Courtesy of the Sousa Archives and Center for American Music, the University of Illinois at Urbana-Champaign.*

these amateur and semiprofessional bands into account, then, by the 1930s Hawaiian musicians and dancers came to comprise only a small fraction of the "Hawaiian" bands performing in the United States.

Hawaiian musicians became all too familiar with hāole obsessed with Hawaiianness, and they had to develop strategies for dealing with them. Most considered this interest in their music to be potentially productive for their careers, and they also recognized the opportunity to encourage appropriate Hawaiian genres and compositions, as opposed to the offensive pseudo-Hawaiian music increasingly filling the airwaves. Many Hawaiian musicians likewise welcomed the curiosity of non-Hawaiians truly interested in their musical technologies and techniques. As Rudy Waikuiki said of Brother Oswald's stalking, "I didn't mind. He was welcome any time. I was glad to help him."[117]

Many professional Kanaka musicians seemed to demonstrate a genuine patience, if not an eager willingness, to share their knowledge with others. While the documentation of such relationships in this period is not easy to come by, a few anecdotal recollections and letters provide us with a glimpse into these exchanges. Ernest Deale benefited from a great deal of generosity by a number of Hawaiian musicians passing through Washington, DC. Deale was already taking banjo and standard guitar lessons in 1919 when he attended a staging of *Bird of Paradise* in a local theater. "Although I couldn't see the steel player (from where I sat)," he recalled, "I knew by that sound that I wanted to play the steel."[118] Later that night, his music instructor introduced him to two members of the troupe, Ben Hokea and Duke Kahananui. "The next day I bought a $10 Stella guitar, extension nut, bar and picks. I made very little headway that first year. At that time [I had no access to] instruction books on steel guitar."[119] When the production returned in 1920, Ernest insisted the troupe come to his house. They not only agreed but also stayed there for a week (which certainly defrayed their lodging expenses) and gave him lessons for the duration. Ben Hokea encouraged him to buy a songbook by (Hawaiian composer) Charles E. King and to listen to the playing of Pale K. Lua and David Kaili, then recording with Irene West's Royal Hawaiians. When West's troupe performed in DC, Ernest got to go backstage to meet them.[120] As Ernest recalled, "Being young and American and playing their music made us as much of a novelty to them as they were to people who came to see them the first time."[121] The guitarists and some of the female hula dancers taught Ernest additional hapa haole songs, including, "Hula Blues," "Honolulu Hula Girl," "Maui Girl," and "Forget Me Not." Deale befriended touring steel guitarist Charles Opunui and learned much more from him, before forming his own band, the Honolulans. They performed a regular show on radio WRC and played bootlegger parties, vaudeville houses, and movie theaters (before talking pictures eliminated the sites as venues), all while donning leis and featuring a white dancer in a grass skirt, who received hula lessons from Opunui's wife, June. As Deale recalled, "The Hawaiian boys knew we were sincere in our love for the music and for their friendship, and they were always glad to help us."[122]

It is impossible to ascertain Hokea's and Opunui's feelings about Deale and his all-white Hawaiian troupe, but according to Deale, Opunui eventually asked him to perform with his troupe on a Matson ship headed to Hawaiʻi. Deale could not accept the offer, and in fact, just as so many others like him, he never visited the Islands that became his musical obsession.[123] It seems clear, however, that many Hawaiian performers appreciated the sincerity of a number of these enthusiasts, even if they "played Hawaiian" onstage; at the very least, they understood it as a mutually beneficial phenomenon. For some it could become even more meaningful. Walter Kolomoku, the steel player for the first continental production of *Bird of Paradise*, died young, in 1930. His son died shortly after, leaving Walter's widow Anita "Goldie" Kolomoku despondent. She continued to manage Hawaiian troupes from New York City, however, and in the years following her husband's and son's deaths, tuned into Eddie Alkire's Oahu Serenaders whenever she could. She corresponded with Alkire regularly over the years, praising his program and song selection and sending him some of Walter's compositions to perform over the air.[124] She became lifelong friends with Alkire, long after he had retired from radio. Part of her approval of the group resulted from the ability of its standard guitarist from Maui, Alex Hoapili, to sing in ʻŌlelo Hawaiʻi, but Hoapili's partnership with Alkire also spoke to a mutual admiration of each other's abilities to perform Hawaiian music.

In fact, a number of Native Hawaiian steel guitarists opened local instructional studios in North America, beginning with the studio that Joseph Kekuku opened in San Francisco soon after he arrived in 1904 (he would later give lessons or open studios in Los Angeles, London, Paris, Chicago, and several other cities).[125] These schools provided musicians with an opportunity to gain an income when not on the road, while others focused on full-time teaching as a more stable livelihood. Their work in local conservatories further extended the reach of the instrument into the hands of local non-Hawaiians fascinated with Hawaiian music. By the mid-1910s and 1920s, guitar schools operated by Hawaiians or their students began to pop up throughout the country. As we saw in chapter 3, two of Kekuku's first American students, Myrtle Stumpf and C. S. DeLano, either opened schools or produced instructional manuals for steel guitars based on his teachings.[126] Kekuku's cousin, Sam Nainoa, opened a Hawaiian conservatory in Los Angeles, while Walter Kolomoku opened the First Hawaiian Conservatory of Music in New York City's Woolworth building.[127] Kolomoku, like several others, produced correspondence courses on the Hawaiian guitar, providing an even greater reach into rural areas with no access to a conservatory (see fig. 10 in chap. 2). Kolomoku's nephew Charles, who earlier had toured Chautauqua circuits with the Vierra brothers, opened a studio in Fort Wayne, Indiana, in the 1940s.[128] Alex Hoapili, Alkire's partner in the Oahu Serenaders, also taught lessons on Spanish and Hawaiian guitar in Cleveland.[129] Another player from the Islands, Sam Kainoa, opened a studio in Baltimore.[130] Robert Matsu, a member of several troupes from the Islands, opened a studio in Little Rock in the teens or early twenties.[131] Charles Kama Valera opened the Moana Hawaiian Studios in San Antonio in 1932.[132] The list seems endless, as the diaspora continued to expand into small towns and cities throughout the continent. During the 1930s brothers Jack and Jimmy Kahauolopua taught at a Hawaiian guitar school in Philadelphia. It seems that Jack's radio broadcasts inspired Philadelphia resident Troman Eason to take lessons at the Kahauolopua studio in order to adapt the steel guitar for sacred performances in his church. Eason's work launched the "sacred steel" phenomenon, a movement in two national African American churches, now called the House of God and the Church of the Living God, that continue to make inspirational electric steel playing fundamental to the worship experience.[133]

The Kahauolopua brothers, like Hoapili, taught in the Hawaiian guitar school franchises that began to proliferate in the late 1920s. Hoping to latch onto the rage for Hawaiian guitars, Harry G. Stanley and his half brother George Bronson opened the first Honolulu Conservatory of Music in Cleveland in 1926. Bronson and Stanley soon parted ways and eventually became competitors, but Stanley quickly franchised the conservatory and launched the Oahu Publishing Company to provide the students (enrolled in local conservatories or in correspondence courses) with instructional materials, sheet music, and steel guitars and accessories.[134] During the mid-1920s through the 1940s the company came to supply perhaps 1,200 studios, mostly in the United States, while the schools graduated around 200,000 students.[135] Interestingly, however, Harry Stanley's extraordinary success with Hawaiian guitar schools had nothing to do with his background or musical training. His given name was Glen Smeeman, and in 1916 he and Bronson were arrested for auto theft in St. Louis and sentenced to two years in prison. While Bronson served his term, Smeeman fled the state while out on bond. The next year he was arrested for another auto theft in Denver and sentenced to three and a half years, but he escaped while working on a prison road gang and fled to Cleveland.[136] He started a new life, and a new company, while knowing absolutely nothing about the steel guitar. He simply knew to trade on its immense popularity at the time, and the popularity of his schools was reflected in the devotion of his students: by the time the law caught up with him in 1933, his arrest broke nationally, and the judges in his case received 750 letters urging his pardon, which was granted in both states.[137]

The success of the business is surprising, given that neither Stanley nor Bronson were steel guitarists themselves, and that the business grew the fastest at the height of the Great Depression. Yet while piano production dropped by 61 percent between 1930 and 1932, Hawaiian guitar production increased by 15 percent.[138] Part of the steel guitar's success lay in the great popularity of Hawaiian music during this period, a popularity that only expanded with the advent of radio. But the success also derived from Oahu's business model: door-to-door salesmen and women roamed the countryside and signed students up for a year of lessons, with the promise that at the end of the year, the students would then receive a "free" guitar — the guitar that was loaned to them during their first lesson. After luring them in, the company sold the student all of the needed equipment — equipment built or licensed by Oahu. Oahu steel bars, Oahu acoustic guitars, and then their electric guitars, amplifiers, and cords flooded the market in the 1930s. The company issued a monthly magazine, the *Hawaiian Guitarist*, that featured inspirational passages to encourage the students to forge ahead in their lessons, along with photographs of hundreds of students in their schools or in Hawaiian guitar competitions, all to inspire the sense of a national Oahu community.

As in previous decades, nearly all of the professional performers on the steel guitar during this period were men. While many women worked professionally as vocalists in the popular genres coalescing at the time, men policed a line around the bandstand, asserting a masculine aura of professional instrumentalists in the popular music scene. At the same time, hula, practiced in the Islands by men and women, became on entertainment circuits an exclusively female domain.[139] The world of amateur musicians, however, was much different, and if women struggled to break down the barrier that kept them in the audience or on the dance floor, their interest in the instrument was as profound as that of men, if not more so. In looking at student enrollments, and the hundreds of photos in the Oahu periodicals, this much is clear: at least as many females enrolled in the Hawaiian guitar lessons in the 1920s through the 1950s as did males.[140] Moreover, through the schools many of these female students found a way to become professional guitarists — as teachers of the instrument rather than as paid performers.[141] Meanwhile, the Hawaiian guitar conservatories and correspondence schools worked to make the instrument into an appropriate medium for any form of music, popular or classical. This strategy served as a means to expand the schools' business by attracting as many clients as possible, regardless of their degree of interest in Hawaiian music.

Thus, the schools solicited boys and girls, men and women, to enroll in

FIGURE 39. *Boys and girls enrolled in Hawaiian guitar schools all over the United States in the 1930s and 1940s. This conservatory appears to have been located in Omaha, Nebraska. Courtesy of the Sousa Archives and Center for American Music, the University of Illinois at Urbana-Champaign.*

FIGURE 40. *The Electone-Settes, an all-girl band active in the mid-1940s, featured two Eddie Alkire students and a nice variety of steel guitars: a Gibson double-necked console on the left, four Epiphone Electars, and a double-necked National console on the right. Courtesy of the Sousa Archives and Center for American Music, the University of Illinois at Urbana-Champaign.*

Hawaiian steel guitar lessons. The Oahu Company used a variety of rhetorical strategies to sell its guitars and lessons to parents of prospective students. Some salespeople, for example, would tout the instrument as a means to develop wholesome activities in the household or to enhance the children's self-confidence. In addition, Oahu's *Hawaiian Guitarist* regularly promised that learning the instrument would increase one's popularity.[142] The schools were not marketed necessarily to train professional performers, although riches were promised through the *teaching* of Hawaiian guitar, for those who paid for and completed the Oahu student and instructor courses. In fact, Oahu encouraged students who finished the courses to buy studios and sell Oahu materials to the next round of students. Because of this pyramid-like business model, some referred to Oahu as "the Amway of Hawaiian guitar."[143]

During the Depression, many families were made intimately aware of the Hawaiian guitar through the efforts of door-to-door salespeople. After Eddie Alkire left Oahu and the Honolulu Conservatory of Music in Cleveland to form his own company and compete against them, he distributed to his teachers a guide for selling the instrument (and his lessons) to parents. It provides them with a strategy for getting in the door: "When you start to work in the morning (8:00 to 9:00 A.M.) and make your first call, find out about the next several houses that have children. A successful approach is to say, 'Good morning, Mrs. Blank. I came to talk with you about your children. Do you folks like music? Are your children interested in music?' Thus conveying an interest in the mother's children, which is the easiest way to arouse the mother's interest in your case."[144] The salesperson is then instructed to find out when the husband will be home, and to schedule an evening appointment when both parents are available. The guide presupposes that women are staying home and men are working, demonstrating not only gendered assumptions about the family but also a targeting of the middle class. At the evening meeting, the guide then instructs the salesperson to

> go to work immediately *with the child*. . . . Point out to the child the advantages and the pleasure that can be obtained from studying music, the entertainment which the whole family can enjoy, etc. Furthermore, a child has practically no sales resistance. You can sell a child almost anything. *You must sell the child first*. . . . After having sold the child, give your attention to the parents. You might open with, "Would you, Mr. and Mrs. Blank, like to see your child have a musical education? Your child is at a good age to begin learning. He (or she) seems very much interested and wants to learn to play. Don't you, Junior?" And when the child tells the parents, "Yes," he wants to learn to play, the parent's [*sic*] can't do much else but consent, unless for some reason or another they absolutely cannot *afford* the lessons. If you think the parents can pay for lessons, continue your sales talk.[145]

The guide then instructs the salesperson to show the child an extremely simple Alkire composition, "Music of Hawaii," designed to lure in the parents and the children.[146] The salesperson, in bringing the sale home, should then convince the parents that each new lesson will be as easy to grasp as the first.

Of course, the point was to sell as many lessons to as many families as possible while giving the parents no sense of the complexity of the instrument.

Many professional country and western swing steel guitarists such as Lloyd Green, Herb Remington, and Buddy Emmons were in fact first exposed to the instrument through the Oahu school, but the students' capacity and interest to learn varied considerably, as did the duration of their enrollments. Green (1937–) recalled it this way: "Well, I started playing guitar—Hawaiian guitar, in those days—at the age of seven. And I'm from Mobile, Alabama, and I lived in a housing project, and this gentleman came around to different houses, and he was giving these demonstrations—auditions—to get students. He would give you the little audition, and tell your parent whether you were good enough to warrant further instruction. Naturally, nobody was turned down; everybody warranted further instruction."[147] Kay Koster (aka Kostrzewski, 1918–2014) first learned of the Hawaiian guitar near her home of Peshtigo, Wisconsin, when her grandmother took her to a medicine show featuring a Kanaka guitar duo in 1928: "I told my grandmother, 'I don't care whatever else I do in this world, grandma, I want to play like *that*.'"[148] Sometime later, her parents enrolled her in lessons. She recalled, "Guys would go around and knock on doors and ask if children could come on tour. . . . [The salespeople would ask the parents if they would like to see their children perform on "tour" at Hawaiian guitar conventions in Chicago and elsewhere. The idea excited many parents and they would ask to learn more]." She continued, "These were booze-soaked sales guys. I mean they were old drunks and fat and burpy, but they were good sales people. They were selling guitar lessons. If you signed up for a year, you got a free guitar at the end of the 52nd lesson."[149] Koster exceeded the abilities of her instructor after six weeks. At that point, he asked her to begin to teach for Oahu. Eventually she took over that studio, then moved to other Oahu franchises.

In the 1940s and 1950s, Koster brought hundreds of students to the Hawaiian guitar conventions of the Oahu Company and other music organizations. At the Oahu conventions, sometimes seventy-five students would play a recital on Hawaiian guitar—simultaneously. Koster recalled placing a forty-student Hawaiian guitar orchestra on a bus to play in New York City and in Cleveland. Often parents joined them, for many their first trip outside the town limits. Twins Joanne Parker and Janice Crum (1930–) began attending the conventions in the early 1940s; when asked what seventy-five Hawaiian guitars sounded like at one time, they exclaimed, "Beautiful!," though they also acknowledged that sometimes a badly prepared or poorly trained orchestra could "sound like a symphony tuning up for a concert."[150] Billy Tonnessen (1929–) first took up the instrument through a door-to-door salesman for a West Coast Hawaiian guitar school when he was around ten; a few years later he joined 500 Hawaiian guitarists for a simultaneous performance at the Hollywood Bowl.[151] Similarly, in the 1930s the annual Banjo, Mandolin, and Guitar (BMG) conferences began to feature 60- to 100-piece community steel guitar bands. At the 1937 meeting in Detroit, twenty-nine such bands competed against one another, including the eighty-five-piece Elgin (Illinois) Hawaiian Guitar Band. The meetings thrilled the students. Elgin member Marguerite Piegorsch recounted the competition to her friend who was unable to attend: "I played an electric in the contest. . . . The Minneapolis bunch played first. I no more than played four bars of 'Hilo March[,]' our warm-up number[,] when I broke a string. And kiddo I got so nervous I thought I'd faint right up there onstage. Well at the start of Swanee Echoes I took Glenn's guitar and the frets are different on that and when we had to play that squeaky part, you know 21-19-17 I couldn't find 21. Did I ever frizzle it. Oh I'm telling you I wished I were dead."[152] Piegorsch quickly recovered, however, when the Elgin band won first place.

The nature of the Hawaiian guitar by the 1940s had come to mean, for many of the Oahu, Alkire, and other students, an after-school activity or an exciting family trip to the big city. Piegorsch regaled her friend with descriptions of her thirteenth-floor hotel room's running ice water, radio, and daily delivered newspapers.[153] The lesson plans quickly began to emphasize American popular music and standards over Hawaiian music. Students would learn "Yankee Doodle Dandy," or a Stephen Foster song, or a Brahms lullaby.[154] By the 1940s such songs far outnumbered those even only thematically tied to Hawai'i. Amateurs, as always, comprised the vast majority of musicians, on Hawaiian guitar as they did on the piano, and most correspondence schools and studios catered to them through providing tablature for songs rather than requiring them to learn staff notation.[155] As Tim Miller argues, the large Hawaiian guitar companies such as Oahu and Alkire's demonstrated, "through [their] aspirations toward a universal, forward-looking music, the steel guitar's absorption into the mainstream of the philosophical, educational, and aesthetic model that grew from the United States' European heritage."[156]

During the course of these changes, the instrument continued to generate interest among students and their families, but not for the same reasons that it excited Ernest Deale or Jerry Byrd. In the students' imaginations, the Hawaiian guitar began to evoke not so much the Islands as recitals and other such social events. For some, perhaps coerced by parents into enrolling in the schools, it represented not much more than their weekly music lessons, which happened to be practiced on a Hawaiian guitar. For Harry Stanley, who had no investment in Hawaiian music and no knowledge of how to play the instrument, it meant nothing more than business. His goal was to transform the Hawaiian guitar into the country's next piano — but one vastly less expensive — "free," in fact, if one paid for fifty-two weeks of lessons. Eddie Alkire, in contrast to Stanley, maintained close contact with a number of Hawaiian musicians throughout his lifetime, and he dedicated a great deal of his energy to technological innovations of the instrument, as well as to his thousands of students. In 1939 he named one of his most important innovations — a ten-string electric steel guitar — the EHARP. The name, derived from eha, the number 4 in ʻŌlelo Hawaiʻi, represented the three fingers and thumb required to play it.[157] His first love remained Hawaiian music, but even his schools and correspondence lessons featured fewer and fewer Hawaiian mele as the years progressed.

Meanwhile, significant innovations in techniques and technologies by a new cadre of professional steel guitarists and builders revealed just how out of touch the instructional offerings by Stanley and Alkire became with younger generations. Steel guitarists long outside of the southern and even Hawaiian genres, such as Roy Smeck and Alvino Rey, developed exciting new sounds for the steel guitar. Rey even developed a "talk box" that allowed him to speak through the notes that sounded in his amplifier. By the late 1930s, builders began to sell exotic and intimidating multinecked steel guitars to accommodate the multiple tuning preferences of both Hawaiian and non-Hawaiian musicians. One steel guitarist from South Alabama, Neal "Pappy" McCormick, even built a four-sided steel guitar that rotated on an axle to accommodate his four tunings, and used a Ford Model T crank to bring each neck to the top.[158] Up and coming guitarists such as Noel Boggs began to break up the verses in country hits with complicated jazz passages, while Wesley "Speedy" West created atomic age, sci-fi sounds that leaped into the stratosphere. Both profited from the work of Leo Fender, who began building double-, triple-, and quadruple-necked steels, bolted together laterally, and from one of Fender's lead designers and builders, Kanaka guitarist Freddie Tavares (1913–90).

Tavares, in fact, took a lead role not only in designing Fender's Stratocaster — perhaps the most iconic standard electric guitar ever built — but also in developing Fender's first "pedal steel" guitars.[159] Pedal steels, which emerged in various incarnations during the 1940s and 1950s, provided a new set of options for steel guitarists; builders joined cable pulleys, or later an intricate set of rods underneath the body of the guitar, to up to ten pedals on the floor. The depressed pedals raised various combinations of string pitches, thus pro-

FIGURE 41.
Eddie Alkire designed and licensed many guitars over the years. Here Alkire steel guitar teacher Laura Grassie proudly holds an Alkire EHARP. Built in the 1940s, the EHARP featured ten strings—an innovation now standard on most pedal steel guitars. Courtesy of the Sousa Archives and Center for American Music, the University of Illinois at Urbana-Champaign.

viding the players with entirely new sets of chord possibilities. Builders had already begun to expand the number of strings on each neck to eight, and then ten (and later, to twelve and fourteen), and on pedal steels they soon attached knee levers underneath the body as well (some guitars today feature ten knee levers) to provide additional options for raising and lowering string pitches to create different chord combinations and transitions between them. Their efforts revolutionized the steel guitar, and most non-Hawaiian players quickly adopted the new technologies and never looked back. However, very few Hawaiian guitarists adopted the pedal steel, opting instead for the simplicity and original techniques associated with the kīkā kila, which soon became known in country music as the "non–pedal steel guitar."

By the 1960s, when a new generation of country music stars rose to the

FIGURE 42.
In the recording studio or at home one could simply retune the guitar to find different voicings; however, many players found doing so onstage impractical. Steel guitar manufacturers began adding more necks to the instrument in order to provide additional tuning options. Here Noel Boggs stands behind his quadruple-necked Fender Stringmaster. Courtesy of the Sousa Archives and Center for American Music, the University of Illinois at Urbana-Champaign.

fore, the role of Hawaiian guitarists in shaping the sounds of modern country began to wane from public consciousness. The unprecedented virtuosity of pedal steel players in the country field, such as Buddy Emmons, Jimmy Day, and Curly Chalker, seemed to eclipse any sense of tradition associated with the instrument, at least the tradition that linked it with Hawaiian practices. As Nashville became the genre's epicenter and a handful of elite pedal steel guitarists soon handled practically every session in town, Hawaiians found little room within the genre that they had played such a fundamental role in sonically defining. Yet many changes indeed were afoot for the legacy and cultural vitality of the Hawaiian steel guitar during that period.

The earlier rise of the Oahu Publishing Company demonstrates a remarkable integration of the Hawaiian steel guitar into the continent's musical culture; the instrument, having conquered stage shows, radio broadcasts, and the recorded music industry's most popular genres, had now generated an equally impressive reach into the business of amateur music, from local studios to far-reaching correspondence courses. Just as suddenly, the instrument's Kanaka origins faded from the view of North American youth in the 1950s and 1960s. They were transfixed by the vibrant cultural icons that emerged in new genres such as rock 'n' roll, rhythm and blues, and soul—genres that continued to incorporate Hawaiian sounds and technologies but that only further entrenched the biracial logic demanded by industry marketing. Everyone continued to listen to the Hawaiian guitar, and many continued to play it, but its indigenous history began to disappear.

A particularly poignant example of this took place in 1959, when the brothers Santo and Johnny Farina recorded their instrumental "Sleep Walk" at a small studio in Manhattan. "Sleep Walk" was electrifying and quiet; immediately nostalgic and blindingly modern sounding, as Santo, a twenty-one-year-old Italian American from Brooklyn, cut a searingly beautiful melody into the wax with his instrument, a state-of-the-art Fender electric steel guitar. The recording did not sound particularly "Hawaiian," yet the instrument had arrived in Santo's hands only through the efforts of the Hawaiian guitarists who preceded him. "Sleep Walk" reached the top of the Billboard charts on September 21—it remains the highest-charting steel guitar instrumental in history—only a few months after the U.S. government declared Hawai'i a state.

For teenagers and young adults raised in the 1950s and 1960s, the instrument became less and less familiar by name or sight, despite the fact that its various iterations were heard on an ever-greater number of recordings during this period, in all genres, southern or otherwise. Even Jerry Garcia of the Grateful Dead recorded pedal steel on Crosby, Stills, Nash, and Young's 1970 hit "Teach Your Children Well." By this time most of the instruments' practitioners no longer turned to Hawaiian music or musicians for their inspiration. To this generation of teens, rock 'n' roll and rhythm and blues proved much more alluring than the Hawaiian music that their parents listened to, and the role of Hawaiians in the southern musical wellspring from which such genres originated eluded them.

Despite the success of Santo and Johnny and the ever-increasing use of the steel guitar on popular commercial recordings in the United States, enrollments in Hawaiian guitar schools began to decline in the late 1950s and never

FIGURE 43. *In the midcentury, Hawaiian steel guitars were familiar sights in the United States, yet they became associated less and less with Hawaiian musicians. In this photograph from 1953, three boxing champions clown around at Jack Dempsey's restaurant. Dempsey is playing bass, Rocky Graziano is on guitar, and former heavyweight champion Joe Louis assumes duties behind the steel guitar.* © Bettmann/CORBIS

recovered. Though the Oahu Publishing Company did not close its doors until 1985, the interest in steel guitars on the continent had flatlined long before that. Ninety-four-year-old Kay Koster was still giving Spanish guitar lessons at her studio in Rockford, Illinois, when I interviewed her in 2012, but as for steel guitar lessons? She hadn't seen a student in over a decade. As she put it, "The steel guitar is deader than a doornail."[160]

7 *Banishment, and Return*

SEEKING THE STEEL GUITAR IN THE HAWAIIAN RENAISSANCE

In the 1960s and 1970s the sound of the pedal steel became an enduring and iconic fixture in country music. In blues, folk, and rock, the slide guitar surged, first through the 1960s blues and folk revivals that featured "rediscovered" elders like Son House and seasoned electric guitarists like Elmore James, and then through the recorded output and celebrity of young guitarists such as Duane Allman, Ry Cooder, and Bonnie Raitt. Meanwhile, the popularity of Hawaiian guitar schools and Polynesian-themed clubs continued to decline steadily. By the 1970s, few young people in the United States knew what a steel guitar looked like, much less its relationship to Hawaiians, even though they likely heard the steel (including its descendants) on a daily basis on hit records by Neil Young, Dionne Warwick, Jackson Browne, Gladys Knight, Joni Mitchell, the Rolling Stones, the Eagles, and countless more. The steel guitar had become a vital tool for producers and artists to generate excitement or pull heartstrings across the radio dial, yet the number of its practitioners plummeted, and the instrument itself began to sink into anonymity.

Thus the contradiction in the 1960s and 1970s: the steel guitar seemed to become endlessly adaptable to the full spectrum of genres and American radio formats, just as the instrument began its migration from the center to the dark wings of the stage and eventually out of public consciousness altogether. But during this turn of events, what was happening to the instrument and its role in the Islands? Certainly it would retain a prominent role in the ʻāina, from the tourist stages of Waikīkī to the rural areas. Yet dramatic changes were well under way for the steel guitar in Hawaiʻi as well. It seems that Kay Koster's damning appraisal, that the steel guitar was "deader than a doornail" in 2012, would have sounded familiar to Hawaiians in the Islands, more than forty years before she uttered those words.

The threat of the steel guitar's loss seemed to be just a symptom of a larger problem, however: beginning in the late 1960s, alarming headlines began to creep in between the newspapers' municipal concerns: "Is Hawaiian Music Pau?" "Must We Bid Sad Aloha to Hawaiian Music?"[1] In a 1971 *Honolulu*

Advertiser editorial, Hawaiian music and cultural scholar George Kanahele warned readers, "Hawaiian music is in its death throes."[2] He reported that only a "handful" of steel players remained in the Islands, and they were far along in their years; only one radio station in the Islands played Hawaiian music regularly; and even in the tourist areas, only one hotel featured Hawaiian music.[3] Another contemporary observer recalled, "We were down to the last falsetto singer, Joe Keawe. We were down to the last steel guitarist, Billy Hew Len. You could go down the line, and we were down to our last guys, and they were old men and women."[4] Hawaiian music, "once so popular throughout the world," Kanahele later recalled to a gathering of the Polynesian Voyaging Society, "was all but dead."[5]

The culprit, Kanahele and others identified, was music from beyond the Islands, new sounds that had robbed Hawaiian youth of any interest in their forebears' music. The younger generations, he lamented, were awash in a sea of rock 'n' roll: "Of all the signs, it is Aquarius that may spell the finish for Hawaiian music, for in this Age of Rock with its turned on frenzy and violent, menacing symbolism, there is no room for the moonlight-and-palm-tree sentimentality of Hawaiian music. Ask any kid in Hawai'i and he will say Hawaiian music is a drag—it's out; it's dead. Which means that rock 'n' roll has virtually captured the musical allegiance of nearly a whole generation of Hawaiians who most likely couldn't care less about the fate of Hawaiian music."[6]

It seemed that Hawaiian music was in a crisis state by the late 1960s. Neither Hawaiian nor non-Hawaiian kama'āina, nor even haole tourists, seemed to express much interest in the formerly celebrated troupes of Hawaiian musicians. The concerns voiced by Kanahele and others were genuine and grave. Hawaiians had already suffered threats to their cultural practices, beginning with the haole religious and political interventions of the nineteenth century. Without immediate intervention, many worried, Hawaiians might lose their language and cultural integrity. Such apprehension, however, soon met a powerful response, a "Hawaiian Renaissance," as it became known—a movement unmatched in strength since Kalākaua's similar call to cultural arms nearly a century before—a movement that would rejuvenate traditional Hawaiian music.

Yet so many types of arguably "traditional" Hawaiian music existed by the 1970s. What sort of traditional Hawaiian music spoke to the architects of the movement? Would they turn to the chants accompanied by 'ūkēkē, the stringed instrument developed prior to the arrival of Europeans? Or to hula ku'i, which took the Islands by storm during Kalākaua's reign? Or to the Royal Hawaiian Band, which was over a century old and a tradition unto itself by this time? Would they revive the practice of strolling through the city, performing the love songs of the aliʻi nui? Would they turn to the intimate voices of the kuaʻāina singing mele in remote island valleys? Or to the hapa haole songs crafted by Kanaka songsmiths? Would they tap into the history of the innumerable Hawaiian string bands driven by the steel guitar, which had traveled the world since the turn of the twentieth century? Each could claim to be an exemplar of "traditional" Hawaiian music by the time that Kanahele raised his alarm.

This chapter will return our focus to the Islands as we explore the history of the steel guitar in its homeland, from the "death throes" of Hawaiian music through the 1980s. During this period, the politics of Hawaiian music, no matter how "sentimental" in sound, became deafening in practice, and the steel guitar was implicated in them from the start.

Up until the 1960s, the steel guitar had retained a prominent position in the music of the Islands, from Waikīkī and the downtown Honolulu bars that locals frequented to the valleys deep in the heart of the Island of Hawaiʻi. In Lāʻie, Joseph Kekuku had directly inspired Pale K. Lua and became a legend for Tau Moe, but others continued to develop innovations after Kekuku left the Islands. For example, Alex Hoapili, who played the Spanish guitar in the Cleveland-based Oahu Serenaders, first witnessed someone using a cylindrical, rounded steel bar (rather than the rectangular bar with a rounded edge that Kekuku originally developed) when a player from Molokaʻi arrived in Honolulu around 1910. Hoapili recalled, "Honolulu, as you know, is the capital; and any time a group of musicians wished to present their act to the public, they would come to this city. It was there that I saw him use the round steel. It was the talk of the town. Everywhere you went you would hear people remarking, 'Say, have you heard that boy from Molokaʻi play? He uses a round steel to play with!' After that, several others tried using a round steel but found it difficult to hold. Undoubtedly [he] had been practicing at home for some time."[7] That "everywhere you went" suggests a greatly expanded familiarity with the instrument in the Islands, only a few years after it was developed. Tau Moe listened to wax cylinder recordings featuring Kekuku only a few years later, revealing how musicians who had left the Islands continued to impact local music.

By the late 1930s guitarists in the Islands were avidly experimenting with tunings and instruments. "Most all of the Island boys here are using the Rickenbacker Electric Guitars," reported Honolulu music storeowner Richard Choy in 1938, five years after the electrics were introduced. The Hawaiian

FIGURE 44. *The steel guitar was quickly incorporated into family luaus and other informal gatherings. The steel guitar in this photograph, circa 1930, is accompanied by a standard guitar, a ʻukulele, and an ipu drum. Courtesy of Bishop Museum.*

players opted against the double-necked guitars just entering the market, though: "The Hawaiian boys do not use the double neck guitars here in the Islands. Only that sometimes the boys take turns in playing the instruments and every now and then they'll switch and in this way they divide the numbers between them[,] some in the modified tuning and the rest in E7th tuning."[8] Local players by that time expressed little interest in the A major tuning that most novices on the continent were taught in Hawaiian guitar schools and primers: "Nearly all the players here including the beginners are demanding the E7 tuning," Choy wrote. He continued, "Here in the Islands one third uses the A minor tuning and [a] few use the A minor 7th tuning, about two thirds use the E7th tuning. These boys here think the A Major is old fashioned."[9] The C# minor tuning, first popularized by Sol Hoʻopiʻi, also attracted much attention in the Islands.[10] The concept of adding pedals to the steel guitar was not

FIGURE 45. *Few women worked as professional steel guitarists, but Emma Kaimana (seen in the center of the seated row) performed with the much-celebrated Royal Hawaiian Girls Glee Club. The organization formed in 1927 to entertain at the Royal Hawaiian Hotel in Waikīkī. Given that she was not yet playing an electric steel guitar, this photograph likely was taken sometime before the mid-1930s. Courtesy of Hawaiʻi State Archives.*

exclusive to the continent either, as Choy himself in 1940 worked to create a single-necked instrument that, with pedals deployed, could produce major, minor, and 7th tunings.[11] As for technique, Choy reported that players in the Islands seemed most interested in "improvising instead of chord work and use[d] plenty of single notes"; he also observed the admonition of the local players who believed that knowing "the meaning of all the Haw[aiia]n words in the song [is necessary] to perform it like it should be played."[12]

Despite the success of some professional female steel guitarists such as Thelma Kaʻai, Nani Makakoa, and Emma Kaimana, Choy never strayed from

FIGURE 46. *Through the midcentury the steel guitar remained popular in the Islands for amateur and semiprofessional as well as professional musicians. In this 1937 photo, firefighting musicians from Honolulu's Central Fire Station at Fort and Beretania Streets strike a pose. The steel guitarist, seated in the center, is playing a state-of-the-art Rickenbacker B6. Courtesy of Bishop Museum.*

referring to the local steel guitarists as "the boys," and indeed, men took nearly all of the jobs offered to steel guitar, bass, and ʻukulele players in Waikīkī's hotels (professional female vocalists such as Lena Machado and Lizzie Alohikea, however, also secured jobs).[13] During the 1930s and 1940s, the work in Waikīkī was steady; orchestra leader Johnny Noble had long featured some of Oʻahu's best steel players at the Moana Hotel, including Joe Lopez, Freddie Tavares, and M. K. Moke, the latter of whom also ran the Hawaiian guitar school in Honolulu where Tau and Rose Moe and others enrolled.[14] Harry Owens's orchestra at the Royal Hawaiian Hotel in the 1930s introduced a number of steel guitarists, including Alvin Kaleolani Isaacs Sr. and Ernest and Freddie Tavares.[15] Sam Kaʻapuni and Walter Moʻokini each performed for the

Islanders at the Royal Hawaiian Hotel, which featured a large cast of players and several orchestras from the 1930s to the 1950s.[16]

At the same time, steel guitarists secured steady jobs in the cafés, bars, and small clubs that catered principally to Hawaiians and other kamaʻāina, particularly in the days before jukeboxes, when live music was the only option in such venues. Walter Moʻokini was born on Maui in 1917 and learned the instrument both from his father and through listening to Sol Hoʻopiʻi recordings.[17] By the time he started performing in clubs in the late 1930s, "steel guitarists were evident everywhere," he said, rattling off the names of a dozen players and a number of local venues.[18] Famed slack key guitarist Gabby Pahinui recalled even more venues featuring guitarists near Bethel Street alone, including the Wonder Bar, the Log Cabin Inn, the Rialto Café, the Hoffman Café, the Black Cat Café, and others.[19] Steel guitars had integrated very quickly into the Honolulu string band scene that had been prevalent since the late 1800s, and by the 1930s, you could find them in nearly any venue that hosted live entertainment, for either locals or tourists.

Beginning in the 1930s, steel players also could gain local and international fame without ever leaving the Islands by performing on a globally broadcast radio program, *Hawaii Calls*. The brainchild of Webley Edwards, a car salesman who moved to Oʻahu from Oregon, the radio program launched from underneath the banyan tree at the Moana Hotel on July 3, 1935, and began broadcasting via shortwave radio to the West Coast.[20] Edwards said that he was disappointed by the musicians performing "jazzed up" music on the West Coast and sought to broadcast instead "an accurate, faithful, and authentic presentation of the music of the Islands" (it is unclear if he was reacting to "jazzed up" music by Hawaiian or non-Hawaiian performers).[21] He and the musicians who performed on the program began collecting songs from their families and other sources; the collection surpassed 3,000 by 1965. *Hawaii Calls* continued until 1975, after an extraordinary 2,083 programs. In the meantime, the *Hawaii Calls* organization secured significant funding from the territorial and later, the state legislature for its promotion of tourism, it issued numerous records, and it was relayed by 750 stations at its peak in 1952, reaching many millions of listeners.[22]

Over 300 of the best musicians and performers in the Islands performed on the show.[23] The steel players alone represented the top talent of their day, and over the years included Alvin K. Isaacs, Freddie Tavares, David Keliʻi, Jake Keliʻikoa, Jules Ah See, Billy Hew Len, Barney Isaacs, Danny Stewart, Eddie Pang, and Joe Custino.[24] Maui-born David Keliʻi performed on the show from

FIGURE 47. Hawaii Calls *broadcast from Waikīkī from 1935 to 1975. During its peak, around the time this photograph was taken, it was relayed around the world via 750 stations, reaching millions of listeners each week. The steel guitar was always prominently featured in the programs. Of the three steel players shown here, Sonny Nicholas is on the left, Barney Isaacs is in the center, and Bob Kauahikaua is on the right. Photograph by Laurence Hata, courtesy of Bishop Museum.*

1935 through 1952 and won singular praise for his technique and tone from fans abroad as well as in the Islands.[25] Richard Choy remarked to Eddie Alkire in 1940, "David Keli'i is considered *the world's greatest steel guitarist today. I mean just that*. I think he can cut everyone to ribbons when it comes to steel guitar playing. . . . He's genius."[26] During the show Keli'i would use two guitars, one tuned to E7 and the other to A minor: "He see saws back and forth on two instruments, and believe me, he goes places."[27] It seems clear that, with few exceptions, musicians were honored to perform on the show.[28] *Hawaii Calls* certainly provided them with regular work and an unprecedented platform; they could select from an expansive list of mele to perform on one of the world's most popular radio programs.

Yet, if the performers maintained 3,000 songs at their fingertips, with 1,500 songs memorized and ready to perform, as some claimed, then how did they select their repertoire for a half-hour program each week?[29] And how could they ensure that their selections would please their audiences both at home and overseas? Simply put, they could not. From almost the beginning, the repertoire faced criticism from many sides, particularly after Edwards began featuring more songs in English than in Hawaiian, along with "jazzed up" renditions — the kind that he originally rejected in order to distinguish the show from its rivals on the continent — all done, purportedly, to broaden the show's appeal in North America.[30] Although Kamehameha graduate and composer Charles E. King (1874–1950) originally lent Edwards and Harry Owens (the first music director) his music library, he quickly turned against the program, arguing that it was not authentic enough.[31] A musical protégé of Lili'uokalani, King rejected hapa haole music, which he felt was infected by Tin Pan Alley aesthetics or syncopation. "Hawaiian songs," he said, "should have Hawaiian lyrics, the subject should be about Hawai'i, and the melodic quality nahenahe (sweet) and not 'jazzed up.'"[32] Entertainer and composer Johnny Almeida (1897–1985) seemed to concur about language, preferring to write songs and perform in 'Ōlelo Hawai'i during the peak in popularity for hapa haole songs; certainly others felt the same way.[33]

King was outspoken in his criticism of *Hawaii Calls*, in part because he could speak his mind on his own English-language radio show. On the air, he ranted that all those responsible for *Hawaii Calls* were "pepping up" and "murdering" Hawaiian music: "You cannot improve the melodious and gripping songs of our Islands by the new-style treatment. Don't try it! Harry Owens, at public expense, has done more harm by doing it — orientalizing and even 'Dardenella-izing' our island songs is a sheer waste of time."[34] When Al Kealoha Perry took over the music directorship from Owens, King remained unimpressed. On his show he compared the sales of Perry's pepped up rendition of "Lili'u Ē" to one recorded in the original, slower tempo. The latter, he defiantly declared, outsold the former by four to one. He also reported the observations of the Louise Akeo Serenaders and Amelia Guerrero's troupe, just back from a continental tour, that the audiences preferred songs at a slow tempo, from "Ua Like No a Like," to "Nā Lei O Hawai'i," to "Imi Au Iā 'Oe."[35]

Thus, quite soon after their introduction, "jazzed up" arrangements of mele as well as hapa haole compositions generated intense debate in the Islands.[36] "Let's have enough pride in our own music," King urged, "to keep it pure."[37] Of course the "purity" of music lies in the eye of the beholder, and King's legacy as a Hawaiian composer demonstrates some ambivalence in his feelings toward hapa haole music and pepped up tempos. One of his biggest hits from 1934, for example, was a comedic number called "Pidgin English Hula (Ah-Sa-Ma-La-You)." He wrote over a dozen English-language songs about the Islands, and one composition from 1916, "Honolulu Maids," was even "mildly syncopated," with ragtime piano accompaniment.[38]

Thus while King consistently condemned "unpure" Hawaiian music, his own compositions revealed the difficulty of policing music's cultural boundaries. The line separating hapa haole, "partly foreign," songs from "authentic" and "pure" Hawaiian music remained (and remains) blurry, contentious, and ill-defined. The same music that musicians and dancers took great cultural pride in performing on *Hawaii Calls*, for example, could attract criticism from their neighbors. In the years to come, such distinctions only grew more volatile, even after the rock 'n' roll invasion eviscerated the interest of most younger Hawaiians in Hawaiian music, hapa haole or otherwise. The steel guitar became symbolic and deeply implicated in these debates.

In the 1960s it seemed as if all forms of Hawaiian music had begun to lose their appeal among audiences both abroad and in the Islands. *Hawaii Calls* then fell under criticism, not for its promotion of new "jazzed up" hapa haole songs but for being "too slow and old-fashioned."[39] During that decade the program lost stations as well as financial support and its local audience and continued to decline until it went off the air in 1975. Meanwhile, Hawaiian youth, and many of their parents, turned on to the rock 'n' roll and pop pulsing out of the continent. So did a number of the most significant tourist hotels: the Royal Hawaiian Hotel, in the past one of the most vital venues for Hawaiian musicians in Waikīkī, replaced its Hawaiian acts with generic lounge acts and even a three-ring circus.[40]

The decade also witnessed the meteoric rise of Don Ho, a sentimental balladeer from Kāneʻohe, Oʻahu, who commanded both international *and* local audiences in the mid-1960s, but whose band, the Aliʻis, purposefully abandoned the traditional ʻukulele and steel guitar accompaniment in Hawaiian troupes for vibes, a piano, and Ho's electric organ. While Ho occasionally performed select hapa haole songs, he was much better known for saccharine pop numbers such as "Tiny Bubbles" or even Willie Nelson's "Nightlife," neither of which had anything remotely to do with Hawaiʻi, in their lyrical content, at least. As one critic put it, "The Don Ho Show [at Duke Kahanamoku's] became increasingly bloated with hoax and hype—middle-aged tourist women stepping onstage to be kissed by the entertainer and staying there to be taught, and dance, the 'traditional' hula. . . . [This was the] spectacle that commercial Hawaiian music and culture had become."[41] Indeed, Ho became the international icon of Hawaiian music during that period, and was "one of the last Hawaiian or hapa haole entertainers (of any style) to be signed by a major mainland record label and subsequently register on any of the six major *Billboard* charts."[42]

This musical backdrop in the late 1960s and early 1970s convinced George Kanahele and others to sound the alarm. "Hawaiian music is in its death throes," Kanahele warned in his 1971 editorial. "Add it to the necrology of Hawaiiana, for soon it may be buried alongside the ancient mele."[43] Hawaiian music, as he understood it, was nearly extinct, and steel guitarists in the Islands, already aging and with no protégés waiting in the wings, were also a dying breed.

Of course, music was only one concern—arguably a minor concern among many—for Hawaiian people, who faced increasing political, social, and economic marginalization in the Islands in the aftermath of World War II. More hāole and Japanese had moved to the Islands than ever before, increasing competition for jobs, diminishing access to land and resources, and weakening Hawaiians' political voice, all while the U.S. military expanded its grip in the Islands. Spurred by these concerns and buoyed by the recent apparent success of decolonization and rights movements elsewhere, an ever-larger number of Hawaiians—young and old, urban and kuaʻāina—followed their forebears in the wake of the overthrow and fought back.[44]

The Hawaiian Renaissance was comprised of several political and cultural movements, tactics, goals and ideas, not always agreed upon by all involved. Yet, as Kanahele put it, "it has reversed years of cultural decline; it has created a new kind of Hawaiian consciousness; it has inspired greater pride in being

Hawaiian; it has led to bold and imaginative ways of reasserting our identity; it has led to a new political awareness; and it has had and will continue to have a positive impact on the economic and social uplifting of the Hawaiian community."[45] It led to organized protests over the evictions of Hawaiian residents from their homes in the name of "development." It led to the occupation (and eventual reclamation) of Kahoʻolawe, a Hawaiian island that the U.S. military had turned into a pockmarked bombing range. It precipitated the 1975 voyage of the *Hōkūleʻa*, a double-hulled canoe in which Hawaiians sailed to Tahiti with no modern navigational instruments, generating immense pride that celebrated long-standing indigenous technologies and knowledge. It led to the revival of the male hula and the creation of dozens of hālau hula (hula schools) and other cultural, business, and philanthropic organizations. It led to significant efforts to expand the diminishing number of Hawaiian-language speakers. And it profoundly changed the music scene in Hawaiʻi.[46]

"We don't play 'Tiny Bubbles,'" declared a member of the Sunday Manoa. "We don't play 'Little Brown Gal,' and we don't play 'Melancholy Baby.' What we do play is a different kind of Hawaiian music."[47]

"If you go and see the Brothers [Cazimero] and even whisper 'Sweet Leilani,' a bouncer would throw you out."[48]

"Dis song tell how them stu-u-pid hāole fight ovah land, when it not theirs to fight ovah. It ours, yeah!," exclaimed Israel ("Iz") Kamakawiwoʻole before his band, the Mākaha Sons of Niʻihau, launched into "Waimānalo Blues."[49] "Someone tell me some haoles in dis place," he continued. "Poor haoles, don' unnerstan' dose Hawaiian words," he shook his head. "Hey, I got it. You guys, you go down Waikīkī. You unnerstan' *all* the words down there, yeah!" In a lowered voice, he then added, "You unnerstan' us soon enough."[50]

The material, social, and political concerns in the Islands, and the nationalist verve that they generated for Hawaiians during the 1970s required a new soundtrack, with attitude. Music seemed to become as politically charged in this era as it had in the immediate aftermath of the overthrow, when Ka Bana Lahui performed "Mele ʻAi Pōhaku" ("Stone-Eating Song") at the Hawaiian Hotel before 5,000 people.[51] Hawaiian-language performances, in particular, had always reminded both Hawaiian and non-Hawaiian audiences of the kingdom—of the enduring presence of an indigenous population living under a territorial and then state regime.[52] But in the 1970s, a large contingent of Hawaiians began to identify new targets in their performances, from Waikīkī, to the tourists who thronged there, to hapa haole music, to Don Ho, and to the steel guitar.

The call to arms arose from activists and intellectuals as well as musicians. "I hate tourists," proclaimed Walter Ritte. "Oh, I don't hate the tourist *person* — I hate the industry. We have no control over that industry. It's like a giant malignant cancer and it's eating up all our beaches, all the places that are profound for our culture. It's grabbing them. They take the best."[53] Hawaiian intellectual Haunani-Kay Trask concurred, "When you take the land away from Hawaiians, you've cut them off from who they are. What's the alternative? You want us to go dance in the hotels and keep prostituting our culture? Is that being Hawaiian? Don't talk to me about the aloha spirit. That was the invention of Arthur Godfrey."[54] She added later, "The cultural revitalization that Hawaiians are now experiencing and transmitting to their children is as much a *repudiation* of colonization by so-called Western civilization in its American form as it is a *reclamation* of our own past and our own ways of life. . . . The distance between the smutty and the erotic is precisely the distance between Western culture and Hawaiian culture. In the hotel version of the *hula*, the sacredness of the dance has completely evaporated, while the athleticism and sexual expression have been packaged like ornaments. The purpose is entertainment for profit rather than a joyful and truly Hawaiian celebration of human and divine nature."[55]

Musicians who had performed hapa haole music during its heyday were being charged by some as taking on "'fake culture' and the impact of its negative images of Hawaiians as part of their heritage."[56] If they were not duped, then, they had, perhaps worse, sold out. Soon sociologists from the continent, sympathetic to this critique, began to weigh in: "One group of musicians in Hawai'i has chosen to remain identified with the commercial, hapa haole sound," protested George H. Lewis. "They have chosen the rewards of a higher income and steady work over the respect of the Hawaiian audience and of fellow musicians who have refused to play, or stopped playing, the supper clubs and lounges of Waikīkī." He accused musicians who played in groups like the Royal Hawaiian Serenaders or the Waikiki Beachboys as taking band names that made them appear as "happy-go-lucky brown lackeys."[57] As Charles K. L. Davis, a local performer, remarked about Don Ho, "He's the one, I'm sure, that brought [Vegas-style lounge acts to Waikīkī]. God, have you seen his TV show lately? Auwe! I don't think that can keep on much longer. Is it going off the air soon? I think it should. It's the most frightening thing I've ever seen. I watched it about three times, just to see it. I sat through it, and it was just dismal. God, it was awful! It's absolute amateur hour."[58] Local music writer John Berger recalled, "With the coming of statehood in 1959, attitudes changed. By the mid-1970s, Lei Day seemed to be falling from favor. It may have been unintended, but as the Hawaiian Renaissance fueled interest in identifying the most 'traditional,' 'grass-roots' Hawaiian music, a tendency developed to reject Hawaii's rich repertoire of hapa-haole (part-foreign, part-Hawaiian) music as kitschy, old-fashioned or even demeaning to local people."[59]

The polarization within the Hawaiian community over the local music scene troubled many of the entertainers who either witnessed it or found themselves under personal attack. Kahauanu Lake (1932–2011) was perplexed: "Younger people don't want to do it. They feel that playing hapa-haole music is going against the culture for some reason or other. Hawaiian people have spoken English for over one hundred years and what's wrong with singing it? If it was good enough for the Royal family, then it's good enough for me. Hapa music was composed by Hawaiian people and has been on the Hawaiian scene since before I was born."[60] Don Ho, for his part, expressed ambivalence. On the one hand, he said in a 1982 interview, "So what if my show's for tourists? What's wrong with tourists? I mean, why are local people so prejudiced against tourists?" On the other hand, he added later in the same interview, "I don't like it. I do it because people pay me a lot of money to do it. I'd much rather be in a quiet place with my friends. . . . Just let me have a place to go where my friends — mainly local people — can come and enjoy the freedom of expression. . . . I'm not free to express my style here. . . . But I will not argue the point because they pay me very well to do what they want me to do."[61]

One significant casualty of the criticism of hapa haole music, Waikīkī venues, and tourists, was the Hawaiian steel guitar. In 1966 a headline in the *New York Times* announced, "Moaning Sigh of Steel Guitar on Wane in Hawaii."[62] Reflecting on the period, Hawaiian music scholar Amy K. Stillman, an active participant in the Renaissance, recalled, "Younger musicians shunned conventional sounds, especially those of steel guitar and 'ukulele."[63] John Berger added, "When Hawaiian music began to experience a local revival in the early 1970s[,] . . . Island residents evidently did not identify Hawaiian music with the steel guitar. Some, particularly the young, thought of steel guitar either as part of the country music popular with haole servicemen or the 'old-fashioned tourist music' played for tourists in Waikīkī."[64] "[The kids] think a steel guitar sounds like it's from Nashville, all the cowboy music. No, no. It's a Hawaiian instrument. [A] Hawaiian invented it," Benny Kalama protested.[65] When asked years later about the shunning of the instrument, musician Keola Beamer confirmed, "We sort of have Hollywood to — I don't want to find blame here — but Hollywood sort of trivialized some of the marvelous aspects of the Hawaiian guitar. People thought of it as lightweight."[66] As a result, another remarked that the instrument was "treated like an illegitimate child in Hawai'i."[67] Thus, the Hawaiian steel guitar, an innovation engineered by Kānaka nearly 100 years earlier, an instrument that generated a unique voice, perfectly suited to the mele and hula ku'i traditions of the late nineteenth century, an instrument that in the hands of Hawaiian musicians had revolutionized music traditions around the world, seemed to lose all resonance during the Hawaiian Renaissance. Seen as a tool to ridicule and delegitimize Kānaka political concerns rather than articulate them, the instrument had lost its indigenous voice.

Such views of hapa haole music, the musicians who performed it in Waikīkī, and the steel guitar, as we will see, were by no means universal among Hawaiians. However, they tapped into a powerful feeling, buoyed by the protest spirit of the 1960s folk music movement on the continent, that the time was ripe for a reimagining of Hawaiian music. This reimagining generated an extraordinary wellspring of creativity by musicians, especially the younger ones who had earlier shunned hapa haole for the Beatles, Joan Baez, Bob Dylan, and the Rolling Stones. Yet what would their new music sound like? How could they channel their energies into a music that demonstrated long-standing and, for them, essential Hawaiian values and aesthetics, at the same time that it spoke to their own contemporary music sensibilities?

To begin with, the new bands—such as the Sunday Manoa, the Sons of Hawaii, and the Mākaha Sons of Ni'ihau—performed a repertoire overwhelmingly in the Hawaiian language. They discovered old songs, songs tied to the 'āina, which could speak directly to contemporary political and environmental concerns. They sought language instruction from kūpuna (elders). Many also embraced the percussive instruments long-standing in Hawaiian music traditions, including the ipu, 'ili 'ili, and pahu. Often these instruments were blended with contemporary instruments and sentiments that spoke to their generation. And overwhelmingly, they turned to the kī hō'alu, or slack key guitar.

The practice of kī hō'alu had continued throughout the twentieth century, but it was typically performed at luaus and other family gatherings, and very rarely on public stages. For the most part it had escaped the attention of hāole in the Islands, and was known by very few of them on the continent. It seemed then, to many, the perfect antidote to the hapa haole songs and instrumentation associated with tourists and Waikīkī, and more than that, it was beautiful.

Specific references to the style in early written records are sparse, but guitarist Alex Hoapili spoke of the tradition in a 1934 interview:

> Before the steel method of playing the guitar was known, musicians would sit on the beach playing the old hulas in the regular Spanish manner. In those days the accompanist would tune his guitar to the regular Spanish tuning, and the melody player used what was known to the boys as "slack key" tuning. As you know, the second, third, and fourth strings of a Spanish Guitar are tuned to the same ratio as the second, third, and fourth strings of a Hawaiian Guitar. However, they are all exactly one tone lower. Instead of raising the second, third, and fourth strings up one tone so as to have the guitar in A Major, they would lower the first, fifth, and sixth strings a tone, placing the guitar in G Major. In this way, when they played pieces in the regular A position, they were really producing tones of the G scale. The idea of this "slack key" tuning was to enable the accompanist to play in the more appropriate keys, such as C, G, and F, while the melody guitar played in D, A, and G. As far as the rhythm, harmony, and melody are concerned, these hulas played on the Spanish Guitar resembled the modern hulas played on the Hawaiian Guitar.[68]

Hoapili discussed only one tuning, but dozens and perhaps even more became personal to families (and often were carefully protected).[69] The tunings and the technique involved created unique voicings for the instrument that effortlessly accompanied the mele singer. However, by the 1960s the tradition, like that of steel guitar, remained in the hands of only a few guitarists. One of them, however, soon began to attract the interest of the younger generation. Eventually he became the best-known face, indeed the "folk hero," of the new Hawaiian music movement. His name was Philip "Gabby" Pahinui (1921–80).[70]

Pahinui had been around the Honolulu music scene for a long time, and his immersion in it begins to complicate for us the stark, anti–hapa haole, anti–steel guitar position that colored Hawaiian Renaissance discourse. He grew up in the Ward Street area of Kakaʻako, and had to quit school in the fifth grade in order to help support his family. After selling papers and shining shoes, he picked up the guitar and began to learn songs and techniques from local musicians. By the 1930s he was playing Hawaiian music in downtown cafés and bars, as well as in Waikīkī. He became interested in slack key in the late 1930s or early 1940s, when he encountered a kī hōʻalu guitarist named Herman.[71] He found occasion to enter local recording studios, and in 1946 he cut a slack key rendition of "Hi'ilawe" for Bell Records. Pahinui's music career faced ups and downs, and eventually he took a full-time pick-and-shovel job for the Honolulu City and County Road Department, where he worked the next fourteen years until an accident forced his early retirement.

Pahinui continued to play, however, and in 1960 he joined a new group, the Sons of Hawaii, who recorded what came to be recognized as the foundational records for the Hawaiian Renaissance movement. They were the first to perform with a stripped-down, rural sound; they tracked down Hawaiian-language mele, learned pronunciations and meanings from kūpuna Mary Kawena Puku'i and Pilahi Pākī and soon began to attract a great deal of attention from locals, far from the glitz of Waikīkī. They first booked a working-class bar — the Sandbox — located across the lagoon from Honolulu International Airport. As the biographer of Sons of Hawaii 'ukulele player Eddie Kamae described it, the band "played Thursday, Friday, and Saturday nights. By the second weekend the place was packed, with customers waiting outside to get in. The club's neighborhood regulars were soon surrounded by listeners from all layers of island life — cab drivers and college students, beach boys and politicians, attorneys and fellow musicians, bank officers and corporate executives, side by side with truckers and husky stevedores from the docks who came in straight from work and stayed until closing time. The boys in the band were playing for audiences unlike any they'd seen in their combined years in Waikīkī."[72] As Kamae recalled, "They stood for hours in lines that went out the door. I had no idea there was such enthusiasm for pure Hawaiian music, which was all we were playing."[73] Their records, ironically produced by veterans of the Waikīkī music scene, served as the most significant touchstone just a few years later for the next generation of musicians seeking their new, "pure" sound.

Indeed, Gabby Pahinui, the slack key guitarist the younger generation would embrace as their guide for their new musical aesthetic, was not only a veteran of the Waikīkī scene — he played as a member of Andy Cummings' popular Hawaiian Serenaders band for eighteen years in the 1940s and 1950s. Cummings worked diligently to incorporate Hawaiian-language repertoire into the band's sets, but hapa haole was fundamental to their sound as well. Gabby had played it nearly all his life. He recalled, "I think that the most exciting years were when they had the cottages in back of the Moana. It was not only fun, but the people were so appreciative. If you played 'Sweet Leilani,' 'Blue Lei,' well, then you were the greatest. You know, all those hapa haole songs."[74] He also recognized such labor as "a job," however, a particular type of performance that might not give "that feeling": "I'd rather play outside with a few grass shacks here and there and the feeling of the ocean water and a beautiful luau outside," he conceded, echoing the sentiments of Don Ho.[75] But he approached composer and entertainer Johnny Almeida's work, hapa haole and otherwise, with extreme respect (Pahinui regarded him as "the dean of Hawaiian music"), as he did the artistry of Genoa Keawe, an extraordinary falsetto singer who had recorded several popular hula albums, full of steel guitar, and who regularly performed both Hawaiian-language and hapa haole songs in Waikīkī. Pointing to those examples he said, "There is Hawaiian music, and yet people don't really accept it," alluding to the rejection of steel guitars and hapa haole music that remained in vogue during the 1970s.[76] In fact, Pahinui recalled to many interviewers that he originally had no interest in Hawaiian music and only came to appreciate it through steel guitar recordings, often of hapa haole songs: "Don't get me wrong, I like Hawaiian music. But I got to like Hawaiian music when I heard Sol Ho'opi'i and Eddie Bush and the Biltmore Trio. Eddie Bush played all the hapa-haole things. Sol Ho'opi'i played all the Hawaiian things. Then in their days, they had like a competition among themselves."[77]

The recordings of Ho'opi'i and Bush instilled in Pahinui his first real passion for Hawaiian music; it should come as little surprise, then, that for the majority of his career Gabby Pahinui was perhaps best known in the Islands as a steel guitarist. He was mentored in the 1930s by Charley "Tiny" Brown, who played regularly at the Central, the Hoffman, and other downtown cafés.[78] Pahinui developed his own style of playing steel, however, which was heavily influenced by Benny Goodman, Artie Shaw, Count Basie, Duke Ellington, and other popular jazz artists of the day. By 1937 or 1938 Pahinui was performing the steel regularly in clubs such as the Sky Room, Fisherman's Wharf, and the Ramona Café, though his style was considered too sophisticated by many of the orchestra leaders, who were playing "traditional" hapa haole and Hawaiian music.[79] "I studied with Andy Cummings then," Pahinui recalled, "and the style I wanted to play on my steel just wasn't accepted for Hawaiian music. They would just shake their heads and say, 'Do you think you could just play one or two strings and gives us a little Hawaiian flavor?'"[80] Pahinui continued: "I liked [jazz playing] because there was chord work, and young as I was, I liked that style of music. But when Andy Cummings told me, 'This is not da t'ing for you Gabby. We're playing Hawaiian music. Just change your style.' I played with Ted Dawson's band in Waikīkī at Lau Yee Chai. When I took the audition, I used to do all that rippling stuff on the steel. But when I began playing they said, 'Well, you're not the guy I heard, Gabby.'"[81] Pahinui's steel playing on commercial records and bootlegs sounds quite exceptional and indeed

FIGURE 48. *Gabby Pahinui (second from left) playing his Fender steel guitar at home in Waimānalo with family and friends, ca. 1972. Surrounding him (left to right) are James "Bla" Pahinui, Leland "Atta" Isaacs, Philip Pahinui, Cyril Pahinui, Martin Pahinui, and Manuel "Joe Gang" Kupahu. Courtesy of Panini Records.*

unique compared to that of many other guitarists in the Islands at the time.[82] "I was flabbergasted," recalled Barney Isaacs of the first time he saw Gabby play steel in the mid-1950s. "That guy was so tremendous with the steel."[83] As his son Cyril Pahinui, now a veteran slack key performer, put it, "My dad's favorite instrument was the steel guitar."[84] Fellow slack key guitarist Ray Kane added, "Steel guitar is pure Gabby."[85] Pahinui, then, a musical figurehead of the Hawaiian Renaissance movement, was intimately tied to hapa haole, jazz, and the steel guitar, and he held genuine affection for them all.

When one begins to look more closely at the most significant bands of the Hawaiian Renaissance, in fact, the steel guitar never entirely disappeared. On the landmark Sons of Hawaii records, it is actually a featured component; however, it sounds quite different from the style heard more commonly in those days on *Hawaii Calls*. When the band first formed as a ʻukulele, bass, and slack key guitar trio in 1960, the members quickly acknowledged the need for a steel player. The bass player knew the perfect candidate, David "Feet" Rogers.[86] Rogers, like so many others, came from a family of musicians. His father,

George, was known as an "elder statesman of the Hawaiian steel guitar," and his uncle Benny Rogers had played for years in Honolulu and recorded steel on Genoa Keawe's now classic albums.[87] What Feet Rogers brought to the Sons of Hawaii's recordings was his almost minimalist approach. As Kamae and his biographer reflected, "There is a busy, flashy way of playing steel that tries to fill each measure with as many notes as possible. Feet's music was the opposite of that. He had no desire to draw attention to himself or be the star. He played with reserve and understatement, with an exquisite purity of tone."[88] His unusual D major tuning was only played by his family. "How we tune the steel," he said, "is kind of like a chant or a family song, you know. It belongs to us, and we have to take care of it, or else it will change like everything else. It's just like my steel, too. It belongs to my father, and I never played one that has the same sound."[89] His playing and his philosophical approach perfectly suited the accompaniment of Pahinui's slack key picking and ipu-pahu rhythms, and the exquisite subtleties of their vocal performances. One observer remarked, "The inclusion of the steel guitar at a time when it was no longer popular among Hawaiian groups was what Kamae wanted."[90] Kamae simply stated, "Hawaiian music without the steel is not really Hawaiian music."[91]

We see, then, that the younger generation's rhetorical rejection of hapa haole music and the steel guitar coincided with the continued embrace of both by some of the Renaissance movement's most significant musicians. Their entanglement displays the ambiguities, the ambivalence, and the economic imperatives that have continued to weigh heavily in the figuring of professional opportunity as well as the aesthetics of expressive culture for Hawaiian musicians since the late nineteenth century. Hawaiians created the steel guitar, just as they crafted the hapa haole genre. While created independently of one another, Kānaka considered both to be intimately associated, if not synonymous, with Hawaiian music. Yet both just as quickly became wed to the tourist market, the only market in the Islands that generated meaningful income for Hawaiian musicians.[92] While the steel continued to increase in popularity among both Hawaiians and hāole, by the 1930s Charles King began to allege that hapa haole music did not represent a "pure" Hawaiʻi, even while he continued occasionally to pen his own hapa haole compositions. The precise definition of what constitutes "hapa haole music" was never quite agreed upon, but claims of authenticity continued to figure into the rhetoric of composers as they vied for authority in the marketplace. Meanwhile, Hawaiians such as Gabby Pahinui arrived at Hawaiian music *through* the hapa haole genre, and maintained a loving respect for it. Likewise, Hawaiian musicians enjoyed the opportunity that *Hawaii Calls* and the tourist market provided them, and hapa haole music and the steel guitar continued to thrive. By the 1960s, though, a younger generation grew increasingly alienated from the Hawaiian music that had filled the Waikīkī hotels, and soon, even the hotels began to respond to fading tourist interest by instead offering Don Ho and other alternative entertainments. In the 1970s, when increasing numbers of young Hawaiians embraced the folk aesthetic of kī hōʻalu and aligned Hawaiian music with their political activities, many rejected hapa haole music and the steel guitar outright. Whereas the steel guitar thrived in the Islands during the first round of hapa haole criticism, it reached its nadir during the second, despite the decision by some of the most iconic musicians of the movement to use the instrument in their recordings.

The far-reaching global embrace of Hawaiian steel guitar technology, then, ultimately planted the seeds of its undoing at home. The damage rendered by its growing association with haole tourism or alternatively with country music grew significantly, such that the steel guitar artistry of Gabby Pahinui and Feet Rogers was overshadowed by the adoration that the 1970s generation lavished on Pahinui's more authentically understood slack key and ipu-pahu rhythm guitar workmanship.[93] Pahinui continued to release albums on his own and with others in the 1970s that featured kī hōʻalu.[94] The explosion of interest in slack key guitar was reflected in a 1975 observation in the *Haʻilono Mele* newsletter, the print media arm of the music movement: "There are hundreds of persons studying kī hōʻalu in classes that have sprung up like mushrooms all over town."[95] As the interest in kī hōʻalu grew exponentially in the Islands, the kīkā kila began to drift into obscurity.

Fortunately, the aesthetics of the Hawaiian Renaissance did not spell the end of the Hawaiian steel guitar. As we have already seen, ambiguities and ambivalence prevented its total elimination from the scene. In addition, two key developments led to the cultivation of a very small but accomplished young cohort of professional players. The first was the support of the steel guitar by the Hawaiian Music Foundation (HMF). While many involved in the cultural revitalization of the 1970s dissociated the steel from "traditional" Hawaiian music, George Kanahele and his HMF embraced it. Having founded the HMF in 1971 to support the advancement of knowledge regarding Hawaiian music, and to launch a series of initiatives to cultivate and support Hawaiian music and its musicians, the HMF organized a series of well-attended concerts. The first, a slack key concert held in 1972, was a resounding success, and the HMF followed up the next year with a falsetto concert and then with a steel guitar concert.[96] Kanahele understood the steel guitar as an important instrument indigenous to Hawaiʻi that seemed destined for extinction if the HMF did not intervene. Accordingly, the HMF raised funds to provide scholarships for young people interested in learning how to play it. Scholarship recipients tutored with David Keliʻi, of *Hawaii Calls* fame, as well as with a recent arrival to the Islands, Jerry Byrd.

Jerry Byrd, as we saw in chapter 6, had first heard a Hawaiian steel guitarist at a tent show outside of Lima, Ohio. He went on to devote his life to the instrument, eventually becoming one of the most significant steel guitarists in country music. His country playing style closely mirrored the prevailing aesthetics of Hawaiian musicians, and he never abandoned his interest in Hawaiian music. When he moved to Oʻahu in the early 1970s, he could not believe how few people, especially young people, were playing the instrument. Although he had officially retired from the music industry, he decided to teach, as he put it to Eddie Alkire, "with the emphasis on the young Hawaiian boys and girls—that's where [the Hawaiian steel guitar] will live in the future."[97] Word traveled fast that he was in the Islands and eager to teach. Often encouraged by older musicians in their families who were familiar with Jerry Byrd's reputation, a number of young men and women eventually contacted him. Many either did not have family members to teach them the steel or had only limited resources to afford lessons, and Byrd did his best to accommodate them. He was, by all accounts, an extraordinarily gifted and demanding teacher. By the mid-1970s, he was teaching enough successful students to organize three-dozen of them to perform on one stage as a steel guitar band. This was a remarkable feat, given the near total absence of interest in the instrument by young people only a few years before. In fact, in his first years of teaching lessons on Oʻahu, five of his students—Alan Akaka, Owana Salazar, Casey Olsen, Greg Sardinha, and Paul Kim—became so adept that they were soon playing professionally at various venues throughout the Islands. For a time, it seemed as if the steel guitar was making a significant comeback in Hawaiʻi. But who were these new steel players, and whose influences were most important to them? As young men and women swept up in the political climate of the early 1970s, what did Hawaiian music and the steel guitar mean to them?

Alan Akaka was one of Byrd's first and best-known students, and his recollections of the period shed some light on how the steel guitar was regarded as he came of age and how he was drawn to it. Akaka (1956–) grew up in a musical family, and for a time his father was the minister of music at Kawaiahaʻo

Church. Most of Kawaiahaʻo's music was sung in Hawaiian; as Akaka recalled, "It was a Hawaiian church. We did Hawaiian anthems, they also did luaus where the choir played secular songs, you know, the Hawaiian standards, in the traditional Hawaiian way, like Aunty Genoa [Keawe], that style. I grew up with all of that." To Akaka the Kawaiahaʻo Church did not represent a challenge to Hawaiian culture; rather, he believed, it harbored Hawaiian culture, particularly in regard to language and music. The church did not feature steel guitarists, but he saw steel guitars during the 1960s in other social settings: "[At the luaus] steel was much more common then, much more. There were a lot of players in those days, not necessarily [big] names, [but] they were players." "I did not know what it was called," he continued. "I didn't even know what it was. I knew the sound when I heard it." Akaka took up a number of instruments in his youth, including the ʻukulele, clarinet, bass, and piano. He resisted his peers' interest in rock 'n' roll (which he said nauseated him when he listened to it in the car); meanwhile, he said, "with Hawaiian music, I felt very comfortable, and so I clung to Hawaiian music way back then."[98]

Around 1970, Alan Akaka's brother, along with so many other young Hawaiians, took up slack key guitar. Alan wanted to play something different, however, so he began to run a clarinet barrel along the strings of a guitar in order to experiment with the steel guitar technique. He adapted a slack key tuning and began playing along to the final Sons of Hawaii album, *The Folk Music of Hawaii* (1971). He recalled, "I started to copy 'Feet' Rogers's style. . . . I [could] actually follow 'Feet' Rogers and do it, and so someone at church, a calabash uncle — calabash means, not related — he found out I was interested in the steel guitar, so he let me use his." Eventually Alan and his brother formed a group, and they began playing with their father: "My dad formed a group with two of my cousins, and he included my brother and me. My brother played slack key and I played steel guitar. My father encouraged me. So there was a lot of music around me, growing up, and plus, going to Kamehameha Schools, there was a lot of music there." He soon began collecting older songs and searching for steel guitar primers, but he made little progress until he was awarded a scholarship to work with Jerry Byrd.[99]

He had already heard of Byrd by that time. One of Akaka's early mentors, Aunty Nona Beamer, shared with him copies of Byrd's diagram music for the steel guitar. "And then I met him," Akaka recalled. "He moved here in the early '70s. . . . I knew he was in town because my uncle . . . said, 'Wow, you gotta meet this Jerry Byrd — He can play two parts at the same time!'" Akaka was a sophomore in high school and had been granted an HMF scholarship to learn from Pua Almeida. Almeida was too busy, however, so the foundation asked Byrd to take Akaka on.[100]

Memories of Byrd's lessons continue to inspire awe among the students who worked with him. He demanded a great deal, but he also generated excitement among his young students for the steel guitar. He taught private lessons in addition to those coordinated with the HMF's music education program, Hālau Mele Hawaiʻi, as well as night classes in community colleges outside of Honolulu. The most meaningful thing that Byrd conveyed to Akaka was the notion of "musicality": "It's what happens between the notes," Akaka said, "that makes the music." Akaka, meanwhile, was also consuming everything he could find that had to do with the steel guitar: "I would go to Ala Moana Shopping Center, where you could listen to demo records, [and would] be there for hours listening [to] . . . 49th State records, Benny Rogers solos, Eddie Kamae and the Sons of Hawaii, Bill Lincoln, there were so many, just rows and rows of albums. . . . Then I would go to the state library and borrow records."[101]

Akaka began not only following the musicians who inspired him but also playing with them. He had to work his way up, however: "So in the mid- to late seventies, normally I played bass. Every now and then if there were younger players playing, I could play steel. But if I was playing with 'old timers,' I would be playing the bass." He eventually was hired by Genoa Keawe, which landed him a Waikīkī gig seven nights a week, at least for a time, with some of the biggest players in the Islands: Benny Kalama, Jerry Byrd, Walter Moʻokine, Norman Isaacs, Sonny Kamahele, and others. He would share rides with Benny Kalama in order to tease stories out of him about recordings or players: "If I was driving I could put in a cassette, and he would just start talking about the recordings. Memories would come out. And so I got all these stories."[102]

Aside from Sol Hoʻopiʻi and Jerry Byrd, Akaka's greatest inspirations on the steel guitar, in fact, were players who rarely left the Islands, such as David Keliʻi, Jake Keliʻikoa, and Billy Hew Len. Billy Hew Len's superb playing was made even more exceptional by the fact that he only had one hand: a local doctor had fabricated a prosthetic for him with a steel bar welded in place. From Hew Len, Akaka learned to play and sing at the same time (very few steel guitarists today can do both at once, but it was commonplace in the days of Sol Hoʻopiʻi, when all musicians were expected to sing in parallel or harmony). He used to watch Keliʻi play on the street in a rented area by the Princess Kaiulani Hotel: "And so I would watch David, and talk story with him, and his advice was, 'Let's see your hands. . . . They're gold. Keep them in your pockets. Protect your hands.'" Akaka continued, "And then David did something. I was watch-

FIGURE 49. *Alan Akaka sought out and worked with musicians from previous generations to learn their techniques and listen to them talk story.* Left to right: *Akaka, Benny Kalama, and Sonny Kamahele. Courtesy of Alan Akaka.*

ing him playing, and I saw him turning the [tuning] keys—he was retuning, while playing. And then I started doing that, too. Single neck, I will do that. I'll go, hey, wait a minute, this song will sound better with a different tuning, and I'll change it."

In the late 1970s Akaka's work in Waikīkī continued to pick up as a few more clubs and restaurants began to once again feature Hawaiian music. Waikīkī served as boot camp for young players like Akaka, who were not raised on the steel guitar but who came to it in their teens.[103] Akaka considered the music, which typically included many hapa haole compositions, as "traditional": "I play music from the forties and fifties. We call it traditional, but you know there was a style before that, and a style before that, and a style before that. If I can call Aunty Genoa's style traditional, it has to do with the type of instruments used. Not the bongos, not the electric guitar, not an electric bass, but an upright bass, 'ukulele, steel guitar, guitar—the standard combo. And maybe, um, sticking to more basic chords, standard turnarounds. Like how we do the vamps in between . . . harmony. For what we normally do, we go parallel [not counterpoint]; we're breaking the rules of standard theory that you learn in university. Parallel chords makes it sound Hawaiian. I'm playing in C7, and the voices are singing in A minor. Sounds perfectly fine. It fits. It's what sounds pleasant to our ears."[104]

Akaka admitted, however, that most of the people he played for in the 1970s and 1980s were tourists, with few locals. They were mainly from Japan, North America, and Europe.[105] His audience also reflected a hard reality: while the HMF and Byrd succeeded in identifying a strong cohort of students in the early 1970s, the phenomenon did not replicate itself in the years following. Today, the youngest professional players in the Islands, with Jeff Au Hoy being an important exception, are in their late forties or fifties—they are the players who got their start studying under Jerry Byrd. Bobby Ingano and Greg Sardinha fit in this category, and by the 1980s they were the "go to" players for anyone in the Islands looking to add steel to a record. "When a steel guitarist was heard on a recording by a contemporary island group," reported one observer, "it was almost always either Ingano or Sardinha."[106] As a member of the rock 'n' roll generation, Ingano, tellingly, got turned onto the steel guitar not by Hawaiian music but by Santo and Johnny's smash 1959 recording, "Sleep Walk."[107]

Thus, while the steel guitar was retrieved from brink of obscurity in the Islands, it by no means has recovered the ground that eroded so quickly during the rock 'n' roll revolution and the Renaissance. This concerns many players: "When locals think of steel guitar they might perceive of it as a Waikīkī instrument for hapa haole music, but the steel guitar is more than that. Just look at 'Feet' Rogers, and what he did," protested Akaka in the *Honolulu Star-Advertiser* in 2010. "The simplicity of his style fits slack key (and the) Sons of Hawaii perfectly."[108] Sardinha reported that he "has been wondering in recent years when (and whether) the next generation of local steel guitarists will make themselves known."[109]

The Hawaiian steel guitar—developed in the midst of excruciating political upheaval in the late nineteenth century—was an instrument that enabled Hawaiians to nurture and protect their expressive culture by vastly expanding its reach, and their diaspora, throughout the world. It was an instrument that revolutionized vernacular music traditions in the Islands and beyond. An indigenous, Kanaka technology, it spurred the transformation of the guitar into a featured lead melodic instrument, and it inspired landmark achievements in acoustic, mechanical, and electrical amplification. It changed the way that the modern world understood the guitar, and changed the sound of much of its music. Yet a century later, this same instrument continues to reckon with the perception that it wrought damage in the land of its birth. Like a Pan, it lured hāole to the Islands—it domesticated the image of Hawaiians in the United States and thus enabled the continued cooptation of lands in the name of military or economic necessity. It underwrote the development of pseudo-Hawaiian, Tin Pan Alley songs; it brought shame to Native Hawaiians in hapa haole lyrics. Its journey has been long and circuitous, breathtaking and indirect; and it is not over yet.

EPILOGUE *Remembrance and Kuleana*

Alan Akaka welcomed me one morning into his Hawaiian music school, Ke Kula Mele Hawai'i. The school is located on the first floor of his home in Kailua, situated in the middle of a pleasant but crowded neighborhood near Enchanted Lake. A few days earlier I had seen his students perform a recital. It was "Hawaiian Steel Guitar" month at the Waikīkī Beach Walk, so that evening three of his upright bass players, four 'ukulele players, and six of his young steel players, boys and girls, had performed at the walk for around 300 onlookers. As I followed him inside his house, he told me that he was wrapping up a lesson and led me to the main classroom, comprised of two rows of seats with panels for writing musical notation. The walls are filled with tapestries that featured images of his students, who range in age from four to over seventy and who represent the great diversity of the Islands' population.

I had seen Alan play the previous night at the Waikiki Beach Marriott Resort's Moana Terrace, an outdoor venue beside a pool, separated from the Pacific by the bustle of Kalākaua Avenue, about twenty feet below. That night Alan was playing, just as he had for years, with the Keawe 'Ohana—an ensemble celebrating the legacy of the late Genoa Keawe and featuring Alan along with several members of Keawe's family. The music included exquisite falsetto singing by Genoa Keawe's granddaughter Pōmaika'i Keawe Lyman and parallel harmonies indicative of this style of Hawaiian music; the repertoire ran from very old kingdom mele to several of the now "classic" hapa haole variety. Before the night was over, and in the midst of a much welcome rainstorm that did not seem to deter anyone from playing on the stage (or listening under canopies), the musicians traded instruments with one another and welcomed others to join them. This night George Kuo stepped up, a master of the slack key guitar, as well as David Doucet, a member of the Grammy-winning Cajun band Beausoleil, who is also an avid slack key player and was in town to perform in a local theater. Pōmaika'i's young daughter Mālie occasionally stepped in front of the stage to hula; she is now also one of Alan's steel guitar students.

This morning, however, Alan's classroom was empty. We continued to walk through the ke kula mele to his office, where around a dozen instruments—ʻukuleles, standard guitars, and several steel guitars—surround his desk. On the wall hangs an original Rickenbacker "frying pan" Hawaiian guitar, the first electric steel guitar ever sold. In the office Alan sat at his computer to resume work with the student via Skype. On the computer monitor I see the protruding abdomen of an older man perched behind an electric steel guitar; the man had aimed his computer's camera that way in order to provide Alan with a view of his hands as they hovered above the instrument. Bill was a retiree living about thirty miles west of Phoenix. Now in his seventies, he had grown up listening to Hawaiian music via *Hawaii Calls* and other Hawaiian radio programs. After learning about Alan's online instruction, Bill had recently decided to pursue his lifelong dream of learning to play the steel guitar.

Bill was struggling. In fact, he had been working on the steel guitar turnarounds on the same mele for months. These are the students who can try instructors' patience, yet Alan displayed no sign of weariness. Bill played the passage again. And again. And again. "Hanohano try again. Hanohano try again," Alan encouraged. His students range broadly in talent and location. "I have a sixteen-year-old student in Illinois who learns every song I teach him in a week." Another lives in Moscow, which requires Alan to log into Skype at 11:00 P.M. in order to provide his lesson. Day and night, Alan is working to reintroduce not simply the Hawaiian guitar but also fundamental Hawaiian repertoire and technique to new students, both local and far-flung.[1]

The challenge is great, but not because the steel guitar has disappeared from contemporary music. Today the Hawaiian steel guitar signals, more quickly than any other sound, the country music format of an American radio or satellite network channel. In countless Hollywood films it accentuates the melancholy of a sad scene, or pulls audience heartstrings in soaring celebration; slide guitars continue to sear leads into all sorts of rock formats. Steel guitarists such as Debashish Bhattacharya continue to tour the world; he is continuing where Tau Moe's students left off, reimagining Indian ragas on his Hawaiian guitar.

Yet the indigeneity of the instrument—its associations with Hawaiian history, if not with Hawaiian musicians—remains firmly outside public consciousness, at least beyond the Islands. In the Islands, the instrument never regained the prominence it once held—in the 1980s, "Jawaiian" music, a local genre steeped in reggae, began a long tenure as the anthemic music for Hawaiian youth, with hip hop soon to follow. The kī hōʻalu now reigns supreme, by contrast, on Waikīkī poolside stages and on mall speakers; it also filled the soundtrack of *The Descendants*, a successful 2011 George Clooney film set in the Islands. Gabby Pahinui's slack key recordings, and not his (or anyone else's) steel guitar, provided the sonic foundation for the film. If you listen carefully, however, you can hear his bandmate Feet Rogers playing steel on one song, "He'eia," and even Sol Ho'opi'i on another, "Ka Mele Oku'u Puuwai."

Despite these challenges, the kīkā kila continues to find dedicated adherents in the Islands, and as Akaka's and others' work attests, its future remains vibrant with possibility. Its indigenous heritage, at least for some Hawaiians, has become one to celebrate, protect, and nurture. In 2014, for example, Akaka, also an avid 'ukulele player, led a campaign *against* a bill that had been proposed in the state legislature to decree the 'ukulele as the "official state musical string instrument" of Hawai'i.[2] The only, truly Hawaiian instrument, he testified before the legislature, is the Hawaiian steel guitar. News of the bill and Akaka's efforts to derail it quickly filtered through a variety of online instrument forums. The legislature was deluged with submitted testimony from all over the world, both for and against the bill. As one state senator remarked, "It's surprising that with all the huge, substantive bills that we're discussing here, 'ukulele is one of the more controversial bills this Legislative session."[3] The bill died in the senate, generating a surprising amount of national media attention in the process.[4] Slowly but surely, Akaka believes, the Hawaiian steel guitar will gain its historical due, and in the process reclaim its proper place in the consciousness of people in the Islands and beyond.[5]

In Lā'ie, meanwhile, even if memories of Joseph Kekuku have faded, the steel guitar has long remained a mainstay of the community. Kekuku's nephew Merle took up the instrument and played in venues on O'ahu for decades. One of the best-known and most-beloved Lā'ie steel players of the mid- to late twentieth century was "Uncle Five Cents," Thomas Au. Au's formal education ended in the eighth grade; by then, like many of his classmates, he had begun to labor, for fifty cents per day, in the sugarcane fields of the Mormon Church's plantation at Lā'ie.[6] Laboring as a child for menial wages on the LDS plantation did not stifle his faith, however. Au's decision to take up the steel guitar, in fact, came about *because* of his faith, as a means to support the church after it began hosting fundraisers with Hawaiian music ensembles in the 1940s and 1950s. As he recalled decades later, "I start learning to play the steel when I was going on thirty-three years old. But, so strong was the Church program, I really wanted to learn the steel."[7] In 1991, during a tribute to Joseph Kekuku in a small chapel in Hau'ula, just a few miles south of Lā'ie, Uncle Five Cents suffered a fatal heart attack while playing "Beautiful Kahana."[8]

More recently, Lā'ie Elementary School began hosting Hawaiian steel guitar lessons for its students. Ka'iwa Meyer raised the money to provide twenty guitars and after-school lessons for as many boys and girls each year, so that they may learn the instrument of her great uncle Joseph Kekuku. She glows in wonderment when she thinks about Joseph's travels throughout the world. Even before she retired to the Waimānalo homestead on O'ahu, after working many years on Maui, she labored intensively to teach the residents of Lā'ie about the innovations and adventures of one of its most famous but, until recently, nearly forgotten residents. Kekuku's family in Lā'ie, of course, has maintained stories of his youth. But Meyer felt that his legacy was dissipating in Lā'ie, and she felt an urgency to foster a new generation of players in his honor. Her work gained attention in the community, and, in 2014, LDS officials at Lā'ie's Polynesian Cultural Center, one of the biggest tourist draws on O'ahu, commissioned a bronze statue of Kekuku for placement just outside the main entrance, in front of the Hukilau Marketplace.[9]

From Hau'ula, where Uncle Five Cents passed away while delivering his own homage to Kekuku, one can travel just a few miles further south to a hairpin turn along the highway that cradles Kahana Bay, the namesake of Uncle Five Cents's final mele. There at the bend, a stone's throw down Trout Farm Road, we find Joseph Kekuku's birthplace. Kekuku's mother raised him in Lā'ie, but she lived here, at Kahana Bay, during the time that Joseph was born. She and others formed the Kahana Hui in order to purchase the ahupua'a from her Pākē husband, Ahmee, who was returning, without her, to China. Rural Hawaiians had formed similar huis all over the Islands in the late nineteenth century as they sought to collectively bargain for the return of the common lands taken from them during and after the Great Māhele.[10] The Kahana Hui was particularly concerned to restore its members' relationship to the 'āina, and was emboldened by a recent, infuriating decision rendered by the missionaries at Lā'ie. In 1874, a few months before Joseph Kekuku was born, the missionaries had disfellowshipped several Hawaiians for refusing to respect a ban on the growing of 'awa. 'Awa was a cash crop of economic importance for maka'āinana in the mid-nineteenth century, and one with strong and longheld cultural value, as it was also locally consumed in a mildly narcotic, ceremonial drink.[11] After their banishment from the church at Lā'ie, they built their own at Kahana, and formed the hui. Within this context of profound cultural determination, Kekuku was born.

FIGURE 50. *In the spring of 2015 the Polynesian Cultural Center in Lāʻie unveiled a statue that honors Joseph Kekuku. Several steel guitarists performed during the event, including Mālie Lyman, pictured here. Lyman, the great-granddaughter of Genoa Keawe, is one of Alan Akaka's students. Highly motivated and talented, she is one of several young people now embracing the steel guitar in the Islands.* Courtesy of Pōmaikaʻi Lyman.

Recently the chapel built by the Kahana Hui members of this 1874 "ʻAwa Rebellion," as it became known, was condemned and torn down. Likewise, the state of Hawaiʻi condemned the entirety of the Kahana ahupuaʻa in the 1960s, declaring it a state park.[12] Ron Johnson and his family still live there, however; he had grown up in the church built by those disfellowshipped members.[13] When the remaining residents of Kahana were threatened with their own eviction following the condemnation of their lands, they fought back. In a highly unorthodox settlement with the U.S. Park Service, the thirty-one families who call Kahana home are now required by state law to engage in twenty-five hours of "distinctly Hawaiian" cultural practices per month in order to remain. The settlement frustrates Johnson, a fisherman, taro farmer, and retired firefighter, who would have been doing such things anyway: "I just don't like being mandated to do it as a condition of being here. I'd do it out of aloha, not because we had to."[14]

Johnson is also a steel guitarist. He, like Alan Akaka, Casey Olsen, Greg Sardinha, Owana Salazar, and several others of his generation, studied with Jerry Byrd. His grandmother traveled the United States as a kumu hula. In fact, he was born in New Orleans and performed Hawaiian shows in Atlantic City with his mother and grandmother until he was five, wearing the white pants, white shirt, and red sash that Kekuku and his predecessors donned for decades in their troupes. Johnson returned to Kahana with his family the next year and has remained ever since.

As a Kanaka Maoli cultural practice, the steel guitar is as deeply significant to him as is the toil in his Kahana taro patch. As he puts it, "It's totally unique. And I think Hawaiians don't get credit for being as inventive as they are, and as talented as they are. I've seen Hawaiians do amazing things. And steel guitar is one of them." He thought for a moment and continued,

> But, you know, even like planting taro—I've seen my grandmother make it rain when I needed rain, and I've seen her stop the rain when I had too much rain. All in the prayer, the Hawaiian oli, the Hawaiian chant. . . . So the steel guitar is like that. It's a part of us—it's a part of our culture. It's not meant for everybody. In old Hawaiʻi not everyone did hula, not everyone practiced like the kāhuna, did the medicine. Not everybody fished, not everybody farmed. But everybody had their particular jobs. . . . You would know how to do several things, but you had particular responsibilities in old Hawaiʻi—things that you were an expert in. That was your kuleana—that was your responsibility—to do these particular things. I treat this as my

FIGURE 51.
Ron Johnson lives by Kahana Bay, on the windward side of Oʻahu, where Joseph Kekuku was born. He studied with Jerry Byrd and considers the survival and nurturance of the steel guitar as his kuleana, or responsibility. Sitting in his music room, he shows off one of his most prized instruments, a vintage Rickenbacker "Panda" B6. Courtesy of the author.

> responsibility, to learn and try to teach as best I can. And if I'm not good enough to teach anyone, I can at least perpetuate it, pass it on, play it as much as I can every day and share that along the way.[15]

Kuleana. Responsibility. Tradition. And change. From the gentle flowing waters of Kahana Bay, the steel guitar is home. Yet from a Skype lesson to Moscow, to an embroiled legislative debate, to a Marriott stage in Waikīkī, it moves from space to space, staking an ongoing and dynamic relationship between tradition and innovation. It figures at the center of a long series of crossroads. It represents the zenith of Hawaiian ingenuity that characterized the music of the ʻāina during the nineteenth century. It led many Hawaiians out of the Islands during the economic, social, and political trauma that surrounded the overthrow. It served as a tool to strengthen the diaspora and facilitate mele tradition. It created the modern sounds of twentieth-century music genres around the world.

Certainly, it became fundamental to the crafting of modern American music. In the United States, the instrument is now much more frequently associated with non-Hawaiian musicians. Beyond the pedal steel guitars that continue to signify country music, the Dobros that resonate in bluegrass, and the slide guitars that scream in the blues or rock, the most visible steel guitarists are instrumentalists such as Ben Harper or Robert Randolph. The three-time Grammy-winning Harper is a multi-instrumentalist, singer, and songwriter whose work transgresses numerous styles, but he is best identified with a lap steel or a Weissenborn-style Hawaiian guitar in hand. Randolph, a blazingly gifted guitarist who trained in the African American sacred steel gospel tradition, now tours the world with the funky Family Band. Another is Nels Cline, the genre-leaping lead guitarist in Wilco, who onstage still plays the vintage Gibson electric steel guitar originally inherited from a family friend who bought it during the height of the Hawaiian guitar craze.[16]

As the versatility of the instrument became apparent, its history of indigeneity was lost in the fray to most. Likewise, the instrument's origins ebbed in people's consciousness in the Islands. It became associated with a hapa haole genre disparaged by many as the soundtrack of colonization, or otherwise became unfashionable to younger generations of Hawaiians who had become taken with the possibilities that other instruments and genres offered them. At some point along the way, however, the Hawaiian guitar also became kuleana. The recent efforts by Kaʻiwa Meyer, Alan Akaka, and Ron Johnson attest to this, and their work on behalf of the instrument's legacy and future is determined, resonant, and sound.

NOTES

ABBREVIATIONS USED IN THE NOTES

AMPAS	Margaret Herrick Library, Academy of Motion Picture Arts and Sciences, Beverly Hills, CA
UNC	University of North Carolina at Chapel Hill
BMLA	Bishop Museum Library and Archives, Honolulu, HI
BYUH	Brigham Young University–Hawai'i, Lā'ie
CMHF	Country Music Hall of Fame, Nashville, TN
COHUHM	Center for Oral History, University of Hawai'i at Mānoa
HLUHM	Hawaiian Collection, Hamilton Library, University of Hawai'i at Mānoa
HSA	Hawai'i State Archives, Honolulu
HSL	Hawai'i State Library
KSA	Kamehameha School Archives, Honolulu
NARA	National Archives and Records Administration
UIL	University of Iowa Libraries, Iowa City
UIUC	University of Illinois at Urbana-Champaign
VAMA	Victoria and Albert Museum, London, UK
YU	Yale University, New Haven, CT

PREFACE

1. B. B. King, interview with Terry Gross, *Fresh Air*, National Public Radio, 1996, re-aired May 15, 2015.

2. King, *Blues All Around Me*, 163. Like many others, King refers to the pedal steel guitar, an iteration of the Hawaiian steel guitar, as the "steel pedal."

3. Throughout the book I will interchangeably use the terms *Kanaka Maoli*, *Kanaka*, *Hawaiian*, and *Native Hawaiian* to refer to individuals with a direct ancestral connection to the Islands that predates the earliest arrival of Europeans. Hawaiian people have used the term *Kanaka* to refer to themselves consistently across the previous two centuries. *Kanaka Maoli* is a term that, over the most recent decades, resonates particularly strongly among Hawaiian nationalists working to defend Hawaiian sovereignty and to restore the kingdom and the 'āina to the Hawaiian people. I will attempt to deploy my usage of these terms to reflect

the preferences of the individuals under discussion, and I apologize in advance for any inconsistencies in this effort. The use of the kahakō, or macron, in some nouns, such as *kānaka* and *hāole*, typically denotes the plural form. People with no Hawaiian ancestry but who were born or resided in the Islands are never referred to here as "Hawaiians." They can be considered kama'āina, however, which commonly refers to anyone residing in the Islands, Kanaka or otherwise.

INTRODUCTION

1. Kānaka and their neighboring Pacific Islanders have navigated the seas, islands, and continents for millennia, and had long labored along the Eastern and Western shores of North America, with some working as musicians and dancers, by the time these musicians followed in their wake. However, as this book will suggest, the overthrow provided some Kānaka with a new rationale for leaving the Islands. For an introductory overview of the Hawaiian diaspora in North America prior to the overthrow, see Okihiro, *Island World*, 135–68. See also Kauanui, "Diasporic Deracination."

2. Asensio, "Language Policy," 12; Lucas, "E Ola Mau Kākou I Ka ʻŌlelo Makuahine," 8.

3. Adria Imada has published extraordinary work on the female hula performers who labored on these global entertainment circuits. This study seeks in some ways to complement her book, *Aloha America*, by focusing on the lives of professional Hawaiian guitarists, most of whom were men.

4. To view the clip, see http://www.criticalpast.com/video/65675023647_US-troops_guitar_American-Indian-Woman. For more information on Blackstone's life and professional career, see Troutman, *Indian Blues*, 201–44.

5. Recent scholarship has emphasized the density and interconnectedness of historical Pacific Ocean human geography. See Hau'ofa, "Our Sea of Islands."

6. For an excellent political history of the Kingdom of Hawai'i from 1840 through 1887, see Osorio, *Dismembering Lāhui*. For studies on nineteenth-century land tenure, including the Great Māhele (as the Kānaka call the loss of their land during the middle of that century), see Kame'eleihiwa, *Native Land and Foreign Desires*. For another view of the significance of the Great Māhele and the following process by which Kānaka were divorced from their lands by non-Hawaiians, see Stauffer, *Kahana*. For an early and insightful cultural and political history of the Islands, see Malo, *Hawaiian Antiquities*. See also Buck, *Paradise Remade*. For a history of Native Hawaiian resistance strategies in the years surrounding the overthrow, see Silva, *Aloha Betrayed*. On intimately related, ongoing colonial struggles and the modern sovereignty movement, see Kauanui, *Hawaiian Blood*; Goodyear-

Ka'ōpua, Hussey, and Wright, *A Nation Rising*; and Haunani-Kay Trask, *From a Native Daughter*. See also Yamashiro and Goodyear-Ka'ōpua, *The Value of Hawai'i*, vol. 2. Older but still useful volumes on Hawaiian Kingdom history and settler history in the Islands include Kuykendall, *The Hawaiian Kingdom, 1778–1854*; Kuykendall, *The Hawaiian Kingdom*, vol. 2; Kuykendall, *The Hawaiian Kingdom, 1874–1893*; and Daws, *Shoal of Time*.

7. Dye, "Population Trends in Hawai'i before 1778," 1–2; Schmitt, *Demographic Statistics of Hawaii*; Schmitt, *Historical Statistics of Hawaii*; Bushnell, *The Gifts of Civilization*.

8. Hawaiians gained visual and written literacy in the Hawaiian language very quickly during the mid-nineteenth century. According to the 1910 U.S. Census, which defined illiteracy as the inability to write, regardless of the ability to read, the illiteracy rate of Native Hawaiians stood at only 4.7 percent, while the illiteracy rates for people of mixed Hawaiian and Caucasian or Hawaiian and Asian ancestry were even lower, at 1.3 and 1.8 percent, respectively. Meanwhile, the average illiteracy rate in the Islands for "all races" combined was 26.8 percent. Thrum, *Hawaiian Almanac and Annual for 1915*, 22.

9. For excellent studies and discussions of missionary proselytization efforts, see Kame'eleihiwa, *Native Land and Foreign Desires*; Osorio, *Dismembering Lāhui*; and Aikau, *A Chosen People, a Promised Land*.

10. Amy Ku'uleialoha Stillman's foundational work on Hawaiian music and dance, and the inestimable significance of repertoire and context, has deeply informed my work. For histories of mele hula and dance, see Stillman, "Re-membering the History of Hawaiian Hula"; Stillman, "Globalizing Hula"; Stillman, "Hula Hits, Local Music and Local Charts"; Stillman, "Hawaiian Hula Competitions"; and Stillman, "Not All Hula Songs Are Created Equal." For a particularly interesting examination of resistance through song, see Stillman, "History Reinterpreted in Song." See also Silva, "He Kānāwai E Ho'opau I Nā Hula Kuolo Hawai'i"; Tatar, "Toward a Description of Precontact Music in Hawai'i"; and Tatar, *Nineteenth-Century Hawaiian Chant*. See also Bacon and Napoka, *Nā Mele Welo = Songs of Our Heritage*; Kaeppler, "Music, Metaphor, and Misunderstanding"; Kaeppler, *Hula Pahu*; Kaeppler, "Acculturation in Hawaiian Dance"; Pollenz, "The Puzzle of Hula"; Pukui, "Hawaiian Poetry and Music"; Roberts, *Ancient Hawaiian Music*; Smith, "Folk Music in Hawai'i"; Solberg, "Hawaiian Lyrics, Chant, and Dance"; and Solberg, "Hawaiian Music, Poetry, and Dance." For an authoritative study of hula performance and its relationship to tourism and U.S. imperialism from the late nineteenth through the mid-twentieth century, see Imada, *Aloha America*.

11. For a very helpful breakdown of mele hula and mele oli genres, see Stillman,

"Textualizing Hawaiian Music." Her highly anticipated book on these genres without doubt will serve as a foundational resource on Hawaiian music.

12. On the hula bans, see Silva, "He Kānāwai E Ho'opau I Nā Hula Kuolo Hawai'i." Hawaiian-language newspapers published hundreds of mele during the second half of the nineteenth century and into the twentieth century. In addition, in the early 1920s ethnologist Helen Roberts transcribed hundreds of mele from family mele books shared with her. These books were comprised of mele written or transcribed by family members in the mid-nineteenth through the early twentieth centuries. In these books they developed a new means for preserving and remembering mele in the Islands. Helen H. Roberts, "Report of Work Accomplished for the Hawaiian Legend and Fo[l]klore Commission on the Islands of O'ahu and Kaua'i, Covering Five Months," box 2, folder 62, Helen Heffron Roberts Collection, YU.

13. Emerson, "Unwritten Literature of Hawaii."

14. As a cultural phenomenon, guitars generate a great deal of scholarship on their own. Books particularly relevant to this study include Brookes, *Guitar: An American Life*; Noonan, *The Guitar in America*; Gioia, *The Guitar and the New World*; and Stone, *Sacred Steel*. Large-format, even self-published books on particular guitar companies form a cottage industry that supplies a large community of guitar enthusiasts; those that particularly relate to the history of the Hawaiian steel guitar include Brozman, *The History and Artistry of National Resonator Instruments*; Noe and Most, *Chris J. Knutsen*; Makin, *Palm Trees, Señoritas . . . and Rocket Ships!*; and Johnston and Boak, *Martin Guitars*.

15. British scholars Kevin Dawe and Andy Bennett originally coined this phrase to refer to the particular adoption of the guitar by musicians in several locales throughout the world; their explanation of the concept bears repeating here: "The guitar exists in cultural space nuanced by the convergence of both local and global forces. The guitar's material form and sound are relatively standardized in global circulation, yet at the same time it is the object of assimilation, appropriation and change in local settings by quite specific means and in quite specific ways. Indeed, the range of discourses that continue to emerge from the performance and reception of guitar music . . . show the instrument to be embedded, located and placed within communities that attach a similar but nevertheless distinct set of values to the guitar. Although the cultures of the guitar are in every respect both globally and locally constituted, the guitar's position in 'global music culture' is underscored by a seemingly infinite range of historical, cultural, and musical contingencies." Their edited volume studies the "guitar makers, guitar players, and audiences who imbue guitar music and the instrument itself with a range of values and meanings through

which it assumes its place as a cultural icon." It features essays on guitar cultures all over the world, including those found in India, Papua New Guinea, and Brazil, but strikingly, it omits a chapter on Hawai'i. Dawe and Bennett, *Guitar Cultures*, 1–2.

16. Tranquada and King, in *The 'Ukulele*, provide a wonderful, definitive history of the 'ukulele's development in Hawai'i and subsequent proliferation in the world. I am indebted to their work, and to Jim Tranquada's correspondence and generous sharing of primary documents with me. As they argue, the historical arc of the 'ukulele begins in similar fashion to that of the Hawaiian steel guitar; the two instruments developed around the same time and typically traveled within the same Hawaiian troupes in the early twentieth century. The 'ukulele also generated wildly popular fads in the United States and elsewhere. However, the 'ukulele, as Tranquada and King also demonstrate, ultimately remained a "second class" instrument and failed to gain significant and lasting incorporation into non-Hawaiian music genres, while the steel guitar continued to gather widespread adoption in a variety of other music traditions for decades to come. Perhaps for that reason, then, the 'ukulele remained more widely understood during the second Hawaiian Renaissance of the 1970s as an indigenous instrument, while the steel guitar, associated by the 1970s with many popular, "haole" genres, especially that of country music, seems not to have been as immediately embraced by young Hawaiians.

17. Mitchell, *Kika Kila*.

18. Ruymar, *The Hawaiian Steel Guitar*, 19. Lorene Ruymar's sourcebook comprises an invaluable collection of letters, interviews, articles, and photographs documenting the history of the instrument.

19. For example, see "He Loea Hookani Gita Me Ke Kila," *Kuokoa*, October 27, 1927, 4; translated by nupepa-hawaii.com: http://nupepa-hawaii.com/2013/03/14/daniel-akana-ku-jr-musician-1927/ (accessed May 19, 2015). See also "Holomua Ia Poe Keiki Hawai'i Hookani Pila," *Kuokoa*, August 15, 1919, 2; translated by nupepa-hawaii.com, http://nupepa-hawaii.com/2014/03/10/lei-o-ke-aloha-band-making-music-abroad-1919/ (accessed May 19, 2015). Documents in 'Ōlelo Hawai'i (the Hawaiian language) have provided stunning contributions to this project. The staff, partners, and volunteers for Ho'olaupa'i, Awaiaulu, the OHA's Papakilo Database (www.papakilodatabase.com), and Ulukau (http://ulukau.org) deserve accolades for their work, as do the individuals who care for the nupepa (newspaper) and other document collections maintained by the Bishop Museum, the Hawai'i State Archives, and the University of Hawai'i at Mānoa. The staff at www.nupepa-hawaii.com provided translations for many key documents. They modestly requested that I not single anyone out for gratitude but instead direct readers to their website. Together they are inventorying and analyzing an unparalleled archive of indigenous

experience. Adopting Robert H. Stauffer's approach in *Kahana: How the Land Was Lost*, when I use Hawaiian words in this book, I alter spellings in order to reflect contemporary usage if the pronunciations and meanings are fairly well understood, unless I am quoting from documents. See Stauffer, *Kahana*, ix. This typically translates into adding the ʻokina or kahakō when they are absent in a text. Please accept my apologies in advance for improper syntax or deployment of the language, as I am bound to have made mistakes.

20. Few scholars have explored the history of the steel guitar in depth. For one who has, see Ruymar, *The Hawaiian Steel Guitar*. See also the chapters regarding the development of Chris Knutsen's hollow-necked Hawaiian guitars in Noe and Most, *Chris J. Knutsen*, as well as Kahn, "Steel Guitar Development," parts 1–3, and Tatar, "History of Steel Guitar according to Charles E. King." Some scholars have published encyclopedic entries, chapters, or articles on the instrument or its better-known players. See Hood, "Musical Ornamentation as History"; Kanahele and Berger, *Hawaiian Music and Musicians*; Brookes, "Hawaiian Invasion"; Mitchell, *Kika Kila*; Mitchell and Kanahele, "Hawaiian Steel Guitar"; Okihiro, *Island World*, 169–205; and Todaro, *The Golden Years of Hawaiian Entertainment*. Folklorist Robert L. Stone recently published a book on a unique American religious tradition that emerged from the Hawaiian steel guitar, *Sacred Steel*. A musicologist and a folklorist have recently published dissertations on a descendent of the Hawaiian steel guitar, the pedal steel guitar. See Miller, "Instruments as Technology and Culture," and Barker, "The American Pedal Steel Guitar."

21. Many steel guitarists in the Islands learned to improvise the crafting of finger-picks through cutting metal or repurposing trade goods such as hairpins. "George E. K. Awai Fueled the Hawaiian Music Craze"; Halfon, "The Moe Family," appendix D, "Moe Family Film Outline," 1.

22. A number of monographs and biographies have recently expanded our understanding of the experiences of people of color laboring in the early twentieth-century culture industries. See Brooks, *Lost Sounds*; Brown, *Babylon Girls*; Brundage, *Beyond Blackface*; Chapman, *Prove It on Me*; Chude-Sokei, *The Last "Darky"*; Forbes, *Introducing Bert Williams*; Garon and Garon, *Woman with Guitar*; Gilbert, *The Product of Our Souls*; McGinley, *Staging the Blues*; Miller, *Segregating Sound*; Ovalle, *Dance and the Hollywood Latina*; Sotiropoulos, *Staging Race*; and Troutman, *Indian Blues*. See also Suisman, *Selling Sounds*.

23. Many studies effectively demonstrate the value of making objects of material culture, including musical instruments, the focus of their historical inquiry. See Spector, *What This Awl Means*; Gura and Bollman, *America's Instrument*; Conway, *African Banjo Echoes in Appalachia*; McNeil, *Inventing the Sarod*; Noonan, *The Gui-*

tar in America; Tranquada and King, *The 'Ukulele*; and Waksman, *Instruments of Desire*.

24. The most authoritative study on the influence of Portuguese and Madeiran laborers and luthiers on the emerging Hawaiian guitar culture is Tranquada and King, *The 'Ukulele*. Vaquero culture in the Islands contributed to the paniolo (Hawaiian cowboy) song tradition that arose after the introduction of cattle to the Islands. Trimillos, *Nā Mele o Paniolo*. Musical practice in the Islands was impacted dramatically in the nineteenth century by the musical culture of sailors and the arrival of professional minstrels from the United States. For this history, see Carr, *Hawaiian Music in Motion*, and Wittmann, "Empire of Culture."

25. For an exceptional history of the music industry in the early twentieth century and its relationship to segregation, see Miller, *Segregating Sound*. On the origins of the modern industry genres and their early artists, see also Mazor, *Ralph Peer and the Making of Popular Roots Music*, and Wynne, *In Tune*.

26. For a history of the idea of "Hawai'i" and the stereotypes that proliferated around it in popular American music during the early twentieth century, see Garrett, *Struggling to Define a Nation*, 165–214. See also Tatar, *Strains of Change*; Imada, *Aloha America*; and Imada, "Hawaiians on Tour." For studies of tourism in the Islands, and its relationship with Hawaiian cultural practices, see Brown, "Beautiful, Romantic Hawaii"; Desmond, *Staging Tourism*; Schmitt, *Hawai'i in the Movies*; Bacchilega, *Legendary Hawai'i and the Politics of Place*; and Fojas, *Islands of Empire*.

27. For engaging first-person accounts of the music of the second Hawaiian Renaissance movement, see Burlingame and Kasher, *Da Kine Sound*, and Houston and Kamae, *Hawaiian Son*. On the relationship of that music to protest and sovereignty movements, see Lewis, "Don' Go Down Waikiki"; Lewis, "Storm Blowing from Paradise"; Lewis, "The Politics of Meaning"; Lewis, "Music, Culture and the Hawaiian Renaissance"; Lewis, "Beyond the Reef"; and Lewis, "Da Kine Sounds." For a related study of cultural expression and resistance, see Walker, *Waves of Resistance*.

CHAPTER 1

1. Siddall, *Men of Hawaii*, 215. See also Iaukea, *The Queen and I*.

2. Iaukea, "Whaling in the Days of the Kingdom," 1. Iaukea recalled with fondness that the "Lahaina folk and gentry" particularly enjoyed round and square dances at that time. According to Jim Tranquada, "Since these were Azorean musicians likely playing the twelve-string *viola de dos corações*, the square dances Iaukea refers to might have been the Azorean *chamarrita*." Personal correspondence with Jim Tranquada, May 25, 2015.

3. Or perhaps the guitars Iaukea described were in fact *guitarras portuguesas*, a

variety of instrument related to Spanish guitars but by that time long made to hold five or six pairs of steel strings.

4. Daws, "Honolulu in the 19th Century," 77.

5. Ibid.

6. Ibid., 77–78; Bushnell, *The Gifts of Civilization*, 216–17.

7. Daws, "Honolulu in the 19th Century," 78.

8. Ibid.

9. Bushnell, *The Gifts of Civilization*, 217.

10. Ibid., 217–18.

11. Quoted in ibid., 218.

12. Ibid., 219.

13. Vincent, *Through and through the Tropics*, 92.

14. Nordhoff, *Northern California, Oregon, and the Sandwich Islands*, 28.

15. For a particularly harrowing account, see Bennett, *Honolulu Directory*, 37.

16. Daws, "Honolulu in the 19th Century," 88–89.

17. Fischer, "Cattle in Hawaiʻi," 350, 363; Bergin, *Loyal to the Land*, 33–36.

18. "It seems that the guitar was brought to the Islands from Mexico at a time when there was considerable intercourse between the two countries, in the early part of the century." Quoted in Tatar and Berger, "Slack Key Guitar," 749. For a remarkable description of Hawaiian paniolos driving cattle onto an offshore schooner, see Vincent, *Through and through the Tropics*, 94–95.

19. Trimillos, *Nā Mele o Paniolo*.

20. Tranquada and King, *The ʻUkulele*, 27.

21. Tatar and Berger, "Slack Key Guitar," 749.

22. Ibid.

23. In 1846 an ensemble of students at the Royal School—quite possibly including one or more of the future monarchs Kamehameha IV, Kamehameha V, Kalākaua, and a young Liliʻuokalani, all enrolled at the school at the time—performed on guitar and piano for U.S. Navy chaplain Walter Colton. In 1867 the *Honolulu Advertiser* featured advertisements for guitar lessons by the flamboyant owner-operator of the Royal Hawaiian Theatre, Charles Derby; in the same year, a San Francisco agent of C. F. Martin and Company began marketing guitars to the Islands. Tranquada and King, *The ʻUkulele*, 4.

24. Ibid., 72.

25. "Buke Himeni," *Ka Nupepa Kuokoa*, September 21, 1872, 3; *Guitar without a Master*.

26. "Ka Aha Mele O Kawaiahao," *Ka Nupepa Kuokoa*, May 16, 1868, 3.

27. Henri Berger remarked in 1885 that "at Kaumakapili and Kawaiahao

Churches much enjoyable congregational singing is heard—every one present, chiming in, young and old. Taken altogether, I may say that, although the choir singing is better in the foreign churches, that the congregational singing is far better in the native ones." Berger, "Music in Honolulu," 72. The now long-standing tradition of Hawaiian falsetto singing may have developed in part through the instruction of haole musical instructors and bandleaders in the 1880s such as Theodore Richards at the Kamehameha School for Boys and Henri Berger, then the leader of the Royal Hawaiian Band. Tatar and Berger, "Falsetto," 136–37. According to one recollection, years later, "It was not long [after Richard's arrival] before the class songs and yodels (this latter a nu-hou) of the Kamehameha boys became the talk of the town, and their annual concerts at Kawaiahao church were eminently popular." Thrum, *The Hawaiian Annual for 1925*, 40. Hawaiian composer Charles E. King concurred that Richards used "many native songs" as choir instructor and that he taught (or perhaps encouraged) choir members to yodel. Quoted in Tatar and Berger, "Falsetto," 136.

28. When Yale University ethnomusicologist Helen H. Roberts conducted fieldwork on the south side of Kaua'i in 1923 and 1924, she reported that "perhaps ten people loaned me their books of meles which had been written out in long hand, and most of which had never been published. These I copied on the typewriter and returned the originals promptly. They constitute probably two thirds of my entire Kaua'i collection." Helen H. Roberts, "Report of Work Accomplished for the Hawaiian Legend and Fo[l]klore Commission on the Islands of O'ahu and Kaua'i, Covering Five Months," n.d., Helen Heffron Roberts Papers, group no. 1410, series 1, box 2, folder 62, Sterling Memorial Library, YU, 6.

29. Quoted in Carr, *Hawaiian Music in Motion*, 106.

30. Daws, "Honolulu in the 19th Century," 81.

31. Twain, *Mark Twain's Letters from Hawaii*, 65.

32. Osorio, *Dismembering Lāhui*, 18.

33. Ibid., 10.

34. Ibid.

35. Vicente Diaz writes thoughtfully on the similar relationship between the indigenous Chamorro of Guam and the Catholic church: "One must keep in mind that those who did embrace Catholicism did so under a range of political and social forces, coercive and noncoercive, in ways that force us to remember that the benefits, opportunities, and costs of conversion to Catholicism were not always the same, and were not always the same for everybody. While some Chamorros converted (and did so enthusiastically), others did not. Some profited; others lost out. We must also keep in mind that Chamorros did not necessarily view their conversion to

Christianity and their Chamorro sense(s) of self as mutually exclusive. . . . If Native political and cultural continuity finds expression within the very intrusive systems typically viewed as hostile toward local tradition, the results can be surprising. . . . Recalcitrant Chamorros realized the need to relocate Native cultural and spiritual practices (especially those that were denigrated and demonized by the padres) to someplace safe, somewhere they could not be identified and finally destroyed. . . . In the barrios that became parishes, in the new Catholic calendar of rituals and practices, Chamorros found refuge within the Catholic Church. The refuge can also be seen as a virtual inoculation against the Church itself. . . . This history is illustrated well in the ways that the physical structures of the parish churches, *conventos*, and missionary schools served as literal refuges in times of natural disasters like typhoons (which were understood in providential terms by Spaniard and Native alike) and not-so-natural disasters, like enemy invasions." Diaz, *Repositioning the Missionary*, 20–21, 27–28.

36. Osorio, *Dismembering Lāhui*, 12–13. Jonathan Osorio attributes this idea to Kame'eleihiwa, *Native Land and Foreign Desires*.

37. Osorio, *Dismembering Lāhui*, 11.

38. For examples of Hawaiians who condemned the hula through Christian conventions, see Imada, *Aloha America*, 34.

39. As missionary Gerrit P. Judd derisively wrote, Liholiho, "educated by the Mission, most of all dislikes the Mission. Having been compelled to be good when a boy, he is determined not to be good as a man. Driven out by morning prayer meeting, Wednesday evening meeting, monthly concert, Sabbath school, long sermons, and daily exhortations, his heart is hardened to a degree unknown to the heathen. Naturally he chooses associates whose feelings and practices are in union with his own." Quoted in Daws, "The Decline of Puritanism," 32.

40. Carr, *Hawaiian Music in Motion*, 110.

41. Named Lot Kapuāiwa at birth, Kamehameha V perpetuated the royal rebuke of the Calvinists, in part because a personal aversion to Americans had festered in him since his days as a prince of Hawai'i. At a dinner table aboard a Connecticut River steamboat in 1849, as Frank Vincent Jr., recounted in his travel memoirs years later, Prince Lot was asked to rise from his seat, "as 'no nagurs were allowed to eat with the white folks at the table.'" The prince, Vincent continued, "never forgave the insult." Vincent concluded by stating that Lot's disgust of Americans was only exacerbated by his observations of Gerrit Judd, the condescending missionary who had earlier criticized Liholiho's attitude toward the Calvinists. Vincent, *Through and through the Tropics*, 62.

42. Greer, "Grog Shops and Hotels," 37–38. Clientele and operators comprised

an extraordinary array of individuals from all over the world. One of the earliest tavern owner-operators in Waikīkī, for example, was an escaped slave named Anthony Allen, who, upon fleeing his bondage in German Flats, New York, in 1810, sailed to Oʻahu on a trade ship bound for China. Carr, *Hawaiian Music in Motion*, 103.

43. Daws, "The Decline of Puritanism," 34–35.

44. Pollenz, "Changes in Form and Function of Hawaiian Hulas," 228. At least one early tavern was owned and operated by Hawaiians; Kamoa and Napihi "built a house with a long counter," or a bar, sometime before 1825 on the corner of King and Nuʻuanu Streets, less than two blocks from the waterfront. It is quite possible, for example, that the early hula performances said to have occurred in the entertainment district took place here or in other establishments operated by Hawaiians. Greer, "Grog Shops and Hotels," 52–53. Carr makes this assertion in *Hawaiian Music in Motion*, 105–6.

45. Beattie was Kamehameha I's "chief 'block-maker,' that is, a shipwright specializing in pulleys." Carr, *Hawaiian Music in Motion*, 107.

46. Daws, "The Decline of Puritanism," 32.

47. Ibid.

48. Certainly inquisitive about these technologies and sounds, the aliʻi nui in the first half of the century nonetheless maintained a guarded interest in these productions. After the HMS *Blonde* delivered the measles-stricken bodies of Kamehameha II and Queen Kamāmalu back to the Islands following their fatal visit to London, young Kauikeaouli, next in line to the throne, delighted in a magic lantern and band performance by the ship's crew. Immediately, however, he "was dragged kicking and screaming away from the performance by representatives of the American mission and Queen Kaʻahumanu." Despite the influence of Protestant moral precepts, the lure of such entertainments continued to attract Hawaiians, makaʻāinana and aliʻi nui alike. Carr, *Hawaiian Music in Motion*, 108.

49. Ibid., 108–9, 128. The band featured percussion, brass, and reed instruments. Originally led by African American bandleaders, it enhanced royal events with monarchical pomp and circumstance and remains a fixture in Hawaiʻi through the present day.

50. Wittmann, "Empire of Culture," 107–8.

51. Advertisement, "Royal Hawaiian Theatre!," *Honolulu Advertiser*, June 14, 1879, 2.

52. Blackface minstrelsy emerged on ship decks, in waterfront taverns, and at other crossroads throughout the world, as entertainers established foreign markets for diasporic audiences. Blackface minstrelsy was a form pregnant in significance, as many scholars have considered it principally as a comic class critique of pretension

and elitism, but its inescapable celebration of white supremacy makes it a somewhat unlikely candidate for transference to indigenous peoples in such occupied or colonized regions. While the performances principally lured U.S. and British whites living abroad, however, at least some elements of the performances, especially the instrumentation, attracted indigenous populations in this period. Evidence also demonstrates that some Hawaiian troupes performed minstrel songs in the Islands, while less evidence suggests their use of blackface. James Carr's excellent *Hawaiian Music in Motion* provides the most informative study of minstrel performances in the Islands, and he found at least one mention of a Hawaiian minstrel act "blacking up" their faces for a show; he found another review of the act, by a haole journalist, claiming that the group represented "perfect specimens of Sambos" (167–68). Clearly, however, donning blackface was not common among Kanaka performers, particularly after the 1870s. See also Cole, "Reading Blackface in West Africa," and Waterhouse, "Ripping Yarns of the Pacific." According to Matthew Wittman's "Empire of Culture," blackface minstrelsy was first introduced to the Islands by a troupe on its way to California in 1849 (111). Wittman discusses Hawaiians performing minstrelsy (with no mention of them donning blackface) in an 1862 performance (125).

53. "We were shown yesterday, at the ware rooms of C. E. Williams, a beautiful guitar made entirely of Hawaiian wood, by Mr. Coleman, who has amused himself during his leisure hours, for the past few months, in making this instrument to test not only his own mechanical ingenuity, but the adaptability of our native woods for the manufacture of musical instruments. In both respects Mr. C. has succeeded, no doubt, beyond his own expectation, as he has made an instrument out of native wood which is not only beautiful to look at, but pronounced, by those who know, to be of very fine tone. Eight different kinds of wood have been used in the manufacture of this instrument, all of which has been well seasoned, and a part of it has been known to have stood over 20 years in a house, recently taken down. Persons passing the corner of Fort and Hotel streets, will, for a few days, be able to see the guitar in question, in the show window of Mr. Cleghorn, at that place." "Home Manufacture," *Honolulu Advertiser*, March 5, 1870, 3.

54. Advertisement, *Hawaiian Star*, June 10, 1893, 2.

55. Their introduction to the continent in the 1850s had attracted scant attention beyond that of the U.S. Treasury officials charged with levying a duty on this novelty. "Guitar Strings (Treasury Circular)," *Hunt's Merchant's Magazine and Commercial Review*, July–December 1858, 109.

56. Data on string preferences in this period is admittedly scant, but on the continent, it seems that when steel strings did take on, their selection or rejection ulti-

mately demonstrated class divisions. Middle-class members of the banjo, mandolin, guitar (BMG) movement preferred the soft but expressive sounds of gut even well after the 1920s; in contrast, African American and white rural players seemed to prefer steel-strung guitars, particularly if they played house parties and in dance halls, where they needed the increased volume that steel strings generated in this era before electronic amplification. Noonan, *The Guitar in America*, 118, 135–36. Jim Tranquada notes "one indirect clue about the use of steel strings on the mainland: Sears' 1894 catalog warranted each guitar sold for one year, 'provided no steel strings are used.' The 1897 catalog has this proviso: 'The efforts of the manufacturers are directed toward the production of a rich mellow tone, and in order to accomplish this result they use a sensitively constructed sounding board, which is not made to withstand the strain of wire strings. By using great care some of them will stand this heavy strain without serious detriment, but we wish it understood that we will not be responsible for the failure of a guitar where steel strings are used.' Both the 1894 and 1897 catalogs carried steel, gut, and silvered wire on silk strings." Personal correspondence with Jim Tranquada, May 25, 2015.

57. "The Symphony Club," *Daily Bulletin*, July 10, 1883, 2.

58. Ibid.

59. Tatar and Berger, "Slack Key Guitar," 754–56. Elizabeth Tatar and John Berger also describe the "ornamentals" of the slack key guitar, including chimed harmonics, but early on these ornamentals were exploited to an even greater extent by Hawaiian steel guitarists. See Hood, "Musical Ornamentation as History."

60. As early as the 1870s, Honolulu shops stocked guitars, accordions, banjos, violins, harmonicas, concertinas, tambourines, and more. "New Music Store," *Hawaiian Gazette*, July 24, 1878, 2.

61. Tranquada and King provide the definitive study of this phenomenon in *The 'Ukulele*.

62. Advertisement, *Evening Bulletin*, February 7, 1899, 5.

63. Houston and Kamae, *Hawaiian Son*, 108.

64. Photograph PP-32-9a.023, #2178; and PP-32-9a.016, #20,250, Hawaiians: Hula Dancers & Musicians, Groups-early, Photo Collection, HSA. As Adria Imada recounts, Kaihumua lived a tragically short life, succumbing to mental illness after her institutionalization in a "hale pupule," or insane asylum, in 1897. Imada, *Aloha America*, 145–46.

65. Kaihumua also was a fiercely independent woman and may have been institutionalized for this reason; in her blog, "365 Days of Aloha," Noelani Arista astutely notes that "'Sweet' may have been ironically attached to her name, since her actions in spurning an honest suitor in favor of other men of lesser character, while having

power over even their 'iwi,' gave rise to [the popular mele written about her, 'Aia i Hilo One']. Through it all, this man's affection remained unflagging. . . . Given the mores of Victorian times, it makes 'sense' that spirited, accomplished, and self sufficient women might be punished for their inability to yield to male domination and find themselves among those classed as 'insane.' Other nupepa articles suggest that Emalia may also have been sent to Kalaupapa as a leper (1906)." See https://www.facebook.com/groups/892879627422826/975194872524634/?notif_t=group_activity; accessed May 19, 2015. For insightful analysis of some of the mele written about or by Kaihumua, see Silva, *He Aloha Moku o Keawe*.

66. Quoted in Tranquada and King, *The 'Ukulele*, 52.

67. Photograph PP-32-9a.022, #2214, ID# 01238, Hawaiians: Hula Dancers & Musicians, Groups-early, Photo Collection, HSA. Other photographs of women holding guitars include Photograph PP-32-9a.018, #21,543, Hawaiians: Hula Dancers & Musicians, Groups-early; Photograph (#25454 Copy Negative), PA 11 Photo Album, Hawaii-Around 1900, Photo Collection, HSA.

68. Photograph PP-32-9a.022, #2214, ID# 01238, Hawaiians: Hula Dancers & Musicians, Groups-early, Photo Collection, HSA. Imada, *Aloha America*, 44. For more on hula ku'i, see Stillman, "Hula Reinterpreted in Song."

69. Marques, "Music in Hawai'i Nei," 58.

70. Imada, *Aloha America*, 44. She was also known as Kini Kapahu and Jennie Wilson.

71. Tatar and Berger, "Slack Key Guitar," 750–54. Though the guitar was the dominant accompanying instrument, hula ku'i was also accompanied by the 'ukulele, the taro-patch fiddle, the mandolin, and, in a parlor setting, even the piano. Emerson, "Unwritten Literature of Hawaii," 251.

72. Tatar and Berger, "Slack Key Guitar," 750.

73. Ibid., 752.

74. Ibid., 753. Some of the guitar-driven hula ku'i songs from the late nineteenth century that remain popular today include "'Anapau," "Nā Hala O Naue," "Moanalua," "Maunawili" (derived from a Portuguese song, according to Tatar and Berger), and "Pa'ahana." Ibid.

75. Worrall simultaneously copyrighted the song "Sebastopol," arranged for an open D tuning—both of these tunings became standard in the blues tradition. Obrecht, "Blues Origins." Famed African American classical guitarist Justin Holland (1819–87) published a transcription of "Spanish Fandango" in the 1860s. Perlak, "Justin Holland and the Classical Roots of the American Guitar Sound."

76. Tatar and Berger, "Slack Key Guitar," 751. *'Ohana* translates as "family."

77. Imada, *Aloha America*, 33. As Iaukea's recollection at the beginning of the

chapter indicated, guitars populated the labor camps of non-Hawaiians as well, revealing the changing demographics of the Islands, and the prominent role of the guitar in nearly all of the newly arrived laboring populations and the locals with whom they interacted. According to Ronald Takaki, on holidays such as New Year's Eve, Portuguese singers and instrumentalists "strolled through the [labor] camps dressed in masks and comic costumes, serenading their friends." One might find Native women socializing with these men at "taxi dance halls," where laborers would congregate on paydays. String bands would provide the music, while the foreign laborers "purchased tickets that offered them a momentary escape, three minutes to touch, hold, and dance with a woman." Particularly given the ravages of disease, female survivors sometimes turned to the dance halls to find a much larger pool of marriageable partners. The Hawaiian guitar culture provided them with a new space, and a lightened mood, in which they could interact with these newly arrived Chinese, Portuguese, and Filipino men. Hawaiian musicians seem to have shared the passion for strolling with their instruments. Takaki, *Pau Hana*, 103, 113.

78. Taylor, "Musical Status of Hawaii," 165.

79. Meriwether, *The Tramp at Home*, 280.

80. Taylor, "Musical Status of Hawaii," 164, 166.

81. Berger, "Music in Honolulu," 72.

82. Smith, "Correspondence," 60. Their repertoire included mostly hīmeni and mele, including "Ka'ahupāhau," which over the next century became better known as the beloved "Pūpū A'o 'Ewa," and was performed in a translated version as "Pearly Shells." Tatar and Berger, "Pūpū A'o 'Ewa," 665.

83. The club broke up after Sam Nainoa left for the mainland. By 1944, perhaps the only member still alive was David Kalama, leader of the Kawaiahao church choir. "Editor at Large, That Steel Guitar Story," *Honolulu Advertiser*, October 21, 1944, 4. According to one story, the band was named Kawaihau in honor of a female American missionary who would only drink icy water. "Kawaihau," http://ulukau.org/elib/collect/nawahi/index/assoc/D1.dir/doc137.pdf; accessed May 20, 2015. The Kawaihau Glee Club left strong impressions on those who heard it. Both English- and Hawaiian-language newspapers such as *Ka Lahui Hawaii* covered Kawaihau Glee Club performances, which seemed quite popular in the 1870s. See, for example, "Ka Hui Pu Ana O Ka Hooilina," *Ka Lahui Hawaii*, October 25, 1877, 3; "Huakai ike Makanina a ka Hooilina Moi ke Alii Ka Mea Kiakia Lilikuolani, i ka poe o Hilo i hoopilikia ia e ke Kai Hoee," *Ka Lahui Hawaii*, May 31, 1877, 3. Years later the guitar ensemble would be remembered as an arbiter of "proper," authentic Hawaiian music: a 1911 editorial in the Hawaiian-language newspaper *Kuokoa*, while criticizing some current performers for "following haole style singing" and singing

with an improper vibrato (hoohaalulu), nostalgically praised the music famously rendered by the Kawaihau group in the "old days" and lauded the "many groups [that] in some places around Hawaii nei still practice that way of singing Hawaiian songs." "Pehea E Hoohepaia Mai Nei Na Himeni Hawaii!," *Ka Nupepa Kuokoa,* September 8, 1911, 4; translated by nupepa-hawaii.com: http://nupepa-hawaii.com/2014/06/04/hawaiian-music-and-editorial-1911/; accessed May 20, 2015. Even surfing legend Duke Kahanamoku was at one time a member. See the Spring 1982 issue of *Ha'ilono Mele* for more information on the glee club.

84. "A Rural Fete," *Hawaiian Gazette,* December 11, 1888, 1.

85. "The Choral Club," *Honolulu Advertiser,* December 23, 1898, 2.

86. "Hopes to Revive Musical Hawaii," *Honolulu Star Bulletin,* March 8, 1928, 5.

87. Takaki, *Pau Hana,* 3.

88. Ibid., 4–7.

89. Quoted in ibid., 5.

90. Ibid.

91. Ibid., 7–12.

92. Ibid., 10.

93. Ibid., 11.

94. Jarves, *Scenes and Scenery in the Sandwich Islands,* 102–3.

95. Takaki, *Pau Hana,* 22.

96. Quoted in ibid.

97. Jim Tranquada notes that the family of guitars in the Islands, including the ʻukulele and taro-patch fiddle, generated similar indictments. Personal correspondence with Jim Tranquada, May 25, 2015.

98. "Hawaiian Characteristics," *American Monthly Review of Reviews,* July–December 1899, 213. Abbott goes on to argue that "the Hawaiians are better workers in the canefields than Chinese, Japs, Portuguese, or even whites," and explains his paradoxical description of a lazy, yet hard-working race by claiming that "both of these apparently diametrically opposite characteristics come from the same mental trait—that is, lack of foresight. . . . This lack of forethought and readiness to yield to the desire of the moment makes the Kanaka an ungrateful friend and an unreliable servant, but it also makes him the most hospitable of mankind. . . . As a servant, he goes to his work and does it well for five days. But on the sixth, perhaps a disgust for labor seizes him, and foregetful [*sic*] alike of obligation and future, he lounges or bathes all day without a qualm." Ibid.

99. De La Vernegne, *Hawaiian Sketches,* 74–75.

100. Silva, "He Kānāwai E Hoʻopau I Nā Hula Kuolo Hawaiʻi," 31.

101. Ibid., 33.

102. Ibid., 36.

103. Ibid., 40.

104. "Philippine Tariff Bill," *Far Eastern Review: Engineering, Finance, Commerce*, July 1906, 51–63, 59.

105. "Bonham Herald: A Lot of These Loafing Guitar Pickers Ought to Be Transformed into Active Cotton Pickers," *Galveston Daily News*, October 1, 1904, 6.

106. The Hawaiian Kingdom opened a Honolulu hotel in 1871, and a second hotel opened, this time in Waikīkī, in 1874. Before that, one traveler wrote, "a stranger landing in Honolulu had either to throw himself on the hospitality of the citizens, take his lodgings in the Sailors' Home, or go back to his ship." Nordhoff, *Northern California, Oregon, and the Sandwich Islands*, 20. Despite the "Long Branch" and "Newport" claims in the 1880s, "amenities were primitive in the extreme by comparison with those of the celebrated watering places on the east coast of the United States." Daws, "Honolulu in the 19th Century," 81 n. 19.

107. McGregor, *Nā Kuaʻāina*, 78. Regarding busking, one San Francisco reporter from the period criticized a foreign guitar troupe performance in his city by arguing, "I have heard [guitar-playing] as well done by native boys in Honolulu serenading for a 'hapalua' [half dollar]." Quoted in Tranquada and King, *The ʻUkulele*, 28.

108. While professional Hawaiian musicians occasionally competed with Portuguese ensembles, by the early 1890s most of the professional string bands in the Islands were constituted of Kanaka musicians. *Kamaʻāina* refers to residents of the Islands, regardless of their ancestry.

109. "Hawaiian Hotel: Quintette Club Concert," *Daily Bulletin*, March 30, 1887, 3.

110. Krout, *The Memoirs of Hon. Bernice Pauahi Bishop*, 27. The school was operated by the American Board of Commissioners for Foreign Missions. Osorio, *Dismembering Lāhui*, 160.

111. Liliʻuokalani et al., *The Queen's Songbook*, 2–3. When Leleiōhoku died, Kalakaua named Liliʻu as his successor and composed a mele inoa to commemorate the occasion, "He Inoa No Kalanikauikamoku, Liliʻuokalani." This act lengthened her name to Liliʻuokalani. Ibid., 11.

112. Schoolmaster Amos Starr Coke reported to the mission board that music "is attended to not as a study but as an amusement. It has charms for [the students] and many of their hours of leisure are spent playing on the pianoforte, accordion, and flute. . . . It is very delightful to hear them play on their instruments as accompaniments to their voices. The king, when he visits us, always insists upon their singing and playing." Quoted in Liliʻuokalani et al., *The Queen's Songbook*, 3.

113. Liliʻuokalani et al., *The Queen's Songbook*, 3.

114. According to Mary Krout, the students "were taught in both English and Hawaiian." Krout, *The Memoirs of Hon. Bernice Pauahi Bishop*, 28.

115. Quoted in Tatar and Berger, "Slack Key Guitar," 750. The word *guitar* was often written in English in the papers belonging to the ali'i nui, rather than the Hawaiian word for the instrument, *kīkā*.

116. Quoted in Tranquada and King, *The 'Ukulele*, 31.

117. Kanahele and Berger, "Leleiōhoku, William Pitt," 501.

118. How their interest was first cultivated remains a mystery. There is no indication, for example, that the Royal School provided guitar lessons to the ali'i children who attended. The children often received invitations to board foreign vessels, exposing them to shipboard musical bands; perhaps it was onboard these foreign vessels that they first cultivated their interest in the instrument. Regardless, by the time she reached adulthood, Lili'uokalani, like her brother Leleiōhoku, favored the guitar, as did Kalākaua. Tatar and Berger, "Slack Key Guitar," 750; Lili'uokalani et al., *The Queen's Songbook*, 3. Lili'uokalani also played the autoharp, organ, piano, and the 'ukulele. Even while imprisoned after the overthrow and a failed attempt to restore the monarchy, she composed songs with her guitar and autoharp. Lili'uokalani et al., *The Queen's Songbook*, 8, 16; Tranquada and King, *The 'Ukulele*, 49, 31.

119. Smith, "Correspondence," 60.

120. Lili'uokalani, *Hawaii's Story*, 52–53.

121. Most of Leleiōhoku's popular compositions, Lili'uokalani asserted, were never written down or properly attributed to him, but his more famous songs have endured for over a century, including "Adios ke Aloha" and "Moani ke Ala." Lili'uokalani, *Hawaii's Story*, 52–53.

122. Kanahele and Berger, "Lili'uokalani," 505.

123. Tranquada and King, *The 'Ukulele*, 31.

124. Pukui, "Songs (Meles) of Old Ka'u, Hawai'i," 247–58. Adria Imada argues that "Kaona, as a tactic of enclosure and revelation, demarcated those who could interpret and those not meant to know. Hawaiian performers, I suggest, deployed kaona as a cultural and political resource in their colonial performances and travels; it served as a productive disguise for subtle and more dramatic political critiques and struggles against colonial incorporation." Imada, *Aloha America*, 18–19. See also Arista, "Navigating Uncharted Oceans of Meaning," 663–69.

125. Lili'uokalani et al., *The Queen's Songbook*, 7; Tranquada and King, *The 'Ukulele*, 31.

126. Buck, *Paradise Remade*, 118.

127. Quoted in ibid., 118–19.

128. For the relationship of aupuni and lāhui to concepts of nationhood, see Osorio, *Dismembering Lāhui*, 41.

129. Ibid., 147.

130. Ibid., 157.

131. Ibid., 166–82; Tranquada and King, *The ʻUkulele*, 50.

132. Quoted in Osorio, *Dismembering Lāhui*, 178.

133. Pollenz, "Changes in Form and Function of Hawaiian Hulas," 229.

134. Osorio, *Dismembering Lāhui*, 200.

135. These included a lei niho palaoa, kāhili, or feather standards associated with Hawaiian royalty, as well as an ʻahu ʻula, or feather cloak, that traced to the family of Kamehameha. Ibid., 202.

136. Ibid., 205. Alexander, *History of Later Years of the Hawaiian Monarchy and the Revolution of 1893*, 9.

137. Osorio, *Dismembering Lāhui*, 203–4.

138. Ibid., 224.

139. Ibid., 203.

140. Some Hawaiians were offended by the revival of hula as well. A Hawaiian member of the legislature, George Pilipō, provided the court with what he considered to be the obscene hidden meanings behind the "Hula Kui" and the "Mele inoa." Ibid., 204–5.

141. Quoted in ibid., 203.

142. Ibid., 204.

143. Ibid., 205.

144. Emerson, "Unwritten Literature of Hawaii," 250.

145. Quoted in Imada, *Aloha America*, 44–45.

146. E. W. Barrett, "In the Far East," *Atlanta Constitution*, May 12, 1895, 4.

147. Quoted in Tranquada and King, *The ʻUkulele*, 48.

148. Meriwether, *The Tramp at Home*, 277.

149. Carr establishes the affinity of instrumentation between minstrel groups and Kalākaua's "Singing Boys" in *Hawaiian Music in Motion*, 174–75. Carr refers to the "Singing Boys" as Kalākaua's "own version of a minstrel troupe" because many of their instruments, particularly the bones, likely derived from the minstrelsy tradition imported to the Islands. This claim is quite provocative, and it is clear that Kalākaua attended and enjoyed occasional minstrelsy performances. However, Carr acknowledges that their repertoire beyond Hawaiian mele remains undocumented; whether or not the "Singing Boys" ever performed minstrelsy songs or donned blackface also remains unknown, as no evidence supports either assertion. Ibid.

150. Hopkins, "Ioane 'Ukēkē," 5.

151. One such particular request was made by a man named Ioane, perhaps the famed "Hawaiian dandy" and hula master who often organized Kalākaua's hula events, who requested to stage a "Hawaiian show" on Maui. Ibid.

CHAPTER 2

1. Ruymar, *The Hawaiian Steel Guitar*, contains some brief but helpful accounts of Kekuku's career; no publications on the steel guitar or on Joseph Kekuku include information on his family or childhood.

2. Aikau, *A Chosen People, a Promised Land*, 57.

3. Ibid., 58.

4. Quoted in ibid., 58.

5. Quoted in ibid.

6. Ibid.

7. Stauffer, *Kahana*, 1.

8. Ibid., 4.

9. Aikau, *A Chosen People, a Promised Land*, 60. Stauffer, *Kahana*, 5. See also Preza, "The Empirical Writes Back."

10. Stauffer, *Kahana*, 1. The results of this land tenure "reform" are comparable to the land loss experienced by American Indians through the General Allotment Act of 1887, another privatization scheme that worked to alienate Native people from their homelands.

11. See ibid.

12. Genealogical data maintained by his grandniece, Ka'iwa Meyer, identifies his birthplace at Kahana, O'ahu. I have identified conflicting dates for his birthdate. Meyer's data has his birthdate as December 29, 1875. However, his World War I draft card gives his birthdate as October 19, 1874. On his 1919, 1920, 1922, and 1924 passport applications, he writes his birthday as December 19, 1874. Genealogical records in author's possession, provided by Ka'iwa Meyer, March 1, 2012, registration state California, registration county Los Angeles, roll 1530906, draft board 8, NARA, via http://home.ancestry.com; accessed May 20, 2015; Passport Applications, January 2, 1906–March 31, 1925, collection number: ARC identifier 583830/MLR number A1 534, series M1490, roll 796, NARA, via http://home.ancestry.com; accessed May 20, 2015.

13. Stauffer, *Kahana*, 242.

14. Ibid., 46.

15. Ibid., 61, 68. Keohokālole and her husband, Kapa'akea, created a trust to hold the land with their son, David Kalākaua, in 1856. Ibid., 84.

16. Keohokālole—the mother of King David Kalākaua, Queen Lili'uokalani, Princess Likelike, and Prince Leleiohoku—soon after mortgaged the property. She sold the property through the trust described in the previous note. AhSing was also known as Ahakana or Apakana. Stauffer, *Kahana*, 89.

17. Fujikane and Okamura, *Asian Settler Colonialism*, 17; Nordhoff, *Northern California, Oregon, and the Sandwich Islands*, 74.

18. Nordhoff, *Northern California, Oregon, and the Sandwich Islands*, 71–72.

19. Stauffer, *Kahana*, 87–90.

20. Ibid., 88–89. H. Ahmee was also referred to in legal documents as Ah Mee or Ahmi.

21. Stauffer, "An Early L.D.S. Family of Kahana and Lā'ie," 49. Her granddaughter Viola Kehau Kawahigashi placed Miliama Kaopua's birth at Ka'ao, Honoka'a, Hawai'i. Kawahigashi to "Dearest Missionaries, My Other Brethren & Sisters," March 9–13 and April 1978, MSSH Kawahigashi's Letters, MSSH 245, box 40, Joseph F. Smith Archives and Special Collections, BYUH.

22. Stauffer, "An Early L.D.S. Family of Kahana and Lā'ie," 49.

23. "ma muli o ka noho haku 'ana o ka'u kāne e noho pū ana ia wā 'o ia ho'i 'o Ahmi." Translated by and quoted in Stauffer, *Kahana*, 119. Ahmi's "return to China" should instead refer to his "move to China," if other oral tradition, identifying AhSing and a Kanaka wahine, Mele, as his parents is correct. An alternative scenario to that described here by Miriam, according to oral tradition within the family, is that Ahmee (also referred to in the written record as Ahmi) died in Kahana in 1875, rather than moved to China. Personal e-mail communication from Ka'iwa Meyer, February 2, 2013.

24. Stauffer, "An Early L.D.S. Family of Kahana and Lā'ie," 50–51.

25. This lineage is supported by written communication between the author and Ka'iwa Meyer, the grandniece of Joseph Kekuku. Personal e-mail communication from Ka'iwa Meyer, January 31, 2013. His niece Viola Kehau Kawahigashi noted that "Tutu Miliama's oldest son was one-half Chinese whom Tutu Kane accepted as his son & gave him his name, Joseph Kekuku." Kawahigashi to "Dearest Missionaries, My Other Brethren & Sisters," March 9–13 and April 1978, MSSH Kawahigashi's Letters, MSSH 245, box 40, Joseph F. Smith Archives and Special Collections, BYUH. Additionally, see Stauffer, *Kahana*, 89. It is important to note when researching Joseph K. Apuakehau that throughout his life he was often listed in census and city directories under two surnames, Apuakehau and Kekuku.

26. "Qualifications for Appointment," *The Friend*, August 1931, 188.

27. Quoted in Stover, "The Legacy of the 1848 Māhele and Kuleana Act of 1850," 27–28.

28. According to Jeffrey Stover, Keliiwaiwaiole owned 4.79 acres out of Lā'ie's total parceled acreage of 84.39575 acres. See Stover, "The Legacy of the 1848 Māhele and Kuleana Act of 1850," 162. Though Keliiwaiwaiole reluctantly filed a claim only three days before the deadline, according to Stover, "Cy Bridges, in a discussion with [Stover], stated that Keliiwaiwaiole received his name 'the chief with no property ('aina)' because he declined a land endowment from the King." Ibid., 28 n. 5.

29. "Qualifications for Appointment," *The Friend*, August 1931, 188.

30. 1900 U.S. Census, Koolauloa, O'ahu, Hawaii Territory, roll 1837, page 13B, enumeration district 0036, FHL microfilm 1241837, NARA, via http://home.ancestry.com; accessed May 20, 2015. His high status was also acknowledged by his sister's granddaughter, Ka'iwa Meyer, who stated to me that Joseph K. Apuakehau "was probably the wealthiest man in Lā'ie and respected with his ali'i ranking as well as Peni Keliiwaiwaiole. . . . Miriam was probably high class and of ali'i rank herself coming from Kohala." Personal e-mail communication from Ka'iwa Meyer, February 2, 2013.

31. Personal e-mail communications from Ka'iwa Meyer, January 31, 2013, and February 2, 2013. For his work as luna at Kahuku, see, for example, *Honolulu, Hawai'i, City Directory, 1917*, accessed via http://home.ancestry.com, May 20, 2015. For his work as deputy assessor for Ko'olau Loa and agent to grant marriage licenses in Lā'ie, see, for example, *Honolulu, Hawai'i City Directory, 1905*, accessed via http://home.ancestry.com, May 20, 2015. For listings of Joseph K. Apuakehau as "taro planter," see the 1900 and 1920 census records, where he is identified as Joseph Kekuku. Apuakehau's employment with the Kahuku plantation was noted in city directories under the name Joseph K. Apuakehau and the misspelling Joel K. Apuakehau for several years, while in the same directories his role as assessor was listed under the name Joseph Kekuku. Ka'iwa Meyer, his grandniece, assured me that all these names referred to him and that he held multiple positions and jobs. Personal e-mail communications from Ka'iwa Meyer, January 31, 2013, and February 2, 2013. The 1900 U.S. Census indicates that Joseph K. Apuakehau (listed as Joseph Kekuku) could not read English but was fluent in written and spoken Hawaiian.

32. 1900 U.S. Census, Koolauloa, O'ahu, Hawaii Territory, roll 1837, page 13B, enumeration district 0036, FHL microfilm 1241837, NARA, via http://home.ancestry.com; accessed May 20, 2015. It appears that the senior Kekuku continued to strongly support the LDS Church, even after the disaster at Iosepa. This support led to questionable decisions on one occasion in 1905. He was convinced by the mission president and plantation manager, Samuel E. Woolley, to purchase some kuleana lots from residents and then turn them over to the LDS plantation for a commission. Stover, "The Legacy of the 1848 Māhele and Kuleana Act of 1850," 92.

33. Personal e-mail communication from Ka'iwa Meyer, February 7, 2013b.

34. 1920 U.S. Census, Lā'ie, Honolulu, Hawaii Territory, roll T625_2037, page 7A, enumeration district 142, image 679, NARA, via http://home.ancestry.com; accessed May 20, 2015. During his later years he and his daughter Ivy, who worked at the family store in Lā'ie, reared two of his granddaughters. The granddaughters in the home at that time included Viola, Ivy's daughter, and Eunice, the daughter of Ivy's sister Harriett. Personal e-mail communication from Ka'iwa Meyer, February 7, 2013a. Joseph K. Apuakehau finally retired, either in 1929 or 1930. Honolulu, Hawai'i, City Directories, 1929 and 1930, via http://home.ancestry.com; accessed May 20, 2015.

35. A small community of Native LDS members were living in Lā'ie already, which enhanced the interest of the LDS church in the Lā'ie property. Also attractive to the church was the fact that Lā'ie, as a classic ahupua'a, contained a water source and fertile land stretching to the sea, in addition to productive crops that could immediately generate income for the church. Aikau, *A Chosen People, a Promised Land*, 66.

36. In 1854, the church bought property on Lāna'i, but Lā'ie was particularly attractive to the LDS because its plantation could better "financially support the proselytizing aspects of the mission while also serving as models of industry and wholesome living for Hawaiians." Aikau, *A Chosen People, a Promised Land*, 57, 63.

37. It is clear that Miriam Kekuku regularly sang at church functions and possibly composed music as well. For examples, see "Hawaiian Mission Conference," *Deseret News*, 18; and "Jensen's Travels," *Deseret News*, 13. Joseph Kekuku's sister Violet played organ solos for the congregation as well. See "Conference in the Hawaiian Mission," *Deseret News*, 27. The LDS mission at Lā'ie had employed a music teacher by 1885 named Isaac Fox. "Conferences on the Sandwich Islands," *Deseret News*, 14.

38. Aikau, *A Chosen People, a Promised Land*, 55.

39. An important exception to this assessment, however, is the 1873 effort by the new mission president at Lā'ie, Fredrick A. Mitchell, to ban the production of 'awa (kava), a tuber that Hawaiians harvested as a secondary cash crop (it was believed to provide medicinal benefits; if consumed in large quantity, it also had a narcotic effect). His action caused several families at Lā'ie, facing disfellowship for their refusal to stop growing 'awa, to leave Lā'ie; they established an Ahupua'a Hui to purchase communal lands for their continued production of the crop in Kahana. After the disfellowshipped members petitioned Brigham Young in Salt Lake City to protest Mitchell's actions, Mitchell was relieved of his position as mission president. Ibid., 76. Kester, *Remembering Iosepa*, 147 n. 244.

40. The 1862 Morrill "Anti-bigamy Law," passed in the United States and tar-

geting the LDS, banned "plural marriage" practices and "restricted churches in the territories of the United States from owning land worth more than fifty thousand dollars." The church began to look beyond the United States for opportunities to purchase large tracts of land; it eventually identified Hawaiʻi for this purpose. Aikau, *A Chosen People, a Promised Land*, 65.

41. For a fascinating treatment of the LDS impact on Oʻahu, including the development of the Polynesian Cultural Center, see ibid.

42. Quoted in Barrère, Pukui, and Kelly, "Hula," 47.

43. Smith, "Correspondence," 60.

44. See, for example, "Hawaiian Mission Conference," *Deseret News*, November 10, 1894, 18; and "Hawaiian Mission Jubilee," *Deseret News*, November 19, 1900, 4.

45. ʻAwa was in fact banned in Lāʻie for some time beginning in 1874 by a new, inexperienced haole mission president. Many residents of Lāʻie relocated to Kahana that year in protest, which coincides with the period when Joseph Kekuku was born. Miriam Kekuku, already in Kahana, seems to have played a prominent role in the success of the Kahana Hui, the collective, comprised largely of the disfellowshipped Mormon Kānaka from Lāʻie, that organized to purchase the Kahana ahupuaʻa from her first husband, Ahmee. Stauffer, "An Early L.D.S. Family of Kahana and Lāʻie," 50–51. For information on the "ʻAwa Rebellion," as it became known, and Miriam Kekuku's role, see Kester, *Remembering Iosepa*, 70–73.

46. Harold Davis places the number at "about forty adults and ten children." Davis, "The Iosepa Origin of Joseph F. Smith's ʻLāʻie Prophecy,ʼ" 101.

47. Kester, "Race, Religion, and Citizenship in Mormon Country," 58. Jonatana Nāpela, the first Mormon convert, was also the first Hawaiian Saint to journey to Salt Lake City. A few more "sporadic and temporary" visits by others followed, but it was not until the late 1880s, when Joseph and Miriam brought their children to Utah, that a significant migration of Hawaiians to Utah occurred. Aikau, "Indigeneity in the Diaspora," 486–87.

48. Miliama was pregnant during the journey to Iosepa; she gave birth three months after they arrived, but the female infant died a short time later. Davis, "The Iosepa Origin of Joseph F. Smith's ʻLāʻie Prophecy," 101.

49. They may have had well-informed expectations, however, as Miriam's parents, Ikeole and Kaheana, traveled to Salt Lake City around 1881. Stauffer, "An Early L.D.S. Family of Kahana and Lāʻie," 51.

50. Kester, "Race, Religion, and Citizenship in Mormon Country," 71–72. James Kester writes that this was part of a larger effort to disenfranchise Mormons in Utah, justified here through a racial citizenship calculus. He documents the intense racism against Hawaiians that shaped the Utah media at this time.

51. Ibid., 68–69.

52. Quoted in ibid., 73.

53. Ibid., 75.

54. "Appendix A: Indigent Hawaiians in Samoa and Utah," in Hawai'i Department of Foreign Affairs, *Report of the Minister of Foreign Affairs*, 64–65.

55. Ibid., 65.

56. Interview notes with Viola Kawahigashi, Lā'ie, June 1, 1977. Ken Baldridge faculty file, box 4, Iosepa, BYUH.

57. Stover, "The Legacy of the 1848 Māhele and Kuleana Act of 1850," 85.

58. Bishop also funded a Kamehameha School for Girls, which opened in 1894.

59. Szego, "Musical Meaning-Making in an Intercultural Environment," 63.

60. In her will, Bishop directed her estate's trustees to "devote a portion of each year's income to the support and education of orphans, and others in indigent circumstances, giving the preference to Hawaiians of pure or part aboriginal blood." "1881–1887 Highlights." http://kapalama.ksbe.edu/archives/Archives/Founding,_Boys.html, accessed May 20, 2015.

61. Quoted from correspondence provided by Tom Walsh to the author, May 17, 2013. The story is reproduced in the book on Martin 'ukuleles that Walsh coauthored with John King, *The Martin Ukulele*, 96.

62. Quoted in Ruymar, *The Hawaiian Steel Guitar*, 16.

63. Kupihea had earlier maintained the royal fishponds and was a well-known 'ukulele player. Kupihea identified Hoa also as the "first Hawaiian bandmaster" and noted that he "served under Kamehameha V, Lunalilo, and Kalākaua." Kupihea's claims are questionable, given that no one named James Hoa had ever served as a bandmaster for the Royal Hawaiian Band. Hawaiian music scholar George Kanahele has refuted both the Hoa and Davion claims (see the next paragraph), arguing that if the steel guitar had been in the Islands since 1876, and particularly if it had been featured in the Jubilee celebration, then it would have surfaced somewhere in the written record in the fifteen years or so before Kekuku's introduction. It was simply too novel a style and sound not to have attracted attention: "If Hoa indeed invented the steel guitar in 1876," Kanahele wrote, "why did no other Hawaiian musicians pick it up?" I agree with Kanahele's arguments, for when the steel guitar *does* emerge in the written record years later, notices of the technique spread like wildfire because of its sheer novelty and foreignness. By then, it is already attributed to the adolescent from the Kamehameha School for Boys, Joe Kekuku. Quoted in Ruymar, *The Hawaiian Steel Guitar*, 4. The newspaper article appears in the *Honolulu Advertiser*, January 24, 1932. Kanahele and Berger, *Hawaiian Music and Musicians*, 788–89.

64. Undated program, Charles E. King, Radio Scripts of Bina Mossman's Glee Club, KHU Radio, Sunday, August 2, 1936, to December 16, 1940, H 780 K58r, KSA, 375, 378.

65. See, for example, "Cases Set for the Present Court Term," *Maui News*, March 22, 1918, 8, and "Real Estate Transactions," *Hawaiian Gazette*, March 13, 1908, 7.

66. Ancestry.com, *U.S. City Directories, 1821–1989 (Beta)* [database on-line] (Provo, UT: Ancestry.com Operations, 2011), via http://home.ancestry.com, accessed May 20, 2015.

67. Radio broadcast, March 3, 1939, Charles E. King, Radio Scripts of Bina Mossman's Glee Club, KHU Radio, Sunday, August 2, 1936, to December 16, 1940, H 780 K58r, KSA, 151.

68. Year: 1900; Census place: Honolulu, Oʻahu, Hawaii Territory; roll 1836; page 15A; enumeration district: 0001; FHL microfilm: 1241836; via http://home.ances try.com; accessed May 20, 2015.

69. Year: 1910; Census place: Honolulu, Honolulu, Hawaii Territory; roll T624 _1753; page 12B; enumeration district: 0019; FHL microfilm: 1375766; via http:// home.ancestry.com; accessed May 20, 2015.

70. For a comprehensive survey of the global trafficking of Indian indentured servants, see Tinker, *A New System of Slavery*. My thanks to Indira Karamcheti for directing me to this resource.

71. Undated radio broadcast, Charles E. King, Radio Scripts of Bina Mossman's Glee Club, KHU Radio, Sunday, August 2, 1936, to December 16, 1940, H 780 K58r, KSA, 382.

72. Kanahele and Berger, "Gōttuvādyam," *Hawaiian Music and Musicians*, 203–4.

73. McNeil, "A Mouse, a Frog, the Hawaiian Guitar and World Music Aesthetics," 87.

74. "Troubadours Swap Guitars for Saxophones, Says Charles King," *Honolulu Star Bulletin*, July 16, 1925, 1.

75. Kapua, "Joseph Kekuku."

76. Ibid.

77. Alkire wrote in an unpublished manuscript, likely dating to the 1930s, "There was a popular and widely believed story that a certain Hawaiian player was repairing his Spanish guitar with a railroad spike along the railroad one day when he accidentally touched the strings. There are those who will tell you that this story was manufactured many years after the start of the Hawaiian style and simply served as an introduction in a published method book." Untitled manuscript, folder 7, box 105,

Elbern H. "Eddie" Alkire Personal Papers and Music Instrument Collection, 1926–1997, series 12/9/101, Sousa Archives and Center for American Music, University of Illinois Archives, UIUC. C. S. DeLano claimed that Kekuku told him he had "accidentally" vibrated on his guitar strings a "rusty bolt" that he picked up while walking along a road. After this, DeLano reported, Kekuku began to experiment with the back of a pocketknife, and then with a metal comb. DeLano, "Hawaiian Music."

78. Quoted in Mitchell, Kanahele, and Berger, "Steel Guitar," 790.

79. Noble, "Origin of the Steel Guitar," 34.

80. Roberts, *Ancient Hawaiian Music*, 10.

81. "The History of the Hawaiian Steel Guitar," 7.

82. Cortese, *Roy Smeck*, 11. In oral histories and newspaper interviews with Native Hawaiian steel guitarists, I have found, without fail, support for the claim that Kekuku was the originator of the instrument. See, for example, ʻIwalani Hodges, "Oral History Interview with Benny Kalama," April 29, 1986, Lanikai, Oʻahu, tape no. 12-78-1-86, Center for Oral History, University of Hawaiʻi at Mānoa. See also a 1916 interview with Hawaiian musician James Kahoano and others on the road in El Paso: "Hawaiian Music Made in Germany," *El Paso Herald*, August 24, 1916, 12.

83. "Editor at Large," *Pacific Commercial Advertiser*, October 21, 1944, 4.

84. Ibid. In an unpublished manuscript, Hawaiian guitarist and manufacturer Eddie Alkire, who performed with Alex Hoapili, relayed another version of the origin story: "A more plausible story has been given me by Alex Hoapili whose parents and grandparents vouched for it and knew the families concerned. All of us are acquainted the manner of placing tissue paper on a comb and humming through it. This little trick was popular with Hawaiians and could be heard with Spanish guitar accompaniment wherever parties were in session. The Hoapilis say that at one such party the Spanish guitarist grabbed a comb from a girl's hair and in a playful mood *slid* it up and down the strings. Right there he got an 'idea' which he guarded secretly and began to practice. What he was *up to* leaked out, though, as these things do and a *relative* started on secret practice. So by 1897 there were two families working on the same idea." Based on Hoapili's published 1934 interview (also presumably conducted by Eddie Alkire), we may assume that the two unnamed individuals in this rendition of the story are Joseph Kekuku and Sam Nainoa. Untitled manuscript, folder 7, box 105, Elbern H. "Eddie" Alkire Personal Papers and Music Instrument Collection, 1926–1997, series 12/9/101, Sousa Archives and Center for American Music, University of Illinois Archives, UIUC; emphasis in original. Interestingly, Alex Hoapili reported that after Sam Nainoa began performing with the steel guitar some years later in North America, he claimed to have invented the instrument

himself. However, Hoapili saw this as "sales talk," and said that Nainoa later acknowledged as much and said that it was Kekuku who indeed developed the technique on his own. "The History of the Hawaiian Steel Guitar," 7.

85. Sis Kehau Kawahigashi, letter dated August 25–28, 1973, Lāʻie, Oʻahu, in MSSH Kawahigashi's Letters (1967), MSSH 245, box 40, Joseph F. Smith Archives and Special Collections, BYUH.

86. Meyer interview.

87. "Editor at Large," *Pacific Commercial Advertiser*, October 21, 1944, 4. Bluegrass musicians playing Dobro guitars tend to prefer the Stevens (or a like) bar, which provides a vertical grip for the fingers. "Slide" guitarists distinguish their craft from Hawaiian guitarists now by placing a finger inside a glass or metal tube rather than using a solid bar.

88. D. Kilolani Mitchell, George Kanahele, and John Berger note that Kekuku and his contemporaries developed the raised nut and "designed finger and thumb picks cut out of metal and shaped to fit their fingers." George E. K. Awai knew Kekuku and learned to play the instrument around the turn of the century. He "remembered as a young boy making his own wooden adapter [raised nut] and picks out of metal." Mitchell, Kanahele, and Berger, "Steel Guitar," 791.

89. Roberts, "Hawaiian Music," 76.

90. Elizabeth Tatar, "Slack Key Guitar," 754–56. Mantle Hood suggested that the "glide up to pitch" that characterizes Hawaiian melodies, as performed by singers and steel guitarists, parallels similar ornamentals on the pisendin or rebab in Javanese traditions. Hood, "Musical Ornamentation as History," 143–44.

91. Malcolm Johnson, "Cafe Life in New York: Kanui, Hawaiian Band Leader at the Bossert, Sings Swing in Chinese-Notes," *New York Sun*, August 15, 1939; clipping courtesy of Les Cook.

92. Roberts, *Ancient Hawaiian Music*, 10.

93. Ibid.

94. Imada, *Aloha America*, 108. These firms included Castle and Cooke, C. Brewer, American Factors, Theo H. Davies, and Alexander and Baldwin. Kent, *Hawaiʻi*, 69–72.

95. Jim Tranquada noted in correspondence (May 17, 2015) that the PG relied heavily on the Portuguese population to maintain political power. The Portuguese were considered a separate racial category, neither haole nor white.

96. The 1899 Hawaiian Almanac observed this phenomenon, for example, when it reported "a large number of Hawaiian organizations which go out in serenading parties. They play a combination of instruments, such as the guitar, mandolin, banjo, flute and violin." Thrum, *Hawaiian Almanac and Annual for 1899*, 165.

97. Mohr, *Plague and Fire*, 139.

98. For examples, see "The Choral Club," *Honolulu Advertiser*, December 23, 1898, and Thrum, *Hawaiian Almanac and Annual for 1899*, 165–66.

99. One visitor to the Hawaiian Hotel in 1896, for example, reported that tourists danced "to the music of four Kanaka men, who sing and play at the same time. The instruments are a violin, a banjo, and two guitars." Quoted in Tranquada and King, *The 'Ukulele*, 57.

100. "Church Gets Copy of Hotel March," *Honolulu Advertiser*, February 17, 1905, 10. This dress, of white cloth with red sashes around the waist and ties, became the uniform of Hawaiian string bands from the 1890s well into the twentieth century. Amy K. Stillman notes that this "was a kind of formal wear 'uniform' for entertainers working in the major upscale hotels. The Halekulani's House Without a Key still maintains the dress code." Amy Ku'uleialoha Stillman, *Daily Mele*, August 25, 2015. http://amykstillman.tumblr.com/post/30155134012/august-25-2012-the-red-carnation-lei-on-eddie; accessed May 20, 2015.

101. "Shanghai Hotel Wants a Hawaiian Quintette Club," *Honolulu Advertiser*, February 2, 1905, 1.

102. "The Band Is Now a Big Glee Club," *Honolulu Star Bulletin*, May 10, 1906, 1, 5.

103. Guitars were long associated with women's domestic roles in the United States. See Macleod, "Whence Comes the Lady Tympanist?," 292.

104. Adria Imada writes that "men, including māhū, occupied the highest echelons of hula; they comprised the teachers as well as the elite class of ho'opa'a, the chanters and musicians who may receive further training and advance to kumu hula. Women, on the other hand, occupied an elementary order of hula — they were certainly skilled as dancers, but ordinarily did not undergo secondary and tertiary stages of training as ho'opa'a and kumu hula. Women were not considered the cultural reproducers of hula; men and māhū instead became the favored inheritors of hula genealogies." Imada, *Aloha America*, 39.

105. With few exceptions, women were excluded from professional orchestras in the United States until well into the twentieth century. Macleod, "Whence Comes the Lady Tympanist?," 292. The exceptions included women such as Thelma Ka'ai, who performed steel guitar in the 1920s with the bands of her uncle Ernest Ka'ai. See, for example, "Big Success of the Hawaiian Troupe," *Straits Times*, November 29, 1921, 10.

106. Adria Imada's work provides us with remarkable accounts of how female dancers reacted to the overthrow. See Imada, *Aloha America*.

107. "Will Follow the Band," *Boston Daily Globe*, February 25, 1893, 10.

108. "Hawaiian Music Will Live." The *Paradise of the Pacific* article, rather than providing the reason for the musicians' departure, refers to their action as a "rotten banana shower [that] interrupted the progress of Hawaiian music. . . . When the Republic days arrived [Berger] found himself without the Hawaiian members who had previously made up practically its entire personnel" (122). Another article gives the date as February 2, 1893, after their performance or the departure of the steamship *Australia*. "Will Follow the Band," *Boston Daily Globe*, February 25, 1893, 10. Jim Tranquada identified the five who remained as David Naone, Robert S. Kapua, Gomes, Santana, and Lakala or Lokala. Personal correspondence with Jim Tranquada, May 23, 2015.

109. Tranquada and King, *The ʻUkulele*, 52.

110. Amy Stillman discovered a previously unknown publication of the song in 1895, attributed to the director of the band, Jose S. Libornio. Stillman, "ʻAloha Aina.'"

111. Quoted in Nordyke and Noyes, "ʻKaulana Nā Pua,'" 28. It is possible that they adopted the phrase of eating stones to spite Henri Berger, who, according to one newspaper account, allegedly told them that "later you will eat stones" after they refused to sign the oath. "Hoolaulea Kanalima Makahiki," *Ka Makaʻainana*, August 6, 1894, 1; translated by nupepa-hawaii.com: http://nupepa-hawaii.com/2015/04/18/henry-bergers-50th-birthday-and-commentary-on-eating-stones-1894/#more-18267; accessed June 8, 2015.

112. The song was earlier known variously as "He Lei No Ka Poʻe Aloha ʻAina" ("A Symbol of Affection for the People Who Love Their Land"), "Mele ʻAi Pōhaku" ("Stone-Eating Song"), and "Mele Aloha ʻĀina" ("Patriot's Song"). Ibid., 27.

113. Translated in Elbert and Mahoe, *Nā Mele o Hawaiʻi Nei*, 63–64.

114. "Rousing Ovation," *Daily Bulletin*, March 23, 1893, 2.

115. Ibid.; quoted in Tranquada and King, *The ʻUkulele*, 52.

116. Of these hula kuʻi, 144 were published in 1895. Stillman, "History Reinterpreted in Song," 2; translation by Stillman.

117. Adria Imada describes the significance of these mele as performed by a hula and string band troupe that traveled to the United States in the 1890s: "Poʻe hula and musicians deliberately performed chants and compositions written by or for aliʻi of the Kalākaua line, those who had been deposed through military force and annexation. The Hawaiian musicians performed songs that soon became popular with American audiences, such as ʻAloha ʻOe,' ʻKuʻu Pua i Paolakalani,' and ʻLei Poni Moi.' These mele were indelibly associated with the deposed queen Liliʻuokalani, who had composed them, while they activated ties between the performers and their sovereigns." Imada, *Aloha America*, 124–25.

118. Musicians also sang mele with kaona, or hidden meanings, while Liliʻuokalani published mele in the newspaper *Ka Makaʻainana* while she was imprisoned in order to offer Hawaiians support and reassurance. Tranquada and King, *The ʻUkulele*, 52.

119. Asensio, "Language Policy," 12; Lucas, "E Ola Mau Kākou I Ka ʻŌlelo Makuahine," 8.

120. Quoted in Lucas, "E Ola Mau Kākou I Ka ʻŌlelo Makuahine," 8.

121. Ibid., 9.

122. Imada, *Aloha America*, 75–76.

123. Ibid., 49–50.

124. Ibid., 50.

125. Kanahele and Berger, "Mekia Kealakaʻi," 459–60; "Hawaiian Music Will Live," 122.

126. Quoted in Imada, *Aloha America*, 114–15. George Kanahele dated the encounter with Sousa to an 1895 tour with Ka Bana Lahui, but Imada's research suggests otherwise. Imada, *Aloha America*, 303 n. 43. Despite Kealakaʻi's stated fondness for Berger, his departure from the band may have been hastened by the fact that Berger, as Kealakaʻi recalled, "hit him on the head with his baton so often that he grew a callus." Kanahele and Berger, "Mekia Kealakaʻi," 459. "Hawaiian Music Will Live," 122.

127. Kealakaʻi was born in the barracks of King Kamehameha V, as his father was a sergeant major in the royal guard at the time. *Mekia* translates in English as "Major." "Notes and Comments," *Paradise of the Pacific*, October 1905, 21; "Hawaiian Music Will Live," 122.

128. Quoted in Tranquada and King, *The ʻUkulele*, 64–65.

129. Quoted in ibid., 65–66.

130. Liliʻuokalani's sentence was commuted, but she was forced to live under house arrest in one room in ʻIolani Palace for several months, then under house arrest at her private home. She was forbidden from leaving Oʻahu for another eight months. "Queen's Imprisonment," http://www.iolanipalace.org/SacredPlace/History.aspx; accessed May 20, 2015.

131. Ernest Kaʻai (1881–1962), who played several stringed instruments, became Honolulu's "top impresario" of Hawaiian string bands by the early 1900s and eventually toured the world, from Australia to India, Burma, Java, China, and the U.S. continent. He was closely linked to the monarchy, being the son of Simon Kaʻai, Kalākaua's one-time minister of interior and finance, a member of the House of Nobles, and an ardent royalist. July Paka (1874–1943), one of the most important first-generation kīkā kila players, and one we will discuss further in the next chapter, was also tied to the monarchy. The son of Juliana Walanika from Mānoa Valley,

O'ahu, a favorite singer and dear friend to Kalākaua and Lili'uokalani, Paka came of age in Kalākaua's court. Walanika performed on O'ahu throughout the 1880s and during Kalākaua's Jubilee festivities in 1886; a little over ten years later, her son July (aka Iolai) left the Islands as the guitarist and vocalist who would come to introduce, with Joseph Kekuku, some of the first steel guitar sounds to the United States. "Hawaiian Music Will Live," 122; Kanahele, "Ernest Ka'ai," 3; Tranquada and King, *The 'Ukulele*, 59; U.S. Selective Service System, World War I Selective Service System Draft Registration Cards, 1917–1918, M1509, registration state: Wisconsin; Registration, NARA, via http://home.ancestry.com; accessed May 20, 2015; "The Tableaux," *Daily Herald*, November 29, 1886, 3.

132. "Hookohu Peresidena Nui," *Ka Maka'ainana*, December 7, 1896, 1, 7; see also "Ahahui Aloha Aina," *Ka Maka'ainana*, November 30, 1896, 1.

133. "Kue: The Hui Aloha Aina Anti-annexation Petitions, 1897–1898," Hawaiian Collection, HLUHM, http://libweb.hawaii.edu/digicoll/annexation/petition/pet801.htm; http://libweb.hawaii.edu/digicoll/annexation/petition/pet800.html; http://libweb.hawaii.edu/digicoll/annexation/petition/pet259.html; accessed May 21, 2015. All of the Kekukus signed the petition in Lā'ie's district of Ko'olauloa; one Joseph Kekuku is listed in the petition as a thirty-nine-year-old, which reveals this Kekuku to be the guitarist's father, Joseph Kekuku'upenakana'iaupuniokamehameha Apuakehau, who was born in 1857. The other is listed as twenty-one years old, which places him within one or two years of his presumed (though unverified) birth month of December 1874. No other Joseph Kekuku of near this age lived on the island of O'ahu at this time. Therefore this, beyond reasonable doubt, is the guitarist. On the significance of the Hui Aloha 'Āina petition, see Silva, *Aloha Betrayed*, 123–63.

134. Kester, *Remembering Iosepa*, 147. Unfortunately, by the 1920s, much of those resources were again lost to hāole as the Kahana hui and others were liquidated. Stauffer, *Kahana*, 125.

135. Cluff, "The Hawaiian Islands and Annexation," 435.

136. Ibid., 442–43. According to Cluff, Kekuku and most of the others agreed that if no country in the world would help them restore the queen, then they would accept annexation.

137. Ibid., 436.

138. Ibid., 446.

139. Ibid., 443.

140. Many Honolulu musicians were "young men who have not had the opportunity to receive the best education, and their occupations do not command big wages. The opportunity to play and sing in quintet clubs opens the way to earn all

the way from $1.50 to $3 a night, affording a fund with which they can almost support a family." "To License Quintet Clubs," *Hawaiian Gazette*, February 2, 1909, 2. Thanks to Jim Tranquada for sharing this article with me.

141. "Before Judd, C. J., Tuesday, April 28," May 5, 1891, *Hawaiian Gazette*, 5.

142. "Robertson McFarren Family History and More," http://myfamilyjourneys.com/RobertsonMcFarrenGenealogy/f600.htm#f4020; accessed May 29, 2012.

143. Advertisement, *Evening Bulletin*, July 14, 1897, 5. Interestingly, a 1917 pamphlet from Bergstrom Music Company in Honolulu suggests that the steel guitar did not take hold in the Islands until 1913 or 1914. This timing is contrary to the accounts of Kekuku's classmates and others who recounted the steel guitar's rapid popularity in the Islands immediately following his development of the instrument. It is possible that this pamphlet instead acknowledges the instrument's growing popularity following the introduction of hundreds of Hawaiian guitar recordings produced between 1909 and 1916. R. A. D. Beaty, *Hawaiian Music and Musical Instruments*. I thank Jim Tranquada for bringing this pamphlet to my attention.

144. For examples, see "Hawaii Ponoi," *Evening Bulletin*, December 26, 1901, 2; "Concert by Natives," *Evening Bulletin*, October 9, 1902, 2.

145. "How Keliimiola Took the Witness Stand," *Honolulu Republican*, September 15, 1900, 1; "Mrs. Tewksbury Given Freedom," *Evening Bulletin*, September 13, 1900, 1; Census records: Year: 1900; Census place: Honolulu, Oʻahu, Hawaii Territory; roll 1837; page 10A; enumeration district: 20; FHL microfilm: 1241837; via http://home.ancestry.com; accessed May 20, 2015. Treasury Department, *Report of the Treasurer of the Territory of Hawaii*, 120. The U.S. Census indicates that he was living at 103 Rice Mill Road, whose name, according to Stauffer, seems to have been changed to Trout Farm Road some years later. Stauffer, *Kahana*, 149.

146. "Gone to Frisco," *Hawaiian Star*, July 16, 1904, 5; "Local Brevities," *Hawaiian Gazette*, July 19, 1904, 4.

147. "Local Brevities," *Hawaiian Gazette*, July 19, 1904, 4.

148. "Kekuku's New Method," *Evening Bulletin*, July 22, 1904, 1.

CHAPTER 3

1. Both traveled there with fellow Hawaiian musicians Tony Zablan, Tommy Silva, and David Makuakane, under the direction of William Kualii Sumner Ellis. Topolinski, "Ellis Brothers," 131. Rockwell, *Hawaiian and Hawaiian Guitar Records*, ix.

2. Personal correspondence with Jim Tranquada, May 23, 2015; Rockwell, *Hawaiian and Hawaiian Guitar Records*, 917.

3. "Some Tales from Buffalo," *Pacific Commercial Advertiser*, December 5, 1901, 3; Tranquada and King, *The 'Ukulele*, 80.

4. Kanahele and Berger, "William Miles," 546. Albert G. Duck of Waynesburg, Ohio, filed an intriguing patent application in 1894 for a guitar-like instrument that featured an open tuning and a bar very closely resembling some of the early, flat, rectangular steel bars that the first generation of Hawaiian guitarists developed. It is unclear whether he had visited the Islands or whether he developed the concept independently, but it did not, apparently, move beyond the conceptual or prototype stage. Patent no. 587,089, filed June 30, 1894, patented July 27, 1897, U.S. Patent Office.

5. Berger, "Frank Ferera," 152. What is less clear is whether Ferreira mastered the steel guitar before or after his arrival in the continental United States. The same uncertainty applies to Paka and Puni.

6. Quoted in "Hawaiian Boys Are Best Ever," *Hawaiian Gazette*, July 7, 1905, 5.

7. "Sonny Cunha's Singers Do Well at Santa Cruz," *Pacific Commercial Advertiser*, June 30, 1905.

8. W. D. Adams traveled along the West Coast, East Coast, and through the Midwest of the United States during the summer of 1916. At all the summer resorts, cabarets, and theaters he visited save one, he heard Hawaiian music. "Those who visited the San Francisco fair," he wrote, "will agree that that one institution is more responsible [f]or the craze for our music and instruments that is now sweeping the country than any other agency. The medium through which our music gets its best advertisement, no doubt, is through the Victor Talking Machine Company's efforts in this direction." That year Adams spoke at a "jobber's" convention in Atlantic City, a national gathering that attracted record and Victrola machine distributors and dealers from throughout the country: "I . . . took this opportunity," he wrote," to ask this body of men what records had had the biggest sale over the past twelve months. Every jobber was unanimous in stating that the Hawaiian records placed on the market the last year had reached larger sales with them than any other popular records." Adams, "The Popularity of Hawaiian Music and Musical Instruments," 142–43. The September 1916 issue of the *Edison Phonograph Monthly* likewise reported that "the biggest popular hits of this season are all Hawaiian songs and the demand for records of these is widespread and insistent." "Hawaiian Music Universally Popular," *Edison Phonograph Monthly*, September 1916, 3.

9. "Advertised Letters," *Aberdeen Herald*, April 5, 1906, 1; advertisement, "Pantages Theater," *Bellingham Herald*, March. 7, 1907, 7. I thank Jim Tranquada for sharing these newspaper references with me.

10. "Hawaiian and Guitar," *San Jose Evening News*, April 23, 1907, 3.

11. Ibid.

12. "Thaw Case at the Unique," *Los Angeles Herald*, June 11, 1907, 5.

13. Knutsen's given name was Johan Christian Kammen.

14. Noe and Most, *Chris J. Knutsen*, 7–15.

15. Ibid., 48.

16. One such student was Paul Goerner, while another, in Los Angeles, was Charles S. DeLano. Goerner became a music teacher in Seattle in 1910 and attributed his instruction to Kekuku in a Gibson instruments catalog, while DeLano became deeply involved in fueling the Hawaiian steel guitar craze through his performances, compositions, and publishing of sheet music and method books. Manuel Nunes, one of the best-known builders of ʻukuleles in the Islands, had been producing koa wood Hawaiian steel guitars in Honolulu since at least 1910. Ibid., 48, 51.

17. Ibid., 48–51.

18. Knutsen likely secured his first samples of koa wood from the supply available in the Hawaii Building at Seattle's 1909 Alaska-Yukon-Pacific Exposition, where Ernest Kaʻai's Hawaiian troupe, and likely Kekuku himself, played for many of the 3.7 million attendees. Ibid., 45, 51. Knutsen's earliest Hawaiian guitars that remain intact are dated to 1909 and feature convertible necks that can be quickly adjusted to raise and lower the strings in relation to the fretboard, allowing the instruments to be played in the conventional or Hawaiian steel style. Ibid., 53. On the strength of hollow-neck guitars, see Cundell, "Across the Pacific," 29.

19. Teves interview. U.S. Selective Service System, World War I Selective Service System Draft Registration Cards, 1917–1918, M1509, registration state Wisconsin, registration county Douglas, roll 1674993, draft board 1, NARA, via http://home.ancestry.com; accessed May 20, 2015.

20. "The Tableaux," *Daily Herald*, November 29, 1886, 3; "Come One! Come All! Grand Concert," *Daily Bulletin*, December 14, 1883, 3.

21. Topolinski, "Ellis Brothers," 131.

22. Tranquada and King, *The ʻUkulele*, 69. The troupe included Kanaka musicians William Ellis, Tom Hennessey, William Kai, and Thomas Kiliwa.

23. Ibid.

24. Imada, *Aloha America*, 114.

25. "Lei Awapuhi" sheet music, box 6, folder 34, John Henry Wilson Papers, HSA. See also Imada's discussion of the song in *Aloha America*, 149–50.

26. Bierley, *Hallelujah Trombone*, 35. Note that this book incorrectly names Hannah's husband in 1904 as Ned, not July. Ned was the name of her son with her first husband, Will Whitford. My thanks to Barbara Roddy for sharing her research on her family. Personal correspondence with Barbara Roddy, April 18, 2013.

27. They married on October 21, 1903; his surname was listed incorrectly as "Parker." Personal correspondence with Barbara Roddy, February 25, 2010; April 18, 2013.

28. "Under the Tents," *New York Clipper*, May 20, 1905, 335.

29. Bierley, *Hallelujah Trombone*, 38–39; "Notes from Wm Altherr's Dog and Pony Circus," *New York Clipper*, November 18, 1905, 986.

30. Advertisement, *Bellingham Herald*, December 14, 1906, 6.

31. Tranquada and King, *The 'Ukulele*, 80–83. For more information on the Ellis Brothers Quartet and Glee Club, see Topolinski, "The Sumner Family."

32. It is unclear whether Paka knew Kekuku when both lived on O'ahu.

33. See, for example, advertisement, "The Atlas," *Cheyenne Daily Leader*, August 19, 1908, 5.

34. Revell, "The Dance Spectacle Dominates Vaudeville," 212; "New Acts of the Week," *Variety*, September 19, 1908; Lee and Casey, *Making the Irish American*, 408.

35. "New Acts of the Week," *Variety*, September 19, 1908.

36. "Toots Paka's Hawaiians," *Variety*, May 15, 1909.

37. For Kanahele and Berger's chronology of Hannah and July's workplaces their first collaborative efforts at 1899, see their "Toots Paka's Hawaiians," 826. I believe that Hannah and July likely first met around 1902, somewhere in the Midwest. Given newspaper coverage of their performances, I date their contract with Pat Casey to either shortly before or soon after their September 1908 debut on the New York vaudeville stage.

38. "Hawaiian Stars in Musical Comedy," *Hawaiian Gazette*, May 17, 1910.

39. Not every review of Kekuku's "The Rosary" performance was positive, though most were. Percy Hammond, the high-minded Chicago critic whose reviews consistently disdained the Paka troupe and their audiences, wrote that "they change the melody of 'The Rosary' into an imitation of somebody seasick, and their nauseous and discordant strains are much approved. Four handclaps win an encore." Hammond, "In Vaudeville and Elsewhere," *Chicago Daily Tribune*, January 12, 1916.

40. Kapua, "Joseph Kekuku."

41. "Bassie McCoy Begins Tomorrow," *Philadelphia Inquirer*, October 30, 1910; *Los Angeles Times*, May 27, 1912.

42. "Good Bill at Brighton," June 15, 1909, *Brooklyn Daily Eagle*, 5.

43. Ibid.

44. "Practice and Patience All That Is Necessary to Play Hawaiian Airs," *Atlanta Constitution*, August 16, 1916, 6.

45. "Hawaiian Music Made in Germany," *El Paso Herald*, August 24, 1916, 12. "Kulainoheo" is certainly a misspelling of her surname, which I have been unable to identify.

46. Ibid.

47. Ibid.

48. "This Week," *Los Angeles Times*, May 19, 1912, III:1–2.

49. Though the Hawaiian musicians knew she was haole, Hannah Jones seems to have told a variety of stories in the mainland U.S. press that linked her to the Islands. In the most informative interview on this matter that I have located, she told a reporter, "Oh, yes, I guess I'm a haoli [*sic*]! . . . I guess I'm two peoples. But when I'm dancing, I feel Pele, goddess of thunder and the volcano, is true; and in my sun-dance, I worship like my mother." The reporter later claimed that her mother was "principal dancer" to Queen Lili'uokalani, and that her father was American: "When she was a tiny child, her father brought her over here. But the lure of the elemental was too strong for her. Ten months she dresses and eats and behaves like other people. Then [she] must go back to her people." Kingsley, "Says, Toots, 'Thees Li'l Danze Are Vur Much Many Li'l Danze.'"

50. "Joseph Kekuku," *Los Angeles Times*, May 27, 1912, II:5.

51. Smith, *Bert Williams*, 8–9. Williams was born in Nassau, the Bahamas, but was raised first in New York City, then in Riverside, California.

52. "This Week," *Los Angeles Times*, May 19, 1912, III:1–2. A theater gossip column in a 1911 edition of the *Washington Post* remarked that "Toots Paka was one of the most stylishly gowned young women on F Street more than one afternoon last week." "Playhouse Patter," *Washington Post*, April 30, 1911, 37.

53. "Kekuku's Hawaiian Quintet," *Wray Rattler*, November 16, 1916, 1.

54. Commercially available Hawaiian music was then in quite limited circulation, but it included sides by the Honolulu Students and ones recorded in Honolulu by Victor in 1905.

55. Kekuku is listed in Edison promotional materials by the name of Joseph Kakuku. "Advance List of Hawaiian Edison Records," *Edison Phonograph Monthly*, December 1909, 28. Rockwell, *Hawaiian and Hawaiian Guitar Records*, 917; "Toots Paka's Hawaiians," *Edison Phonograph Monthly*, July 1911, 10.

56. Cunha (1879–1933) was born Albert R. Cunha.

57. Kanahele and Berger, "Albert R. 'Sonny' Cunha," 114–16. Cunha attended Yale Law School from 1898 to 1900 but returned to the Islands before he could graduate. He toured the U.S. continent several times. Personal correspondence with Jim Tranquada, May 23, 2015; Noble, "Hawaiian Musicians in the Jazz Era," 22.

Cunha's first hapa haole composition was "My Waikiki Mermaid" (1903), while the very first hapa haole composition as identified by Kanahele and Berger is "Eating of the Poi" (1888). Kanahele and Berger, "Albert R. 'Sonny' Cunha," 115.

58. Lucas, "E Ola Mau Kākou I Ka 'Ōlelo Makuahine," 8.

59. Rockwell, *Hawaiian and Hawaiian Guitar Records*, 917–20. The song titles included "Aloha Oe," "Wai'alae," "Pulupe," "Tomi Tomi," "Kaowe Ake Kai," "Lia Ika Wai Mapuna," "Ahi Ahi Poakolu," "Kamawae," "Popoakalu," "Liaika Wai Mapuna," "Rain Tuahine," "Lei Rose O Kawika," "Moanikeala," "Ko Maka Palupalu," "Aw Auaula," "He Lei No Kaieulani," "Hula O Kilauea," "Adios Kealoha," "Lei Ohaoha," "Lei Aloha," "Lanihuli," "Hoo Mau," "He Inoa No Waipio," "Kalai O Pua (Dedicated to King Kalākaua)," "Aloha No Mau I Ko Maka," "Poli Pumehana," "Halona," "Ho'omana'o Oe A Hiki Oe," "Akahi Hoi" (Kalākaua), "Lei Awapuhi," "Ko Maka Palupalu," "Aw Aiaula," "Aloha No Mau I Ko Maka," "Halona," "Kai Malino," "Ipu Lei Manu," "Paahana," and "Ua Like No A Like." It was not until their final sessions of 1919 and 1920, long after Kekuku had left the group and shortly before they retired the act, that the Pakas ventured any further into recording songs by non-Hawaiians.

60. Samoan Hawaiian steel guitarist Tau Moe recounted listening to a wax cylinder featuring Kekuku in 1918, while living on O'ahu. Ruymar, *The Hawaiian Steel Guitar*, 21.

61. "Hoots! Toots Paka and July in Town," *Hawaiian Gazette*, June 14, 1912, 7.

62. According to the *Pacific Commercial Advertiser*, she spent a few months on O'ahu in 1909 "in order that [she] could learn something of the Hawaiian music and dances at first-hand. She studied the music carefully, and acquired an intimate knowledge of the hula, and became an accomplished dancer." "Hawaiian Singers Make Big Hit on Broadway," *Pacific Commercial Advertiser*, March 17, 1910.

63. Kingsley, "Says, Toots, 'Thees Li'l Danze Are Vur Much Many Li'l Danze.'" It is unclear whether she trained with a kumu hula (hula master). Hula ku'i were the dances associated with mele composed with or for the accompaniment of guitars, 'ukuleles, and other instruments. 'Pūili, and kāla'au refer to split bamboo rattles/sticks and hard wood rhythm sticks, accordingly. 'Ōlapa, or dancers, use both to accompany oli, or chants.

64. Ibid. Hula 'āla'apapa is lesser-known hula genre of the Kamehameha dynasty that predates the modern hula kui of the Kalakaua era. Stillman, *Sacred Hula*.

65. "Hawaiian Boys Who Left Islands for Outside World Are 'Making Good' All Over Mainland," *Honolulu Star Bulletin*, January 4, 1913, 5.

66. Advertisement, *Variety*, October 17, 1908, 23.

67. MacKenzie, *Tandy*, 45–46.

68. "Hawaiians on the Mainland Do Well," *Hawaiian Gazette*, August 30, 1912, 4.

69. Ibid.

70. Ibid.

71. "Old Kam" refers to the Kamehameha School for Boys on Oʻahu.

72. "Hawaiian Boys Who Left Islands for Outside World Are 'Making Good' All Over Mainland," *Honolulu Star Bulletin*, January 4, 1913, 5.

73. The eighteen-month-old daughter of Aeko and his wife was named Momi. "Hawaiian Baby Christened," *New York Times*, March 14, 1912, 11.

74. Balme, "Selling the Bird."

75. Quoted in Tranquada and King, *The ʻUkulele*, 77.

76. "*Passers-By* Most Promising of New Plays in Other Cities," *Christian Science Monitor*, September 16, 1911, 12. Debuting in September of that year, local critics chronicled the revisions and generally heaped much praise on the play. Julian Johnson, "Illington Real Juliet," *Los Angeles Times*, September 18, 1911, II:5.

77. After another staging in Rochester, New York, Tully found producers and investors willing to run the play on Broadway. It debuted at Daly's Theater before quickly relocating to Maxine Elliot's Theatre. Kanahele and Berger, "'The Bird of Paradise,'" 78.

78. Honolulu, Hawaii, 1912 City Directory, 213, ancestry.com. *U.S. City Directories, 1821–1989* [database on-line] (Provo, UT: Ancestry.com Operations, 2011), via http://home.ancestry.com, accessed May 20, 2015.

79. The Victor recording notes, detailing their three sessions in April 1913 as the Hawaiian Quintette, provide this assignment of their instruments, although it is clear that many of these musicians were well-versed in a variety of stringed instruments. The "banjo ukulele" the notes refer to may in fact be a taro-patch fiddle. "Walter Kolomoku," *Discography of American Historical Recordings*, http://victor.library.ucsb.edu/index.php/talent/detail/57880/Kolomoku_Walter_instrumentalist_steel_guitar; accessed May 21, 2015.

80. Kanahele and Berger, *Hawaiian Music and Musicians*, 79.

81. "Hawaiian Boys Who Left Islands for Outside World Are 'Making Good' All Over Mainland," *Honolulu Star Bulletin*, January 4, 1913, 5.

82. Kanahele and Berger, "'The Bird of Paradise,'" 78.

83. "Belasco—'The Bird of Paradise,'" *Washington Post*, December 24, 1912, 5; "News Notes of the Stage," *Washington Post*, March 21, 1915, 67.

84. "'Bird of Paradise' Coming," *Nevada State Journal*, November 2, 1913, 2; "Coming Attractions," *Anaconda Standard*, December 7, 1913, 2.

85. Advertisement, *Indianapolis Sunday Star*, September 6, 1914, 38; "'Bird of Paradise' of the Victoria," *Xenia Daily Gazette*, October 4, 1915, 3.

86. "Chats Over the Tea Cup," *Des Moines Daily News*, July 30, 1916, 5.

87. "The Bird of Paradise," *Daily Democrat-Times*, March 14, 1918, 4.

88. Advertisement, *Anniston Star*, March 31, 1918, 2. See also advertisement, *Daily Democrat Times*, March 5, 1918, 7.

89. "No Lazy Man's Place," *Hartford Republican*, August 30, 1918, 6.

90. Desmond, *Staging Tourism*, 66.

91. Kanahele and Berger, "Panama-Pacific International Exposition," 634.

92. Todd, *The Story of the Exposition*, 323.

93. Ibid.

94. "Fully seventy-five per cent of the boys got east aboard the American-Hawaiian fleet. They shipped out of Honolulu in the crew and after getting their discharges were able by degrees to get started into the more agreeable line of music." "Hawaiian Boys Who Left Islands for Outside World Are 'Making Good' All Over Mainland," *Honolulu Star Bulletin*, January 4, 1913, 5.

95. The Hawaiian Pavilion committee became consumed with the matter, which seemed to escalate into a politically volatile concern. In November of that year it requested the leading contenders, the Ka'ai Glee Club and Jonah Kumalae's Glee Club, to audition in a contest before them. Ernest Ka'ai at first refused the request, asking the committee members to instead attend an upcoming performance at the Moana Hotel. Ka'ai's string band dominated Honolulu at the time but clearly (and wisely) felt threatened by Kumalae's group, which featured Keoki "George" Awai on steel guitar. Kumalae, for his part, distrusted Ka'ai, and even accused Ka'ai in the press of hiring Honolulu's highest-priced players for the contest, knowing that he would replace them with cheaper musicians if he won. Kumalae also contended that Ka'ai attempted to "buy him off" so that Kumalae would drop out of the competition. After he was given unfamiliar music by the committee to perform for the judges, Kumalae once again objected, urging simply that instead of the haole committee's deciding the merits of their performance, both clubs instead should "perform before ex-Queen Lili'uokalani and that the commission accept her decision." The "hot fight" between the bands seems to have been won by Kumalae's group. However, over the next two months the Hawaiian Pavilion committee continued to debate which string band should represent Hawai'i in the pavilion. In February, it selected a third group, led by the rising singer and composer Henry Kailimai, to perform in the pavilion. Meanwhile, Jonah Kumalae and his band also worked at the fair, performing and selling Kumalae's guitars, 'ukuleles, and taro patches in a booth next to the lecture room. I thank Jim Tranquada for clarifying much of the "hot fight" drama for me. Minutes, November 12, 1914, folder 1: Minutes of Commission Meetings, handwritten, 1914, Panama Pacific International Exposition, 1915—

Files, HSA; "Musicians Sound Discordant Note to Commission," *Honolulu Star Bulletin*, January 1, 1915, 2; "Fair Orchestra Still Puzzling Commissioners," *Honolulu Star Bulletin*, January 8, 1915, 7. Jim Tranquada to the author, November 7, 2014.

96. "George E. K. Awai Fueled the Hawaiian Music Craze"; Mitchell, Kanahele, and Berger, "Steel Guitar," 791.

97. "Hawaiians Bring 'Witching Music,'" *Evening Herald*, June 8, 1916, 1; Tranquada and King, *The 'Ukulele*, 95.

98. Noble, "Hawaiian Musicians in the Jazz Era," 23.

99. Awai, *The Superior Collection of Steel Guitar Solos*.

100. Ibid., 9–11.

101. He taught "the Hawaiian style of playing the guitar with [a] steel bar, which produces that enchanting, exquisite Music for which the Natives are famous." Advertisement, "Free Instruction on Hawaiian Steel Strung Guitars and Ukuleles," *Los Angeles Times*, May 16, 1914.

102. Alohikea, *"Hawaiian Method" of Playing Guitar Self Taught*.

103. Stumpf, *Original Hawaiian Method for the Steel Guitar*. "Hawai'i Proves Inspiration for Guitar Author," *Honolulu Star Bulletin*, August 21, 1917, 6.

104. Kapua, "Joseph Kekuku."

105. Ruymar, *The Hawaiian Steel Guitar*, 6. Nainoa recorded four extremely rare discs of instructional and informative material that corroborated his cousin's invention of the instrument sometime in the 1930s or 1940s.

106. Walter Kolomoku to Eddie Alkire, September 5, 1925, box 79, folder 7, Elbern H. "Eddie" Alkire Personal Papers and Music Instrument Collection, 1926–1997, series 12/9/101, Sousa Archives and Center for American Music, University of Illinois Archives, UIUC.

107. Miller, *Segregating Sound*, 185.

108. Ibid., 158.

109. I am deeply indebted here to Karl Hagstrom Miller for his work in unearthing this history of the U.S. music industry in *Segregating Sound*.

110. "Our San Francisco Letter," *Hawaiian Star*, May 13, 1912, 9.

111. Ibid.; my emphasis.

112. Rockwell, *Hawaiian and Hawaiian Guitar Records*, 917–20.

113. Cook, "Pale K. Lua," 512–13.

114. "Irene W. Peterson," obituary, *San Bernardino County Sun*, March 17, 1966. Thanks to Les Cook for locating this obituary.

115. "Pale K. Lua," *Discography of American Historical Recordings*, http://victor.library.ucsb.edu/index.php/talent/detail/42299/Lua_Pale_K._instrumentalist_

guitar; accessed May 22, 2015. See also Rockwell, *Hawaiian and Hawaiian Guitar Records*, 740–72. Pale Lua's middle name in some sources is listed as Kauhi. By June 1917 he was working as "musician-guitarist traveling" for Charles S. Wilshim[n?] at 1585 Broadway, New York. Pale Kauhi Lua, WW1 Registration Card, June 5, 1917; World War I Selective Service System Draft Registration Cards, 1917–1918, registration state Hawaii, registration county Hawaii, roll 1452096, draft board 1, NARA, ancestry.com, U.S., World War I Draft Registration Cards, 1917–1918 [database on-line] (Provo, UT: Ancestry.com Operations, 2005).

116. Les Cook notes that Lua may have left the Islands for Cleveland as early as 1910, when he was only fifteen years old. Cook, "Pale K. Lua," 513.

117. Les Cook, "Irene West," 513. Personal correspondence with Les Cook, April 11, 2013. The date and cause of Lua's death remain unknown. Although he was originally believed to have died in 1917 in New York City, newspaper clippings now reveal that he remained active until at least 1920. His photograph is found in Queenie Kaili's scrapbook from 1923–24 (see chap. 4), but the photograph may have been taken before their 1923 departure.

118. Rockwell, *Hawaiian and Hawaiian Guitar Records*, 247–330.

119. Ibid., xiii.

120. Gracyk and Hoffmann, *Popular American Recording Pioneers: 1895–1925*, 120. U.S., World War II Draft Registration Cards, 1942 Record for Frank Ferreira, Ancestry.com. *U.S., World War II Draft Registration Cards, 1942* [database on-line] (Provo, UT: Ancestry.com Operations, 2010), via http://home.ancestry.com; accessed May 20, 2015.

121. "Hawaiian Boys Who Left Islands for Outside World Are 'Making Good' All Over Mainland," *Honolulu Star Bulletin*, January 4, 1913, 5.

122. Ferreira's great-grandson fielded my questions regarding Ferreira's life before and after his recording career and passed on to me answers from Ferreira's daughter, Mary, in May 2013. Personal correspondence with Jonathan Vecchi, May 14, 2013.

123. Gracyk and Hoffmann, *Popular American Recording Pioneers*, 120. 1940 Census Records, Census place: New York, Queens, New York, Roll T627_2739, 3A, enumeration district 41-1007, NARA, via http://home.ancestry.com; accessed May 20, 2015.

124. Quoted in Gracyk and Hoffmann, *Popular American Recording Pioneers*, 120. This reference to the Hawaiian style of playing guitar may in fact be referring to Ferreira's 'ukulele playing, though he was never known while a recording artist as a 'ukulele player, despite the fact that he recorded a few sides on the 'ukulele in August and September 1922. Rockwell, *Hawaiian and Hawaiian Guitar Records*,

282–83. A 1915 publication indicates that Ferreira introduced the steel guitar to California when he arrived from the Islands in 1900. "Palakiko Ferreira," *Edison Phonograph Monthly*, October 1915, 14.

125. "Hawaiian Boys Who Left Islands for Outside World Are 'Making Good' All Over Mainland," *Honolulu Star Bulletin*, January 4, 1913, 5.

126. Rockwell, *Hawaiian and Hawaiian Guitar Records*, 248–49.

127. Though a steamship company representative said that the ship "was steaming in fine weather with the sea as smooth as a mill pond," her family believed that she accidentally "washed overboard." "Seattle Musician Lost at Sea: Versions of Mystery Conflict," *Seattle Daily Times*, December 19, 1919, 15.

128. Rockwell, *Hawaiian and Hawaiian Guitar Records*, 251–52.

129. Ibid., 251–97.

130. Ibid., 298–330.

131. Personal correspondence with Jonathan Vecchi, May 14, 2013. Tranquada and King, *The 'Ukulele*, 135.

132. Interestingly, although Ferreira had stopped recording before the development of electric steel guitars, he played an Epiphone Electar Zephyr model six-string electric steel guitar in later years. It is possible that he performed publicly with it, though his daughter indicated that his playing in this period was restricted to audiences of family and friends. When he died, his family placed his steel bar in his coffin. Personal correspondence with Jonathan Vecchi, May 14, 2013.

133. It is possible that his record for steel guitar recordings has been surpassed by Nashville's premier Dobro session musician, Jerry Douglas.

134. "The Hawaiian Duo, introducing Joseph Kekuku and John Pa'aluhi [unclear], guitar players, were well liked, though the soft music of the instrument was difficult to hear in the rear of this house. Mr. Kekuku plays the guitar as no other musician does, laying it over his knees and picking with the first two fingers of his hand." "Coney Island: Henderson's Music Hall," *New York Clipper*, July 30, 1910. In 1909 Kekuku and a quartet of Hawaiian musicians played a clambake at Long Beach, Long Island. It is unclear whether or not this group included the Pakas and Pa'aluhi, the latter of whom was a long-standing member of the Toots Paka troupe. "Long Beach Will Have Carnival at Casino," *New York Herald*, August 22, 1909, Brooklyn Section, 4.

135. It is not uncommon to find many of the musicians residing near one another in census records. For example, the 1920 U.S. Census reported that Hannah and July Paka lived in a Manhattan apartment located directly between those of two other Hawaiian musicians, including the guitarist David Kaili. 1920 Census, Census place

Manhattan Assembly District 10, New York, New York, roll T625_1204, 6A, enumeration district 799, Image 527, NARA, via http://home.ancestry.com; accessed May 20, 2015.

136. Joseph Kekuku and William Kamoku, passport application, June 6, 1919, Passport Applications, January 2, 1906–March 31, 1925, collection number: ARC identifier 583830/MLR number A1 534, NARA series M1490, roll 796, via http://home.ancestry.com; accessed May 20, 2015. Tranquada and King state that Kealakaʻi was also aboard their ship, the SS *Baltic*, that June. Tranquada and King, *The ʻUkulele*, 111.

CHAPTER 4

1. "Hawaiian 'Music Boys.' About 1890," EC Hawaiian Music and Musicians, folder 2, CP 77360, BMLA.

2. Scrapbook belonging to Queenie Kaili, 1978.237.01, 1978.237.02, Donor: Mrs. Gay Slavsky, BMLA.

3. The donation was by Mrs. Gay Slavsky. For a reference to Slavsky as an appraiser, see Kanai, "From Our Files."

4. Two scholars who have investigated the complex role of tourism in indigenous peoples' lives include Imada, in *Aloha America*, and Teaiwa, in "Militarism, Tourism and the Native."

5. By the fall of 1920, as he entered his eighteenth year, steel guitarist Kiwini Panui and his older brother, Keoni, had made their way to the American Midwest, where they were performing under the management of Mildred Leo Clemens Schenck and her husband, Robert. Kiwini Panui, U.S. passport application 119584; Keoni Panui, U.S. passport application 119583, Passport Applications, January 2, 1906–March 31, 1925, collection number: ARC identifier 583830/MLR number A1 534, NARA series M1490, Roll 1435, NARA.

6. "He Leke Na Ke Keiki I Ka Makuahine," *Ka Nupepa Kuokoa*, March 25, 1921, 3; translated by the staff of Hoʻolaupaʻi: Hawaiian Newspaper Resource, in "London, a 1920 Hawaiian Boy Writes Home," *Ka Wai Ola*, March 2011, 20.

7. Ibid.

8. Ibid.

9. Ibid.

10. Manifest of the SS *Manoa*, Sailing from San Francisco to Honolulu, T.H., May 25, 1921, List of United States Citizens, Passenger and Crew Lists, 1900–1959, Arrivals, June 1921, 199, ancestry.com, *Honolulu, Hawaii, Passenger and Crew Lists, 1900–1959* [database on-line] (Provo, UT: Ancestry.com Operations, 2009).

11. "Some Tales from Buffalo," *Honolulu Advertiser*, December 5, 1901, 3. By 1905

he was referred to as a manager of Hawaiian troupes. See "Public and Promotion Matters," *Hawaiian Gazette*, November 14, 1905, 7.

12. "Joseph Puni, Wanderer for 40 Years, Glad He's Home," unidentified newspaper, December 11, 1940, 13, Newspaper Clipping and Pamphlet File, HSL. Marsden, "Hawaiian Music in Great Britain," 223. Their Paris act was called "The Hawaiians with Miss Leilani." Ibid. According to Les Cook, "William Kanui might have been the 1st steel player in Europe when he came to France with Joe Puni in November 1913. April 1914 saw Kanui, Puni relocate to the UK for the duration of WW1 bringing with them the French girl Lucie Schmidt. Known as 'the Hawaiians and Miss (sometimes Mlle) Leilani' or 'the Hawaiian Serenaders,' they toured the British isles extensively. At the end of the war Kanui and Schmidt settled in Paris, renamed the act Kanui and Lula and performed across Europe and the Middle East." Personal correspondence with Les Cook, May 31, 2015.

13. "Joseph Puni, Wanderer for 40 Years, Glad He's Home," unidentified newspaper, December 11, 1940, 13, Newspaper Clipping and Pamphlet File, HSL.

14. Balme, "Selling the Bird," 8.

15. The names of the cast are included in a program discovered at the Victoria and Albert Museum. *The Bird of Paradise*, Lyric Theatre, program, Theatre and Performance Archives, Blythe House, VAMA. Lily Moa was born in Batavia, New York, while John was born in Hilo. Their 1919 passport applications name the couple as John and Lily Moore, but because Kiwini Panui refers to John Moa as a Hawaiian living abroad, and a fine poi chef at that, I assume that Moore was an "Americanized" name they sometimes used in the States. A *B.M.G.* magazine in 1965 identified the musicians in a photograph from the first production, which correlates to the image of the musicians featured in the original program. The article lists John Moa and Diamond Kekona on 'ukulele, Joseph Puni and Gabriel Papaia on Spanish guitar, and William Kamoku on steel. It is unclear why Papaia is identified in this photograph and yet not listed in the program. Perhaps Papaia took over for William Kamoku during the run at the Lyric. *B.M.G.*, December 1965, 73. Papaia married a British woman while working in England. Cook interview. Diamond Kekona discusses his enlistment in the British army and his marriage in a letter published in the newspaper *Ka Nupepa Kuokoa*. "Leta Mai Pelekane Mai," *Ka Nupepa Kuokoa*, February 18, 1916, 2; translated by nupepa-hawaii.com: http://nupepa-hawaii.com/2012/08/04/a-touching-letter-from-diamond-kekona-in-far-away-britain-to-his-father-in-hawaii-1916/; accessed May 20, 2015. The staff at nupepa-hawaii.com in fact translated a series of letters, originally published in *Ka Nupepa Kuokoa*, that were sent to Hawai'i by Diamond Kekona and his wife during the war. These letters offer a fascinating glimpse into the lives of Hawaiians both working and

serving in militaries abroad; http://nupepa-hawaii.com/tag/diamond-kekona/; accessed May 20, 2015.

16. "Certificate of Registration of American Citizen," Cardiff, Wales, 1916, via http://home.ancestry.com; accessed May 20, 2015.

17. "The Theatres," *Times* (London), February 2, 1920, 10.

18. Balme, "Selling the Bird," 8.

19. For the list of ali'i nui who visited England, see Marsden, "Hawaiian Music in Great Britain," 222.

20. Imada, *Aloha America*, 299 n. 170.

21. Ibid., 98.

22. "Na Keiki Hawaii Himeni Ma Amerika," *Kuokoa Home Rula*, September 5, 1912, 2; translated by nupepa-hawaii.com: http://nupepa-hawaii.com/2012/09/06/more-on-hawaiians-performing-in-lands-afar-1912/; accessed May 23, 2015. The letter indicates that Mr. and Mrs. David Kalaukoa, Alfred K. Jones, and John K. Pa'aluhi performed in Europe. This may reference the May 1910 London appearance of the Hawaiian Band and Chorus led by Alice Raymond, a cornetist form the United States. Marsden, "Hawaiian Music in Great Britain," 223.

23. Pale K. Lua, Irene West, and the rest of the troupe—Willie Kahakalau, Julia Anelika Willing, John K. Pa'aluhi, and Louise Rose Kamakea—together appeared to apply for passports in March 1914. Pali Luau, passport application, March 21, 1914, Passport Applications, January 2, 1906–March 31, 1925, collection number: ARC Identifier 583830/MLR number A1 534, series M1490, roll 796, NARA, via http://home.ancestry.com; accessed May 20, 2015. The troupe embarked at Liverpool sailing for New York on August 22, 1914. Passenger Lists, 1820–1857, via http://home.ancestry.com; accessed May 25, 2015.

In her book of poetry, Irene West noted that she had returned from London after the declaration of war. That December, the Irene West Royal Hawaiians recorded a few sides in New York City for Victor Records. West, *A Soul's Appeal and Other Poems by the Actress Convert*, 17.

24. Thompson was born in Honolulu on April 22, 1882. His aliases, according to British Hawaiian music researchers Les Cook and John Marsden, include Luvaun Tawmsen, Keouli Tawmsen, Carlo Luvaun (likely a misspelling of Keouli), Lu Thompson, Lui Thompson, Keouli, Professor Keouli, Segis Luvaun, and Juan Akoni. It is unclear why he took on such a variety of names, but he left behind a significant combined legacy of European recordings. Before arriving in Europe, he performed as a member of the "Honolulu Students" and toured throughout the U.S. continent. Marsden, "Hawaiian Music in Great Britain," 223, 235. Speech given on

anniversary of the founding of the Kamehameha School, folder 21, Political Correspondence, 1947, John Henry Wilson Papers, 1871–1956 (M-182), HSA.

25. Marsden, "Hawaiian Music in Great Britain," 223; advertisement, *B.M.G.*, February 1920, iii.

26. The witness for Kekuku's and Kamoku's passport application was Joseph Puni, who swore on the application that he had known both of them for twenty-five years as a family friend. The passports were sent to the Pontiac Hotel on Broadway, in New York, which was Puni's listed address. It is possible that Puni, who by then had been managing Hawaiian troupes for twenty years, arranged for Kekuku's earliest European tours. Joseph Kekuku and William Kamoku, passport application, June 6, 1919, Passport Applications, January 2, 1906–March 31, 1925, collection number: ARC identifier 583830/MLR number A1 534, series M1490, roll 796, NARA, via http://home.ancestry.com; accessed May 20, 2015. Tranquada and King state that Kealaka'i also sailed that June on their ship, the SS *Baltic*. Tranquada and King, *The 'Ukulele*, 111.

27. His address in Paris in late 1920 was the Hôtel Excelsior, rue Pigalle 59. Joseph Kekuku, passport application, November 29, 1920, Passport Applications, January 2, 1906–March 31, 1925, collection number: ARC identifier 583830/MLR number A1 534, NARA, series M1490, roll 1423; Joseph Kekuku, passport application, November 1, 1922, Passport Applications, January 2, 1906–March 31, 1925; collection number: ARC identifier 583830/MLR number A1 534, series M1490, roll 796, NARA, via http://home.ancestry.com; accessed May 20, 2015. Kekuku confirms a role in *Bird of Paradise* in an instructional materials pamphlet reprinted in Ruymar, *The Hawaiian Guitar*, 11. Kapua, "Joseph Kekuku"; DeLano, "Hawaiian Music." Joseph K. Kealoha served as a witness for Kekuku's application, noting that he had known Kekuku for twenty-seven years. Kealoha and Kekuku were working in Spain when he applied. It is possible that this Kealoha is in fact July Kealoha Paka. If this is indeed the case, then we know more about the Paka's whereabouts in the 1920s, and also, perhaps, that Kekuku had known Paka since around 1895. Kealoha listed his permanent address as 1440 Broadway, New York City. Kekuku eventually returned to the United States and began offering lessons in Chicago. Advertisement, "Hawaiian Guitar," *Chicago Daily Tribune*, Aug. 4, 1929, 11.

28. For example, see Kapua, "Joseph Kekuku," and "To Harrods from Honolulu," *Times* (London), October 15, 1923, 10. Kekuku developed his vaudeville routine with Alvin Keech, a haole born in Hawai'i, who was often billed, nevertheless, as a Hawaiian. According to Jim Tranquada, Keech was "a star pupil in Ernest Ka'ai's music school" before moving to San Francisco and then Los Angeles. He relocated

to the United Kingdom in 1921 with his brother Kelvin, where he invented a hybrid instrument called the "banjolele." Personal correspondence with Jim Tranquada, May 25, 2015. In one article, Keech was referred to as "an Hawaiian," and Kekuku was referred to as "a tall, dusky skinned man, whom one . . . I suppose, would mistake for one of the 'all blacks.'" "The Talk of London," *Daily Express* (London), January 1, 1925, 4. Kekuku gave 'ukulele lessons as well, and performed at the London Hippodrome off and on for nine months in 1924 in the cast of *Leap Year*, starring George Robey. Marsden, "Hawaiian Music in Great Britain," 226.

29. Moe interview.

30. Ibid.

31. Moe family genealogical information posted on ancestry.com corroborates the information provided by Tau and Dorian Moe. See http://trees.ancestry.com/tree/25114994/person/1611294369 and http://trees.ancestry.com/tree/25114994/person/1611294383; accessed May 20, 2015. Dorian Moe says that Tau's parents were prompted to move to Lā'ie to serve as missionaries. Moe interview. Though the U.S. death index indicates a 1909 birth year, Lorene Ruymar provides an alternative birthday for Tau Moe of August 13, 1908. Ruymar, *The Hawaiian Steel Guitar*, 33. Tau Moe himself indicates in one interview a 1908 birthdate, during "The Aloha Four."

32. Halfon, "The Moe Family," appendix D, "Moe Family Film Outline," 2. I would like to thank Les Cook for sharing this grant proposal with me. For more comprehensive estimates on losses resulting from influenza in Western Samoa, see Tomkins, "The Influenza Epidemic of 1918–19 in Western Samoa," 181–97.

33. Halfon, "The Moe Family," appendix D, "Moe Family Film Outline," 2.

34. Ibid., appendix C, "Treatment," 5.

35. Ibid., appendix D, "Moe Family Film Outline," 1. Moe described the cylinder as "a round disc like a glass that we drink water in. . . . The color of the glass record was I think dark brown or black." Tau Moe to Lorene and Art Ruymar, August 26, 1990, reproduced in Ruymar, *The Hawaiian Steel Guitar*, 21. In one interview, Tau indicates that he had learned how to play Spanish guitar in Samoa, before his family arrived at Lā'ie. "The Aloha Four."

36. Halfon, "The Moe Family," appendix D, "Moe Family Film Outline," 1.

37. He first tuned his guitar to E-A-E-A-C#-E, the "low bass" A tuning, which was one of the earliest steel tunings, if not *the* earliest. Halfon, "The Moe Family," appendix D, "Moe Family Film Outline," 1–2.

38. M. K. Moke (also known as Moses Keakalauloa McCallum Jr.) recorded "Moana Chimes" both under his name and under "Johnny Noble's Hawaiians featuring M. K. Moke with the Moke Trio." The trio likely included Sampson Akaka

on guitar and Raymond Kinney on ʻukulele. It appears in Malcolm Rockwell's discography to most likely have been recorded during or soon after March 1928. Rockwell, *Hawaiian and Hawaiian Guitar Records*, 838, 879.

39. Halfon, "The Moe Family," appendix C, "Treatment," 8.

40. Ibid., appendix D, "Moe Family Film Outline," 4.

41. Tau Moe to John Marsden, January 18, 1978, courtesy of John Marsden. Moe referred to the song as "Maui Chimes," but most likely he was referring to Moke's hit recording of "Moana Chimes."

42. Halfon, "The Moe Family," appendix D, "Moe Family Film Outline," 5.

43. "Mort de Claude Rivière," newspaper clipping dated January 26, 1972, courtesy of Les Cook.

44. Halfon, "The Moe Family," appendix D, "Moe Family Film Outline," 7. Tauivi, Pulu Moe, and Fuifui Moe are referred to by Tau and his daughter in interviews as Tau's uncles. One account of the family suggests that they were the children of Tau's father's brother. Ibid., 6.

45. The house stood opposite McKinley High School at 1136 S. King St. in Honolulu. Halfon, "The Moe Family," appendix D, "Moe Family Film Outline," 7; Ruymar, *The Hawaiian Steel Guitar*, 33. For Tau Moe's recollections of the house, see "The Aloha Four."

46. Tau Moe to John Marsden, July 9, 1982, courtesy of John Marsden; Ruymar, *The Hawaiian Steel Guitar*, 33. According to Tau Moe, "I am [Tauvivi, Fuifui, and Pulu's] nephew, as My Grand Father MOE first wife have two children My Father & one Sister then my Grand Father Moe married again then come Pulu, Tauivi and Fuifui, Masaga and others, so they are my half Uncle, but of course in the show we are the MOE BROTHERS." Tau Moe to John Marsden, November 17, 1978, courtesy of John Marsden. The descendants of his half uncles remained in the business. By 1980, Tau Moe could report that one of Tauivi's sons and daughter had "their own Hawaiian show in Texas," and his other son "Pat Moe and his wife are now working with the Lani Moe Show in Ohio[.] Lani is Pulu Moe's son." Tau Moe to John Marsden, March 11, 1980, courtesy of John Marsden.

47. Halfon, "The Moe Family," appendix D, "Moe Family Film Outline," 6.

48. Keiki died in a prisoner of war internment camp in Japan in 1945. General Records of the Department of State, record group RG59–entry 205, box number 1876, box description: 1945–1949 Japan A—S, NARA, ancestry.com, Reports of Deaths of American Citizens Abroad, 1835–1974 [database on-line] (Provo, UT: Ancestry.com Operations, 2010).

49. Halfon, "The Moe Family," appendix C, "Treatment," 10.

50. Moe interview.

51. Tau Moe to John Marsden, April 27, 1977, Courtesy of John Marsden.

52. The troupe also featured two Filipina dancers and singers with the stage names Feilani and Lei Ilima. Lei Ilima was originally known as Louisa Reyes. She joined the troupe once it arrived in Manila in January 1929. Eventually she married Pulu Moe. Halfon, "The Moe Family," appendix D, "Moe Family Film Outline," 9. The troupe may have included four additional musicians and dancers who sailed with them from Honolulu. "List or Manifest of Outward-Bound Passengers," SS *President Jefferson*, Honolulu to Manila, December 27, 1928, Crew Lists of Vessels Arriving at Honolulu, Hawaii, August 1912–November 1954, National Archives Microfilm Publication A3510, roll 73, record group title: Records of the Immigration and Naturalization Service, 1787–2004, record group number 85, NARA. Dorian Moe said that as many as eight or ten originally traveled in the troupe. She said Tau Moe's family "let him go. Because he was lucky, he had a lot of siblings behind that could take care of the family. So basically he was the wanderer. And he wandered off into a foreign country [laughs]!" As for Rose, she asked her father what she should do when he was sick in the hospital. Dorian recalled Rose telling her that her father said, "'Okay, look. You go. You want to go? That's fine. But come back the same person you are. I don't want you to change. But you go.' So he let her go." Moe interview. For Moke's gift to Tau of a Martin guitar, see Tau Moe to John Marsden, October 25, 1978, courtesy of John Marsden.

53. The session in Tokyo in September 1929 yielded an interesting mixture of Hawaiian, Samoan, and popular American songs: "Goodbye My Felina," "Ellis March," "Lau Lupe Ua Sola," "Paahana Hula," "Fort Street Rag," "Mama E," "Mountain of Samoa," "Tofa Leve Ta," "He Aloha No O Honolulu," "Aue Si Ta'e," "Maikai No Kauai," "Tofa Sole Oe," and "Lei I Ka Mokihana." Rockwell, *Hawaiian and Hawaiian Guitar Records*, 835.

54. "The Aloha Four."

55. Halfon, "The Moe Family," appendix C-I, "Tau Moe Family Chronology," n.p.

56. See Troutman, *Indian Blues*, for multiple examples of this production trope in federal Indian boarding schools as well as on professional entertainment circuits.

57. Halfon, "The Moe Family," appendix C, "Treatment," 12.

58. Tau and Rose saved Rivière from financial ruin in Bombay and supported her for two years as their own group established itself. Halfon, "The Moe Family," 11.

59. Photocopies of programs from the Moe scrapbooks, now lost, are included in Halfon, "The Moe Family," appendix C, "Treatment."

60. Quoted in Ruymar, *The Hawaiian Steel Guitar*, 35. Halfon, "The Moe Family," appendix D, "Moe Family Film Outline," 10.

61. In one source, Tau also attributed their departure to the trust that Rivière placed in him to distribute the band's pay. According to Tau, the others squandered their earnings each week and grew jealous of his control over the funds. A year later, his uncles, stranded in Calcutta, reached out to him for help. He bought them tickets to Bombay, arranged a contract for them, and eventually, having reconciled, they played together again in Europe. Halfon, "The Moe Family," appendix D, "Moe Family Film Outline," 10–12. In another source, Tau suggested that his family's departure from his half uncles was amicable. He wrote, "In 1934 after our contract in Calcutta, India, I told Pulu, Louisa, Fuifui, Tauivi and their Families that I have decided to return back to Hawaii for the Education of my young Son Lani Moe." Tau Moe to John Marsden, undated letter, courtesy of John Marsden.

62. Tau Moe to John Marsden, undated letter, courtesy of John Marsden. Halfon, "The Moe Family," appendix C-I, "Tau Moe Family Chronology," n.p.

63. "Tau Moe: A Hawaiian Odyssey," part 1; Halfon, "The Moe Family," appendix C-I, "Tau Moe Family Chronology," n.p. Rivière took a job at the French embassy in Shanghai, leaving the Moes without an agent. They secured an Indian agent, but this agent died and the contracts fell through, leaving the family in dire straits. Halfon, "The Moe Family," appendix D, "Moe Family Film Outline," 14. A letter from Tau Moe on this period does not mention that the agent died and the contracts fell through, nor that they were in dire straits; instead, it notes that the contract as originally signed was on good terms: "The Agent from Cairo saw us [at the Taj Mahal Hotel in Bombay] and He immediately gave us six months contract in Egypt for such a Fantastic condition in those days that we Immediately accepted it and sailed for Alexandria." Tau Moe to John Marsden, undated letter, courtesy of John Marsden.

64. Photocopies of programs from the Moe scrapbooks, now lost, are included in Halfon, "The Moe Family," appendix C, "Treatment."

65. Clippings in Halfon, "The Moe Family," appendix C, "Treatment."

66. Quoted in Ruymar, *The Hawaiian Steel Guitar*, 36; my emphasis.

67. Halfon, "The Moe Family," appendix C-I, "Tau Moe Family Chronology," n.p.

68. Quoted in Ruymar, *The Hawaiian Steel Guitar*, 34–35.

69. Quoted in ibid., 35.

70. "Tau Moe: A Hawaiian Odyssey," part 1.

71. "Tau Moe," Obituaries, *Times* (London), July 5, 2004, 24.

72. Halfon, "The Moe Family," appendix D, "Moe Family Film Outline," 16; Moe interview.

73. "Tau Moe's Haiwaiian-Trio: Eine Exotische Revue-Attraktion des Welt-

Varietés." Clipping in Halfon, "The Moe Family," appendix C, "Treatment." Thanks to my colleague Richard Frankel for providing this translation.

74. Quoted in Ruymar, *The Hawaiian Steel Guitar*, 34.

75. Tau Moe recalled these events to have taken place in October 1938; while this is possible, it is more likely that they took place in November. Halfon, "The Moe Family," appendix D, "Moe Family Film Outline," 16.

76. Halfon, "The Moe Family," appendix D, "Moe Family Film Outline," 16.

77. The precise nature of these "passports" is unclear, but they provided some sort of documentation that enabled the troupe's safe passage in and out of Germany. "Tau Moe: A Hawaiian Odyssey," part 1. That part of Samoa was once a German protectorate may have facilitated their navigation of Nazi bureaucracy as well. Halfon, "The Moe Family," appendix D, "Moe Family Film Outline," 17.

78. Moe interview.

79. Halfon, "The Moe Family," appendix D, "Moe Family Film Outline," 17.

80. Ibid.

81. Moe interview.

82. "Tau Moe," Obituaries, *Times* (London), July 5, 2004.

83. Moe interview.

84. Quoted in Ruymar, *The Hawaiian Steel Guitar*, 35.

85. Ibid., 35; Tau Moe to John Marsden, undated letter, courtesy of John Marsden.

86. Quoted in Ruymar, *The Hawaiian Steel Guitar*, 35.

87. Tau Moe to John Marsden, undated letter, courtesy of John Marsden.

88. "Tau Moe: A Hawaiian Odyssey," part 1.

89. Moe interview.

90. Ibid. See also Tau Moe to John Marsden, November 11, 1980, courtesy of John Marsden.

91. Moe interview.

92. Ibid.

93. Ibid.

94. Quoted in Ruymar, *The Hawaiian Steel Guitar*, 36.

95. Ibid.

96. McNeil, "A Mouse, a Frog, the Hawaiian Guitar and World Music Aesthetics," 84. Ernest Ka'ai's troupe first toured India for five months in 1922. Personal correspondence with Jim Tranquada, May 25, 2015.

97. Moe interview.

98. McNeil, "A Mouse, a Frog, the Hawaiian Guitar and World Music Aesthetics," 85.

99. Das interview.

100. McNeil, "A Mouse, a Frog, the Hawaiian Guitar and World Music Aesthetics," 85.

101. Ibid. See also "Mahima: Debashish Bhattacharya and Bob Brozman," http://www.bobbrozman.com/mahima.html#mahima3; accessed May 20, 2015.

102. Ellis, "The Secret World of Hindustani Slide." According to Adrien McNeil, Kabra's tuning, a modification from Hawaiian tunings, "reflects the emphasis of the melodic, as opposed to the harmonic, character of Hindustani music, in the manner of a solo voice. Kabra states that he tunes the first three strings, which are the main playing strings on his guitar, to *sa pa sa* (in his case Eb, Bb, Eb) respectively. The fourth, fifth, and sixth strings act as drones and are tuned according to the raga chosen. He plays mostly only on the first string sa or Eb in performances, but even so this arrangement gives his guitar a range of three octaves, which is today considered standard for Hindustani string instruments. Added to these changes Kabra has also included a chikari string tuned to the tonic but at an octave above the first main string. This string runs across the bridge and is affixed to a peg half-way down the side of the top side of the fingerboard. Its specific function is to punctuate the main melody and to enable the important jhala section of a raga to be realised, in which the right hand quickly alternates between the side and main strings of the instrument in a series of complex stroking patterns." McNeil, "A Mouse, a Frog, the Hawaiian Guitar and World Music Aesthetics," 86.

103. Ellis, "The Secret World of Hindustani Slide."

104. Ibid.

105. "Filmi" refers to music produced for films. "Tagore music" refers to renditions of compositions by the poet and musician Rabindranath Tagore, winner of the Nobel Prize in Literature in 1913. Nazrul was also a famous musician and poet from Bengal, where audiences of "millions of people on the east coast of the subcontinent" listened to steel guitarists' versions of his and Tagore's work. McNeil, "A Mouse, a Frog, the Hawaiian Guitar and World Music Aesthetics," 85. For samples of these artists and LP art, see http://radiodiffusion.wordpress.com/2010/01/24/van-shipley/; accessed May 24, 2015.

106. Bhattacharya's encounter with the Moe family was confirmed to me by Basil Henriques. Personal communication with Basil Henriques, July 27, 2013.

107. Two of the early twentieth century's most dynamic Hawaiian steel guitarists, Pale K. Lua and Sam Ku, passed away while on the road. Ku (whose surname likely was Kuanoni) had been touring Asia and Europe for several years when, in 1930, his health began to decline because of an undetermined illness. Admitted into Paris's American Hospital, fellow Kanaka entertainers and Paris residents Joe Puni

and Billy Kanui visited him and served him poi before he died on September 8 of that year. He was twenty-three years old. The date and place of Pale K. Lua's death are unknown, but he likely died sometime between 1921 and 1924, when he would have been no older than twenty-nine. Cook, "William ('Bill') Kanui [William Kulii Kanui]," 448. Cook, "Sam Ku West," 872, 877. Tau Moe describes Puni and Kanui's care for him in the hospital in a transcription of a letter from Tau Moe to John Marsden, January 1, 1981, courtesy of Les Cook.

108. "Joseph Puni, Wanderer for 40 Years, Glad He's Home," unidentified newspaper, December 11, 1940, 13, Newspaper Clipping and Pamphlet File, HSL.

109. Cook and Berger, "Pale K. Lua," 512–14. Pale K. Lua, Irene West, and Sam Ku (aka Sam Ku West) have each received extensive, and exceptional, biographical treatment by UK Hawaiian researcher Les Cook. While any errors are my own, my discussion of these three individuals relies heavily on the research that Cook has published and generously shared with me through personal correspondence.

110. Presumably they toured nearby countries with Ka'ai's troupe before heading to Australia in 1924. For a review of a Singapore show, see "Ka'ai's New Hawaiian Troubadours," *Singapore Free Press and Mercantile Advertiser*, March 14, 1923, 7. Based on these early reviews, it is clear that Thelma Ka'ai, Ernest Ka'ai's daughter, had long before introduced local audiences to the steel guitar. Documentation of this in Singapore goes back to 1921. "Big Success of the Hawaiian Troupe," *Straits Times*, November 29, 1921, 10. It seems that David Kaili at first accompanied Thelma Ka'ai on Spanish guitar, as he had Pale K. Lua, and then gradually integrated his own steel playing into the Ka'ai act. "Hawaiian Troubadours," *Straits Times*, March 16, 1923, 10.

111. Coyle and Coyle, "Aloha Australia," 34.

112. "Real Hawaiians," *Mirror* (Perth, Australia), March 15, 1930, 11; "The Royal Hawaiians," *Morning Bulletin* (Rockhampton, Australia), July 15, 1924, 8; "Bijou—Vaudeville," *Argus* (Melbourne, Australia), October 12, 1925, 14; "Hawaiian Music: A Night in Honolulu," *Freeman's Journal* (Sydney, Australia), March 5, 1925, 26.

113. A promotional photograph in a Parramatta, Australia, newspaper features Kaili holding such an instrument, while a photograph in their scrapbooks reveals two individuals strumming similar guitars, with the caption "Home-made steel guitars." For that reason, it is undetermined who built his instrument for that tour. "A Night in Honolulu," *Cumberland Argus and Fruitgrowers Advocate* (Paramatta, Australia), February 24, 1925, 4; Scrapbook Belonging to Queenie Kaili, 1978.237.01, 1978.237.02, Donor: Mrs. Gay Slavsky, BMLA; Coyle and Coyle, "Aloha Australia," 36. Knutsen and Weissenborn guitar expert George Tom Noe examined the photo-

graph of the "Home-made steel guitars" and observed, "They are not 'home-made.' They have slotted headstocks, pyramid bridges, and an unusual fretboard profile extending into the sound hole. So they are not Weissenborns, Knutsens, Schiresons, or Oscar Schmidt Hilos. However, there were a number of short-lived manufacturers of Hawaiian steel guitars during the 1922–1925 boom years." Personal correspondence with Tom Noe, May 16, 2015.

114. "Entertainments: Luxor Theatre," *West Australian* (Perth, Australia), September 3, 1928, 16.

115. "Real Hawaiians," *Mirror* (Perth, Australia), March 15, 1930, 11.

116. They continued to tour, however. In 1937, they had even signed a contract with Irene West, and, along with their partner George Kalani (whom West had fired years earlier from Sam Ku's troupe) and Queenie's "Beautiful Hula Girls," were touring Singapore as "Kaili's Hawaiian Troubadours." "Raffles Hotel," advertisement, *Singapore Free Press and Mercantile Advertiser*, January 13, 1937, 1.

117. As Queenie Kaili recalled to the *Honolulu Advertiser* on her return, "they beat me constantly, stuck bamboo slivers which had been soaked in salt water under my finger and toe nails, used any part of my body they fancied for putting out their cigarette butts." Damon, "Four Years of Hell in Manila Described by 'Queenie' Kaili."

118. Queenie Kaili reported, "David came back to me after only five days at the fort, he looked like a man about 150 years old. His hair was snow white and his face deeply lined. Besides innumerable beatings, he had been given the electric rod and water hose treatment, but he wouldn't ever speak of it to me," she continued. "Every time I asked him about the Fort, he would put his finger over his lips. He knew he was dying, the electric shocks had been too much for his heart, but he insisted that I carry on" (ibid.).

119. Bernardo Endaya, quoted in Ruymar, *The Hawaiian Steel Guitar*, 29. Ruymar published a wonderful collection of accounts of the instrument's arrival in several countries. Ibid., 39–46.

120. Bob Brozman, quoted in "Tau Moe: A Hawaiian Odyssey," part 2.

121. Ruymar, *The Hawaiian Steel Guitar*, 42.

122. Kubik, *Theory of African Music*, 245.

123. Kubik, liner notes to *African Guitar*, 58–59.

124. See in particular the King Sunny Adé albums from 1977 forward, including *Synchro Chapter 1* (1977), *African Beats in London* (1977), *Sound Vibration* (1978), *Chapter 3* (1978), *Private Line* (1979), and *The Golden Mercury of Africa* (1979), for examples of steel guitar playing by Adepoju. After that year he switched to pedal

steel. For an excellent example of his pedal steel playing with King Sunny Adé, listen to the latter's *Ju Ju Music*. The Inter-reformers Band, led by fellow juju music giant Chief Commander Ebenezer Obey, featured Lai Yinusa Dauda on steel guitar.

CHAPTER 5

1. Eddie Bush is an exception to this rule, as he was born in the continental United States to parents who had already left the Islands. Other successful guitarists from this generation include Sol K. Bright, Bob Pauole, and Sam Koki.

2. Dodge, liner notes to *Honolulu to Hollywood*, 4. "Dude" Miller was Edward K. Kaleleihealani Miller, a champion surfer and fisherman as well as musician; his band began performing at the Moana soon after it opened in 1901. The Royal Hawaiian Hotel opened in 1927. Ejiri, "The Development of Waikīkī," 178–79.

3. Stewart, "The Hollywood Record Company Store."

4. Solomon Hoopii Kaaiai, October 26, 1918, World War I draft registration card, registration state Hawaii, registration county Hawaii, roll 1452096, draft board 1, via http://home.ancestry.com; accessed May 20, 2015. Rockwell, "Sol Hoopii"; Rockwell, "Hawaiian Steel Guitar Pioneer Sol Hoopii." I am indebted to Malcolm Rockwell for his extensive research on Hoʻopiʻi's early life and career. Honolulu *City Directory, 1920*, ancestry.com, U.S. City Directories, 1821–1989 [database online] (Provo, UT: Ancestry.com Operations, 2011), via http://home.ancestry.com; accessed May 20, 2015.

5. Rockwell, "Sol Hoopii."

6. Quoted in Rockwell, "Hawaiian Steel Guitar Pioneer Sol Hoopii."

7. Todaro, *The Golden Years of Hawaiian Entertainment*, 145.

8. After his discovery, he served as a "workaway" in order to pay for his passage. Rockwell, "Sol Hoopii."

9. Todaro wrote that Hoʻopiʻi was "pretending" to be a professional boxer in order to secure "preliminary bookings to feed the trio and pay the rent." Todaro, *The Golden Years of Hawaiian Entertainment*, 145.

10. Rockwell, "Sol Hoopii." One of the earliest mentions of Hoʻopiʻi (listed as Solomon Hoope) in the *Los Angeles Times* comes in an advertisement for an open house at the Pasadena Furniture Company. Thanks to Jim Tranquada for bringing this ad to my attention. Advertisement, *Los Angeles Times*, December 18, 1920, II:3.

11. "K-H-J, the Times," September 19, 1922, *Los Angeles Times*, II:6; Rockwell, "Sol Hoopii."

12. "String Trio Meets Emergency: Native Island Airs Hum over Radio," August 10, 1923, *Los Angeles Times*, II:3.

13. Ibid.

14. Other early on-air collaborators included Sammy Kenelle, Richard Makinikaea, Laui Makinikaea, Joseph Mikila, Albert Wiliama, and Joe Nawahi. "K-H-J, the Times," September 19, 1922, *Los Angeles Times*, II:6. For Nawahi, see "KHJ Features 'The Wayfarer,'" September 8, 1923, *Los Angeles Times*, II:2.

15. Advertisement, July 12, 1924, *Los Angeles Times*, 4.

16. These brilliant first recordings by Sol Hoʻopiʻi in Southern California on the small Sunset label were reissued recently. See *Sol Hoopii in Hollywood: His First Recordings 1925*, Grass Skirt Records GSK 1002, 2007. Rockwell assesses the jazz elements of Hoʻopiʻi's early recordings in his "Hawaiian Steel Guitar Pioneer Sol Hoopii."

17. Todaro, *The Golden Years of Hawaiian Entertainment*, 145.

18. Brozman, *The History and Artistry of National Resonator Instruments*, 116.

19. Cundell, "Across the Pacific," 62–63; Hood, "Musical Ornamentation as History."

20. Hoʻopiʻi, *Sol Hoopii in Hollywood*; Hoʻopiʻi, *Sol Hoopii and His Novelty Quartette*.

21. In 1938, Hoʻopiʻi became a born-again Christian and joined Aimee Semple McPherson's "crusade." He continued to record and tour, but he rarely played anything other than religious songs from then until his death in 1953. Brozman, *The History and Artistry of National Resonator Instruments*, 116.

22. Dodge, liner notes to *Honolulu to Hollywood*.

23. "Beautiful Girls Sail for Hawaiʻi," *Los Angeles Times*, June 17, 1928, B 2; Rockwell, "Hawaiian Steel Guitar Pioneer Sol Hoopii."

24. "Hoopii Musical Troupe Is Back," *Star Bulletin*, July 21, 1928; Rockwell, "Hawaiian Steel Guitar Pioneer Sol Hoopii."

25. See, for example, "Hawaiian Music to Feature Brief Radio Day," *Los Angeles Times*, March 3, 1924, A 8.

26. Noonan, *The Guitar in America*, 118. Exceptions exist: Chris Knutsen was building x-braced harp guitars that could withstand steel strings by the 1890s. Noe and Most, *Chris J. Knutsen*, 17.

27. "The authors believe that the hollow-square-necked Hawaiian steel guitar in the shape that we all recognize was a Hawaiian innovation. It is apparent that Knutsen patterned his early Hawaiian steel guitars after those crafted by the Hawaiians." Noe and Most, *Chris J. Knutsen*, 51.

28. Ibid., 101.

29. In 1912 Ybarra was recruited with many other young women in Mexico to work in Los Angeles's new nonunion garment industry. She married Weissenborn in 1915 and became his business partner, investing today's equivalent of $30,000 in

the business. My thanks to Tom Noe for sharing his research on Concepción Ybarra and the genesis of Weissenborn guitars. Personal correspondence with Tom Noe, May 19, 2015 and May 24, 2015. Weissenborn by the early 1920s was fielding such demand for his koa wood, hollow-necked Hawaiian guitars that today practically all hollow-necked acoustic guitars are referred to as "Weissenborns."

30. Personal correspondence with Tom Noe, May 24, 2015.

31. Noe and Most, *Chris J. Knutsen*, 101, 81. Advertisement, "Free Instruction on Hawaiian Steel Strung Guitars and Ukuleles," *Los Angeles Times*, May 16, 1914, II:1. Sam Nainoa, Kekuku's cousin, later opened a Hawaiian music conservatory in Los Angeles and offered steel guitar lessons. Ruymar, *The Hawaiian Steel Guitar*, 6.

32. Rudy and John emigrated in 1908 with their family (three siblings already had emigrated to the United States). When war in their homelands seemed imminent, the family rushed to relocate. Veru, "The National-Dobro Guitar Company," 32.

33. Dopyera, "Dad: Some Personal Reflections," 9.

34. The instruments are so striking, and have become so iconic in design, that their patina became a metaphor for Paul Simon, whose song "Graceland" opens with the memorable refrain, "The Mississippi Delta was shining like a National guitar."

35. According to Bob Brozman, Hoʻopiʻi was originally offered $500, but after gambling this money away during the first night of the party, he was paid another sum to keep his trio at the party. He also was given two tricone guitars, including one with his name engraved on the body. Brozman, *The History and Artistry of National Resonator Instruments*, 27, 115.

36. Ibid., 27.

37. For example, his trio introduced the industry to the instrument at the 1927 Western Music Trades Convention in San Francisco. Ibid., 27; *National String Instruments*.

38. The company soon began making metal ʻukuleles, mandolins, and Spanish guitars, which also took the stringed instrument industry by storm.

39. Veru, "The National-Dobro Guitar Company," 42–43. The Dobro instruments featured a wood body, a single, large cone for amplification, and two screened sound holes to regulate the bass. The guitar generated more warmth and sustain than the tricones, and to this day, Dobros, as all instruments similar in design to theirs became known, have commanded the acoustic steel guitar field in the U.S. genres of both country and bluegrass. The leaders of the Ro-Pat-In Company also included Paul Barth and C. L. Farr. Brozman, *The History and Artistry of National Resonator Instruments*, 36.

40. According to a letter from George Beauchamp, the Electro frying pan debuted "in the hands of Jack Miller, now with George Olsen's 'Band of Tomorrow,' in the prologue of the preview of *Rain*, starring Joan Crawford, at Sid Grauman's Chinese Theatre in Hollywood; having also been used in the filming of the picture." This preview took place on September 9, 1932. George D. Beauchamp to Eddie Alkire, September 24, 1937, series 3, sub 1, folder 9, box 79, UIUC.

41. For an unknown reason, Sol did not arrive in DC with a Rickenbacker, so he had to borrow an Epiphone Electric Hawaiian steel guitar with a similar "horseshoe" magnetic pickup to at least demonstrate proof of concept. Because the company was so late in filing, Epiphone by that point had had the opportunity to produce a similar electric steel guitar. The patent was awarded to Rickenbacker following Sol Ho'opi'i's visit. Personal correspondence with Lynn Wheelwright, June 30, 2015. Rickenbacker scholar Matthew Hill found the telegram regarding Sol's need for an instrument.

42. Lynn Wheelwright has spent decades studying the early history of electric instruments. Until very recently it was assumed that the Rickenbacker frying pan was the first electric guitar sold on a production scale. Others had experimented with ideas for electrically conducting the sound of acoustic guitars, but none had succeeded to the extent that they began selling electric guitars. However, Wheelwright found evidence of one electric standard guitar marketed about three or four months before August 1932, when Rickenbackers became available. The instrument was called the Vivi-Tone and was created by Lloyd Loar of Kalamazoo, Michigan. Vivi-Tone folded after only about four years, however, having sold around 600 guitars during that period. It never produced a steel guitar, only standards. Meanwhile, Rickenbacker's Electric Hawaiian frying pan quickly became popular among guitarists, and featured prominently in their bands. Rickenbacker also introduced a standard electric guitar during this period, which seems to have failed miserably in sales. Personal correspondence with Lynn Wheelwright, June 22, 2015.

43. Don McDiarmid, "Music of the Islands," *Paradise of the Pacific*, September 1947, 11.

44. The other two members of the trio were non-Hawaiians named Bill Seckler and Paul Gibbons.

45. Vogel, "Eddie Bush: 1911–1969 (Part 1)," 24–25. Thanks to Les Cook for providing me with a copy of this article. Thank you to Jay Munns for sharing with me his extensive earlier research on and photographs of Eddie Bush and the Biltmore Hotel Trio.

46. Vogel, "Eddie Bush: 1911–1969 (Part 1)," 26.

47. Ibid.

48. Other films include the 1930 productions of *Flying Fool*, *Children of Pleasure*, *Spring Is Here*, *Just Imagine*, and *With a Song in My Heart*. Ibid., 28.

49. Quoted in Vogel, "Eddie Bush: 1911–1969 (Part 2)," 23. The Ambassador Hotel hired Eddie away from its rival, the Biltmore, in 1930, and he assembled a new trio. Soon he established residencies in several cities, from engagements in Honolulu, to the Hurricane Restaurant in New York, to several Polynesian clubs in Los Angeles, including a sixteen-month residency at the Seven Seas, from 1938 through 1940.

50. Philip K. Scheuer, "Deluge of Eating Spots and Dance Emporiums Hits Hollywood; Stars Seen at Many Favorite Haunts," *Los Angeles Times*, July 18, 1937, C 1.

51. Advertisement, *Los Angeles Times*, October 22, 1937. Machado (1903–74) was born Lena Ualani Wai'ale'ale on O'ahu.

52. McIntire interview. Her father, Alfred, was born in 1906 and died in 1960. His siblings were Victor Lani McIntire (1904–51), Dixon Ka'aihu McIntire (1902–51), and Ellen Kealoha McIntire (1910–74?). According to an ancestry.com family tree, his parents were Hattie Ka'aihue and William Dixon McIntire. William McIntire is reportedly buried at the U.S. Army's Schofield Barracks, near Wahiawā. He seems to have passed away in early January 1920. It is unclear when Hattie Ka'aihue died. http://trees.ancestry.com/tree/35444029/person/18861304316/fact/142390762195; accessed May 23, 2015.

53. McIntire interview.

54. Rockwell, "Hawaiian Steel Guitar Pioneer Sol Hoopii." Another account suggests an alternative story, which is that she may have listened to his records instead: according to Sol Bright, "Mary Pickford [used] his steel guitar to make her cry at the appropriate moments in scenes from the film, *Roses of Picardy*." "Solomon Hoopii Influenced the World," 1.

55. Ruymar, *The Hawaiian Steel Guitar*, 90.

56. Clipping, *Variety*, June 26, 1939, 2, "Hawaiian Nights," Motion Picture Association of America, Production Code Administrative Records, AMPAS.

57. As the next chapter attests, influential Nashville steel guitarist Jerry Byrd spent considerable time repeatedly watching scenes from such movies in order to view precious seconds of Sol Ho'opi'i and other steel guitarists.

58. L. Andrews to G. M. Shurlock, October 24, 1941, censor report, "Song of the Islands," Motion Picture Association of America, Production Code Administrative Records, AMPAS; Production Code Administration to Colonel Jason S. Joy, October 25, 1941, censor report, "Song of the Islands," Motion Picture Association of America, Production Code Administrative Records, AMPAS.

59. Ruyman, *The Hawaiian Steel Guitar*, 78.

60. McIntire interview.

61. "Musicians," *Variety*, June 18, 1930.

62. McIntire interview.

63. "Back-Slapping," *Variety*, July 16, 1930, 58.

64. When looking through her extensive photo albums, Lani Ellen McIntire identified many Kanaka musicians working in Los Angeles in the 1930s and 1940s, including Pua Almeida, George Kainapau, Gary Speare, Sol Ho'opi'i, Jimmy Haulani (aka Jimmy Tai), Eddie Bush, Anthony Ah Sam, Danny Stewart, Allen Kela, Danny Kuaana, Sam Koki, Archie Kehanu, Freddie and Ernie Tavares, Alfred Apaka, Sam Kaieo, Sol K. Bright, and others. McIntire interview.

65. Ibid.

66. Advertisement, *Variety*, October 12, 1937, 4.

67. The McIntire brothers had long felt it important to stick together. When their father died in 1920, the three already were living together in the "Oriental Barracks" at the U.S. Army's Schofield Barracks near Wahiawā in central O'ahu. Tired of laboring at the post laundry, Lani and Dick soon joined the U.S. Navy and served on the USS *Birmingham*. The navy brought them to West Coast, where they began their music careers in earnest. While Lani took up work in Los Angeles by the early 1920s as a guitarist for Sol Ho'opi'i's group, Dick McIntire opened a Hawaiian club in Tijuana, and eventually began broadcasting on San Diego's radio station, KFSD, until his brother Al heeded their call to join them for work stateside. Al McIntire remembered his mother, Hattie Ka'aihue, for her guitar playing and singing ability. McIntire interview. Ruymar's book dates their naval enlistment to 1919, though the 1920 U.S. Census does not suggest it. Ruymar, *The Hawaiian Steel Guitar*, 99; "K-H-J, the Times," *Los Angeles Times*, September 19, 1922, II:6; Ruymar, *The Hawaiian Steel Guitar*, 99; McIntire interview; Lis, "The Steel Guitar in Early Country Music," part 2, chap. 4, sec. 1, 16.

68. Press release, Harry Brand, Director of Publicity, *Song of the Islands*, 20th Century Fox 1942, Production Notes, Synopsis, Press Releases, AMPAS.

69. Ibid.

70. Ibid.

71. No date exists on the release, other than a stamp indicating its receipt on December 3, 1941, by the Library of the Academy of Motion Picture Arts and Sciences. Ibid.

72. McIntire interview. Eddie Bush reference quoted in Vogel, "Eddie Bush: 1911–1969 (Part 2)," 23.

73. The steel guitar, however, quickly transcended these constraints through its

appropriation by non-Hawaiian musicians, as we will see throughout the next chapters.

74. According to hula dancer Raylani Kinney, African Americans were not welcome in New York's Lexington Hotel Hawaiian Room, where she and her father, Ray Kinney, worked for years. Imada, *Aloha America*, 177.

75. Ibid.

76. Garrett, *Struggling to Define a Nation*, 175. Additional examples of early hapa haole songs include Henry Clark's "Ona Ona," Harry Kahanamu's "Mauna Kea," Jack Heleluke's "Fair Hawaii," and G. H. Stover and Henry Kailimai's smash 1915 hit, "On the Beach at Waikiki." For these and other examples, see Garrett, *Struggling to Define a Nation*, 186. See also Ejiri, "The Development of Waikīkī," 192–94; and Connell and Gibson, "'No Passport Necessary.'"

77. Garrett, *Struggling to Define a Nation*, 174–75.

78. Ejiri, "The Development of Waikīkī," 197.

79. Charles Hiroshi Garrett writes, "Tin Pan Alley's interest in producing Hawaiian songs had little to do with the pursuit of musical authenticity or the quest for cross-cultural understanding; rather, this venture demonstrates clearly how the politics of representation can play into the formation of American national identity. Creating products that combined hula girl iconography and tropical exoticism, the music industry not only supported the American colonial project but also tapped into America's growing fascination with Hawaiian tourist destinations." He continues, "The use and repetition of short syllabic sounds was understood by non-Hawaiians to be playful, primitive, and redolent of the exotic allure of the Islands. . . . Tin Pan Alley songwriters transformed genuine Hawaiian terms like 'Waikīkī' and 'wikiwiki' into a mishmash of nonsensical lyrics and comic song titles." Garrett, *Struggling to Define a Nation*, 186–87.

80. These examples and others are provided by Garrett in ibid., 187. Whereas Cunha and other Kanaka composers occasionally fetishized wāhine in their compositions, according to Garrett, "what differentiates most Hawaiian-themed Tin Pan Alley songs is that they accentuate not only the gendered but also the racialized dynamics of this encounter, suppressing the Hawaiian female perspective and focusing on the experiences of a white American male protagonist" (189).

81. Quoted in Imada, *Aloha America*, 178.

82. Ibid.

83. Ibid., 198.

84. Ibid., 200.

85. Quoted in ibid.

CHAPTER 6

1. Bjorn Johnsen to the Oahu Serenaders, February 7, 1933, folder 2, box 83, UIUC.

2. Helen B. Ward to the Oahu Serenaders, January 22, 1934, folder 7, box 83, UIUC.

3. "Nashville Listener" to the Oahu Serenaders, January 1934, folder 2, box 83, UIUC.

4. Madge Smith to the Oahu Serenaders, February 13, 1934, folder 2, box 83, UIUC.

5. Elizabeth MacDonald to the Oahu Serenaders, n.d., folder 3, box 83, UIUC.

6. Mrs. J. O. Holbrook to the Oahu Serenaders, January 10, 1934; Bill Winston to the Oahu Serenaders, February 10, 1933, folder 2, box 83, UIUC; emphasis in original.

7. "Those Ryder Gals" to the Oahu Serenaders, September 20, 1933, folder 7, box 83, UIUC.

8. Rose Kua to the Oahu Serenaders, January 19, 1933, folder 2, box 83, UIUC.

9. Edmund R. DeMarch to the Wahu [*sic*] Serenaders, March 23, 1933, folder 3, box 83, UIUC.

10. General Superintendent, Consolidated Coal Mine, to Joe Green, September 10, 1929, folder 7, box 79, UIUC.

11. Alkire worked professionally in the Oahu Serenaders with a Hawaiian musician named Alex Hoapili. Alkire seems to have studied the Hawaiian guitar via Walter Kolomoku's correspondence courses in the early to mid-1920s. Kolomoku owned the First Hawaiian Conservatory of Music, based in New York City, and surviving correspondence indicates that Kolomoku was encouraging Alkire as a student, while also rewarding him for recruiting others in his West Virginia community for Kolomoku's courses. Kolomoku to Alkire, August 26, 1925, folder 7, box 79, UIUC.

12. Recent works such as Elijah Wald's *Escaping the Delta* and Karl Hagstrom Miller's *Segregating Sound* demonstrate how southern white and black musicians shared not only vernacular repertoires but also, through sheet music, recordings, and radio, the passion of southern white and black consumers for music generated outside of the South. Diane Pecknold's recent anthology historicizes the making and remaking of the whiteness of country music, despite the consistent presence of African Americans in the genre. Pecknold, *Hidden in the Mix*.

13. As Elijah Wald notes, "Though their motives were different from those of the commercial record scouts, [folklorists] also had a specific agenda, which was to

find survivals of older traditions and 'typical' examples of regional and ethnic styles. Thus, they were uninterested when their informants, whether white or black, sang current hits or anything learned off records, and they often sought out 'white' material such as the British ballads from their Euro-American sources, while mining Afro-Americans for songs that might reveal African or slavery-era connections. As a result, their recordings often reinforce the impression that Southern music could be split along racial lines." Wald, *Escaping the Delta*, 57.

14. A number of blues scholars have long maintained that the slide guitar represented an "Africanism"—a demonstration of cultural retention that survived the Middle Passage. They argue that the slide guitar's ancestor was not the Hawaiian guitar but a one-stringed zither sometimes referred to as a "diddley bow." Some scholars such as David Evans argue that it is more likely that Joseph Kekuku learned the steel guitar technique from an African American sailor who had docked in Honolulu. I critique this argument in my article "Steelin' the Slide." The gist of my argument against these assertions is that they are born from not evidence but a yearning to believe that such a direct cultural retention between Africa and southern African American musicians exists. Diddley bows, which are children's instruments, do not even appear in the historical record until the 1930s. The evidence supporting the influence of Hawaiian guitars on southern guitarists who eventually played a conventionally held guitar with a slide is far more extensive, and this argument, I contend, is much more logical.

15. An excellent recent example of this reassessment is found in the work of musician and scholar Jake Fussell. See his 2013 MA thesis, "Out of This World."

16. I did find one newspaper report from Hattiesburg, Mississippi, that describes an alternative technique to the "Hawaiian style" of playing with a steel bar, but the article was published in 1927, well after Hawaiian guitarists had become a familiar sight in the South, and the technique is identified as originating from the labor of an individual who was convalescing in a veteran's hospital in San Francisco. The *Hattiesburg American* promoted what it claimed is the first local public performance by a player using a bottle rather than a piece of steel as a slide: "What is probably the most novel presentation act ever to be presented on local stages is 'Turner & McCoy'. . . . [It has] proved a knockout in all the largest theatres in the country where it has played. 'Turner and McCoy' . . . have a style all their own for playing guitars, that of using a 'jake' bottle to produce tones and sounds from their instruments that never before have been heard on local stages. . . . McCoy is known in theatrical circles as the Hawaiian guitar specialist. He plays a large steel guitar." "Turner-McCoy Premier Show," *Hattiesburg American*, April 14, 1927, 9. Turner is Lemuel Turner, identified as a white guitarist who recorded four "steel-guitar

solos" for Victor Records in Memphis in February 1928, including "Jake Bottle Blues." Russell, *Country Music Records*, 917. "Jake" refers to a Jamaican Ginger Extract medicine with a high alcohol content; it was frequently consumed by poor and working-class southerners as an intoxicant. The next day's edition of the *Hattiesburg American* provided a biographical sketch of Turner. It reported that he was born in McComb City, Mississippi, and during World War I enlisted in the U.S. Army's Eighty-First Infantry Division. He recounted to the newspaper that after he was gassed in France, he returned to the United States and spent six years in a government hospital in San Francisco. It was there that he began to play guitar and developed this method of playing guitar with a bottle. "King Guitar Player Here," *Hattiesburg American*, April 15, 1927, 2. I have not located any further references to the Turner and McCoy group. Turner's recordings are among the very earliest to feature the guitar presumably played with a bottle rather than a knife or metal bar. It is likely that guitarists Sylvester Weaver or Walter Beasley came to use the bottleneck around this time, too, as together they cut "Bottleneck Blues" in November 1927. What is not clear is whether they were holding the bottlenecks in the same fashion as Hawaiian guitarists held their steel bars, or if they actually placed their finger inside the bottlenecks and held the instrument in the standard fashion. Thanks to Elijah Wald for pointing out to me that we must not assume that these recordings featured the latter technique over the Hawaiian technique. The significance of this coverage by a Hattiesburg newspaper of Lemuel Turner in 1927 is that Turner's use of a bottle seems so new and novel, even in the context of the steel guitar played by McCoy. It suggests, at the very least, that the concept of the "bottleneck slide" was only beginning to take root in Mississippi at this time. Of course, Turner could have lied about the origins, but if a competent and practiced bottleneck slide tradition was in place when Hawaiian guitarists arrived in the South twenty or more years earlier, it seems more likely than not that (a) we would find press coverage of the more talented practitioners, regardless of their skin color, who would presumably seek to profit from their novel ability and (b) the southern press would compare the steel method when it was introduced to a concurrent method of southern origin, rather than declare the degree to which the Hawaiian guitar sound was unique and new.

17. Imada, "Aloha America," 152–56; Imada, *Aloha America*, 60, 81–82, 89; Rockwell, *Hawaiian and Hawaiian Guitar Records*, 3.

18. Personal correspondence with Jim Tranquada, September 14, 2013.

19. "Address Book," box 9, John Henry Wilson Papers, HSA. See also his appointment books from 1899 to 1901. Ibid.

20. Personal correspondence with Jim Tranquada, September 14, 2013.

21. "Hawaiians on the Mainland Do Well," *Hawaiian Gazette*, August 30, 1912, 4.

22. They lived and died in the South, too: in 1906, a member of the Royal Hawaiian Band, who had years earlier toured the United States as a member of the Hawaiian Kawaihau Glee Club, suffered a heart attack in his hotel room in Memphis. "Juan F. Edwards' Body: The Remains Will Be Shipped to Hawai'i for Burial," *Times-Picayune*, August 9, 1906, 13. In addition to writing about Native Hawaiians traveling in the U.S. South, southern newspapers frequently provided coverage of the Hawaiian Islands, including articles on Hawaiian music. For example, see "Hawaiian Music: Elementary Modes of Expressing Musical Ideas Influenced by Incoming Civilization," *Biloxi Daily Herald*, October 15, 1901, 6.

23. "Green Room Gossip," *Times-Picayune*, October 6, 1912, 44; *Times-Picayune*, September 19, 1915, 10; advertisement for Maison Blanche, *Times-Picayune*, February 19, 1917, 34; *Times-Picayune*, October 13, 1917, 13; *Times-Picayune*, May 29, 1921, 13; *Times-Picayune*, December 19, 1921, 3.

24. "Glee Club Trip Success: Fourteen Concerts Given by L.S.U. Men in Ten Days," *Times-Picayune*, March 27, 1918, 11; *Times-Picayune*, August 27, 1925, 17.

25. Venet, "The Hawaiian Tinge," 24–25.

26. Armstrong, liner notes to *King Bennie Nawahi*. See also Venet, "The Hawaiian Tinge," 25. The Armstrong recordings, made in Los Angeles on July 21, 1930, featured African American steel guitarist Ceele Burke, who learned the instrument in California and later cut the steel guitar on Fats Waller's rendition of "My Window Faces the South" (1937).

27. By this time, Kekuku had left the group, and July Paka was singing and playing steel guitar full time for the Toots Paka troupe. "Practice and Patience All That Is Necessary to Play Hawaiian Airs," *Atlanta Constitution*, August 16, 1916, 6. The article erroneously referred to Paka's steel guitar as a banjo: "Atlantans know July Paka as a man who literally can make his banjo talk." There is no evidence that July Paka ever played the banjo, but occasionally critics struggled over the names of the steel guitar and the 'ukulele. The *Constitution* printed three pieces on Paka that week that each commented on his steel guitar playing: heralded by one critic for his ability to play that "insid[i]ous, insinuating" instrument, another commented that "when July Paka places his Hawaiian guitar across his knees it takes little imagination to conjure a fantasy of moonlit Honolulu as its setting. He is a man whose music holds his hearers absolutely spellbound." "Amusements," *Atlanta Constitution*, August 15, 1916, 10; "Forsyth Offers Toots Paka as Headliner This Week," *Atlanta Constitution*, August 13, 1916, B8.

28. Jim Tranquada provided the *Ledger* reference and information on "Professor" Pa'aluhi's lessons at Philip Werlein's store on Canal Street through personal

correspondence, September 14, 2013. See also "He Was Hungry and Stole Watch," *Times Picayune*, September 29, 1919, 14.

29. Pierce, "In Behalf of the 'Popular' Elements in Musical Art," 477.

30. From 1934 to 1939 Frank Vierra served as the director of the Royal Hawaiian Band. Before then, however, he and his brothers organized and/or performed in several Hawaiian troupes over the years. These groups included Vierra's Hawaiian Troupe, the Hawaiian Serenaders, Vierra's Hawaiians, Vierra's Royal Hawaiian Singers, Vierra's Hawaiian Singers and Players, Vierra's Native Hawaiians, and the Royal Hawaiian Quartette. See the biographical information presented in the unprocessed Vierra Family Papers collection at the Hawai'i State Archives. My thanks to historical records branch chief Luella H. Kurkjian and her fellow staff at the HSA for alerting me to the collection's existence and making it available.

31. For example, see advertisement, *Hattiesburg American*, December 6, 1919, 3; advertisement, *Biloxi Daily Herald*, January 31, 1920, 3; "Hawaiians 8:30 Tonight," *Fayetteville Democrat*, April 12, 1918, Fragile Documents Folder, Vierra Family Papers, HSA; advertisement, *Robesonian*, December 18, 1919, Fragile Documents Folder, Vierra Family Papers, HSA; advertisement, *Hattiesburg American*, October 21, 1920, 3; and "Music, Dancing, Singing and Jazz to Be Free Numbers in Exposition's Entertainment," *Fort Worth Star-Telegram*, February 19, 1922, Fragile Documents Folder, Vierra Family Papers, HSA.

32. "Vierra's Hawaiian Singers and Players," *Clarksdale Daily Register*, May 30, 1917.

33. Gulf 1923, box 58, series VII (Financial Records), Redpath Chautauqua Collection, UIL. The Vierra troupe is listed as "Haw" in the ledger book. William O. Thomas, Mgr. Gulf Five-Day Circuit, to Albert S. Vierra, February 10, 1923, Vierra's Hawaiians, box 332, folder 2, series I, Talent Series Correspondence and Brochures, MsC 150 Redpath Chautauqua Collection, UIL.

34. Advertisement, *Biloxi Daily Herald*, February 17, 1917, 4; advertisement, *Laurel Daily Leader*, January 10, 1923, 2; "Radio Programs," *Laurel Daily Leader*, December 24, 1924, 2; "The Radio," *Hattiesburg American*, January 16, 1925, 12; "Radio Programs," *Laurel Daily Leader*, March 26, 1925, 3; Wald, *Escaping the Delta*, 95.

35. Jim Tranquada provided the *Ledger* quote through personal correspondence, September 14, 2013.

36. Advertisement, *Anniston Star*, March 31, 1918, 2; advertisement, *Greenville Daily Democrat Times*, March 5, 1918, 7.

37. Handy, *Father of the Blues*, 34–35.

38. Miller, *Segregating Sound*, 23; Peabody, "Notes on Negro Music," 151.

39. Otto and Burns, "Black and White Cultural Interaction in the Early Twentieth Century South," 410. The authors also acknowledged that "blacks and whites both may have borrowed the [bottleneck or knife] style from Hawaiian guitarists who toured the South in tent shows and fairs in the early twentieth century" (409).

40. McIntire interview. Racial epithets and threats of violence were directed toward Hawaiian musicians both in and out of the South. While living in western Pennsylvania, steel guitarist David Kanui faced a shotgun and a barrage of racial slurs typically directed at African Americans while picking up his young daughter, Ewalani, at her school bus stop. The threats came from a man who told Ewalani to stay away from his daughter, Ewalani's classmate. Personal correspondence with Ewalani Kanui, June 22, 2015.

41. Wilson, "A Royal Hawaiian Love Story," 3.

42. Singletary, *Hilo Hattie*, 75–76. Segregation and abuse was not limited to the South. According to the Hawaiian-language newspaper *Ka Nupepa Kuokoa*, in 1911 several white citizens of Denver complained to the police that Hawaiian musicians were winking at white women at their packed performances in a local hotel. "Condemned for Winking," *Ka Nupepa Kuokoa*, February 17, 1911; translation provided by Hoʻolaupaʻi: Hawaiian Newspaper Resource: https://www.facebook.com/photo.php?fbid=212570525447175&set=a.150883714949190.26988.116857171685178&type=1&permPage=1; accessed May 25, 2015. Tranquada and King found several more such instances in their study of the ʻukulele. See Tranquada and King, *The ʻUkulele*, 213–14 n. 29.

43. "Lizzie Wallace," *Chicago Defender*, December 22, 1917. She may have used her connections to play on both black and white entertainment circuits; earlier in 1917, for example, her Hawaiian troupe performed at the Strand, a major theater in Fort Wayne, Indiana. Advertisement, *Fort Wayne Journal-Gazette*, December 3, 1917, 5. I would like to thank Les Cook for bringing these articles to my attention.

44. Evans, "Afro-American One-Stringed Instruments"; Ferris, *Blues from the Delta*; Kubik, *Africa and the Blues*, 17. Maybe, given the late date when one-stringed zithers are first documented in the South, we have the diddley bow story backward. When Lynn Summers and Bob Scheir asked blues musician Little Milton the leading question, "Was your first instrument the proverbial piece of baling wire strung up on the side of a house?" Milton responded, after first describing drums made out of lard cans, "You had wire [on] the side of the house, on the wall or something, with a brick on one end maybe and a bottle on the other, then you use a nail in a bottle and *you sound like a Hawaiian type*" (Summers and Scheir, "Little Milton," 391; my emphasis). Rather than demonstrating an African retention, perhaps children built diddley bows to mimic the Hawaiian guitar, which we know widespread

audiences of black and white southerners alike had witnessed by the first or early second decade of the century. Based on the existent evidence, such a scenario is at least as plausible as the Africanism theory, if not much more so. In regard to the fabled stories of homemade instruments, Barry Lee Pearson notes, "The homemade guitar has become tied to the bluesman image and is a recognized and at times even a suspect motif of the bluesman's story. What began as a black folk tradition now is part of the bluesman stereotype and, as a stock item of record liner notes and folk festival programs, now serves to authenticate the artist for an essentially white audience" (Pearson, *"Sounds So Good to Me,"* 52).

45. By 1898, at least, the Cable Piano Company in Atlanta was selling steel strings from Germany and distributing them via advertisements throughout the South. Advertisement, *Chipley Banner*, December 17, 1898, 4. However, the C. F. Martin Company did not begin building guitars braced for steel strings until the 1920s, in response to the "lasting, profound effect" of the "Hawaiian craze" on the Martin line. Carter, *The Martin Guitar*, 31. Yet other companies had begun responding to the Hawaiian craze earlier, with some producing improved bracings because of the late nineteenth-century popularity of mandolins. Meanwhile, at least by the 1910s, companies were manufacturing raised nuts that players could place underneath the strings where they contact the fretboard behind the first fret, thus providing the elevation necessary to convert standard guitars into "Hawaiian" guitars. Such modifications may have been the most economical and common option to make a guitar playable in the Hawaiian style, although the guitars would still require significant bracing to hold their intonation, regardless of whether they were played in laps or in the conventional manner documented by some African American artists in the 1930s.

46. Handy, *Father of the Blues*, 74. According to David Evans (personal correspondence, July 15, 2013), in the first draft of Handy's book, the passage read "in a style later popularized by Hawaiian guitarists." Assuming that Handy accurately recalled the 1903 date, then either assertion is correct: the Hawaiian style did not gain wide popularity in the United States for another few years. This difference does not, however, diminish the significance of Handy's primary association of the style with Hawaiians.

47. A number of liner notes and books that discuss Jimmie Tarlton suggest that he learned the method from a local African American musician. However, when we go to their source, a series of interviews with Tarlton by Graham Wickham, this claim turns out to be unfounded, and was likely influenced by Wickham's own assumptions. Wickham writes, "When he was ten he decided to play the guitar as he had *probably* seen or heard Negro street musicians playing; that is, across the

knees or hand-held, with some sort of smooth object, a knife or bottleneck, used for chording and melodies. . . . Jimmie first used a comb but, finding that unsatisfactory, used a bottleneck or a penknife. Years later he used automobile wrist pins." Wickham continues later in the newsletter, "It is not very clear why Jimmie took up the guitar as he does not fully explain this. But, very importantly, he says he found the standard way of playing the guitar too limited, so he began using a 'noter,' something he regards as his own invention. . . . Jimmie does not recall any other steel guitar players in his youth." Whatever the case, Tarlton did not hit the streets (and the road) to busk for money until 1912, when he certainly would have encountered Hawaiian guitarists. Over the next years he traveled throughout the country for various jobs, and ended up in Los Angeles. There he met Frank Ferreira [Ferera], who showed him how to use a steel bar. Wickham notes, "Jimmie learned a great deal from Ferera." Wickham, *Darby and Tarlton*, 7–9, 16; my emphasis. My thanks to Patrick Huber for directing me to this source.

48. Ibid.

49. Odum, "Folk-Song and Folk-Poetry as Found in the Secular Songs of the Southern Negroes"; Odum, "Folk-Song and Folk-Poetry as Found in the Secular Songs of the Southern Negroes (Concluded)."

50. Kahn, liner notes to *Darby and Tarlton*; Olsson, liner notes to *Cannon's Jug Stompers*. Hamilton, *In Search of the Blues*, 29. Bruce Bastin argues that the transition to slide guitar was facilitated by a familiarity with fretless banjos. Bastin, *Red River Blues*, 11–12. The relationship between the fretless banjo and the slide guitar is disputed by banjo scholar Tony Thomas, however: "There is absolutely NO evidence of slide banjo playing being a regular part of banjo playing at any time, much less as a precursor of slide guitar. The one player I know about, Gus Cannon, always said that he picked up slide banjo playing from a slide guitarist he learned a number of songs from around the turn of the century. As far as I know there is no history of slide banjo playing and that the one or two slide banjo players we know of like Gwen Foster and Cannon did this as a novelty under the influence of guitarists in Cannon's case or clearly trying to sound like a Hawaiian guitarist in Foster's case." Personal correspondence with Tony Thomas, June 24, 2014.

51. Non-Hawaiians who visited the Islands in the 1890s began teaching the technique back on the continent soon after. For example, in 1899, William Miles observed Hawaiian guitarist Keoki Akea in Honolulu; while residing in Pasadena, California, in 1902, he took steel guitar lessons from a Mexican guitarist who had learned to play the instrument while living in the Islands. By 1903, Miles was regularly teaching classes and giving public steel guitar demonstrations in Winnipeg. Shilstra and Berger, "William Miles," 546–47. It is also possible that in 1899 July

Paka played the steel guitar on Edison cylinder recordings in San Francisco, though no cylinders from this session seem to have survived.

52. Sutton, "Rediscovering Sam Moore." Moore enjoyed considerable success with this song, which he recorded and released through seven labels in the United States and the United Kingdom in that year alone. Rockwell, *Hawaiian and Hawaiian Guitar Records*, 842.

53. Quoted in Sutton, "Rediscovering Sam Moore."

54. Rockwell, *Hawaiian and Hawaiian Guitar Records*, 842.

55. Malone, *Country Music U.S.A.*, 39.

56. Russell, *Country Music Records*, 424.

57. For an account of the creation of these lists. See Miller, *Segregating Sound*, 198–214.

58. Miller, "Instruments as Technology and Culture," 32–33.

59. Russell, *Country Music Records*, 299–300; Okihiro, *Island World*, 199.

60. Russell, *Country Music Records*, 299–300, 303. Regarding his 1937 session with Lani McIntire, Al McIntire (Lani's father), Bob Nichols, and George Kainapu, Davis recalled, "They were playing at the Lexington Hotel in New York. We went up there, and we recorded this, and I sang, of course, and they came in after, and they did a great job. It was a—well, I thought it was a beautiful record." Interview with Jimmie Davis, July 8, 1976, Nashville, Tennessee, OH40, Oral History Collection, CMHF.

61. Obrecht, "Sylvester Weaver."

62. Tranquada and King, *The 'Ukulele*, 214 n. 43. Personal correspondence with Jim Tranquada, September 14, 2013.

63. Advertisement, Krausgill Piano Company, *Kentucky Kernel*, April 20, 1916, 2.

64. "No Lazy Man's Place," *Hartford Republican*, August 30, 1918, 6; "Miss Gladys Frisbie Entertained," *Central Record*, August 1, 1918, 7; "Famous Hawaiian Troupe of Singers, Dancers, and Steel Guitar Players in *My Honolulu Girl* at the Manring Theatre, April 17," *Middlesboro Pinnacle News*, April 14, 1919, 4; advertisement, *Mt. Sterling Advocate*, July 29, 1919, 3; "'The Royal Serenaders' at Paris Grand Thursday," *Bourbon News*, November 28, 1922, 2. The *Bourbon News* reported that "the guitar and his own ukelele [*sic*] . . . has made the music of these Islands familiar to all." In the early years, newspaper reporters occasionally confused the names of the 'ukulele, with its often brash, staccato rhythmic playing, and the Hawaiian guitar, with its associated soft, glissando slides; thus, the article continued, "The peculiar sliding tone of the ukulele has taken the world by storm, and you can hear almost any familiar tune rendered a la Hawaiian." 'Ukuleles were sometimes confused with steel guitars, but more often audiences recognized the clear distinction

between the two instruments, and early on at that. A review of a local "Field's Minstrels" performance in a 1916 edition of Mississippi's *Greenville Daily Democrat*, for example, states, "One of the new hits of the performance was when Bobbie Henshaw and his little 'Ukulele imitated the music of the Hawaiian steel guitar in a most realistic manner. He pleased the audience wonderfully." This review also reveals that the 'ukulele can be played in a number of styles, not simply in the rapid, staccato manner that was popularized on the U.S. continent in the teens and twenties. "Field's Minstrels," *Greenville Daily Democrat*, October 11, 1916, 4.

65. Harris, "Smoketown Strut."

66. Obrecht, "Tampa Red"; Oakley, *The Devil's Music*; Handy, *Father of the Blues*, 74; Charters, *The Country Blues*, 157; Davis, *The History of the Blues*, 116, 146; Wolfe and Lornell, *The Life and Legend of Leadbelly*, 45, 91; Wardlow, *Chasin' That Devil's Music*, 5, 36; Evans, "Musical Innovation in the Blues of Blind Lemon Jefferson," 93. Handy assumed the guitarist was African American, but we should not discount outright the possibility that the guitarist was instead Hawaiian, waiting for the train to depart for the next stop on the vaudeville circuit.

67. Garon and Garon, *Woman with Guitar*, 20–21.

68. *St. Louis, 1927–1933*; Ma Rainey, "Dream Blues" and "Last Wandering Blues," recorded March 1924 in Chicago, Paramount 12098; *Hokum Blues, 1924–29*.

69. Haden, "Vernon Dalhart," 69.

70. Carlin, *The Big Book of Country Music*, 114; Malone, *Country Music U.S.A.*, 61.

71. Carlin, *The Big Book of Country Music*, 114.

72. Miller, *Segregating Sound*, 122.

73. Rockwell, *Hawaiian and Hawaiian Guitar Records*, 191–93, 285, 287, 304–6, 442, 477, 923.

74. Malone, *Country Music U.S.A.*, 62, 64.

75. Gussow, "Playing Chicken with the Train," 236–37; see also Wald, *Escaping the Delta*, 47–53, 57, 96–97.

76. Lis, "The Steel Guitar in Early Country Music," part 2, chap. 4, sec. 1, 16.

77. Quoted in Volk, *Lap Steel Guitar*, 15.

78. Only four sides were issued. Rockwell, *Hawaiian and Hawaiian Guitar Records*, 372; Lani Ellen McIntire, private scrapbooks. Her scrapbooks contain hundreds of images of not only her life as a professional dancer but also the lives of her father, Hawaiian musician Al McIntire, and her mother, Jean Mayo, a trick rider and actress. Combined in several scrapbooks, Lani Ellen McIntire's collection of images provides an astonishing view into the world Hawaiian musicians and Hollywood celebrity in the 1920s through the 1950s.

79. Okihiro, *Island World*, 205.

80. When searching through stacks of 78 rpm records in southern flea markets, estate sales, and antique malls, I have found it nearly impossible not to come across one of Ferreira's recordings.

81. Barker, "The American Pedal Steel Guitar," 27.

82. Huber, *Linthead Stomp*, 244–45.

83. Interview with Cliff Carlisle, September 21, 1967, Lexington, KY, OH296, Oral History Collection, CMHF; Carlin, *The Big Book of Country Music*, 64.

84. Tom Darby and Jimmie Tarlton, "Little Ola," recorded April 15, 1930, Atlanta, Columbia 15591-D; Cléoma Breaux and Joe Falcon, "Prenez Courage" (Take Courage), recorded April 18, 1929, Atlanta, Columbia 40503-F, OKeh 9003; Cliff Carlisle, "Never No Mo' Blues," recorded July 21, 1930, Richmond, IN, Supertone 9708. I'd like to thank my friend and bandmate Philippe Billadeaux for turning me on to "Prenez Courage."

85. Okihiro, *Island World*, 201.

86. "Bashful Brother Oswald," *Brad's Page of Steel*, http://www.well.com/user/wellvis/oswald.html; accessed May 25, 2015. According to the website, "This page is heavily based on the liner notes by Charles Wolfe from the 1994 Rounder Records album *Brother Oswald*."

87. Ibid.

88. "Man Who Gave Steel Guitar to Nashville Dies."

89. Ibid.

90. "Bashful Brother Oswald," *Brad's Page of Steel*, http://www.well.com/user/wellvis/oswald.html; accessed May 25, 2015.

91. Ibid.

92. I derive my biographical information on Rodgers from Malone, *Country Music U.S.A.*, 77–91. For a photograph of Rodgers and his Hawaiian troupe, see Okihiro, *Island World*, 202.

93. His work with Kanui was never released. Lani McIntire and his band recorded six sides with Rodgers in June and July 1930. It is unknown who played steel guitar at these sessions. Hawaiian music aficionado John Marsden believes that the recordings sound like Bob Keolaokalani Nichols's work, while country music discographer Tony Russell suggests that it was Sam Koki. Lis, "The Steel Guitar in Early Country Music," part 2, chap. 3, part 1, 19; Lis, "The Steel Guitar in Early Country Music," part 2, chap. 4, sec. 2, 21; Russell, *Country Music Records*, 803.

94. Carlin, *The Big Book of Country Music*, 396.

95. Interview with Cliff Carlisle, July 11, 1974, Renfro Valley, KY, OH30-LC, Oral History Collection, CMHF; Ankeny, "Cliff Carlisle."

96. Interview with Cliff Carlisle, July 11, 1974, Renfro Valley, KY, OH30-LC, Oral History Collection, CMHF.

97. Quoted in Obrecht, "Tampa Red." See also Cortese, "Tampa Red," 23; and "Son House," interview by Barry Hansen and Mark Levine, FT-2809 LC, "Interview with Son House in Venice, CA, 1965," part 1 (2001), John Edwards Memorial Collection, UNC; inflected emphasis in interview. I would like to thank Elijah Wald for turning my attention to this interview. For more on Rubin Lacy, see Evans, "Rubin Lacy."

98. National Park Service, "Walter 'Furry' Lewis"; Lewis, White, and Friends, *Party! At Home*.

99. "1542 My Hula Hula Love," *Edison Phonograph Monthly*, November 1912, 16.

100. Wolfe and Lornell, *The Life and Legend of Leadbelly*, 45, 48; quoted in ibid., 38; Brooks, "'Hula Love,' Another Case of Song Larceny," 6.

101. Mitchell, Kanahele, and Berger, "Steel Guitar," 793. Noelani's Hawaiian Orchestra was identified on its first recording with the electric steel as "Noi Lane Hawaiian Orchestra."

102. Russell, *Country Music Records*, 136–37.

103. Malone, *Country Music U.S.A.*, 158.

104. Ibid., 157.

105. Ibid., 128.

106. Interview with Jerry Byrd, October 24, 1988, Nashville, OHC48, Oral History Collection, CMHF.

107. Ibid. For the best biographical treatment of the duo, see the liner notes to *Genial Hawaiians Jim and Bob, plus George Ku and His Paradise Islanders*.

108. Interview with Jerry Byrd, October 24, 1988, Nashville, OHC48, Oral History Collection, CMHF.

109. Ibid.

110. ibid.

111. Boyd, *The Jazz of the Southwest*, 117–18.

112. Malone, *Country Music U.S.A.*, 158.

113. Quoted in Boyd, *The Jazz of the Southwest*, 118. In another interview from 1969, McAuliffe said, "Incidentally, I had written a song that I called the 'Steel Guitar Rag.' This was the first tune that I played for W. Lee O'Daniel [of the Light Crust Doughboys]. This tune was more—it was away from Hawaiian music. I was just—oh, I guess, it was sort of a ragtime type of music, you might say. So I used this to audition for him, and I used it as the first tune that I ever played on the Light

Crust Doughboys program." Interview with Leon McAuliffe, August 19, 1969, Nashville, OH340, Oral History Collection, CMHF.

114. See Sylvester Weaver, "Guitar Rag," 1923, and Sylvester Weaver, "Guitar Rag," 1927. Both versions contain all of the parts found in McAuliffe's version, while the 1927 version contains the exact structure of McAuliffe's rendition. Both recordings are included on *Sylvester Weaver, Vol. 1*. McAuliffe may also have heard Weaver's "Guitar Rag" as recorded by Harvey and Johnson in 1930. Minton, *78 Blues*, 68.

115. Desmond, *Staging Tourism*, 73.

116. Quoted in ibid., 74.

117. "Man Who Gave Steel Guitar to Nashville Dies."

118. Quoted in Emerson, "True Fan Lives across the Sea," 6.

119. Ibid.

120. Ibid.

121. Ibid., 8.

122. Ibid.

123. Ibid.

124. Goldie Kolomoku to Eddie Alkire, May 2, 1933, box 81, folder 22, UIUC. Anita "Goldie" Kolomoku eventually married another famous Hawaiian entertainer working in New York, Johnny Kaonohi Pineapple.

125. See, for example, DeLano, "Hawaiian Music."

126. Kapua, "Joseph Kekuku."

127. Walter Kolomoku to Eddie Alkire, September 5, 1925, box 79, folder 7, UIUC.

128. Charles Kolomoku to Eddie Alkire, September 11, 1945, box 79, folder 18, UIUC.

129. Ruymar, *The Hawaiian Steel Guitar*, 71.

130. 1920 Census, Baltimore Ward 11, Baltimore (Independent City), Maryland, roll T625_661, page 7A, enumeration district 171, image 1018, NARA, via http://home.ancestry.com; accessed May 20, 2015.

131. "Meet One of the Oahu Serenaders."

132. Lis, "The Steel Guitar in Early Country Music," part 2, chap. 5, sec. 3, 7.

133. The definitive history of the sacred steel movement, Robert Stone's *Sacred Steel* identifies the relevant connection between Kanaka instructors and the developers of the genre. For Stone's discussion of the Kahuaolopua (aka Kahanolopua) brothers, Eason's discovery of the instrument, and Stone's argument that it was Hawaiian music and musicians—and not bottleneck slide players who held their guitars in the conventional fashion—who inspired Eason's adoption and play-

ing of the instrument, see ibid., 64–76. Eventually Troman Eason's sons developed a unique style of playing that emphasized the vocal melodies of the gospel songs popular in the church. Early female members of the churches also found Kanaka guitar instructors from whom they took lessons, even in the small town of Ocala, Florida. Ibid., 129.

134. Betty Glynn, quoted in Ruymar, *The Hawaiian Steel Guitar*, 71. The brothers later parted ways; Stanley took full ownership of Oahu, and Bronson formed his own brand of Hawaiian guitar schools and a separate publishing company.

135. Ruymar, *The Hawaiian Steel Guitar*, 70. Eddie Alkire worked as the instructor for Oahu Publishing Company's flagship conservatory in Cleveland, the Honolulu Conservatory. The company claimed that Alkire alone had taught over 4,000 students in the United States and Canada via correspondence courses by early 1933. "Busy?," 7.

136. "Second Pardon Frees Smeeman," February 3, 1933, *El Paso Herald-Post*, 16.

137. Ibid.; "Smeeman Prosecutor in Favor of Pardon," January 23, 1933, *Greeley Daily Tribune*, 1. Stanley's illegal exploits did not end when he founded the Oahu Company. He was fined $1,400 in the early 1930s for copyright infringement. Eddie Alkire to Henry Makua, October 22, 1979, box 58, folder 12, UIUC.

138. "How Popular Is the Hawaiian Guitar?," 3.

139. For the best treatment of female hula dancers on the professional circuit at this time, see Imada, *Aloha America*.

140. Eddie Alkire left the Oahu Publishing Company in the mid-1930s to form his own quite popular schools and correspondence courses. His archives at UIUC contain student enrollments and periodicals. The Library of Congress keeps the majority of the run of Oahu's *Hawaiian Guitarist* periodical.

141. Some women on the continent did break into professional performance on the steel guitar during this period. Kay Koster regularly gigged with all-male dance bands and performed session work, while Letritia Kandle performed in numerous bands in Chicago, including an all-girl Hawaiian band and a stint in Paul Whiteman's orchestra. She gained her knowledge of the instrument and of Hawaiian culture through her mentor, George Kealoha Gilman. The Williams Twins likewise toured the country by themselves for over a year, performing educational shows in schools. As the Williams Twins put it, however, "families came first," and eventually they got married and left the road. They continued to play semiprofessionally, however, up through the date of our interview and beyond. Dickerson, "Letritia Kandle and the Magnificent Grand Letar," 50–52; Parker and Crum interview.

142. See, for example, "Hawaiian Guitar Brings Popularity to These Girls," 7.

143. Stone, *Sacred Steel*, 66.

144. John McGinley, *Increasing Your Enrollments through Personal Selling* (Easton, PA: Eddie Alkire, 1942), 9, box 31, folder 5, UIUC.

145. Ibid.; emphasis in original.

146. Ibid.

147. Interview with Lloyd Green, December 12, 1973, OH65, Oral History Collection, CMHF.

148. Koster interview. At the time that I interviewed her, Koster was ninety-four years old, performing that weekend at the Hawaiian Steel Guitar Association annual convention in Joliet, Illinois, and still teaching at her own music school.

149. Ibid.

150. Parker and Crum interview.

151. Tonnessen interview. See also Tonnessen's comments in "Guinness Steel Guitar World Record to Be Set May 13th," *Steel Guitar Forum*, http://bb.steelguitarforum.com/viewtopic.php?t=223714&highlight; accessed May 25, 2015.

152. Quoted in Carlin, "Elgin Hawaiian Guitar Band," 30.

153. Ibid.

154. Miller, "Instruments as Technology and Culture," 29.

155. Ibid.

156. Ibid., 31.

157. Ruymar, *The Hawaiian Steel Guitar*, 70.

158. Sutton, *The Man behind the Scenes*, 25.

159. Born in Paia, Maui, Freddie Tavares worked for years with Harry Owens's Royal Hawaiian Orchestra at prominent hotels in Honolulu, San Francisco, and Los Angeles. He performed on the steel for the first broadcast of *Hawaiʻi Calls* (see chapter 7). In 1953, after Tavares had settled in Anaheim, California, Leo Fender hired him as more or less his design partner. As Fender chronicler Richard R. Smith put it, "Freddie filled a unique role at Fender and became the ultimate design insider, another lobe in Leo's brain and an indispensable part of his inner sanctum." He designed the split finger mechanism on the Fender 1000 pedal steel. Tavares was known to take very little credit for his contributions to Fender designs, but he is understood by Fender experts today to have made major contributions to the design of Fender's Stratocaster and other guitars, pedal steels, and amps. He was also very active in the Hollywood Hawaiian community and worked on many films, television, and radio shows. His brother Ernest Tavares developed an early prototype of a pedal steel guitar in Honolulu in 1947. Smith, *Fender*, 117, 128; Jon Woodhouse, "Tavares/Stratocaster," *Maui News*, May 26, 2011.

160. Koster interview.

CHAPTER 7

1. Suzuki, "Connect Back to Dis Place," 17. In this MA thesis, Andrea Suzuki contributes excellent research and scholarship on the politics of Hawaiian music during the early 1970s.

2. Quoted in Kanahele, "The Hawaiian Renaissance."

3. Ibid.

4. Harry Soria Jr., quoted in Keany, "One Hundred Years of Hawaiian Music."

5. Kanahele, "The Hawaiian Renaissance."

6. Kanahele, quoted in Suzuki, "Connect Back to Dis Place," 18. As early as 1966, steel guitarist Barney Isaacs saw the writing on the wall: "The kids think Hawaiian music is a drag. . . . They want to play rock 'n' roll." John S. Wilson, "Moaning Sigh of Steel Guitar on Wane in Hawaii," *New York Times*, December 21, 1966, 47.

7. The name of the player was Dave Napihe Burrows, born on Moloka'i in 1898, of Pākē and Hawaiian descent. Hoapili said Burrows was "about eighteen at the time," so perhaps he saw Burrows in Honolulu a few years later than 1910, but before 1917, when Hoapili left for California. Burrows went on to play steel guitar professionally, recording several exemplary sides. "The History of the Hawaiian Steel Guitar," 12.

8. Richard Choy owned the Banjo King Music Store and Studio, located at 1191 Bethel St., in the heart of the downtown music scene of cafés and bars. Richard Choy to Eddie Alkire, May 24, 1938, box 56, folder 12, UIUC.

9. Richard Choy to Eddie Alkire, November 26, 1940, box 56, folder 12, UIUC.

10. Choy relayed the popular tunings in the Islands in 1940: E7 was tuned E B G# E D E, or E B G# E D B; A minor tunings included E C A E C A and E C A G C E. Another tuning, "most promising," was E C A F Eb C. The popular C# minor tuning was E C# G# E B E. Players had observed limits with the C# minor tuning, however: "This tuning is good only can't use Palm Harmonics on the Tonic Chord." Meanwhile, at the Hotel Lexington in New York, both Sam Koki and (with Lani McIntire's band) and Tommy Castro (with Ray Kinney's) preferred C# minor. Richard Choy to Eddie Alkire, January 8, 1940; Eddie Alkire to Richard Choy, April 4, 1941, box 56, folder 12, UIUC.

11. Richard Choy to Eddie Alkire, November 26, 1940, box 56, folder 12, UIUC.

12. Richard Choy to Eddie Alkire, January 8, 1940, box 56, folder 12, UIUC.

13. Burlingame and Kasher, *Da Kine Sound*, 17. Although Choy seemed most interested in the steel work of the "boys," photographs from the Bishop Museum reveal that the steel guitar was *not* the exclusive domain of male performers; wāhine guitarists had embraced the instrument as well, in public and private settings, and Ernest Ka'ai's daughter Thelma performed steel guitar professionally for his troupe

while on tour in Southeast Asia during the early 1920s. "Big Success of the Hawaiian Troupe," *Straits Times*, November 29, 1921, 10.

14. Kanahele and Berger, "John Avery Noble," 606; Ruymar, *The Hawaiian Steel Guitar*, 98, 102, 107.

15. Ruymar, *The Hawaiian Steel Guitar*, 48, 52.

16. Ibid., 63.

17. Ibid., 102.

18. Mo'okini wrote, "David Keli'i was at Hoffman's Café, Tommy Castro at Rathskeller and later with Gigi Royce's Orchestra at the Young Hotel Roof Garden. David Malo playing with the Andy Cummings Group at the Hawaiian Town Night Club and Gabby Pahinui later joined Andy. Jake Keli'ikoa was at Maggie's Inn, and later with Don MacDiarmid's Orchestra and eventually with Alfred Apaka, at the Moana Hotel. Pua Alameida (Almeida) started with his dad Johnny, then formed his own band which played at a night club called Club Pago Pago. His stint at the Moana Hotel came some time after this gig. Dan Ka'eka played with Bill Lincoln's group and Eddie Pang later became the steel guitar player. Joe Custino was in this circuit of players but performed weekly on a radio broadcast called the Transit Hawaiians. The late Fred Tavares played with the Harry Owens Orchestra at the Royal Hawaiian Hotel while Steppy DeRego was the steel guitar performer for the Ray Andrade Orchestra at La Hula Rhumba. Merle Kekuku played with the original Islanders and later formed a group that played at the Moana Hotel. Billy Hew Len was at the Niumalu Hotel." Quoted in ibid., 63.

19. Burlingame and Kasher, *Da Kine Sound*, 14.

20. Kanahele and Berger, "Hawai'i Calls," 267.

21. Ibid., 267–68.

22. Ibid., 267–71. The program was briefly rebooted in 1992. A number of prominent steel guitarists in country music recalled listening avidly to *Hawaii Calls* each week, including Jerry Byrd.

23. Kanahele and Berger, "Hawai'i Calls," 268; Todaro, *The Golden Years of Hawaiian Entertainment*, 141.

24. Ruymar, *The Hawaiian Steel Guitar*, 48.

25. His surname was Keli'iheleua. Todaro, *The Golden Years of Hawaiian Entertainment*, 197.

26. Richard Choy to Eddie Alkire, January 8, 1941 [misprinted as 1940], box 56, folder 12, UIUC; emphasis in original.

27. Ibid.

28. Kanahele and Berger, "Hawai'i Calls," 268.

29. Ibid.

30. Shishikura, "I'll Remember You," 27.

31. Kanahele and Berger, "Hawai'i Calls," 267–69.

32. Quoted in Shishikura, "I'll Remember You," 44.

33. Ibid., 43 n. 9.

34. Radio transcripts quoted in Kanahele and Berger, "Hawai'i Calls," 269. "Dardanella" was a smash hit written in 1919 about a (presumably white) man's love for a Middle Eastern, Islamic woman.

35. Ibid.

36. In a demonstration of the recurrent function of nostalgia in music criticism, a 1911 editorial in the Hawaiian-language newspaper *Ka Nupepa Kuokoa* seemed to place the writing on the wall: "If we were to turn back in time, to many years past, when the Kawaihau Glee Club and many other groups were famous for singing, we will see when comparing them to those performing today, the differences between them.... These days... our singers are following haole style singing; and when songs that we are used to hearing along with their tunes which fill us with energy and enthrallment are changed, when listening to that it is like ridicule, for we are not used to hearing that kind of melody, and Hawaiian songs are not famous for that style of singing." "Pehea E Hoohepaia Mai Nei Himeni Hawai'i!," *Ka Nupepa Kuokoa* (September 8, 1911): 4; translated by nupepa-hawaii.com: http://nupepa-hawaii.com/2014/06/04/hawaiian-music-and-editorial-1911/; accessed July 4, 2015.

37. Ibid.

38. Kanahele and Berger, "Charles Edward King," 476–77. For an excellent treatment of the history of piano in the Islands and in Hawaiian music, see Salā, "Claiming the Colonial and Domesticating the Foreign."

39. Kanahele and Berger, "Hawai'i Calls," 269.

40. Interview with Gabby Pahinui and Peter Moon, in Burlingame and Kasher, *Da Kine Sound*, 21.

41. Lewis, "Storm Blowing from Paradise," 57.

42. Berger, "Don Ho," 311.

43. Quoted in Kanahele, "The Hawaiian Renaissance."

44. For the role of the rural kua'āina in many of these struggles, particularly in the reclamation of the island of Kaho'olawe from the U.S. military, which had used it as a bombing range since World War II, see McGregor, *Nā Kua'āina*, 249–85.

45. Kanahele, "The Hawaiian Renaissance."

46. Ibid.

47. Quoted in Engebretson, "The New Sound of Hawaiian Music," 84.

48. Dwight Hanohano, quoted in Lewis, "Beyond the Reef," 192.

49. Quoted in Lewis, "Don' Go Down Waikiki," 171.

50. Quoted in ibid., 183.

51. Ibid., 172–73. "Mele Ai Pohaku" is also known as "Kaulana Nā Pua." "Rousing Ovation," *Daily Bulletin*, March 23, 1893, 2.

52. When the vote for statehood was called in 1959, residents of Hawai'i were given two options: to vote for continued territorial status or to vote in favor of statehood. At the time, non-Hawaiians, including U.S. military personnel stationed in the Islands, far outnumbered the Hawaiian residents, thus ensuring that a vote to renounce either option would not come to pass. Resistance, however, did take many forms, including a strong vote against statehood by the Hawaiian residents of Ni'ihau, and the expression of antistatehood views by Hawaiian tour bus drivers to their passengers. On the U.S. congressional side of the question, a statehood bill took many years to come to the table, partly because senators from southern states believed that "the island population was far too racially unassimilable." Imada, *Aloha America*, 182, 184, 319 n. 113.

53. Quoted in Lewis, "Role Conflict and the Professional Musician," 193.

54. Quoted in Lewis, "Don' Go Down Waikiki," 171. Godfrey's radio show in the 1930s and 1940s, and his television show in the 1950s, *Arthur Godfrey and Friends*, promoted hapa haole and pseudo-Hawaiian music.

55. Trask, *From a Native Daughter*, 142, 144.

56. Lewis, "Storm Blowing from Paradise," 57.

57. Ibid., 61–62.

58. Quoted in Burlingame and Kasher, *Da Kine Sound*, 92–93.

59. Quoted in Shishikura, "I'll Remember You," 54.

60. Quoted in Burlingame and Kasher, *Da Kine Sound*, 162. Lake's concern over the youths' rejection of hapa haole music, combined with his biography and performance legacy, reveals that the relationship between Hawaiians' political and musical perspectives during the 1970s did not conform easily to simple generational or stylistic divides. Lake's hanai (informally adopted) children included the revered Hawaiian activist George Helm, who disappeared off the coast of Kaho'olawe in 1977 while protesting the bombing of the island by the U.S. military. Helm studied music under Lake before becoming a martyr to the political movements that characterized the Renaissance period. And while Lake criticized the fervent anti–hapa haole sentiment of the 1970s, by the time he died in 2011, he was memorialized as "one of only a handful of performing and recording artists in the field of Hawaiian music who created a new sound yet kept it very traditionally Hawaiian." Keith Haugen, quoted in John Berger, "Kahauanu Lake, 1932–2011: Musician was 'Ukulele Master," *Star Advertiser*, March 8, 2011.

61. Quoted in Lewis, "Beyond the Reef," 194.

62. The newspaper reported, "At 42 years of age, [Barney Isaacs] is part of what may be the last generation of steel guitarists." John S. Wilson, "Moaning Sigh of Steel Guitar on Wane in Hawaii," *New York Times*, December 21, 1966, 47.

63. Quoted in Shishikura, "I'll Remember You," 53.

64. Mitchell, Kanahele, and Berger, "Steel Guitar," 798. Likewise, steel guitarist, entertainer, and arranger Benny Kalama reported facing a young movie soundtrack producer who refused to allow the steel guitar in his soundtrack for *Blood and Orchids* because of its connotations with "cowboy music." 'Iwalani Hodges, "Oral History Interview with Benny Kalama," April 29, 1986, Lanikai, O'ahu, tape no. 12-78-1-86, COHUHM, 1083–1084.

65. 'Iwalani Hodges, "Oral History Interview with Benny Kalama," April 29, 1986, Lanikai, O'ahu, Tape No. 12-78-1-86, COHUHM, 1116.

66. Quoted in Hoover, "Tunes of Steel."

67. Jerry Byrd, quoted in ibid.

68. Alex Hoapili, quoted in "The History of the Hawaiian Steel Guitar," 7.

69. A kupuna slack key guitarist, Alice Namakelua, for example, had "forgotten more tunings than most of the modern-day slack key artists have ever learned." "The State of Guitar in Hawaii," *Guitar Player*, 13.

70. Kanahele and Berger, "Charles Philip 'Gabby' Pahinui," 628. He was born Philip Kunia Kahahawai'i but was hanai'd into the Pahinui family as a young boy. Suzuki gives his middle name as Kapono. Suzuki, "Connect Back to Dis Place," 20.

71. Akamine, "Gabby Tells His Own Story," 1.

72. Houston and Kamae, *Hawaiian Son*, 37.

73. Ibid.

74. Gabby Pahinui and Peter Moon interview in Burlingame and Kasher, *Da Kine Sound*, 24.

75. Ibid., 21.

76. Ibid., 22.

77. Akamine, "Gabby Tells His Own Story," 1. See also Thornton, "Gabby Pahinui," 21.

78. Burlingame and Kasher, *Da Kine Sound*, 14; Gabby Pahinui interview with Dave Guard, 1961, part 1, http://www.kingstontrioplace.com/GabbyPahinuiDaveGuardTrack13.mp3; accessed May 25, 2015. According to Pahinui, "As I was growin' older—I was 15 or 16—I heard this guy 'Tiny,' Charley Brown, from Bethel Street. I used to stay with him. All the time I was learning, I watched him, because he never taught you. You gotta watch him. He used to tune his steel guitar in his room. He got these numbers on the wall where you think it was a telephone number, but it

was not. It was all his steel tunings. Every fret was a number. But I would never know unless I watched him. He was great too, Charley Brown. We called him 'Tiny'; he weighed 600 pounds. A big man. He was well known, he always hung around Bethel Street." Akamine, "Gabby Tells His Own Story," 2.

79. Gabby Pahinui interview with Dave Guard, 1961, part 2, http://www.kingstontrioplace.com/GabbyPahinuiDaveGuardTrack14.mp3; accessed May 25, 2015. Gabby recalled, "At the time, I used to hear all the great bands—sextet, big bands, small combos. Benny Goodman was good, Artie Shaw, Tommy Dorsey, Jimmy Lundsford, Andy Kirk, Glenn Miller, Count Basie, Woody Herman, Stan Kenton and Duke Ellington. I listened to all those records. To give you an idea, when I used to get those records, I used to stay home and listen to that. The first guitar player I liked doing all those Be-bop things was Charlie Christian. I thought he was great. When my family was at home they didn't want me playing those kind of records, they were playing those O.K. records by Kalima Serenaders in the early '20s. When I put on those records, they think I'm nuts." Akamine, "Gabby Tells His Own Story," 1.

80. Gabby Pahinui and Peter Moon interview in Burlingame and Kasher, *Da Kine Sound*, 17.

81. Ibid.

82. For a sampling of Pahinui's steel guitar work, listen to the Maile Serenaders, *Kani Ka Pila*, vol. 2, *Let's Play Music!*, Hula Records (HS 561), 1966.

83. Quoted in Chang, "Steel Guitar Magic," 32.

84. Hoover, "Tunes of Steel."

85. Quoted in Chang, "Steel Guitar Magic," 32.

86. David Rogers was also referred to by many as "Feets" Rogers.

87. Houston and Kamae, *Hawaiian Son*, 34.

88. Ibid., 35.

89. Quoted in ibid.

90. Haugen and Berger, "Sons of Hawai'i," 769.

91. Quoted in ibid., 769. A few other groups associated with the Renaissance continued to integrate the steel following the minimalist approach of Feet Rogers. For an example of Rogers's influence during this period, listen to the work of steel guitarist Elmer "Sonny" Lim Jr. on some of the songs recorded by the Mākaha Sons of Ni'ihau between 1975 and 1978. See also Johnston, "Teaching 'the Steel' to a New Generation," 22.

92. Steady work in Waikīkī hotels could provide full-time employment for musicians. Others worked for wages or tips from a wide variety of venues that attracted

tourists and kamaʻāina alike. Gabby Pahinui reflected on his work in the late 1920s and early 1930s: "We started playing for kitty [at a small restaurant by the Ala Wai Bridge called Chock See's] and after that, they had kitties all over the place, even at the parks. Jessie Kalima was doing the Kuhio Beach. And Charley Cab had a kitty too, in the taxi stand. The music was going there, too. I guess there were three places where they had kitties in the can. People come from all parts of the island, sitting there dropping dimes, bus fare, pennies, quarters, whatever. That was something." Akamine, "Gabby Tells His Own Story," 2.

93. Haugen and Berger, "Sons of Hawaiʻi," 769.

94. Pahinui continued to play steel guitar, and recorded it on some of his own (and others') albums. Yet his continued use of the instrument in recordings ultimately failed to spark much interest among the younger generation.

95. "Musical Diggings." The newsletter was printed by the Hawaiian Music Foundation, an organization that began in 1971 to support research and the advancement of knowledge regarding Hawaiian music. Kanahele's remarkable encyclopedia *Hawaiian Music and Musicians*, first published in 1979, was a product of the efforts of the Hawaiian Music Foundation.

95. Kanahele and Berger, "Hawaiian Music Foundation," 275–77.

96. Jerry Byrd to Eddie Alkire, November 1, 1976, box 56, folder 7, Elbern H. "Eddie" Alkire Personal Papers and Music Instrument Collection, 1926–1997, series 12/9/101, Sousa Archives and Center for American Music, UIUC.

98. Akaka interview.

99. Ibid.

100. Ibid.

101. Ibid.

102. Ibid.

103. Ibid.

104. Ibid.

105. Ibid.

106. Mitchell, Kanahele, and Berger, "Steel Guitar," 799.

107. During a 2011 performance, Ingano recalled that when he used to play rock 'n' roll, the "old-timers" and parents "wanted to throw us in jail [laughs]." https://www.youtube.com/watch?v=xdTa9MzgF6s; accessed June 28, 2015.

108. Mitchell, Kanahele, and Berger, "Steel Guitar," 800–801.

109. Ibid., 799.

EPILOGUE

1. Akaka interview.

2. For a history of S.B. 3107, SD1, HD1, and HB2573, see http://www.capitol.hawaii.gov/Archives/measure_indiv_Archives.aspx?billtype=SB&billnumber=3107&year=2014; accessed May 25, 2015. Alan Akaka is very familiar with the legislative process, as he is the son of former U.S. senator Daniel Akaka.

3. "Move to Make ʻUkulele State Instrument Needs Fine Tuning," *Honolulu Star Advertiser*, April 22, 2014. http://www.staradvertiser.com/news/breaking/20140422_Choosing_Hawaii_state_instrument_proves_difficult.html?id=256256701; accessed May 25, 2015.

4. See, for example, Sam Eifling, "Steel Guitar Makes Hawaii Think Twice on Ukulele," *Washington Times*, April 26, 2014. http://www.washingtontimes.com/news/2014/apr/26/steel-guitar-makes-hawaii-think-twice-on-ukulele/?page=all; accessed May 25, 2015.

5. In 2015, the Hawaiʻi state legislature asked students to research and then cast a vote to select the official ʻauana or modern instrument, and the official kahiko or traditional instrument. Of the 100,000 students who voted, an overwhelming 83,241 selected the ʻukulele as the state's ʻauana instrument. The steel guitar followed far behind, with 11,111 votes, and, surprisingly, the slack key guitar finished third with 7,226 votes. The vote demonstrates that the steel guitar continues to suffer from a lack of recognition and popularity in the Islands. At the same time, the attention that Akaka brought to the steel when the previous bill failed likely caused more students to gain an awareness of the instrument, so much so that it earned several thousand more votes than the slack key guitar. Competing with various percussion instruments and the nose flute, the pahu won the kahiko contest, and the legislature voted to adopt the students' recommendation. http://www.kitv.com/news/ukulele-pahu-now-official-state-musical-instruments/32478576; accessed June 28, 2015.

6. Aikau, "Kanaka Maoli Groundwork in the Crossroads of the Pacific," 28.

7. Quoted with permission in ibid., 34.

8. Paleka, "A Very Personal History," 18.

9. Ely, "Joseph Kekuku Statue Unveiling," 4. Lāʻie has produced an extraordinary number of Hawaiian musicians over the years. In addition to Joseph Kekuku and his cousin Sam Nainoa, other professional steel guitarists from Lāʻie include Pale K. Lua, Tau Moe (who moved to Lāʻie when he was ten), and Barney Isaacs. Additional professional Hawaiian musicians and kumu hula from Lāʻie include Johnny Almeida, Pua Almeida, Alfred Apaka, George Mossman, Genoa Keawe, Gary Aiko, Alvin Isaacs, Napua Stevens Poire, Cy Bridges, Momi Kahawaiolaʻa, Andy Cummings, and dozens more. Mary Kawena Pukuʻi, an extraordinarily im-

portant twentieth-century cultural historian, kumu hula, and Hawaiian-language expert, was also raised in Lāʻie. For a much longer list, see Oler, "LDS Composers, Kulu Hula and Musicians," 77–79.

10. In the 1920s the Hawaiʻi Supreme Court ruled that such hui were illegal. Stauffer, "The Hui of Kahana," 15.

11. Stauffer, "An Early L.D.S. Family of Kahana and Lāʻie," 50–51; Stauffer, "The Hui of Kahana," 15–16. The Kahana Hui, and its plan to leave Lāʻie and purchase the ahupuaʻa from Ahmee, seems to have gelled at the height of this "ʻAwa Rebellion," as it is referred to by LDS historians. The LDS leadership quickly realized the missionaries' error in taking a stand against this traditional practice and released those responsible from service. The membership of those who were disfellowshipped was restored soon after; the story of the rebellion remains clear in the minds of Lāʻie's residents, through the present day. For more on the rebellion, see Chase, "The Hawaiian Mission Crisis of 1874," 87–97.

12. Stauffer, "The Hui of Kahana," 24.

13. Ron Johnson was born in 1949. Johnson interview.

14. Quoted in Susan Essoyan, "Oʻahu Valley Families Get Old-Time Lease on Life," *Los Angeles Times*, February 14, 1994, A5.

15. Johnson interview.

16. Cline interview.

BIBLIOGRAPHY

MANUSCRIPT AND ARCHIVAL MATERIAL

Beverly Hills, CA
- Margaret Herrick Library, Academy of Motion Picture Arts and Sciences
  - Motion Picture Association of America, Production Code Administrative Records
  - Production Notes, Synopsis, Press Releases

Chapel Hill, NC
- University of North Carolina at Chapel Hill
  - Southern Folklife Collection, Wilson Library
    - John Edwards Memorial Collection

Honolulu, HI
- Bishop Museum Library and Archives
  - EC Hawaiian Music and Musicians
- Hawaiian Historical Society
  - Photo Collection
- Hawaiʻi State Archives
  - Manuscripts Collection
    - Panama Pacific International Exposition, 1915
    - Vierra Family Papers (unprocessed)
    - John Henry Wilson Papers, 1871–1956 (M-182)
  - Photo Collection
    - Hawaiians: Hula Dancers & Musicians, Groups
- Hawaiʻi State Library
  - Hawaii & Pacific Reference
    - Newspaper Clipping and Pamphlet File
- Kamehameha School Archives
  - Charles E. King, Radio Scripts of Bina Mossman's Glee Club, KHU Radio
  - Photo Collection
- University of Hawaiʻi at Mānoa
  - Center for Oral History
  - Hawaiian Collection, Hamilton Library

- Iowa City, IA
  - University of Iowa Libraries
    - Special Collections and University Archives
      - Redpath Chautauqua Collection (MsC 150)
- Lāʻie, HI
  - Brigham Young University–Hawaiʻi
    - Joseph F. Smith Archives and Special Collections
      - Ken Baldridge Faculty File
      - MSSH Kawahigashi's Letters
- London, UK
  - British Library
  - Victoria and Albert Museum
    - Theatre and Performance Archives, Blythe House
- Nashville, TN
  - Country Music Hall of Fame
    - Frist Library and Archive
      - Oral History Collection
- New Haven, CT
  - Yale University
    - Sterling Memorial Library
      - Helen Heffron Roberts Collection, MS 1410
- Urbana-Champaign, IL
  - University of Illinois at Urbana-Champaign
    - The Sousa Archives and Center for American Music, University of Illinois Archives
      - Elbern H. "Eddie" Alkire Personal Papers and Music Instrument Collection, 1926–1997, Series 12/9/101
- Washington, DC
  - Library of Congress
    - Music Division
    - Prints and Photographs Division
  - National Archives and Records Administration
    - Passport, Census, and Ship Records Retrieved via http://www.ancestry.com
  - Smithsonian Institution
    - National Museum of American History
      - Archives Center

INTERVIEWS CONDUCTED BY THE AUTHOR

Akaka, Alan. July 29, 2011, Kailua, HI.

Cline, Nels. May 4, 2011, phone interview.

Cook, Les. June 8, 2011, Manchester, UK.

Das, Kay. October 6, 2012, Joliet, IL.

Johnson, Ron. May 31, 2013, Kahana Bay, HI.

Koster, Kay. October 6, 2012, Joliet, IL.

McIntire, Lani Ellen. August 4, 2011, Waimānalo, HI.

Meyer, Ka'iwa. January 26, 2012, phone interview.

Moe, Dorian. May 29, 2013, Lā'ie, HI.

Parker, Joanne, and Janis Crum (professionally known as the Williams Twins). October 7, 2012, Joliet, IL.

Teves, Mona. June 4, 2013, Mānoa, HI.

Tonnessen, Billy. May 31, 2012, phone interview.

POPULAR MAGAZINES, NEWSPAPERS, AND NEWSLETTERS

Aberdeen Herald (WA)

American Monthly Review of Reviews

Anaconda Standard (MT)

Anniston Star (AL)

Argus (Melbourne, Australia)

Aloha: The Magazine of Hawai'i and the Pacific

Atlanta Constitution

Bellingham Herald (WA)

Biloxi Daily Herald (MS)

B.M.G.

Boston Daily Globe

Bourbon News (Paris, KY)

Brooklyn Daily Eagle

Central Record (Lancaster, KY)

Cheyenne Daily Leader (WY)

Chicago Daily Tribune

Chicago Defender

Chipley Banner (FL)

Clarksdale Daily Register (MS)

Cumberland Argus and Fruitgrowers Advocate (Paramatta, Australia)

Daily Bulletin (Honolulu)

Daily Democrat Times (Greenville, MS)

Daily Express (London)

Daily Herald (Honolulu)

Deseret News (Salt Lake City, UT)

Des Moines Daily News (IA)

Edison Phonograph Monthly

El Paso Herald (TX)

El Paso Herald-Post (TX)

Evening Bulletin (Honolulu)

Evening Herald (Klamath Falls, OR)

Far Eastern Review, Engineering, Finance, Commerce

Fayetteville Democrat (AR)

Fort Wayne Journal-Gazette (IN)

Freeman's Journal (Sydney, Australia)

The Friend

Galveston Daily News (TX)

Greeley Daily Tribune (CO)

Greenville Daily Democrat (MS)

Greenville Daily Democrat Times (MS)

Guitar Player

Ha'ilono Mele (Hilo, HI)
Hartford Republican (KY)
Hattiesburg American (MS)
Hawaiian Gazette (Honolulu)
Hawaiian Guitarist
Hawaiian Star (Honolulu)
Hawai'i Observer
Honolulu
Honolulu Advertiser
Honolulu Magazine
Honolulu Republican
Honolulu Star Bulletin
Hunt's Merchant's Magazine and Commercial Review
Ka Maka'ainana (Honolulu)
Ka Nupepa Kuokoa (Honolulu)
Ka Lahui Hawaii (Honolulu)
Ka Wai Ola (Honolulu)
Kentucky Kernel (Lexington)
Kuokoa Home Rula (Honolulu)
Latter-Day Saints' Millennial Star
Laurel Daily Leader (MS)
Los Angeles Times
Maui News
Middlesboro Pinnacle News (KY)
Mirror (Perth, Australia)
Morning Bulletin (Rockhampton, Australia)
Mt. Sterling Advocate (KY)
Nevada State Journal (Reno)
New York Clipper
New York Herald
New York Sun
Old-Time Herald
Pacific Commercial Advertiser (Honolulu)
Paradise of the Pacific (Honolulu)
Philadelphia Inquirer
Philippine Herald
Premier Guitar
Robesonian (Lumberton, NC)
San Bernardino County Sun (CA)
San Jose Evening News (CA)
Seattle Daily Times
Singapore Free Press and Mercantile Advertiser
Star Bulletin (Honolulu)
Straits Times (Singapore)
Times (London)
Times-Picayune (New Orleans)
Tribune (Manila)
Variety
Vintage Guitar
Washington Post
Washington Times
West Australian (Perth)
Wray Rattler (CO)
Xenia Daily Gazette (OH)

BOOKS, ARTICLES, DISSERTATIONS, THESES, AND TRANSCRIPTS

Adams, W. D. "The Popularity of Hawaiian Music and Musical Instruments." In *The Hawaiian Annual: The Reference Book of Hawai'i, 1917*, compiled and published by Thos. G. Thrum, 142–46. Honolulu: Thos. G. Thrum, 1917.

Aikau, Hokulani K. *A Chosen People, a Promised Land: Mormonism and Race in Hawai'i*. Minneapolis: University of Minnesota Press, 2012.

———. "Indigeneity in the Diaspora: The Case of Native Hawaiians at Iosepa, Utah." *American Quarterly* 62, no. 3 (September 2010): 477–500.

———. "Kanaka Maoli Groundwork in the Crossroads of the Pacific." American Studies Association Annual Meeting. November 3–6, 2005.

Akamine, Eldon. "Gabby Tells His Own Story." *Ha'ilono Mele*, May 1977, 1–2.

Alexander, William De Witt. *History of Later Years of the Hawaiian Monarchy and the Revolution of 1893*. Honolulu: Hawaiian Gazette, 1896.

"The Aloha Four." In *The Heritage Series*. Presented by KCCN Hawaiian Radio/ Bank of Hawaii, originally broadcast October 29, 1989.

Alohikea, William K. *"Hawaiian Method" of Playing Guitar Self Taught*. Cleveland: Wm K. Alohikea, 1915.

Ankeny, Jason. "Cliff Carlisle." *All Music*. 2015. http://www.allmusic.com/artist/cliff-carlisle-mn0000126492/biography. Accessed May 25, 2015.

Arista, Noelani. "Navigating Uncharted Oceans of Meaning: Kaona as Historical and Interpretive Method." *PMLA* 125, no. 3 (2010): 663–69.

Armstrong, Robert. Liner notes to *King Bennie Nawahi: Hawaiian String Virtuoso, Acoustic Steel Guitar Classics from the 1920s*. Yazoo, a division of Shanachie Entertainment, compact disc, 2000.

Asensio, Rubén Fernández. "Language Policy in the Kingdom of Hawai'i: A Worldly English Approach." *Second Language Studies* 28, no. 2 (Spring 2010): 1–48.

Awai, Keoki E. *The Superior Collection of Steel Guitar Solos*, vol. 1. San Francisco: Sherman, Clay, 1917.

Bacchilega, Cristina. *Legendary Hawai'i and the Politics of Place: Tradition, Translation, and Tourism*. Philadelphia: University of Pennsylvania Press, 2006.

Bacon, Pay Namaka, and Nathan Napoka, eds. *Nā Mele Welo = Songs of Our Heritage: Selections from the Roberts Mele Collection in Bishop Museum, Honolulu*, translated by Mary Kawena Pakui. Honolulu: Bishop Museum Press, 1995.

Balme, Christopher B. "Selling the Bird: Richard Walton Tully's *The Bird of Paradise* and the Dynamics of Theatrical Commodification." *Theatre Journal* 57 (2005): 1–20.

Barker, Kenneth Brandon. "The American Pedal Steel Guitar: Folkloristic Analyses of Material Culture and Embodiment." Ph.D. diss., University of Louisiana at Lafayette, 2012.

Barrère, Dorothy B., Mary Kawena Pukui, and Marion Kelly. "Hula: Historical Perspectives." *Pacifica Anthropological Records* 30. Honolulu: Department of Anthropology, Bernice Pauahi Bishop Museum, 1980.

Bastin, Bruce. *Red River Blues: The Blues Tradition in the Southeast*. Urbana: University of Illinois Press, 1986.

Beaty, R. A. D., ed. *Hawaiian Music and Musical Instruments: A History.* Honolulu: Bergstrom Music, 1917.

Bennett, Chauncey C. *Honolulu Directory, and Historical Sketch of the Hawaiian or Sandwich Islands.* Honolulu: C. C. Bennett, 1869.

Berger, Henri. "Music in Honolulu." In *Hawaiian Almanac and Annual for 1885*, compiled and published by Thos. G. Thrum, 72. Honolulu: Press Publishing, Steam Print, 1885.

Berger, John. "Don Ho [Donald Tai Loy Ho], Do Ho & the Aliis." In Kanahele and Berger, *Hawaiian Music and Musicians*, 310–16.

———. "Frank Ferera [Frank Ferreira Jr.]." In Kanahele and Berger, *Hawaiian Music and Musicians*, 152–55.

Bergin, Billy. *Loyal to the Land: The Legendary Parker Ranch, 750–1950.* Honolulu: University of Hawaiʻi Press, 2004.

Bierley, Paul E. *Hallelujah Trombone: The Story of Henry Fillmore.* Westernville, OH: Integrity, 1982.

Boyd, Jean A. *The Jazz of the Southwest.* Austin: University of Texas Press, 1998.

Brookes, Tim. *Guitar: An American Life.* New York: Grove, 2005.

———. "Hawaiian Invasion." *American History*, December 2004, 48–57, 76–80.

Brooks, Tim. "'Hula Love,' Another Case of Song Larceny." *Haʻilono Mele*, August 1977, 6.

———. *Lost Sounds: Blacks and the Birth of the Recording Industry.* Urbana: University of Illinois Press, 2004.

Brown, Desoto. "Beautiful, Romantic Hawaii: How the Fantasy Image Came to Be." *Journal of Decorative and Propaganda Arts* 20 (1994): 252–71.

Brown, Jayna. *Babylon Girls: Black Women Performers and the Shaping of the Modern.* Durham, NC: Duke University Press, 2008.

Brozman, Bob. *The History and Artistry of National Resonator Instruments.* Anaheim Hills, CA: Centerstream, 1998.

Brundage, W. Fitzhugh, ed. *Beyond Blackface: African Americans and the Creation of American Popular Culture, 1890–1930.* Chapel Hill: University of North Carolina Press, 2011.

Buck, Elizabeth. *Paradise Remade: The Politics of Culture and History in Hawaiʻi.* Philadelphia: Temple University Press, 1993.

Burlingame, Burl, and Robert Kamohalu Kasher. *Da Kine Sound: Conversations with the People Who Create Hawaiian Music.* Kailua, HI: Press Pacific, 1978.

Bushnell, O. A. *The Gifts of Civilization: Germs and Genocide in Hawaiʻi.* Honolulu: University of Hawaiʻi Press, 1993.

"Busy?" *Hawaiian Guitarist*, February 1933, 7.

Carlin, Bob. "Elgin Hawaiian Guitar Band." *Old-Time Herald*, April–May 2011, 22–36.

Carlin, Richard. *The Big Book of Country Music: A Biographical Encyclopedia.* New York: Penguin, 1995.

Carr, James Revell. *Hawaiian Music in Motion: Mariners, Missionaries, and Minstrels*. Urbana: University of Illinois Press, 2014.

Carter, Walter. *The Martin Guitar: A Complete History of Martin Guitars.* Milwaukee: Backbeat, 2006.

Chang, Thelma. "Steel Guitar Magic." *Aloha: The Magazine of Hawai'i and the Pacific*, October 1989, 32.

Chapman, Erin D. *Prove It on Me: New Negroes, Sex, and Popular Culture in the 1920s*. New York: Oxford University Press, 2012.

Charters, Samuel B. *The Country Blues*. New York: Da Capo, 1975.

Chase, Lance D. "The Hawaiian Mission Crisis of 1874: Character as Destiny." *Mormon Pacific Historical Society* 1, no. 1 (1980): 87–97.

Chude-Sokei, Louis. *The Last "Darky": Bert Williams, Black-on-Black Minstrelsy, and the African Diaspora*. Durham, NC: Duke University Press, 2006.

Cluff, Benjamin R. "The Hawaiian Islands and Annexation." In *Improvement Era, Organ of Young Men's Mutual Improvement Association*, by Church of Jesus Christ of Latter-Day Saints, 1:435–47. Salt Lake City: Published by the General Board, 1897–98.

Cole, Catherine. "Reading Blackface in West Africa: Wonders Taken for Signs." *Critical Inquiry* 23, no. 1 (Autumn 1996): 183–215.

Connell, John, and Chris Gibson. "'No Passport Necessary': Music, Record Covers and Vicarious Tourism in Post-war Hawai'i." *Journal of Pacific History* 43 (2008): 51–75.

Conway, Cecelia. *African Banjo Echoes in Appalachia: A Study of Folk Traditions*. Knoxville: University of Tennessee Press, 1995.

Cook, Les. "Irene West." In Kanahele and Berger, *Hawaiian Music and Musicians*, 870–72.

———. "Sam Ku West." In Kanahele and Berger, *Hawaiian Music and Musicians*, 872–77.

———. "William ('Bill') Kanui [William Kulii Kanui]." In Kanahele and Berger, *Hawaiian Music and Musicians*, 447–49.

Cook, Les, and John Berger. "Pale K. Lua." In Kanahele and Berger, *Hawaiian Music and Musicians*, 512–14.

Cortese, Vincent. *Roy Smeck: The Wizard of the Strings in His Life and Times.* Lincoln: iUniverse, 2004.

———. "Tampa Red: Long Live the Guitar Wizard." *Blues Review Quarterly* 6 (1992): 22–25.

Coyle, Jackey, and Rebecca Coyle. "Aloha Australia: Hawaiian Music in Australia (1920–55)." *Perfect Beat* 2, no. 2 (January 1995): 31–63.

Cundell, Guy S. "Across the Pacific: The Transformation of the Steel Guitar from Hawaiian Folk Instrument to Popular Music Mainstay." M.A. thesis, University of Adelaide, 2014.

Damon, Annabel. "Four Years of Hell in Manila Described by 'Queenie' Kaili." *Honolulu Advertiser*, December 16, 1945, 1, 5.

Davis, Francis. *The History of the Blues*. New York: Hyperion, 1995.

Davis, Harold S. "The Iosepa Origin of Joseph F. Smith's 'Lāʻie Prophecy.'" *BYU Studies* 33, no. 1 (1993): 81–108.

Dawe, Kevin, and Andy Bennett, eds. *Guitar Cultures*. Oxford: Berg, 2001.

Daws, Gavan. "The Decline of Puritanism at Honolulu in the Nineteenth Century." *Hawaiian Journal of History* 1 (1967): 31–42.

———. "Honolulu in the 19th Century." *Journal of Pacific History* 2 (1967): 77–96, 77.

———. *Shoal of Time: A History of the Hawaiian Islands*. Honolulu: University of Hawaiʻi Press, 1978.

DeLano, C. S. "Hawaiian Music: Its Origin and Present-Day Development." *B.M.G.*, April 1932, 145.

De La Vernegne, George H. *Hawaiian Sketches*. San Francisco: H. S. Crocker Company, 1898.

Desmond, Jane C. *Staging Tourism: Bodies on Display from Waikiki to Sea World*. Chicago: University of Chicago Press, 1999.

Diaz, Vicente M. *Repositioning the Missionary: Rewriting the Histories of Colonialism, Native Catholicism, and Indigeneity in Guam*. Honolulu: University of Hawaiʻi Press, 2010.

Dibble, Sheldon. *History of the Sandwich Islands*. Lahainaluna: Press of the Mission Seminary, 1843.

Dickerson, Deke. "Letritia Kandle and the Magnificent Grand Letar." *Vintage Guitar*, August 2010, 50–52.

Dodge, Allan. Liner notes to *Honolulu to Hollywood: Jazz, Blues, and Popular Specialties Performed Hawaiian Style*. Old Masters Label, compact disc, 2008.

Dopyera, John E., Jr. "Dad: Some Personal Reflections." In *The History and Artistry of National Resonator Instruments*, by Bob Brozman, 5–17. Anaheim Hills, CA: Centerstream, 1998.

Dye, Tom. "Population Trends in Hawai'i before 1778." *Hawaiian Journal of History* 28 (1994): 1–20.

Ejiri, Masakazu. "The Development of Waikiki, 1900–1949: The Formative Period of an American Resort Paradise." Ph.D. diss., University of Hawai'i, 1996.

Elbert, Samuel H., and Noelani Mahoe, eds. *Nā Mele o Hawai'i Nei: 101 Hawaiian Songs*. Honolulu: University Press of Hawai'i, 1970.

Ellis, Andy. "The Secret World of Hindustani Slide." *Premier Guitar*, June 8, 2012. http://www.premierguitar.com/articles/The_Secret_World_of_Hindustani_Slide. Accessed March 4, 2015.

Ely, John. "Joseph Kekuku Statue Unveiling." *HGSA Quarterly* 30, no. 116 (Fall 2014): 4.

Emerson, Ken. "True Fan Lives across the Sea, across the USA." *Ha'ilono Mele*, April 1980, 6–8, 13.

Emerson, Nathaniel B. "Unwritten Literature of Hawaii: The Sacred Songs of the Hula." *Bulletin* 38, Bureau of American Ethnology. Washington, D.C.: Government Printing Office, 1909.

Engebretson, George. "The New Sound of Hawaiian Music." *Honolulu*, November 1974, 84–85, 158–63.

Evans, David. "Afro-American One-Stringed Instruments." *Western Folklore* 29, no. 4 (October 1970): 229–45.

———. "Musical Innovation in the Blues of Blind Lemon Jefferson." *Black Music Research Journal* 20, no. 1 (Spring 2000): 83–116.

———. "Rubin Lacy." In *Nothing but the Blues*, edited by Mike Leadbitter, 239–45. London: Hanover, 1971.

Ferris, William R. *Blues from the Delta*. Garden City, NY: Anchor/Doubleday, 1978.

Fischer, John Ryan. "Cattle in Hawai'i: Biological and Cultural Exchange." *Pacific Historical Review* 76, no. 3 (August 2007): 347–72.

Fojas, Camilla. *Islands of Empire: Pop Culture and U.S. Power*. Austin: University of Texas Press, 2014.

Forbes, Camille F. *Introducing Bert Williams: Burnt Cork, Broadway, and the Story of America's First Black Star*. New York: Basic Civitas, 2008.

Fujikane, Candace, and Jonathan Y. Okamura, eds. *Asian Settler Colonialism: From Local Governance to the Habits of Everyday Life in Hawai'i*. Honolulu: University of Hawai'i Press, 2008.

Fussell, Jake X. "Out of This World: Hearing Indigenous and Immigrant Music in the American South." M.A. thesis, University of Mississippi, 2013.

Garon, Paul, and Beth Garon. *Woman with Guitar: Memphis Minnie's Blues*. New York: Da Capo, 1992.

Garrett, Charles Hiroshi. *Struggling to Define a Nation: American Music and the Twentieth Century*. Berkeley: University of California Press, 2008.

Genial Hawaiians Jim and Bob, plus George Ku and His Paradise Islanders. Grass Skirt Records GSK 1005, compact disc, 2012.

"George E. K. Awai Fueled the Hawaiian Music Craze in 1915." *Ha'ilono Mele*, September 1977, 5–6.

Gilbert, David. *The Product of Our Souls: Ragtime, Race, and the Birth of the Manhattan Musical Marketplace*. Chapel Hill: University of North Carolina Press, 2015.

Gioia, Joe. *The Guitar and the New World: A Fugitive History*. Albany: State University of New York Press, 2013.

Goodyear-Ka'ōpua, Noelani, Ikaika Hussey, and Erin Kahunawaika'ala Wright, eds. *A Nation Rising: Hawaiian Movements for Life, Land, and Sovereignty*. Durham, NC: Duke University Press, 2014.

Gracyk, Tim, with Frank Hoffmann. *Popular American Recording Pioneers, 1895–1925*. New York: Routledge, 2000.

Greer, Richard A. "Grog Shops and Hotels: Bending the Elbow in Old Honolulu." *Hawaiian Journal of History* 28 (1994): 35–67.

Guitar without a Master. Boston: Oliver Ditson, 1850.

Gura, Philip F., and James F. Bollman. *America's Instrument: The Banjo in the Nineteenth Century*. Chapel Hill: University of North Carolina Press, 1999.

Gussow, Adam. "Playing Chicken with the Train: Cowboy Troy's Hick-Hop and the Transracial Country West." In Pecknold, *Hidden in the Mix*, 234–62.

Haden, Walter Darrell. "Vernon Dalhart." In *Stars of Country Music*, edited by Bill C. Malone and Judith McCulloh, 64–85. Urbana: University of Illinois Press, 1976.

Halfon, Neal, project director. "The Moe Family." NEH Humanities Projects in Media grant application. Filed 1989.

Hamilton, Marybeth. *In Search of the Blues*. New York: Basic Books, 2008.

Handy, W. C. *Father of the Blues*. New York: MacMillan, 1941.

Harris, Jeff. "Smoketown Strut: Sylvester Weaver's Blues Pt. 1." Big Road Blues, 2008. http://sundayblues.org/archives/230. Accessed March 4, 2015.

Haugen, Keith, and John Berger. "Sons of Hawai'i." In Kanahele and Berger, *Hawaiian Music and Musicians*, 768–71.

Hau'ofa, Epeli. "Our Sea of Islands." In *A New Oceania: Rediscovering Our Sea of Islands*, edited by Epeli Hau'ofa, Vijay Naidu, and Eric Waddell, 2–16. Suva, Fiji: University of the South Pacific in association with Beake House, 1993.

"Hawaiian Guitar Brings Popularity to These Girls." *Hawaiian Guitarist*, February 1933, 7.

"Hawaiian Music Will Live: Threatened Degeneracy of Island Melodies into Cheap Jazz Is Averted by Return of Mekia Kealaka'i to Lead the Royal Hawaiian Band." *Paradise of the Pacific*, December 12, 1921, 121–22, 127.

Hawai'i Department of Foreign Affairs. *Report of the Minister of Foreign Affairs to the Hawaii Legislature, Session of 1892*. Honolulu: Ka Leiali'i, 1892.

"The History of the Hawaiian Steel Guitar." *Hawaiian Guitarist*, July–August 1934, 7–12.

Hokum Blues, 1924–29. Document Records, DOCD-5370, compact disc, 1995.

Hood, Mantle. "Musical Ornamentation as History: The Hawaiian Steel Guitar." In "East Asian Musics," special issue, *Yearbook for Traditional Music* 15 (1983): 141–48.

Ho'opi'i, Sol. *Sol Hoopii and His Novelty Quartette: Classic Hawaiian Steel Guitar Performances, 1933–34*. Origin Jazz Library OJL-3000, compact disc, 2007.

———. *Sol Hoopii in Hollywood: His First Recordings, 1925*. Grass Skirt Records GSK 1002, compact disc, 2007.

Hoover, Will. "Tunes of Steel." *Honolulu Advertiser*, May 31, 1998, E3.

Hopkins, Jerry. "Ioane 'Ukēkē: Hawaiian Dandy, Hawaiian Tragedy." *Ha'ilono Mele*, February 1980, 1–5.

Houston, James D., and Eddie Kamae. *Hawaiian Son: The Life and Music of Eddie Kamae*. Honolulu: 'Ai Pōhaku, 2004.

"How Popular Is the Hawaiian Guitar?" *Hawaiian Guitarist* (February 1933): 3.

Huber, Patrick. *Linthead Stomp: The Creation of Country Music in the Piedmont South*. Chapel Hill: University of North Carolina Press, 2008.

Iaukea, Curtis Piehu. "Whaling in the Days of the Kingdom." *Honolulu Advertiser*, May 7, 1939.

Iaukea, Sydney L. *The Queen and I: A Story of Dispossessions and Reconnections in Hawai'i*. Berkeley: University of California Press, 2011.

Imada, Adria L. "Aloha America: Hawaiian Entertainment and Cultural Politics in the U.S. Empire." Ph.D. diss., New York University, 2003.

———. *Aloha America: Hula Circuits through the U.S. Empire*. Durham, NC: Duke University Press, 2012.

———. "Hawaiians on Tour: Hula Circuits through the American Empire." *American Quarterly* 56, no. 1 (March 2004): 111–49.

Jarves, James Jackson. *Scenes and Scenery in the Sandwich Islands, and a Trip through Central America: Being Observations from My Note-Book during the Years 1837–1842*. Boston: James Munroe, 1843.

Johnston, Patrick. "Teaching 'the Steel' to a New Generation." *Ka Wai Ola* (Office of Hawaiian Affairs), September 1994, 15, 22.

Johnston, Richard, and Dick Boak. *Martin Guitars: A History*. Milwaukee: Hal Leonard, 2008.

Kaeppler, Adrienne L. "Acculturation in Hawaiian Dance." *Yearbook of the International Folk Music Council* 4 (1972): 38–46.

———. *Hula Pahu: Hawaiian Drum Dances*, vol. 1, *Ha'a and Hula Pahu: Sacred Movements*. Bishop Museum Bulletin in Anthropology, no. 3. Honolulu: Bishop Museum, 1993.

———. "Music, Metaphor, and Misunderstanding." *Ethnomusicology* 38, no. 3 (Autumn 1994): 457–73.

Kahn, Daniel. "Steel Guitar Development," part 1. *Ha'ilono Mele*, March 1976, 6–7.

———."Steel Guitar Development," part 2. *Ha'ilono Mele*, April 1976, 4–6.

———. "Steel Guitar Development," part 3. *Ha'ilono Mele*, May 1976, 1–4.

Kahn, Ed. Liner notes to *Darby and Tarlton: Complete Recordings*. Bear Family BCD-15764, 3-CD boxed set, 1995.

Kame'eleihiwa, Lilikalā. *Native Land and Foreign Desires: Pehea La E Pono Ai? How Shall We Live in Harmony?* Honolulu: Bishop Museum Press, 1992.

Kanahele, George S. "Ernest Ka'ai, a Giant in Hawaiian Music." *Ha'ilono Mele*, November 1977, 3–4.

———. "The Hawaiian Renaissance." Speech before the Polynesian Voyaging Society. May 1979. http://kapalama.ksbe.edu/archives/pvsa/primary%202/79%20kanahele/kanahele.htm. Accessed March 5, 2015.

———, ed. *Hawaiian Music and Musicians*. Honolulu: University of Hawai'i Press, 1979.

Kanahele, George S., and John Berger. "Albert R. 'Sonny' Cunha." In Kanahele and Berger, *Hawaiian Music and Musicians*, 114–16.

———. "'The Bird of Paradise.'" In Kanahele and Berger, *Hawaiian Music and Musicians*, 78–80.

———. "Charles Edward King." In Kanahele and Berger, *Hawaiian Music and Musicians*, 476–77.

———. "Charles Philip 'Gabby' Pahinui." In Kanahele and Berger, *Hawaiian Music and Musicians*, 627–31.

———. "Gōttuvādyam." In Kanahele and Berger, *Hawaiian Music and Musicians*, 203–4.

———. "Hawaiian Music Foundation." In Kanahele and Berger, *Hawaiian Music and Musicians*, 275–78.
———. "Hawai'i Calls." In Kanahele and Berger, *Hawaiian Music and Musicians*, 267–71.
———. "John Avery Noble." In Kanahele and Berger, *Hawaiian Music and Musicians*, 606–8.
———. "Leleiōhoku, William Pitt." In Kanahele and Berger, *Hawaiian Music and Musicians*, 500–501.
———. "Lili'uokalani." In Kanahele and Berger, *Hawaiian Music and Musicians*, 504–7.
———. "Mekia Kealaka'i." In Kanahele and Berger, *Hawaiian Music and Musicians*, 459–60.
———. "Panama-Pacific International Exposition." In Kanahele and Berger, *Hawaiian Music and Musicians*, 633–34.
———. "Toots Paka's Hawaiians." In Kanahele and Berger, *Hawaiian Music and Musicians*, 825–26.
———. "William Miles." In Kanahele and Berger, *Hawaiian Music and Musicians*, 546–48.
Kanahele, George S., and John Berger, eds. *Hawaiian Music and Musicians: An Illustrated History*. Honolulu: Mutual, 2012.
Kanai, Maria. "From Our Files." *Honolulu Magazine*, August 2012.
Kapua [Reece], Ken. "Joseph Kekuku: The Originator of the Hawaiian Guitar." *B.M.G.*, August 1933, 238.
Kauanui, J. Kēhaulani. "Diasporic Deracination and 'Off-Island' Hawaiians." *Contemporary Pacific* 19, no. 1 (Spring 2007): 138–60.
———. *Hawaiian Blood: Colonialism and the Politics of Sovereignty and Indigeneity*. Durham, NC: Duke University Press, 2008.
Keany, Michael. "One Hundred Years of Hawaiian Music." *Honolulu Magazine*, September 2010. http://www.honolulumagazine.com/core/pagetools.php?pageid=8151&url=/honolulu-magazine/november-2010/100-years-of-hawaiian-music/&mode=print. Accessed May 20, 2015.
Kent, Noel. *Hawaii: Islands under the Influence*. Honolulu: University of Hawai'i Press, 1993.
Kester, James Matthew. "Race, Religion, and Citizenship in Mormon Country: Native Hawaiians in Salt Lake City, 1869–1889." *Western Historical Quarterly* 40, no. 1 (Spring 2009): 51–76.
———. *Remembering Iosepa: History, Place, and Religion in the American West*. New York: Oxford University Press, 2013.

King, B. B., with David Ritz. *Blues All Around Me: The Autobiography of B. B. King*. New York: Avon, 1996.

Kingsley, Grace. "Says, Toots, 'Thees Li'l Danze Are Vur Much Many Li'l Danze.'" *Los Angeles Times*, May 24, 1912.

Krout, Mary. *The Memoirs of Hon. Bernice Pauahi Bishop*. New York: Knickerbocker, 1908.

Kubik, Gerhard. *Africa and the Blues*. Jackson: University Press of Mississippi. 1999.

———. Liner notes to *African Guitar: Solo Fingerstyle Guitar Music form Uganda, Congo/Zaïre, Central African Republic, Malawi, Namibia and Zambia*. Rounder Records, Vestapol Productions, DVD, 2003.

———. *Theory of African Music*, vol. 2. Chicago: University of Chicago Press, 2010.

Kuykendall, Ralph S. *The Hawaiian Kingdom*. Vol. 1, *1778–1854, Foundation and Transformation*. Honolulu: University of Hawai'i Press, 1965.

———. *The Hawaiian Kingdom*. Vol. 2, *Twenty Critical Years, 1854–1874*. Honolulu: University of Hawai'i Press, 1953.

———. *The Hawaiian Kingdom*. Vol. 3, *1874–1893: The Kalākaua Dynasty*. Honolulu: University of Hawai'i Press, 1967.

Lee, J. J., and Marion Casey, eds. *Making the Irish American: History and Heritage of the Irish in the United States*. New York: NYU Press, 2006.

Lewis, Furry, Bukka White, and Friends. *Party! At Home: Recorded in Memphis in 1968*. Arcola Records, A CD 1001, compact disc, 2004.

Lewis, George H. "Beyond the Reef: Role Conflict and the Professional Musician in Hawaii." *Popular Music* 5 (1985): 189–98.

———. "Da Kine Sounds: The Function of Music as Social Protest in the New Hawaiian Renaissance." *American Music* 2, no. 2 (Summer 1984): 38–52.

———. "Don' Go Down Waikiki: Social Protest and Popular Music in Hawaii." In *Rockin' the Boat*, edited by Reebee Garofalo, 171–84. Boston: South End, 1992.

———. "Music, Culture and the Hawaiian Renaissance." *Popular Music and Society* 10, no. 3 (1986): 47–53.

———. "The Politics of Meaning: Emergent Ideology in Popular Hawaiian Music." *Tracking: Popular Music Studies* 1, no. 2 (Winter 1988): 23–33.

———. "Storm Blowing from Paradise: Social Protest and Oppositional Ideology in Popular Hawaiian Music." *Popular Music* 10, no. 1 (January 1991): 53–67.

Lili'uokalani. *Hawaii's Story*. Honolulu: Mutual, 1990.

Liliʻuokalani, Queen of Hawaiʻi; Dorothy K. Gillet; Barbara B. Smith; and Hui Hānai. *The Queen's Songbook*. Hui Hānai, 1999.

Lis, Anthony. "The Steel Guitar in Early Country Music: Part Two: Jimmie Rodgers's Steel Guitarists; Chapter Three: Joe Kaipo and Billy Burkes, Part One." *Aloha Dream* 6, no. 3 (September 2008): 16–21.

———. "The Steel Guitar in Early Country Music: Part Two: Jimmie Rodgers's Steel Guitarists; Chapter Four: Jimmie Rodgers's Summer 1930 Recordings with Lani McIntire's Hawaiians, Section One: Lani McIntire Background." *Aloha Dream* 7, no. 2 (June 2009): 16–19.

———. "The Steel Guitar in Early Country Music: Part Two: Jimmie Rodgers's Steel Guitarists; Chapter Four: Jimmie Rodgers's Summer 1930 Recordings with Lani McIntire's Hawaiians, Section Two: Details on the Recordings." *Aloha Dream* 7, no. 3 (September 2009): 21–24.

———. "The Steel Guitar in Early Country Music: Part Two: Jimmie Rodgers's Steel Guitarists; Chapter Five: Charles Kama Valera, Section Three: Valera's Career from 1940 to His Death." *Aloha Dream* 9, no. 4 (December 2011): 7–12.

Lucas, Paul F. Nakoa. "E Ola Mau Kākou I Ka ʻŌlelo Makuahine: Hawaiian Language Policy and the Courts." *Hawaiian Journal of History* 34 (2000): 1–28.

MacKenzie, Jean S. *Tandy*. Norfolk Island, Australia: Island Heritage, 1975.

Macleod, Beth Abelson. "'Whence Comes the Lady Tympanist?' Gender and Instrumental Musicians in America, 1853–1990." *Journal of Social History*, Winter 1993, 291–308.

Makin, Mark. *Palm Trees, Señoritas . . . and Rocket Ships!* Nottingham, UK: MBM, 2012.

Malo, David. *Hawaiian Antiquities (Moʻolelo Hawaiʻi)*, translated by N. B. Emerson. Honolulu: Hawaiian Gazette, 1903.

Malone, Bill C. *Country Music U.S.A.* Rev. ed. Austin: University of Texas Press, 1985.

"Man Who Gave Steel Guitar to Nashville Dies." *Haʻilono Mele*, November 1979, 9.

Marques, Augustus. "Music in Hawaiʻi Nei." In *Hawaiian Almanac and Annual for 1886*, compiled and published by Thos. G. Thrum, 51–60. Honolulu: Press Publishing, Steam Print, 1886.

Marsden, John. "Hawaiian Music in Great Britain." In Kanahele and Berger, *Hawaiian Music and Musicians*, 222–35.

Mazor, Barry. *Ralph Peer and the Making of Popular Roots Music*. Chicago: Chicago Review Press, 2014.

McGinley, Paige A. *Staging the Blues: From Tent Shows to Tourism*. Durham, NC: Duke University Press, 2014.

McGregor, Davianna Pōmaikaʻi. *Nā Kuaʻāina: Living Hawaiian Culture*. Honolulu: University of Hawaiʻi Press, 2007.

McNeil, Adrian. *Inventing the Sarod: A Cultural History*. Calcutta: Seagull, 2004.

———. "A Mouse, a Frog, the Hawaiian Guitar and World Music Aesthetics: Vishwa Mohan Bhatt and Ry Cooder Meet by the River." *Perfect Beat* 2, no. 3 (July 1995): 82–97.

"Meet One of the Oahu Serenaders." *Hawaiian Guitarist*, April 1933, 5.

Meriwether, Lee. *The Tramp at Home*. New York: Harper & Brothers, 1889.

Miller, Karl Hagstrom. *Segregating Sound: Inventing Folk and Pop Music in the Age of Jim Crow*. Durham, NC: Duke University Press, 2010.

Miller, Timothy David. "Instruments as Technology and Culture: Co-constructing the Pedal Steel Guitar." Ph.D. diss., University of North Carolina at Chapel Hill, 2013.

Minton, John. *78 Blues: Folksongs and Photographs in the American South*. Jackson: University Press of Mississippi, 2011.

Mitchell, D. Kilolani, George S. Kanahele, and John Berger. "Steel Guitar." In Kanahele and Berger, *Hawaiian Music and Musicians*, 781–801.

Mitchell, Donald D. *Kika Kila: The Story of the Steel Guitar*. Honolulu: Hawaiian Music Foundation, 1973.

Mitchell, Donald D., and George S. Kanahele. "Hawaiian Steel Guitar." *Guitar Player*, July 1980, 32–45.

Mohr, James C. *Plague and Fire: Battling the Black Death and the 1900 Burning of Honolulu's Chinatown*. New York: Oxford University Press, 2006.

"Musical Diggings." *Haʻilono Mele*, June 1975, 2.

National Park Service. "Walter 'Furry' Lewis—Memphis School." *Trail of the Hellhound: Delta Blues in the Lower Mississippi Valley*. http://www.nps.gov/history/delta/blues/people/furry_lewis.htm. Accessed April 20, 2014.

National String Instruments. Benld, IL: Gima Reprints, 1975.

Noble, Johnny. "Hawaiian Musicians in the Jazz Era." *Paradise of the Pacific*, November 1943, 22–24.

———. "Origin of the Steel Guitar." *Paradise of the Pacific*, October 1943, 34–35.

Noe, George T., and Daniel L. Most. *Chris J. Knutsen, from Harp Guitars to the New Hawaiian Family: History and Development of the Hawaiian Steel Guitar*. Everett, WA: Noe Enterprises, 1999.

Noonan, Jeffrey J. *The Guitar in America: Victorian Era to Jazz Age*. Jackson: University Press of Mississippi, 2008.

Nordhoff, Charles. *Northern California, Oregon, and the Sandwich Islands*. New York: Harper & Brothers, 1874.

Nordyke, Eleanor C., and Martha H. Noyes. "'Kaulana Nā Pua': A Voice for Sovereignty." *Hawaiian Journal of History* 27 (1993): 27–42.

Oakley, Giles. *The Devil's Music: A History of the Blues*. New York: Da Capo, 1997.

Obrecht, Jas. "Blues Origins: Spanish Fandango and Sebastapol." 2010. http://jasobrecht.com/blues-origins-spanish-fandango-and-sebastopol/. Accessed May 20, 2015.

———. "Sylvester Weaver: The First Blues Guitarist on Record." July 11, 2012. http://theguitar-blog.com/?p=991. Accessed March 5, 2015.

———. "Tampa Red: The Guitar Wizard." Jas Obrecht Music Archive, 2010. http://jasobrecht.com/tampa-red-the-guitar-wizard/. Accessed December 5, 2012.

Odum, Howard W. "Folk-Song and Folk-Poetry as Found in the Secular Songs of the Southern Negroes." *Journal of American Folklore* 24, no. 93 (July–September 1911): 261, 270.

———. "Folk-Song and Folk-Poetry as Found in the Secular Songs of the Southern Negroes (Concluded)." *Journal of American Folklore* 24, no. 94 (October–December 1911): 363–64, 395.

Okihiro, Gary Y. *Island World: A History of Hawai'i and the United States*. Berkeley: University of California Press, 2008.

Oler, Midge. "LDS Composers, Kulu Hula and Musicians." *Mormon Pacific Historical Society* 12, no. 1 (1991): 77–79.

Olsson, Bengt. Liner notes to *Cannon's Jug Stompers: The Complete Works, 1927–1930*. Yazoo 1082, compact disc, 1992.

Osorio, Jonathan Kamakawiwo'ole. *Dismembering Lāhui: A History of the Hawaiian Nation to 1887*. Honolulu: University of Hawai'i Press, 2002.

Otto, John S., and Augustus M. Burns. "Black and White Cultural Interaction in the Early Twentieth Century South: Race and Hillbilly Music." *Phylon* 35, no. 4 (1974): 407–17.

Ovalle, Priscilla Pena. *Dance and the Hollywood Latina: Race, Sex, and Stardom*. New Brunswick, NJ: Rutgers University Press, 2010.

Paleka, Herman. "A Very Personal History." Mormon Pacific Historical Society Proceedings, Sixteenth Annual Conference, Mormon History in the Pacific. Lihue Stake Center, Llihue Kaua'i, March 18, 1995: 6–24.

Peabody, Charles. "Notes on Negro Music." *Journal of American Folklore* 16, no. 62 (July–September 1903): 148–52.

Pearson, Barry Lee. *"Sounds So Good to Me": The Bluesman's Story*. Philadelphia: University of Pennsylvania Press, 1984.

Pecknold, Diane, ed. *Hidden in the Mix: The African American Presence in Country Music*. Durham, NC: Duke University Press, 2013.

Perlak, Kim. "Justin Holland and the Classical Roots of the American Guitar Sound." 2010. http://www.kimperlak.com/guitar/Holland_Guitar_Project_2010/Holland_Guitar_Project_2010.html. Accessed May 20, 2015.

Pierce, Edwin Hall. "In Behalf of the 'Popular' Elements in Musical Art." *Musical Quarterly* 9, no. 4 (October 1923): 469–81.

Pollenz, Philippa. "Changes in Form and Function of Hawaiian Hulas." *American Anthropologist* 52 (1950): 225–34.

———. "The Puzzle of Hula." *American Anthropologist*, new ser., 50, no. 4, part 1 (October–December 1948): 647–56.

Preza, Donovan. "The Empirical Writes Back: Re-examining Hawaiian Dispossession Resulting from the Māhele of 1848." M.A. thesis, University of Hawai'i, Mānoa, 2010.

Pukui, Mary Kawena. "Hawaiian Poetry and Music." Unpublished transcript of lecture given at Kamehameha Schools. Hawaiian Collection, Hamilton Library, University of Hawai'i, Mānoa, 1945.

———. "Songs (Meles) of Old Ka'u, Hawai'i." *Journal of American Folklore* 62, no. 245 (July–September 1949): 247–58.

Revell, Nellie. "The Dance Spectacle Dominates Vaudeville." *Theatre Magazine* 24 (July 1916): 212.

Roberts, Helen H. *Ancient Hawaiian Music*. Bernice P. Bishop Museum Bulletin 29. Honolulu: Bishop Museum, 1926. Reprint, New York: Kraus Reprint, 1971.

———. "Hawaiian Music." In *The Hawaiian Annual for 1920: The Reference Book of Information and Statistics*, edited by Thomas G. Thrum, 69–80. Honolulu: Thos. G. Thrum, 1919.

Rockwell, T. Malcolm. *Hawaiian and Hawaiian Guitar Records, 1891–1960*. CD-ROM. Kula, HI: Mahina Piha, 2007.

———. "Hawaiian Steel Guitar Pioneer Sol Hoopii." Liner notes to Ho'opi'i, *Sol Hoopii and His Novelty Quartette*.

———. "Sol Hoopii: The Early Years." Liner notes to Ho'opi'i, *Sol Hoopii in Hollywood*.

Russell, Tony. *Country Music Records: A Discography, 1921–1942*. New York: Oxford University Press, 2004.

Ruymar, Lorene, comp. *The Hawaiian Steel Guitar and Its Great Hawaiian Musicians*. Anaheim Hills, CA: Centerstream, 1996.

Salā, Aaron J. "Claiming the Colonial and Domesticating the Foreign: A Native Hawaiian Aesthetic for the Piano in Hula Ku'i Music." M.A. thesis, University of Hawai'i, Mānoa. 2011.

Schmitt, Robert C. *Demographic Statistics of Hawaii: 1778–1965*. Honolulu, 1968.

———. *Hawai'i in the Movies, 1898–1959*. Honolulu: Hawaiian Historical Society, 1988.

———. *Historical Statistics of Hawaii*. Honolulu, 1977. http://www.ohadatabook.com/F01-01-11.pdf.

Shilstra, U. A., and John Berger. "William Miles." In Kanahele and Berger, *Hawaiian Music and Musicians*, 546–48.

Shishikura, Masaya. "I'll Remember You: Nostalgia and Hapa Haole Music in Early Twenty-First Century Hawai'i." M.A. thesis, University of Hawai'i, Mānoa, 2007.

Siddall, John William. *Men of Hawaii: Being a Biographical Reference Library, Complete and Authentic, of the Men of Note and Substantial Achievement in the Hawaiian Islands*, vol. 2. Honolulu: Honolulu Star Bulletin, 1921.

Silva, Kīhea de. *He Aloha Moku o Keawe: A Collection of Songs for Hawai'i, Island of Keawe*. Rev. ed. Kailua, O'ahu, HI: Kīhea de Silva, 1999.

Silva, Noenoe K. *Aloha Betrayed: Native Hawaiian Resistance to American Colonialism*. Durham, NC: Duke University Press, 2004.

———. "He Kānāwai E Ho'opau I Nā Hula Kuolo Hawai'i: The Political Economy of Banning the Hula." *Hawaiian Journal of History* 34 (2000): 29–48.

Singletary, Milly. *Hilo Hattie: A Legend in Our Time*. Honolulu: Mutual, 2006.

Smith, Alma L. "Correspondence." *Latter-Day Saints' Millennial Star*, 1876, 58–60.

Smith, Barbara B. "Folk Music in Hawai'i." *Journal of the International Folk Music Council* 11 (1959): 50–55.

Smith, Eric Ledell. *Bert Williams: A Biography of the Pioneer Black Comedian*. Jefferson, NC: McFarland, 1992.

Smith, Richard R. *Fender: The Sound Heard 'Round the World*. Fullerton, CA: Garfish, 1995.

Solberg, S. E. "Hawaiian Lyrics, Chant, and Dance: An Introductory Note with Bibliography." *MELUS* 6, no. 2 (Summer 1979): 41–45.

———. "Hawaiian Music, Poetry, and Dance: Reflections on Protection, Preservation and Pride." *MELUS* 10, no. 1 (Spring 1983): 39–63.

"Solomon Hoopii Influenced the World." *Ha'ilono Mele*, July 1977, 1.

Sotiropoulos, Karen. *Staging Race: Black Performers in Turn of the Century America*. Cambridge, MA: Harvard University Press, 2008.

Spector, Janet D. *What This Awl Means: Feminist Archaeology at a Wahpeton Dakota Village*. St. Paul: Minnesota Historical Society Press, 1993.

"The State of Guitar in Hawaii." *Guitar Player*, April 1976, 13.

St. Louis, 1927–1933: The Complete Recorded Works of Jelly Roll Anderson, Henry Johnson, Bert "Snake Root" Hatton, Jesse Johnson, "Spider" Carter, Ell-Zee Floyd, Red Mike Bailey, Jimmy Strange, Georgia Boyd. Compact disc. Document Records DOCD-5181, 1994.

Stauffer, Bob. "The Hui of Kahana." *Mormon Pacific Historical Society* 8, no. 1 (1987):13–25.

Stauffer, Robert H. "An Early L.D.S. Family of Kahana and Lā'ie." *Mormon Pacific Historical Society* 12, no. 1 (1991): 49–57.

———. *Kahana: How the Land Was Lost*. Honolulu: University of Hawai'i Press, 2003.

Stewart, David. "The Hollywood Record Company Store." Liner notes to Ho'opi'i, *Sol Hoopii in Hollywood*.

Stillman, Amy Ku'uleialoha. "'Aloha Aina': New Perspectives on 'Kaulana Nā Pua.'" *Hawaiian Journal of History* 33 (1999): 83–99.

———. "Globalizing Hula." *Yearbook for Traditional Music* 31 (1999): 57–66.

———. "Hawaiian Hula Competitions: Event, Repertoire, Performance, Tradition." *Journal of American Folklore* 109, no. 434 (Autumn 1996): 357–80.

———. "History Reinterpreted in Song: The Case of the Hawaiian Counterrevolution." *Hawaiian Journal of History* 23 (1989): 1–30.

———. "Hula Hits, Local Music and Local Charts: Some Dynamics of Popular Hawaiian Music." In *Sound Alliances: Indigenous Peoples, Cultural Politics and Popular Music in the Pacific*, edited by Philip Hayward, 89–103. London: Cassell, 1998.

———. "Of What Use Are Hawaiian Songbooks? Interpreting the Notated Presentation of Modern Hawaiian Songs." *Perfect Beat* 2, no. 2 (1995): 64–82.

———. "Not All Hula Songs Are Created Equal: Reading the Historical Nature of Repertoire in Polynesia." *Yearbook for Traditional Music* 27 (1995): 1–12.

———. "Re-membering the History of Hawaiian Hula." In *Cultural Memory: Reconfiguring History and Identity in the Postcolonial Pacific*, edited by Jeannette Marie Mageo, 187–204. Honolulu: University of Hawai'i Press, 2001.

———. *Sacred Hula: The Hula 'Āla'apapa in Historical Perspective*. Bulletin in Anthropology 8, Honolulu: Bishop Museum Press, 1998.

———. "Textualizing Hawaiian Music." *American Music* 23, no. 1 (Spring 2005): 69–94.
Stone, Robert L. *Sacred Steel: Inside an African American Steel Guitar Tradition.* Urbana: University of Illinois Press, 2010.
Stover, Jeffrey S. "The Legacy of the 1848 Māhele and Kuleana Act of 1850: A Case Study of the Lāʻie Wai and Lāʻie Maloʻo Ahupuaʻa, 1846–1930." M.A. thesis, University of Hawaiʻi, Mānoa, 1997.
Stumpf, Myrtle. *Original Hawaiian Method for the Steel Guitar.* Los Angeles: Frank J. Hart Southern California Music, 1915.
Suisman. David. *Selling Sounds: The Commercial Revolution in American Music.* Cambridge, MA: Harvard University Press, 2009.
Summers, Lynn S., and Bob Schier. "Little Milton." In *The Voice of the Blues: Classic Interviews from "Living Blues Magazine,"* edited by Jim O'Neal and Amy van Singel, 389–408. New York: Routledge, 2002.
Sutton, Allan. "Rediscovering Sam Moore." Updated August 11, 2011. http://www.mainspringpress.com/moore.html. Accessed May 25, 2015.
Sutton, Juanealya McCormick. *The Man behind the Scenes.* Juanealya McCormick Sutton, 1987.
Suzuki, Andrea A. "Connect Back to Dis Place: Music and Identity of the Cultural Renaissance of Hawaiʻi." M.A. thesis, University of Hawaiʻi, Mānoa, 2005.
Sylvester Weaver, Vol. 1. Compact disc. Document Records DOCD-5112, 1992.
Szego, Catherine Susan. "Musical Meaning-Making in an Intercultural Environment: The Case of Kamehameha Schools." Ph.D. diss., University of Washington, 1999.
Takaki, Ronald. *Pau Hana: Plantation Life and Labor in Hawaii: 1835–1920.* Honolulu: University of Hawaii Press, 1983.
Tatar, Elizabeth. "History of Steel Guitar according to Charles E. King." *Haʻilono Mele*, October 1976, 5–6.
———. *Nineteenth-Century Hawaiian Chant.* Honolulu: Pacific Anthropological Records, no. 33, Department of Anthropology, Bishop Museum, 1982.
———. "Slack Key Guitar." In Kanahele and Berger, *Hawaiian Music and Musicians*, 357.
———. *Strains of Change: The Impact of Tourism on Hawaiian Music.* Honolulu: Bishop Museum Press, 1987.
———. "Toward a Description of Precontact Music in Hawaiʻi." *Ethnomusicology* 25, no. 3 (September 1981): 481–92.

Tatar, Elizabeth, and John Berger. "Falsetto." In Kanahele and Berger, *Hawaiian Music and Musicians*, 134–45.

———. "Pūpū A'o 'Ewa." In Kanahele and Berger, *Hawaiian Music and Musicians*, 665–66.

———. "Slack Key Guitar." In Kanahele and Berger, *Hawaiian Music and Musicians*, 748–59.

"Tau Moe: A Hawaiian Odyssey." Part 1. *Close Up*. BBC World Service, originally aired October 6, 2006.

"Tau Moe: A Hawaiian Odyssey." Part 2. *Close Up*. BBC World Service, originally aired October 13, 2006.

Taylor, Wray. "Musical Status of Hawaii." In Thrum, *Hawaiian Almanac and Annual for 1899*, 164–66.

Teaiwa, Teresia K. "Militarism, Tourism and the Native: Articulations in Oceania." Ph.D. diss., University of California, Santa Cruz, 2001.

Thornton, Brian. "Gabby Pahinui: My Life and Hard Times." *Hawai'i Observer*, April 7, 1977, 18–23.

Thrum, Thos. G., comp. and pub. *Hawaiian Almanac and Annual for 1899*. Honolulu: Press Publishing, Steam Print, 1898.

———, comp. and pub. *Hawaiian Almanac and Annual for 1915*. Honolulu: Press Publishing, Steam Print, 1914.

———, ed. *The Hawaiian Annual for 1925: The Reference Book of Information and Statistics*. Honolulu: Thos. G. Thrum, 1924.

Tinker, Hugh. *A New System of Slavery: The Export of Indian Labour Overseas, 1830–1920*. London: Published for the Institute of Race Relations by Oxford University Press, 1974.

Todaro, Tony. *The Golden Years of Hawaiian Entertainment*. Honolulu: Tony Todaro, 1974.

Todd, Frank Morton. *The Story of the Exposition: Being the Official History of the International Celebration Held at San Francisco in 1915 to Commemorate the Discovery of the Pacific Ocean and the Construction of the Panama Canal*, vol. 3. New York: G. P. Putnam's Sons/Knickerbocker, 1921.

Tomkins, Sandra M. "The Influenza Epidemic of 1918–19 in Western Samoa." *Journal of Pacific History* 27, no. 2 (December 1992): 181–97.

Topolinski, John R. "Ellis Brothers." In Kanahele and Berger, *Hawaiian Music and Musicians*, 131–33.

———. "The Sumner Family." *Ha'ilono Mele*, March 1976, 3–6.

Tranquada, James, and John King. *The 'Ukulele: A History*. Honolulu: University of Hawai'i Press, 2012.

Trask, Haunani-Kay. *From a Native Daughter: Colonialism and Sovereignty in Hawai'i*. Rev. ed. Honolulu: University of Hawai'i Press, 1999.
Treasury Department, Territory of Hawai'i. *Report of the Treasurer of the Territory of Hawaii, July 1, 1901 to June 30, 1902*. Honolulu: Robt. Grieve, 1903.
Trimillos, Ricardo D. *Nā Mele o Paniolo: Songs of Hawaiian Cowboys*. Honolulu: State Foundation on Culture and the Arts, Folk Arts Program, 1987.
Troutman, John W. *Indian Blues: American Indians and the Politics of Music, 1879–1934*. Norman: University of Oklahoma Press, 2009.
———. "Steelin' the Slide: Hawai'i and the Birth of the Blues Guitar." *Southern Cultures* 19, no. 1 (Spring 2013): 26–52.
Twain, Mark. *Mark Twain's Letters from Hawaii*, edited by Arthur Grove Day. Honolulu: University of Hawai'i Press, 1975.
Venet, Seva. "The Hawaiian Tinge." *Jazz Archivist* 25 (2012): 3–33.
Veru, Peter T. "The National-Dobro Guitar Company: How the Resonator Guitar Survived the Age of Electric Amplification." M.A. thesis, George Washington University, 2009.
Vincent, Frank, Jr. *Through and through the Tropics: Thirty Thousand Miles of Travel in Oceania, Australasia, and India*. New York: Harper and Brothers, 1876.
Vogel, Dirk (based upon original story by Jay Munns). "Eddie Bush: 1911–1969 (Part 1)." *Aloha International Steel Guitar Club* 11, no. 2 (July–September 1998): 24–25.
———. "Eddie Bush: 1911–1969 (Part 2)." *Aloha International Steel Guitar Club* 11, no. 3 (October–December 1998): 23.
Volk, Andy. *Lap Steel Guitar*. Anaheim, CA: Centerstream, 2003.
Waksman, Steve. *Instruments of Desire: The Electric Guitar and the Shaping of Musical Experience*. Cambridge, MA: Harvard University Press, 2001.
Wald, Elijah. *Escaping the Delta: Robert Johnson and the Invention of the Blues*. New York: Amistad, 2004.
Walker, Isaiah Helekunihi. *Waves of Resistance: Surfing and History in Twentieth-Century Hawai'i*. Honolulu: University of Hawai'i Press, 2011.
Walsh, Tom, and John King. *The Martin Ukulele: The Little Instrument That Helped Create a Guitar Giant*. Milwaukee: Hal Leonard, 2013.
Wardlow, Gayle Dean. *Chasin' That Devil's Music: Searching for the Blues*. San Francisco: Backbeat, 1998.
Waterhouse, Richard. "Ripping Yarns of the Pacific: American Minstrel Performers Travel to Australia, 1850–1914." In *Coast to Coast: Case Histories*

of Modern Pacific Crossings, edited by Prue Ahrens and Chris Dixon, 89–102. Newcastle upon Tyne, UK: Cambridge Scholars, 2010.

West, Irene. *A Soul's Appeal and Other Poems by the Actress Convert*. Huntington, IN: Our Sunday Visitor, 1917.

Wickham, Graham. "Darby and Tarlton." *Blue Yodeler* (Denver) (1967): 7–9, 16.

Wilson, John H. "A Royal Hawaiian Love Story—A Man and His Band." Excerpted in *Ha'ilono Mele*, October 1979, 1–5.

Wittmann, Matthew. "Empire of Culture: U.S. Entertainers and the Making of the Pacific Circuit, 1850–1890." Ph.D. diss., University of Michigan, 2010.

Wolfe, Charles, and Kip Lornell. *The Life and Legend of Leadbelly*. New York: Da Capo, 1999.

Wynne, Ben. *In Tune: Charley Patton, Jimmie Rodgers and the Roots of American Music*. Baton Rouge: Louisiana State University Press, 2014.

Yamashiro, Aiko, and Noelani Goodyear-Ka'ōpua, eds. *The Value of Hawai'i*. Vol. 2, *Ancestral Roots, Oceanic Visions*. Honolulu: University of Hawai'i Press, 2014.

ACKNOWLEDGMENTS

I made many new friends while working on this book; if it merits any praise, it is because of their consistent and profound generosity. Alan Akaka, Les Cook, John Marsden, Lani Ellen McIntire, and Ka'iwa Meyer patiently humored my hundreds of questions. They invited me into their homes and shared their treasure with me—memories, photographs, and so much of their valuable time. Jim Tranquada, another new friend, and Les Cook painstakingly reviewed the manuscript text—their contributions and corrections were invaluable. I also thank them for placing a great deal of trust in me, and for sharing their vast personal collections and historical ideas. I only hope that my efforts here do not weaken terribly the magic and the power of the stories they encouraged me to tell.

Likewise, the book's fruition has been dependent on the enduring relationships of several of my colleagues who believed in it from the beginning. Rayna Green, J. Kēhaulani Kauanui, Karl Hagstrom Miller, and Amy K. Stillman spent time with proposals and/or manuscript drafts at various points of the process and provided support and critical advice along the way. Likewise, my editor, Mark Simpson-Vos, has worked passionately on this project since the very beginning. He exercised wonderful guidance and gracious patience over the years and, like the others, expanded the book's possibilities by leaps and bounds. At UNC Press I would also like to thank Lucas Church, Kim Bryant and her design team, and Stephanie Ladniak Wenzel for all of their hard work on the book. Alex Martin, likewise, performed an extraordinarily thorough job as the copyeditor.

In addition, I would like to thank each of the following individuals for their diverse contributions over the years that served to bring this book to fruition: C. C. Adcock, Hokulani Aikau, Isaac Akuna, Noelani Arista, Pandit Debashish Bhattacharya, Philippe Billadeaux, Evelyn Brue, Carl and Jean Clark, Nels Cline, Janice Crum, Guy Cundell, Kay Das, Ricky Davis, Ben Dickey, Ben Elder, Kevin Fellezs, Richard Frankel, Sahoa Fukushima, Ben Harper, Basil Henriques, Patrick Huber, Adria Imada, Noelle Jakeman, Ron Johnson, Christine Kane, Ewalani Kanui, Jordan Kellman, Lion Kobayashi, Kay Koster, Luella H. Kurkjian, Yolanda Landry, Candace Lee, Anthony Lis, K. Tsianina Lomawaima, Malinda Maynor Lowery, Pōmaika'i and Mālie Lyman, Tim Mech, Pascal Mesnier, Ron Middlebrook, Noah Miller, Dorian Moe, Jay Munns, Tom Noe, James Nottage, Chad Parker, Joanne

Parker, Ranalee Perreira, Dan Phillips, Beth Piatote, Tia Reber, Malcolm Rockwell, Barbara Roddy, John Rumble, Lorene Ruymar, Aaron Salā, Greg Sardinha, David Delgado Shorter, Steve Siegfried, Harry Soria, Mona Teves, Tony Thomas, Grifford "Kamaka" Tom, Billy Tonnessen, James Trussart, Jonathan Vecchi, Seva Venet, Elijah Wald, Lynn Wheelwright, Kealoha Wong, and Wanda L. Wong.

This book was generously supported by the Smithsonian Institution, the University of Louisiana System's Board of Regents, the Andrew W. Mellon Foundation, and the National Endowment for the Humanities. I would also like to thank my amazing colleagues and students at the University of Louisiana at Lafayette, and the community of musicians in South Louisiana who welcomed me into their wonderful world. It is truly a place like no other, where the dancing never ends. *Et toi!*

I owe my greatest intellectual and emotional debts to my family. Mag, Chris, Lynn, and Ron provide Jack with such a loving extended family in Lafayette. Scot, Carly, and Will make family trips the highlights of the year. The same goes for John and Dolores, and Malisa and Chris, who turned the loss of Rebekah into an opportunity to form a much stronger bond with them. I think that would make her happy to no end. And finally, Sara and Jack have created such joy and wonderment throughout this process. Sara's mutual passion for discovery and research, her genuine enthusiasm for an admittedly dorky guitar book, her critical readings and her kind patience over the last eight years was truly something to behold. Jack is my hero, despite, or perhaps, because of the fact that he comes to my gigs with his hands clamped over his ears. He fills our hearts with the loveliest music. I can't wait to hear the next track. This book is dedicated to them, and to the memories of Rebekah and Jillian.

INDEX

20th Century Fox, 145
49th State Hawaii Record Co., 223

Abbott, Osmer, 32
Aberdeen, MS, 161
Abu Qir, Egypt, 117
Accordion, 14, 42, 104, 247 (n. 60), 251 (n. 112)
Acuff, Roy, 175
Adé, "King" Sunny, 129
Adepoju, Demola, 129
Ae'a, Joseph Kapeaeau, 174
Aeko, W. B., 91
Ahahui Aloha 'Āina, 71
Ahchuck, 47
"Ahi Wela," 91
Ahmee, H., 47, 71, 73, 230, 255 (n. 23)
Ahmi. *See* Ahmee
Ah Sam, Anthony, 295 (n. 64)
Ah See, Jules, 206
AhSing, 46–47, 255 (n. 16)
Ahupua'a, 45, 46, 47, 49, 50, 71, 230, 232
Aikau, Hokulani K., 16, 49
Aiko, Gary, 319–20 (n. 9)
'Āina, 39, 45, 46, 49, 200, 214, 230, 234
"'Āinahau," 38
Ainahau, Tommy, 132
Akaka, Alan, 221–25, 224 (ill.), 227–29
Akaka, Sampson, 282–83 (n. 38)
"Akaka Falls," 133
Akea, Keoki, 74
Akeo, Louise, 209
"'A Kona Hema," 150
Akoni, Juan. *See* Thompson, Louis
Akron, OH, 153
Alabama, 92, 161, 163, 164, 165, 192, 194
Ala Moana Shopping Center (Honolulu), 223
Alaska-Yukon-Pacific Exposition of 1909, 269 (n. 18)
Albania, 117
Alexander's (New York City), 87–88
Alexandria, Egypt, 117, 285 (n. 63)
Ali'i, 3, 13, 14, 15, 17, 20, 28, 29, 30, 31, 35, 36, 41, 45, 47, 48, 49, 52, 252 (n. 118), 256 (n. 30)
Ali'i nui, 10, 12, 15, 17, 18, 23, 38, 39, 40, 44, 46, 108, 110, 202, 245 (n. 48), 280 (n. 19)
Alkire, Eddie, 57, 154, 155, 156, 183, 186, 191, 193, 194, 195 (ill.), 208, 221, 310 (n. 135)
Allen, Anthony, 244–45 (n. 42)
Allman, Duane, 200
Almeida, Johnny, 208, 217, 313 (n. 18), 319–20 (n. 9)
Almeida, Pua, 223, 295 (n. 64), 313 (n. 18), 319–20 (n. 9)
"Aloha 'Āina." *See* "Kaulana Nā Pua."
Aloha Boys, 124
Aloha Four (Moe family troupe), 112
Aloha Hawaiian Orchestra, 100
"Aloha No Au I Kou Maka," 124
"Aloha 'Oe," 38, 71, 91, 158, 171, 174, 177, 272 (n. 59)

Alohikea, Lizzie, 205
Alohikea, William K., 74, 79, 80 (ill.), 88, 89, 94
"Aloma," 171
Ambassador Hotel (Los Angeles), 144
American Board of Commissioners for Foreign Missions, 16
American Guild of Variety Artists, 143
Amory, MS, 161
Anaconda, MT, 91
Ancient Hawaiian Music, 57, 63
Andrade, Carlos, 45
Andrade, Ray, 313 (n. 18)
Andy Cummings and his Hawaiian Serenaders, 216–17. *See also* Cummings, Andy
Andy Iona's Islanders, 179
Anglican Church, 16, 17
Aniruddha, Kazi, 125
Annexation of Hawai'i in 1898 by the United States, 3, 7, 10, 29, 37, 42, 45, 64, 68, 69, 70, 71–72, 78, 79
Anniston, AL, 92, 163
Apaka, Alfred, 295 (n. 64), 313 (n. 18), 319–20 (n. 9)
Apuakehau, Joseph Kekuku'upenakana'i-aupuniokamehameha, 43, 47, 48, 48 (ill.), 49, 50–51, 255 (n. 25), 256 (nn. 30, 31), 257 (n. 34), 266 (n. 133)
Apuakehau, Violet. *See* Kekuku, Violet
Armstrong, Lil, 175
Armstrong, Louis, 160, 175
Arnold, James "Kokomo," 169
Astor House Hotel (Shanghai), 65
Athens, Greece, viii, 123, 128
Atherr, William, 81
Atlanta, GA, 83, 159, 160
Atlantic City, NJ, 88, 232, 268 (n. 8)
Au, Thomas "Uncle Five Cents," 229–30
'Auana, 319 (n. 5)
Au Hoy, Jeff, 225
Australia, 19, 104–5, 107, 127
Austrian Philharmonic Orchestra, 123
Autoharp, 252 (n. 118)
Autry, Gene, 140, 172, 182 (ill.)
Avalon Ballroom (Catalina Island), 140
'Awa, 46, 50, 230
Awai, Keoki "George," 93, 94, 274–75 (n. 95)
'Awa Rebellion, 230, 232, 257 (n. 39), 258 (n. 45)

Bacigalupi, Peter, 74
Baez, Joan, 214
Baghdad, Iraq, 120, 123
Baker, Charles, 80 (ill.)
Baker, John, 54–55
Bali (Los Angeles), 138
Bali Grill (Manila), 127
Baltimore, MD, 187
Bamboo hano, 4
Banerjee, Nikhil, 125
Banjo, 7, 11, 19, 25, 27, 28, 42, 91, 104, 113, 135, 166, 185, 193, 246–47 (n. 56), 262 (n. 96), 263 (n. 99), 300 (n. 27), 304 (n. 50)
Banjolele, 281–82 (n. 28)
Banjo, Mandolin, and Guitar (BMG) movement, 193, 246–47 (n. 56)
Basie, William J. "Count," 217
Basra, Iraq, 120
Bass viol, 14, 53, 65, 222
Baty, Harry, 142 (ill.)
"Bayonet Constitution" of 1887, 24, 42, 43, 50, 63
Beachcomber (Waikīkī), 142–43
Beachcombers (Los Angeles), 138
Beamer, Keola, 213

Beamer, Winona ("Nona"), 222
Beatles, the, 214
Beattie, James, 18
Beauchamp, George, 135, 136, 137, 293 (n. 40)
Beausoleil, 227
"Beautiful Kahana," 230
Beiderbecke, Bix, 132
Beijing, China, 115
Beirut, Lebanon, 120, 123
Belasco Theater (Los Angeles), 90
Belgium, 112
Belgrade, 117
Bell Records, 216
Bellingham, WA, 77
Berger, Henri, 29, 65, 66, 67, 70, 265 (n. 126)
Berger, John, 26, 212, 213
Berlin, Germany, 111, 118, 120, 124
Bethel Street (Honolulu), 206, 312 (n. 8), 316–17 (n. 78)
Bhatt, Vishwa Mohan, 125
Bhattacharya, Mohon, 125
Bhattacharya, Pandit Debashish, 125, 126 (ill.), 228
Big Kawa'a Hawaiian Troupe, 159
Biloxi, MS, 161
Biltmore Hotel (Los Angeles), 144
Biltmore Hotel Trio, 137–38, 144, 217
"Bird of Paradise," 76, 88–89, 90, 91, 92, 94, 110, 111, 112, 163, 169, 180, 185, 186, 281 (n. 27). *See also* Tully, Richard Walton
Bird of Paradise (1932), 140
Birkel Co., George J. (Los Angeles), 94
Birmingham, AL, 159
"Birmingham Jail," 174
Bishaw, Henry, 105, 107 (ill.)
Bishop, Bernice Pauahi, 51
Bishop Museum Library and Archives, 104
Black Ace, 169
"Black Boy Blues," 160
Black Cat Café (Honolulu), 206
Blackface minstrelsy, 11–12, 18, 19, 79, 96, 97, 150, 151, 184, 245–46 (n. 52); in Hawai'i, 7, 253 (n. 149)
Black Patti, 164
Blackstone, Tsianina Redfeather, 1, 2, 7
Blake, Blind, 167
"Blount Report," 64
"Blue Hawaii," 141 (ill.), 169
"Blue Lei," 216
Blues (music genre), vii, viii, 7, 96–97, 117, 124, 156, 157, 164, 165, 166, 168, 169, 170, 175, 176, 177, 181, 197, 200, 234, 298 (n. 14), 298–99 (n. 16), 302–3 (n. 44)
"Blue Yodel No. 9," 175
BMG. *See* Banjo, Mandolin, and Guitar
Bob Wills and His Texas Playboys, 181–82
Boggs, Noel, 194, 196 (ill.)
Bohling, W. K. (Kalama), 87, 88
Bollywood, use of Hawaiian steel guitars in, 6–7, 125
Bombay, India, 117, 120, 123, 284 (n. 58), 285 (n. 61)
Bones, 19, 42, 253 (n. 149)
Bonham, TX, 33
Boston, MA, 15, 16, 30, 88, 89
Bow, Clara, 138
Brahms, Johannes, 193
Brand, Harry, 145–47
Brando, Marlon, 140
Breaux, Cléoma, 174
Bridges, Cy, 256 (n. 28), 319–20 (n. 9)
Bright, Sol K., 133, 142 (ill.), 144, 294 (n. 54), 295 (n. 64)

Brito, C. L., 20
Broadway Melody, 138
Bronson, George, 187, 188, 310 (n. 134)
Brookhaven, MS, 161
Brooklyn, NY, 82, 153, 197
Brown, Charley "Tiny," 217, 316–17 (n. 78)
Brown, Milton, 179, 181
Browne, Jackson, 200
Brunswick Records, 133
Bryan, William Jennings, 70
Bryn Mawr College, 114
Buck, Elizabeth, 38
Buke hīmeni, 15
Bulgaria, 117
"Bully Song, The" 163
Burma, 115
Burns, Augustus M., 163
Burrows, David Napihi, 164, 312 (n. 7)
Bush, Eddie, 130, 137–38, 139 (ill.), 143, 144, 147, 172, 179, 217
Byrd, Jerry, 179, 180, 181, 193, 221–23, 225, 232, 233
Byron Bay, Australia, 104–5

Cab, Charley, 317–18 (n. 92)
Cairo, Egypt, 117, 285 (n. 63)
Calcutta, 112, 115, 120, 124, 285 (n. 61)
California, 7, 8, 14, 18, 32, 74, 75, 88, 89, 94, 130–47. *See also* Los Angeles; San Francisco
Call of the Valley, 125
Calvinist church, missionary efforts in Hawai'i, 16–18, 50, 97
Camden, NJ, 100
Canada, 74, 81, 88
Cannon, Gus, 166, 177
Canton, MS, 161
Carlisle, Cliff, 174, 175, 176
Carter, Maybelle, 173–74
Carter Family, 173–74
Casey, Pat, 81, 82
Castle, William, 41
Castro, Tommy, 312 (n. 10), 313 (n. 18)
Catalina Island, 140
Cazimero, Brothers, 211
Ceballos, Al, 143 (ill.)
Cello, 65
Central Café (Honolulu), 217
Chalker, Curly, 196
Chants. *See* Mele oli
Chaplin, Charlie, 138
Charleston, MS, 161
Charlie Chan's Greatest Case, 142
Charlot, John, 38
Chautauqua tours, 102–3, 161, 180, 186
Chemnitz, Germany, 111
Cheraw, SC, 166
Cherry Valley, MA, 153
Chicago, IL, 6, 79, 82, 125, 157, 162, 164, 167, 179, 181, 186, 192, 270 (n. 39)
Chief's Children's School, 35–36, 38
Chikari strings, 125, 126, 287 (n. 102)
China, 13, 19, 47, 65, 71, 103, 115, 255 (n. 23)
Chinatown (Honolulu), 20, 64
Chitravina. *See* Gottuvadyam
Chock See's (Honolulu), 317–18 (n. 92)
Choy, Richard, 202, 203, 204, 208, 312–13 (nn. 10, 13)
Christchurch, New Zealand, 105
Christmas Island, 121
Church of Jesus Christ of Latter-Day Saints (LDS), 16, 17, 36, 43, 49–50, 51, 71, 229
Church of the Living God, 187
Clarinet, 132, 222
Clarksdale, MS, 9, 161, 172, 177
Cleghorn, Victoria Kawēkiu Ka'iulani Lunalilo Kalaninuiahilapalapa, 110

Clement, Sam, 164
Cleveland, Grover, 64
Cleveland, OH, 6, 154, 155, 183, 187, 191, 202, 276 (n. 116), 310 (n. 135)
Cline, Nels, 234
Cline, Patsy, 180
Clooney, George, 229
Club Hawaii (Los Angeles), 138
Club Pago Pago (Honolulu), 313 (n. 18)
Cluff, Benjamin, 71–72
Cocoanut Grove (Los Angeles), 138
Coconut Grove, 142
Collins, Sam, 169
Colorado, 84, 187, 302 (n. 42)
Columbia Phonograph Company, 96, 101, 133, 174
Columbus, GA, 160, 163
"Columbus Stockade Blues," 174
Comet Royal Hawaiian Serenaders, 159
Coney Island, NY, 110, 277 (n. 134)
Considine, John, 88
Constitution, 1887 Kingdom of Hawai'i. *See* "Bayonet Constitution" of 1887
Continental Cabaret (Cairo), 117
Cooder, Ry, 200
Cook, James, 3
Corinth, MS, 161
Country (music genre), 140, 156–57, 171, 173, 174, 175, 176, 179, 181, 182, 195, 196, 200, 213, 220, 221, 228, 234, 239 (n. 16), 313 (n. 22). *See also* Hillbilly
Crawford, Joan, 138, 293 (n. 40)
Crescent Trio, 101 (ill.)
Crosby, Bing, 6, 139, 140, 141 (ill.)
Crosby, Stills, Nash, and Young, 197
Crum, Janice, 192
Cummings, Andy, 216–17, 313 (n. 18), 319–20 (n. 9)
Cunha, Albert R. "Sonny," 75, 81, 85, 91, 98, 148, 271–72 (n. 57)
Custino, Joe, 206, 313 (n. 18)
Cyprus, 123

"Dad Blame Blues," 160
Dalhart, Vernon, 171–72
Dallas, TX, 100, 159, 160, 162, 177
Danny Small & 'Ukulele Mays, 171
Das, Kay, 124
Davion, Gabriel, 53–56, 259 (n. 63)
Davis, Charles K. L., 212
Davis, Jimmie, 168
Daws, Gavan, 13, 18
Dawson, Ted, 217
Day, Jimmy, 196
Deale, Ernest, 185, 193
"Dearie," 77
Decker's Hawaiian Serenaders, 132
"Deep in the Heart of Texas," 172
DeLano, Charles S., 94, 134, 186, 260–61 (n. 77)
Delhi, India, 115
DeMille, Cecil B., 140
Dempsey, Jack, 198 (ill.)
Denmark, 112, 117
Denver, CO, 187, 302 (n. 42)
Derby, Charles, 242 (n. 23)
DeRego, Steppy, 313 (n. 18)
Descendants, The, 229
Des Moines, IA, 91
Desmond, Jane, 183
Detroit, 6, 193
Diaz, Vicente, 243–44 (n. 35)
Dick McIntire's Harmony Hawaiians, 179. *See also* McIntire, Dixon Ka'aihu "Dick"
Diddley bow, 165, 177, 298 (n. 14), 302 (n. 44)

Dixie Jazz Hounds, 160
Dobro guitars. *See* Dobro Manufacturing Company. *See also* Dopyera, John; Dopyera, Rudy
Dobro Manufacturing Company, 5, 60, 135, 175, 176, 234, 262 (n. 84), 277 (n. 133), 292 (n. 39)
Don Ho Show, The, 210. *See also* Ho, Don
Doolittle, Jimmy, 140
Dopyera, John, 135
Dopyera, Rudy, 135
Doucet, David, 227
Douglas, Jerry, 277 (n. 133)
Dover, NJ, 125
Dragon Café (Los Angeles), 132
Duke Kahanamoku's (Waikīkī), 210
Dunn, Bob, 179–80, 181
Dylan, Bob, 214

Eagles, the, 200
Eason, Troman, 187
Edison, Thomas, 102
Edison's National Phonograph Company, 74, 79, 85, 96, 101, 159, 179
Edison studios (new York City), 85
Edwards, Webley, 206
Egypt, 117
EHARP, 194, 195 (ill.). *See also* Alkire, Eddie
Electone-Settes, 190 (ill.)
Electric steel guitar, 5, 8, 135–37, 179, 180, 181, 193, 197, 202, 226, 228
Electro String Instrument Corporation, 135–36, 142 (ill.)
Elgin, IL, 193
Ellington, Edward K. "Duke," 217
Ellis, John (Jack), 75, 81, 88
Ellis, Willie, 88
Ellis Brothers' Quartette and Glee Club, 81
Emerson, Nathaniel, 41
Emma, Queen. *See* Rooke, Emma Kalanikaumaka'amano Kaleleonālani Na'ea
Emmons, Buddy, 192, 196
England, 1, 2, 17, 56, 72, 88, 103, 100, 108, 109–12, 127, 186
Epiphone guitars, 190 (ill.), 277 (n. 132), 293 (n. 41)

Fahey, John, 176
Fairbanks, Douglas, 138
"Fair Hawaii," 296 (n. 76)
Falcon, Joe, 174
Falsetto singing, 15, 44, 62, 201, 217, 221, 227, 242–43 (n. 27)
"Famous Are the Flowers." *See* "Kaulana Nā Pua"
"Farewell to Thee," 177
Farina, Johnny, 197
Farina, Santo, 197
Fender, Leo, 194
Fender Electric Instrument Company, 194, 196 (ill.), 197, 218 (ill.), 311 (n. 159)
Ferera, Frank. *See* Ferreira, Frank, Jr.
Ferera and Franchini, 102. *See also* Ferreira, Frank, Jr.
Ferera's Hawaiian Instrumental Quartet, 171. *See also* Ferreira, Frank, Jr.
Ferera's Hawaiian Serenaders, 102. *See also* Ferreira, Frank, Jr.
Ferera Waikiki Sextette, 102. *See also* Ferreira, Frank, Jr.
Ferreira, Frank, Jr., 74, 89, 100–102, 101 (ill.), 114, 159, 166, 171, 172, 173, 174, 176

Fiddle, 7, 11, 19, 21, 30, 42, 94, 104, 157, 182 (ill.)
Fifth Avenue Theatre (New York City), 81
Filmi (music genre), 125, 287 (n. 105)
First Hawaiian Conservatory of Music. *See* Hawaiian Conservatory of Music
Fisherman's Wharf (Honolulu), 217
Flemington, WV, 154
Flint, MI, 174
Flirtation Walk, The, 142
Florence, AL, 165
Florida, 74, 159, 161, 167, 309–10 (n. 133)
Flute, 28, 70, 78, 251 (n. 112)
Foley, Red, 180
Folk (music genre), 156, 157, 178, 200, 214
Folk Music of Hawaii, The, 222
Footlights and Fools, 138
Ford, John and Mary, 139
"Forget Me Not," 185
Fort Wayne, IN, 186
Foster, Stephen, 193
France, 10, 88, 103, 110, 111, 112, 119, 127, 186, 279 (n. 12), 281 (n. 27), 287–88 (n. 107)
Franchini, Anthony, 101, 102
Frank J. Vierra's Hawaiian Quintet, 81
Frying pan guitar. *See* Rickenbacker guitars: EH "frying pan." *See also* Electro String Instrument Corporation
Funicello, Annette, 140

Gandhi, Mahatma, 117
Ganguly, Sunil, 125
Garcia, Jerry, 197
Garrick Theatre (London), 110
Gennett Records, 101
Georgia, 74, 83, 159, 160, 161, 163, 167, 169
Germany, 88, 108, 111, 112, 117–22, 124
Gibraltar, 123
Gibson, Edmund R. "Hoot," 140, 172–73, 173 (ill.)
Gibson guitars, 190 (ill.), 234
Gigi Royce's Orchestra, 313 (n. 18)
"Git along Little Dogies," 172
Glee Club. *See* Hawaiian string bands
Godfrey, Arthur, 212
Goebbels, Joseph, 118
Goering, Hermann, 118
Goerner, Paul, 269 (n. 16)
Goodman, Benny, 217
Goshute Indians, Skull Valley Band of, 43
Gottuvadyam, 55, 56, 124
Grable, Betty, 145
Grand Ole Opry, vii, 175
Grassie, Laura, 195 (ill.)
Graziano, Rocky, 198 (ill.)
Great Depression, 8, 102, 143, 148, 188
Great Falls, MT, 162 (ill.)
Great Gabbo, The, 138
Great Māhele, the, 45–46, 48
Greece, viii, 117, 120, 123, 128
Green, Lloyd, 192
Greenville, MS, 92, 163
Greenwood, MS, 161, 177
Grog shops, 13, 15, 18, 20
Guerrero, Amelia, 209
Guitar: guitar culture, 4, 12, 64–65; as a focus of study, 12; as a favored instrument in Hawai'i, 14, 19, 20, 21, 64–65; modified in Hawai'i, 19, 64–65, 78; tunings for, 20, 27, 215; use of harmonics with, 20, 62, 114, 124; as appropriation, 29–30; as a form of labor, 33–34,

66–67, 69–70, 130, 142–44, 216–17, 266–67 (n. 140), 317–18 (n. 92); represented as the antithesis of labor, 146–47. *See also* Electric steel guitar; Harp guitar; Hawaiian steel guitar; Hollow-necked guitar; Kī hōʻalu; Non-pedal steel guitar; Pedal steel guitar; Slide guitar; Strings, guitar; Tenor guitar
"Guitar Blues," 168
"Guitar Rag," 168, 181–82, 309 (n. 114)
Guitarras portuguesas, 241–42 (n. 3)
Guitar without a Master, 15
Gulfport, MS, 98, 100, 161, 162
Gullah, 158

Hagstrom Miller, Karl, 96, 171
Hālau hula, 33, 211
Hālau Mele Hawaiʻi, 223
Hāmākua Coast, HI, 47
Hamburg, Germany, 111
Hammond, Percy, 270 (n. 39)
Hanapi, Mike, 133
Handy, W. C., 160, 163, 165–66, 169, 177, 303 (n. 46)
Hankow (Hankou), China, 115
Hanley Brothers (New Orleans), 159
"Hanohano Hanalei," 154
Hansen, Barry, 176
Haole (pl. hāole), definition of, viii, 235–35 (n. 3)
Hapa haole, 8, 75, 91, 93, 98, 101, 127, 133, 138, 148, 150, 151, 154, 155, 160, 167, 168, 171, 173, 183, 185, 202, 217, 219–20, 224, 225, 226, 227; definition of, 7, 85, 209, 219; criticisms of, 208–14, 217, 225, 315 (n. 60)
Harp, 14
Harper, Ben, 234
Harp guitar, 77–78, 134
Hartford, KY, 92, 169
Harvey, Roy, 167
Harvey and Johnson, 309 (n. 114)
Hattiesburg, MS, 161, 298–99 (n. 16)
Haulani, Jimmy, 295 (n. 64)
Hauʻula, HI, 230
Hauyani, 128
Hawaiʻi, statehood of, 197, 315 (n. 52)
Hawaiian Conservatory of Music, 61 (ill.), 94, 297 (n. 11)
Hawaiian Dance Orchestra, 102. *See also* Ferreira, Frank, Jr.
Hawaiian Duet, the, 171
Hawaiian Entertainers, the, 102, 171
Hawaiian Glee Club, 79
Hawaiian guitar. *See* Hawaiian steel guitar
Hawaiian Guitarist, 188, 190
"Hawaiian Harmony Blues," 169
Hawaiian Hotel (Honolulu), 34, 65, 68
Hawaiian Kingdom, 1, 3, 7, 10, 11–13, 35–42; 1893 overthrow of, viii, 63–64; musical response to the overthrow, 67–71, 151, 264 (n. 108), 264 (n. 117), 265 (n. 118). *See also* "Bayonet Constitution" of 1887; Kalākaua, David; Kamehameha I; Kamehameha II; Kamehameha III; Kamehameha IV; Kamehameha V; Lāhui; Liliʻuokalani; Lunalilo, William
Hawaiian language. *See* ʻŌlelo Hawaiʻi
"Hawaiian Method" of Playing Guitar Self Taught, 94
Hawaiian music: early nineteenth-century history of, 4–5; demarcations of "traditional," 7, 201, 202, 208–14, 225, 315 (n. 60). *See also* Hawaiian Renaissance; Hawaiian steel guitar; Hawaiian string bands; Mele hula; Mele oli

Hawaiian Music Foundation (HMF), 220
Hawaiian National Band. *See* Ka Bana Lahui
Hawaiian Nights, 140
Hawaiian Paradise (Los Angeles), 138, 144
Hawaiian Quartette, 102. *See also* Ferreira, Frank, Jr.
"Hawaiian Rainbow," 171
Hawaiian Renaissance (1970s), 8, 201, 210–20
Hawaiian Room (Lexington Hotel, New York City), 148, 149 (ill.), 150, 151, 312 (n. 10)
Hawaiian Sales (Honolulu), 114
Hawaiian Serenaders, 171
"Hawaiian Song" 178
Hawaiian steel guitar: references to in ʻŌlelo Hawaiʻi periodicals, 5; and fingerpicks, 5, 59, 83, 113, 117; and steel bar, 5, 59, 262 (n. 87); fundamentals of, 5–6, 52, 59–60; origins of, 52–59, 260–61 (n. 77), 261–62 (n. 84); as developed specifically to perform Hawaiian music, 62–63; early spread of, 63, 73, 74, 75–76, 81–83; as most popular recorded music in the United States, 77, 91, 95–98, 127, 268 (n. 8); development of hollow-necked steel guitar, 77–78; tunings for, 83, 113, 128, 203, 208, 225, 312 (n. 10), 316–17 (n. 78); early lesson books and instructional manuals for, 94, 112; in early Hollywood films, 138, 140; on the radio, 153–55, 206–9; instruction of in Hawaiian guitar school franchises, 155–56, 187–94; extent of evidence supporting independent development of similar technique in the U.S. South, 165–67, 298 (n. 14), 298–99 (n. 16); decline of in Hawaiʻi, 209–14, 316 (n. 64); role of during the Hawaiian Renaissance, 216–20; slow recovery of in Hawaiʻi, 220–26, 227–34
Hawaiian string bands, 7, 29, 34–35, 37, 64–65, 69, 74, 80–81; competition between for 1915 Panama Pacific International Exhibition contract, 92–94, 274–75 (n. 95); and endurance of segregated facilities in the U.S. South, 164–65; formation of by non-Hawaiians, 183–86. *See also* Guitar; Hawaiian steel guitar
Hawaiian Theatre. *See* Royal Hawaiian Theatre
Hawaiian Town Night Club (Honolulu), 313 (n. 18)
Hawaiian Trio, 102. *See also* Ferreira, Frank, Jr.
Hawaiian Village (Los Angeles), 138
Hawaii Calls, 206–9, 207 (ill.), 220, 221, 228
Hawaiʻi House of Representatives, 33
"Hawaiʻi Ponoi," 38, 91, 94, 98
Hawaiʻi State Archives, 21, 104
Healani (Kalākaua's boat house), 42
"Heʻeia," 229
"He Lei No Ka Poʻe Aloha ʻĀina." *See* "Kaulana Nā Pua"
Heleluhe, Jack, 80 (ill.)
Helm, George, 315 (n. 60)
"He Mele Lāhui Hawaiʻi," 38
Hennessey, Tom, 74
Henry Johnson and His Boys, 169
Hensley, Hairl, 175
Hen Wise's Bronze Review, 164
"Hesitation Blues," 160

Hew Len, Billy, 201, 206, 223, 313 (n. 18)
Hicks, Jimmy, 89
"Hi'ilawe," 216
Hill Billies, The, 167
Hillbilly (music genre), 7, 96–97, 156, 157, 167, 171, 172, 173, 174, 179
Hilo, HI, 36, 64, 88, 161, 279–80 (n. 15)
"Hilo Hanakahi," 114
Hilo Hawaiian Orchestra, 172
"Hilo March," 133, 154, 174, 193
Hilo Serenaders, 172
Himeni (pl. hīmeni), 15, 37, 40, 148
Hiram, Solomon, 89
His Jazz Bride, 140
Hitler, Adolf, 118, 120
Ho, Don, 210, 211, 212, 213
Ho, Walter, 164
Hoa, James, 53, 259 (n. 63)
Hoapili, Alex, 57, 186, 202, 215, 261–62 (n. 84), 312 (n. 7)
Hoffman Café (Honolulu), 206, 217, 313 (n. 18)
Hokea, Ben, 185
Hōkūle'a, 211
Holbrook, J. O., 154
Holland, 112
Hollow-necked guitar, 6, 60, 77–78, 105, 127, 134–35, 137, 269 (n. 18), 291 (n. 27)
Holly Springs, MS, 161
Hollywood, CA, 8, 130–31, 172, 193, 228; community of Pacific Islanders working in, 137–52; labor opportunities in, 142–44; limitations of, 144–47; role of in the decline of the steel guitar in Hawai'i, 213–14
Hollywood Bowl, 193
Hollywood Revue of 1929, 138
Holoua, William, 89
"Home on the Range," 140, 172
Hong Kong, 115, 121
Honolulu, 142
Honolulu: early history of, 6, 12–14, 13; harbor of, 12, 13–14, 43, 54–55, 133; waterfront entertainment district of, 15–16, 18, 29; music scene, 1900–1960s, 202–10; music scene during the Hawaiian Renaissance, 210–20; music scene, 1980s–present, 220–26
Honolulu Conservatory of Music, 155, 156, 187, 191
"Honolulu Hula Girl," 185
Honolulu International Airport, 216
"Honolulu Maids," 209
Honolulu Students, the. *See* Lu Thompson Keouli's Honolulu Students
"Honolulu Tom Boy," 85, 148
Hooper, William, 30
Ho'opi'i, Sol, 8, 114, 117, 130, 131–38, 136 (ill.), 140, 145 (ill.), 147, 151, 152 (ill.), 155, 160, 172, 176, 179, 180, 203, 206, 217, 223, 229
Hoot Gibson's Hawaiian Foursome, 172
House, Eddie James "Son," 6, 176–77, 200
House of God, 187
Huilua Fish Pond, 46
"Hu'i Mai," 140
Hukilau Marketplace (Lā'ie), 230
Hula: in Kalākaua's court, 21, 23; prohibitions against, 32–33; and gender roles, 66, 263 (n. 104); on the vaudeville stage, 86, 97; appropriated by non-Hawaiians, 183–84, 210; in Polynesian-themed clubs, 147–52; during the Hawaiian Renaissance, 211. *See also* Hula 'ālā'apapa; Hula ku'i; Mele hula

Hula ʻālaʻapapa, 86
"Hula Blues," 114, 133, 148, 185
"Hula Hands," 150
Hula Hut (Los Angeles), 138
Hula kuʻi, 24, 26, 27, 28, 36, 40, 41, 44, 66, 68–69, 83, 132–33, 148, 155, 201, 214
Hunter, Alberta, 117
Hurricane, The, 142
Hurricane, the (New York City), 147–48
Hutchison, Frank, 167–68

Iaukea, Curtis Piehu, 10–11, 12, 14
ʻIli ʻili, 214
Ilima, Feilani, 284 (n. 52)
Ilima, Lei, 284 (n. 52)
Illinois, ix, 6, 79, 82, 125, 157, 162, 164, 167, 179, 181, 186, 192, 199, 228, 270 (n. 39)
Imada, Adria, 26, 70, 148, 151
"Imi Au Iā ʻOe," 123, 209
"I'm in the Market for You," 160
Imperial Records (UK), 101
India, 103, 108, 112, 120, 228: popularity of Hawaiian steel guitar in, 6, 124–25; possible relationship to the origins of the Hawaiian steel guitar, 53–56; Tau Moe's influence in, 115, 117, 124–25
Indianola, MS, vii, 161
Influenza epidemic, 113
Ingano, Bobby, 225, 318 (n. 107)
International Cowboys, 173
Inter-reformers Band, the, 289–90 (n. 124)
ʻIolani Palace, 3, 51, 67
Iona, Andy, 133, 142, 179
Iosepa, UT, 43, 51, 71
Ipu, 4, 21, 23, 26, 40, 203, 214, 219, 220
Iraq, 120, 123
Irene West Royal Hawaiians, 81, 99, 100, 112, 127, 179, 185
Isaacs, Alvin Kaleolani, Sr., 205, 206, 319–20 (n. 9)
Isaacs, Barney, 206, 207 (ill.), 312 (n. 6)
Isaacs, Leland "Atta," 218 (ill.)
Isaacs, Norman, 223
Israel, 121, 124
Istanbul, Turkey, 117
Italy, 112, 120
"I've Seen My Baby (And It Won't Be Long Now)," 160

J. M. Webb's Golden Rule Bazaar (Honolulu), 73
Jackson, MS, 161
James, Elmore, 200
Japan, 8, 9, 115, 120, 121, 147, 210, 225
Jarvis, James Jackson, 31
Jawaiian (music genre), 228
Jazz (music genre), vii, 7, 127, 132–33, 148, 155, 160, 179, 194, 206, 208, 209, 217, 218
Jefferson, Blind Lemon, 160, 169, 177, 179
Jim and Bob, 180
Johnsen, Bjorn, 153
Johnson, Henry, 169
Johnson, Lonnie, 169
Johnson, Robert, 156, 177
Johnson, Ron, 232–34, 233 (ill.)
Jones, Alfred K., 87, 88, 280 (n. 22)
Jones, Hannah "Toots," 76, 78, 79, 80–86, 87 (ill.), 97, 131, 159, 179, 271 (n. 52), 277–78 (n. 135)
Judd, Gerrit P., 244 (n. 39)
Juju (music genre), 129, 289–90 (n. 124)

Ka'ai, Ernest, 93, 117, 124, 127, 263, 265 (n. 131), 281–82 (n. 28)
Ka'ai, Thelma, 204, 263 (n. 105), 288 (n. 110)
Ka'ai'ai, Solomon Ho'opi'i. *See* Ho'opi'i, Sol
Ka'ai's Glee Club, 93
Ka'apuni, Sam, 205
Ka Bana Lahui, 67, 68, 69, 70, 159, 164, 211
Kabra, Sri Brij Bhushan, 125, 287 (n. 102)
Kachamba, Daniel, 129
Kachamba, Donald, 129
Ka'eka, Dan, 313 (n. 18)
Ka Hae Hawai'i, 21–23
Kahahawai, Charles Kapono, Jr. *See* Pahinui, Charles Philip "Gabby"
Kahakalau, Willie, 280 (n. 23)
Kahana ahupua'a (Ahupua'a O Kahana), 46, 47, 50, 71, 230, 232
Kahana Bay, HI, 46, 104, 230, 233
Kahana Hui, 47, 230, 232
Kahanamoku, Duke, 88, 210, 249–50 (n. 83)
Kahananui, Duke, 185
Kahananui, Sol, 89
Kahanu, Archie, 143 (ill.)
Kahauolopua, Jack, 187
Kahauolopua, Jimmy, 187
Kahawaiola'a, Momi, 319–20 (n. 9)
Kahea, Bill, 89
Kaho'olawe, HI, 211, 314 (n. 44), 315 (n. 60)
Kahuna (pl. Kāhuna), 3, 69, 232
Kaiawe, Moke, 88
Kaiawe, S. M., 90
Kaieo, Sam, 295 (n. 64)
Kaihumua, Emalia, 21, 22 (ill.), 247 (n. 64), 247–48 (n. 65)
Kaili, David Luela, 99, 102, 105–7, 112, 115, 124, 127–28, 159, 179, 185, 277–78 (n. 135)
Kaili, Mary Louise "Queenie," 104, 105–7, 115, 124, 127–28
Kailimai, Henry, 93, 274–75 (n. 95)
Kailua, HI, 227
Kaimana, Emma, 204
Kainapau, George, 141 (ill.), 295 (n. 64), 305 (n. 60)
Kainoa, Sam, 187
Kaipo, Joseph, 175
Ka'iulani, Princess. *See* Cleghorn, Victoria Kawēkiu Ka'iulani Lunalilo Kalaninuiahilapalapa
Kaka'ako, HI, 131, 215
Kāla'au, 86
Kalaina, Joseph, 74, 89
Kalainaina, Sam Li'a, 21
Kalākaua, David, 10, 23, 35, 36, 37, 38, 42, 43, 44, 50, 85, 91, 94, 98, 110, 111, 112, 150, 201; musicians and dancers in court of, 21, 78; ascendancy of to the throne, 39–40; 1883 coronation ceremony of, 40–41; "Singing Boys" of, 41, 67, 70, 104; Healani (boathouse), 42; 1886 Jubilee Celebration of, 53, 56, 79
Kalākaua Avenue (Honolulu), 227
Kalaluhi, George, 88
Kalaluhi, Miranda, 89
Kalama, Benny, 213, 223, 224 (ill.)
Kalama, David, 249 (n. 83)
Kalama, Sylvester, 98
Kalani, Buddy, 132
Kalani, George, 289 (n. 116)
Kalaukoa, David, 280 (n. 22)
Kaleikoa, David, 87
Kalima, Jesse, 317–18 (n. 92)

Kalo. *See* Taro
Kama, Charles, 175. *See also* Valera, Charles Kama
Kamaʻāina, 34, 54, 65, 89, 201, 206, 235–36 (n. 3)
Kamae, Eddie, 20–21, 216, 223
Kamahele, Sonny, 223, 224 (ill.)
Kamakaʻeha, Lydia Liliʻu Loloku Walania Wewehi. *See* Liliʻuokalani
Kamakaia, Sam K., 70
Kamakani, Henry, 89
Kamakawiwoʻole, Israel, 211, 214
Kamakea, Louise Rose, 280 (n. 23)
Kamāmalu, Queen, 110, 245 (n. 48)
"Kamawae," 85, 272 (n. 59)
Kameʻeleihiwa, Lilikalā, 16–17
Kamehameha I, 3, 13, 14, 18, 38
Kamehameha II, 13, 245 (n. 48)
Kamehameha III, 14, 18, 32, 45, 245 (n. 48)
Kamehameha IV, 10, 17, 244 (n. 39)
Kamehameha V, 10, 17, 35, 38, 39, 244 (n. 39)
Kamehameha Glee Club, 30 (ill.)
Kamehameha School for Boys, 51–52, 57, 58, 59, 63, 64, 72–73, 92
Kamehameha School for Girls, 28 (ill.), 64, 66
Kamehameha Schools, 222
"Ka Mele Okuʻu Puuwai," 229
Kamiki Method, 112
Kamoku, John, 110
Kamoku, William, 110, 111 (ill.)
Kanahele, George S., 36, 53, 74, 201, 202, 210, 220, 221
Kanaka (pl. Kānaka), 235–36 (n. 3)
Kanaka Maoli (pl. Kānaka Maoli), 68, 232, 235–36 (n. 3)
Kandle, Letritia, 310 (n. 141)
Kāne, 66
Kāneʻohe, HI, 210
Kanoho, Philip, 89
Kansas City, KS, 159
Kanui, David, 62, 175, 302 (n. 40)
Kanui, William Kulii, 88, 110, 287–88 (n. 107)
Kaʻohu, Rose. *See* Moe, Rose Kaʻohu
Kaona, 38, 68, 252 (n. 124), 265 (n. 118)
Kaopua, Miliama "Miriam," 43, 47–51, 48 (ill.), 71
Kapa, 46
Kapahu, Kini. *See* Kapahukulaokamāmalu, Kini
Kapahukulaokamāmalu, Kini, 26, 41, 111, 112, 158–59
Kapiolani Park (Honolulu), 131
Kapu, 13, 17, 45
Kapu, William, 74
Kapuāiwa, Lot. *See* Kamehameha V
Karachi, Pakistan, 115
Kasihue, Johnnie, 165
Kauahikaua, Bob, 207 (ill.)
Kauaʻi, HI, 29, 30, 154
Kauikeaouli. *See* Kamehameha III
"Kaulana Nā Pua," 67, 68, 71, 211
Kava. *See* ʻAwa
Kawahigashi, Viola Kehau, 58
Kawaiahaʻo Church, 15, 221–22
Kawaihau Glee Club, 29, 65, 249–50 (n. 83), 314 (n. 36)
"Kawaihau Waltz," 85
"Kawiki," 150
"Ka Wiliwili Wai," 154
Kealakaʻi, Mekia, 53, 70, 79, 80 (ill.), 89, 103, 109, 112, 169, 265 (n. 126)
Kealakekua Bay, HI, 13
Kealoha, Joseph K., 281 (n. 27)
Keawe, Genoa, 217, 219, 222, 223, 227, 231, 319–20 (n. 9)

Keawe, Joe, 201
Keawe ʻOhana, 227
Keech, Alvin, 281–82 (n. 28)
Kehanu, Archie, 295 (n. 64)
Keiki, Frank Jonah, 115
Kekauoha, "Little Joe," 143 (ill.)
Kekona, Diamond, 110, 111 (ill.), 279–80 (n. 15)
Kekuku, Edwin, 51, 57, 72
Kekuku, Hattie, 51, 71
Kekuku, Ivy, 51, 71
Kekuku, Joseph, 6, 7, 30, 43, 45, 60 (ill.), 74 (ill.), 88, 92, 95, 99, 102, 104, 113, 159, 168, 179, 186, 202, 229, 230, 231, 233; birth and family history of, 46–51; time enrolled at Kamehameha School for Boys, 51–52, 57–59, 72–73; and development of the Hawaiian steel guitar, 53–61, 63; and royalist support for Liliʻuokalani's restoration, 64, 71–72; early career of on the West Coast and in the Pacific Northwest, 73–75, 77–78, 131; with Toots Paka's Hawaiians, 78–86; with Kekuku's Hawaiian Quintet, 102, 103 (ill.); European tours of, 112, 281–82 (n. 28); death of, 125–27; return of to the United States, 125–28
Kekuku, Merle, 229, 313 (n. 18)
Kekuku, Violet (Viola), 49, 51, 58
Kekuku's Hawaiian Quintet, 102, 103 (ill.)
Ke Kula Mele Hawaiʻi, 227
Kela, Allen, 295 (n. 64)
Keliʻi, David, 206, 208, 221, 223, 313 (n. 18)
Keliiaihue, Joe, 88
Keliʻikoa, Jake, 206, 223, 313 (n. 18)
Keliiwaiwaiole, Peni, 47
Kenelle, Sammy, 291 (n. 14)
Kenona, Henry K., 88
Keohokālole, Analea, 46
Keouli. *See* Thompson, Louis
Keouli, Professor. *See* Thompson, Louis
Kester, Matthew, 50
Keumi, Moses, 19
KFWB, 132
KHJ, 132
Kia, George, 75, 88, 94, 134
Kī hōʻalu, 8, 20, 24–26, 27, 113, 206, 214–17, 218, 219, 220, 222, 225, 227, 228, 229
Kiilehua, Jennie Keliimiola, 73
Kīkā Kila. *See* Hawaiian steel guitar
Kila, Alan, 142 (ill.)
"Kilima March," 100
Kim, Paul, 221
King, B. B., vii–viii
King, Charles E., 53, 55, 56, 208, 219
King's Singing Boys. *See* Kalākaua, David: "Singing Boys" of
Kinney, Raymond, 151, 282–83 (n. 38), 312 (n. 10)
Kinney, Willie, 89
Kleinmeyer, Ted E., 135
Knight, Gladys, 200
Knutsen, Chris J., 77–78
Knutsen guitars, 60, 77–78, 134, 137
Koa, as material for guitar construction, 6, 19–20, 78, 168, 269 (n. 18)
"Kohala March," 100
Koki, Sam, 142, 145 (ill.), 180, 290, 295 (n. 64), 307 (n. 93), 312 (n. 10)
Kolomoku, Anita "Goldie," 104, 186
Kolomoku, Charles, 186
Kolomoku, Walter Keaumakalani, 61, 88, 90, 91, 94, 99, 102, 105, 180, 185
Kolomoku's Hawaiian Quintette, 91, 99

Kolsiana, Ralph, 172
Komoku, William, 103
Kona guitars, 134
Konohiki, 45, 46, 47, 48
Koʻolau Loa, 46, 47, 48, 49, 73
Koʻolau Mountain Range, 46, 101
Koster, Kay, 192
Kostrzewski, Kay. *See* Koster, Kay
Krausgill Piano Company (Louisville, KY), 168
Ku, George Sam, 164
Ku, Sam, 133, 135, 287–88 (n. 107)
Kua, Rose, 154
Kuaʻāina, 29, 34, 42, 202, 210, 314 (n. 44)
Kuaana, Danny, 295 (n. 64)
Kuala Lumpur, Malaysia, 115, 117, 123
Kubik, Gerhard, 128, 165
Kulainoheo, Luana, 83
Kuleana, 46, 49, 51, 232, 233, 234
Kuleana Act of 1850, 45
Kuleella's Hawaiian Troupe, 159
Kulolio, James, 80 (ill.)
Kulolio, Joseph, 89
Kumalae, Jack, 88
Kumalae, Jonah, 93
Kumalae's Glee Club, 93
Kumu hula, 66, 232
Kuo, George, 227
Kupahu, Manuel "Joe Gang," 218
Kupihea, David M., 53, 56
Kūpuna, 214, 216
Kusa, OK, 180
"Kuʻu Home," 91
"Kuʻu Ipo I ka Heʻe Puʻe One," 38
"Kuʻu Lei Pikake," 154

Lacy, Rubin, 177
Lafayette County, MS, 166
La Fère, France, 110
Lāhainā, HI, 11, 13
Lahainaluna Protestant Seminary, 47–48
Lāhui, 39, 40, 46, 64
La Hula Rhumba (Honolulu), 313 (n. 18)
Lāʻie, HI, 6, 36, 42, 43, 46, 48–51, 57, 58, 71, 72, 73, 94, 99, 105, 112, 113, 115, 125, 202, 229, 230, 231, 319–20 (n. 9)
Lāʻie Elementary School, 230
Lake, Kahauanu, 213, 315 (n. 60)
"Lalawana Lullaby," 171
Lani McIntire and His Hawaiians, 168. *See also* McIntire, Lani
"Laughing Rag," 167
Laurel, MS, 161
Lau Yee Chai (Waikīkī), 217
LDS. *See* Church of Jesus Christ of Latter-Day Saints
Lead Belly. *See* Ledbetter, Huddie
Lebanon, 120, 123
Ledbetter, Huddie, 169, 177–79, 178 (ill.)
Lederer, Hans, 119–20
"Lei ʻAwapuhi," 79, 272 (n. 59)
Lei Day, 213
Lei's Hawaiians, 137
Leleiōhoku, William Pitt, 29, 35, 36, 38, 50, 85
Lemon Brothers Circus, 79, 81
Letuli, Freddie, 140
Levine, Mark, 176
Lewis, Furry, 177
Lewis, George H., 212
Lexington, KY, 168
Lexington Hotel (New York City). *See* Hawaiian Room
Light Crust Doughboys, 181
Liholiho, Alexander. *See* Kamehameha IV
Liholiho, ʻIolani. *See* Kamehameha II

Līhu'e, HI, 29, 154
Lihue Club, 29
Likelike, Princess Miriam Kapili Kekāuluohi, 36
"Lili'u Ē," 209
Lili'uokalani, 3, 10, 37, 38, 44, 71, 78, 79, 91, 92, 98, 104, 110, 158, 171, 174, 177, 208; early music training of, 35–36; 1893 overthrow of, 63–64, 67; support of by royalist musicians after overthrow, 67–71, 83, 84, 151
Lim, Elmer "Sonny," Jr., 317 (n. 91)
Lima, OH, 180, 221
Lincoln, Bill, 223, 313 (n. 18)
"Lindy," 77
"Little Brown Gal," 150, 211
Little Hungary, 88
Little Rock, AR, 187
Log Cabin Inn (Honolulu), 206
Lomax, Alan, 177
Lomax, John, 172, 177
London, UK, 100, 108–12, 127, 186
Long, Andy Aiona. *See* Iona, Andy
Lopez, Joe, 205
Los Angeles, CA, 8, 54, 75, 76, 82, 83, 84, 88, 89, 90, 94, 102, 131–38, 143, 147, 149, 151, 166, 172, 173, 179, 186
Los Gatos, CA, 89
Louis, Joe, 198 (ill.)
Louise, Helen, 101–2
Louise Akeo Serenaders, 209
Louise and Ferera, 101
Louisiana, 154, 158, 159, 160, 161, 164, 168, 169, 175, 178, 232
Louisiana State University's Men's Glee Club, 159
Louisiana Theatre (New Orleans), 159
Louisville, KY, 159, 168
Lua, Pale Kealakuhilima, 71, 99, 99 (ill.), 102, 105, 106 (ill.), 112, 127, 155, 159, 179, 185, 202, 287–88 (n. 107)
Lua and Kaili, 99, 100, 127
Luana, the (Los Angeles), 138
Luka Kamiki Hawaiians, 184
Lumberton, NC, 161
Lunalilo, William, 35
Lu Thompson Keouli's Honolulu Students, 81. *See also* Thompson, Louis
Luvaun, Carlo. *See* Thompson, Louis
Luvaun, Segis. *See* Thompson, Louis
Lyman, Mālie, 227, 231 (ill.)
Lyman, Pōmaika'i Keawe, 227
Lyric Theater (London), 110

MacDiarmid, Don, 313 (n. 18)
Machado, Lena, 138, 205
Machete, 20
Mackie's Queen's Hawaiians, 132
Madame Rivière's Hawaiians, 115, 116
Madeirans: laborers, 4, 7, 20; luthiers, 20
Maggie's Inn (Honolulu), 313 (n. 18)
Māhele of 1848, 45
"Mai Poina 'Oe Ia'u," 154
Maka'āinana, 3, 13, 15, 17, 28, 29, 30, 31, 44, 45, 47, 70, 90, 111, 230
Mākaha Sons of Ni'ihau, 211, 214
Makakoa, Nani, 204
Makia, Betty Puanani, 150
Makinikaea, Laui, 291 (n. 14)
Makinikaea, Richard, 291 (n. 14)
Makuakane, David, 74, 89
Malawi, 128
Malo, David, 313 (n. 18)
Malone, Bill, 179, 180, 181
Malta, 123
Manaku, David N., 88
Mandolin, 19, 28, 29, 33, 50, 64, 66, 78, 193, 292 (n. 38)

Manila, Philippines, 115, 117, 127, 128
Manitowoc, WI, 154
Mānoa Valley, HI, 78, 86, 114
Manu, Henry, 89
Marquis, Auguste, 24–26
Martin, C. F., and Company, 115
Martin, Sara, 168
Matsu, Robert, 133, 187
Maui, 13, 14, 48, 53, 54, 58, 63, 124, 185, 186, 206, 230
"Maui Chimes," 124
"Maui Girl," 185
"Mauna Kea," 296 (n. 76)
Maxine Elliot's Theatre (New York City), 89
Mazumdar, Nalin, 125
McAuliffe, Leon, 179, 181, 182 (ill.)
McCallum, Moses Keakalauloa, Jr. *See* Moke, M. K.
McComb, MS, 161, 298–99 (n. 16)
McComber, William, 80 (ill.)
McCormick, Neal "Pappy," 194
McCoy, James, 177
McGee, Sam, 167
McIntire, Alfred, 132, 138, 141 (ill.), 142 (ill.), 295 (n. 67), 305 (n. 60)
McIntire, Dixon Ka'aihu "Dick," 130, 144, 145 (ill.), 147, 152 (ill.), 179, 295 (n. 67)
McIntire, Lani (Victor Lani), 132, 141 (ill.), 149 (ill.), 168, 172, 173 (ill.), 175, 294 (n. 52), 295 (n. 67), 305 (n. 60), 307 (n. 93), 312 (n. 10)
McIntire, Lani Ellen, 138–40, 142–43, 143 (ill.), 144, 164, 295 (n. 64), 306 (n. 78)
McKinley, William, 70
McNeil, Adrien, 55
McPherson, Aimee Semple, 291 (n. 21)
"Melancholy Baby," 211
"Mele 'Ai Pōhaku." *See* "Kaulana Nā Pua"
"Mele Aloha 'Āina." *See* "Kaulana Nā Pua"
Mele hula, 4, 6, 27, 36–37, 44, 50, 84
Mele oli, 4, 44, 50, 66, 232
Memphis, TN, vii, 159, 177
"Memphis Blues," 160
Meridian, MS, 175
Mexico, 11, 33, 74
Meyer, Ka'iwa, 58, 230, 234
Middlesboro, KY, 169
Midwinter Fair, 1894 in San Francisco, 84
Mikila, Joseph, 291 (n. 14)
Miles, William, 74
Miller, Edward K. Kaleleihealani "Dude," 130, 290 (n. 2)
Miller, Timothy, 193
Milton, Little, 302–3 (n. 44)
Milton Brown and His Musical Brownies, 179, 181
Milwaukee, WI, 137, 153
Minneapolis, MN, 193
Missionary Party, The, 42
Mississippi, vii, 92, 98, 100, 157, 161, 162, 163, 164, 166, 169, 172, 175, 176
Mitchell, Frederick A., 257 (n. 39)
Mitchell, Joni, 200
Mix, Tom, 172
Moa, John, 109, 111 (ill.), 279–80 (n. 15)
Moa, Lily, 110, 279–80 (n. 15)
"Moana Chimes," 114, 124
Moana Hawaiian Studios (San Antonio), 187
Moana Hotel (Waikīkī), 130, 148, 206, 216, 313 (n. 18)
Moana Hotel Orchestra, 148
Moana Terrace (Waikīkī), 227

Mobile, AL, 192
"Mocking Bird, The" 77
Moe, Dorian, 108, 112–25
Moe, Fuifui, 114, 116 (ill.), 285 (n. 61)
Moe, Lani, 115, 118
Moe, Pulu, 114, 116 (ill.), 285 (n. 61)
Moe, Rose Ka'ohu, 112–25
Moe, Savea Aupiu, 113
Moe, Tau, 108, 112–25, 116 (ill.)
Moe, Tauivi, 114, 115, 116 (ill.), 285 (n. 61)
Moe Brothers, the, 115
Moke, M. K., 114, 205, 282–83 (n. 38)
Moki, Solomon, 88
Moku, 45
Molokai'i, 202
Montgomery Ward, 113
Mo'okini, Walter, 205, 206, 223
"Moonlight and Roses," 133
Moonlight in Hawaii, 142
Mooringsport, LA, 178 (ill.)
Mormon. *See* Church of Jesus Christ of Latter-Day Saints
Morrill Anti-Bigamy Act of 1862, 257–58 (n. 40)
Mossman, George, 319–20 (n. 9)
Munich, Germany, 118
Mōʻī, 3, 35
Mōʻī Wāhine, 35
Moore, Sam, 167
Moscow, Russia, 228
Motion Picture Association of America, 140
Munich, 111
Munson, David Kaleipua, 161
"Music of Hawaii," 191
Mwarare, Ndiche, 129
"My Hula Hula Love," 178–79
"My Little Grass Shack in Kealakekua Hawaii," 133, 150
Nahaolelua, George, 89
Nainoa, Sam, 30, 58, 65, 71, 94, 186, 261–62 (n. 84), 275 (n. 105)
"Nā Lei O Hawai'i," 133, 209
Namakelua, Alice, 316 (n. 69)
Nandy, Batuk, 125
Nape, David, 79, 80 (ill.), 85, 89
Nāpōʻopoʻo, HI, 21
Nashville, TN, vii, 9, 153, 196, 213
Nath, Sujit, 125
National guitars. *See* National String Instrument Company
National String Instrument Company, 5, 60, 135–36, 136 (ill.), 184 (ill.), 190 (ill.)
Nawaa, Simeon, 58
Nawahi, "King" Bennie, 58, 160, 173, 291 (n. 14)
Nawahine, Robert, 89
Nawiliwili club, 29
Nazrul (music genre), 125
Nelson, Willie, 210
"Never No Mo' Blues," 174
New Albany, MS, 161
New Orleans, LA, 158, 159, 160, 232
New York City, 2, 76, 81–83, 85, 87–88, 89, 94, 100, 101, 147, 148, 149, 163, 168, 173, 185, 192
New Zealand, 2, 103, 104–5, 107, 127
Nicholas, Sonny, 207 (ill.)
Nichols, Bob Keolaokalani, 141 (ill.), 305 (n. 60), 307 (n. 93)
Nigeria, 129
"Nightlife," 210
"Ninipo," 85
Niumalu Club, 29
Niumalu Hotel (Waikīkī), 313 (n. 18)
Noble, Johnny, 57, 130, 131, 148, 205
Noelani Hawaiian Orchestra, 179

Non-pedal steel guitar, 5, 195
Northrup, George, 161
Norway, 112
Nova Scotia, 158
Nunes, Manuel, 269 (n. 16)
Nuʻuanu Street (Honolulu), 20
Nyss, Garney, 124

Oahu Amateur Theatre (Honolulu), 18
Oahu Publishing Company, 187, 196–97, 310 (n. 134)
Oahu Serenaders, 153–54, 183, 186, 202
Oahu steel guitars and accessories, 188
Oʻahu Theater, 115
Obey, "Chief Commander" Ebenezer, 289–90 (n. 124)
Ocala, FL, 309–10 (n. 133)
Octa-Chord, 167
Odum, Howard, W., 166
"Oh, How She Could Yacki Hacki Wicki Wacki Woo (That's Love in Honolu)," 150
ʻOhana, 27, 45
ʻOhe hano ihu nose flute, 4
Okeh Records, 167
ʻŌkolehao, 18
Okolona, MS, 161
ʻOlapa, 150
Old-time (music genre), 157, 167, 172, 173. *See also* Hillbilly
ʻŌlelo Hawaiʻi, 69; and nineteenth-century literacy rates, 3, 237 (n. 8); use of in congregational worship, 15; prohibition of in Hawaiʻi schools, 69; proliferation of through Hawaiian guitar recordings, 85–86
Oliver, Joe "King," 160
Olsen, Casey, 221, 232
Omaha, NE, 89, 189 (ill.)
"Ona Ona," 296 (n. 76)
O'Neal, Jim, 176
One-stringed zither, 165, 298 (n. 14), 302–4 (n. 44)
"Onipaʻa," 38
"On the Beach at Waikiki," 93, 114
Opunui, Charles, 185
Organ, 210, 252 (n. 118)
Original Hawaiian Method for the Steel Guitar, 94, 95 (ill.)
Orpheum Circuit, 159
Orpheum Theatre (Manhattan), 88
"O sole mio," 124
Osorio, Jonathan Kay Kamakawiwoʻole, 16–17, 40
Osterhaus, Hugo, 89
Oswald, Beecher "Bashful Brother," 174, 175, 185
Otto, John S., 163
Owens, Harry, 140, 205, 313 (n. 18)

Pa, Joseph, 89
Paʻaluhi, John K., 85, 87, 88, 102, 172, 280 (nn. 22, 23)
Paʻaluhi, Joseph, 160
Pāʻauhau, HI, 47
Padigon, John, 89
Pahinui, Charles Philip "Gabby," 206, 215–20, 218 (ill.), 229, 317 (n. 79)
Pahinui, Cyril, 218, 218 (ill.)
Pahinui, James "Bla," 218 (ill.)
Pahinui, Martin, 218 (ill.)
Pahinui, Philip, 218 (ill.)
Pahu, 4, 26, 214, 219, 220
Paka, Iolai Kealoha. *See* Paka, July
Paka, July, 74, 78–86, 80 (ill.), 87 (ill.), 91, 92, 94, 97, 98, 99, 100, 112, 131, 132, 159, 160, 168, 179, 277–78 (n. 135). *See also* Toot's Paka's Hawaiians

Paka, Toots. *See* Hannah "Toots" Jones. *See also* Toot's Paka's Hawaiians
Paka's Hawaiian Quintette, 79
Pākē, 46, 47, 230
Pākī, Pilahi, 216
Pal, Barun Kumar, 125
"Palakiko." *See* Ferreira, Frank, Jr.
Palakiko Pala's Hawaiian Serenaders, 172
Pali, Zachary, 165
Panama Pacific International Exhibition of 1915, 76–77, 92, 95; Honolulu glee club competition for fair contract, 92–94
Pan-American Exposition in Buffalo (1901), 70, 74, 79, 80 (ill.), 112, 159
Pang, Eddie, 206, 313 (n. 18)
Paniolo, 14, 142
Panui, Kiwini, 108, 109, 110, 112, 278 (n. 5)
Paoakalani, John, 89
Papaia, Gabriel, 111 (ill.)
Paradise Isle, 142
Paris, France, 110, 111, 112, 119, 127, 186, 279 (n. 12), 281 (n. 27), 287–88 (n. 107)
Paris, KY, 169
Parker, Joanne, 192
Parsons, Louella, 138
Party Girl, 138
Pasadena, CA, 74
Pathé Records (France), 101
Patton, Charley, 169, 170 (ill.)
Paty, Henry, 14
Paul, Robin, 125
Pauole, Bob, 180
Peabody, Charles, 163
Pearl Harbor, HI, 120, 147
"Pearly Shells." *See* "Pūpū A'o 'Ewa"
Pebbles, the, 171
Pedal steel guitar, viii, 5, 194–96, 197, 200, 203, 234
Peer, Ralph, 167
Pele, 146
Perry, Al Kealoha, 208–9
Perth, Australia, 127
Peshtigo, WI, 192
Peterson, J. A. C., 88
Peterson method of tablature, 94
Philadelphia, PA, 89, 187
Philippines, 8, 9, 33, 97, 115, 127–28
Philippine Tariff Bill, 33
Piano, 11, 77, 87, 134, 168, 175, 188, 193, 194, 209, 210, 222, 252 (n. 118), 314 (n. 38)
Pianofortes, 15, 251 (n. 112)
Pichon, Walter "Fats," 160
Pickford, Mary, 140
"Pidgin English Hula (Ah-Sa-Ma-La-You)," 209
Piegorsch, Marguerite, 193
Pineapple, Johnny Kaonohi, 309 (n. 124)
Pioneer Sugar Plantation, 10
Plantation labor, vii, 1, 3, 7, 10, 20, 30–32, 33, 66, 70, 229
Poi, 89, 109, 279–80 (n. 15), 287–88 (n. 107)
Poi palaoa, 109
Poire, Napua Stevens, 319–20 (n. 9)
Pokipala, Dan, 115
Poland, 117
Polihale, John K., 88
Polynesian clubs, 147–51. *See also* Hollywood, CA
Polynesian Cultural Center, 50, 115, 230, 231
Polynesian Society (Los Angeles), 144
Polynesian Voyaging Society (Honolulu), 201

Pono, 16–17
Port Huron, MI, 79
Port Said, Egypt, 117
Portsmouth, UK, 110
Port Townsend, WA, 77
Portugal, 112, 123
Portuguese: as laborers, 4, 10, 11, 32, 39; as musicians, 20, 25, 28, 34, 100
Prima, Louis, 140
Princess Kaiulani Hotel (Waikīkī), 223
Princess Pauhi and Her Hawaiian Song Birds, 164–65
"Prisoner's Song, The," 171
Provisional Government (Hawai'i) (PG), 1, 49, 64, 66, 67, 68, 69
Pruitt, Milas, 171
"Pua Carnation," 109
Pualoke, 29
"Pua Mohala," 91
Pū'ili, 4, 86, 143
Puku'i, Mary Kawena, 216
Punahele, Joseph Kawehi, 114
Puni, Joseph, 74, 111 (ill.), 281 (n. 26), 287–88 (n. 107)
"Pūpū A'o 'Ewa," 249 (n. 82)

Quebec, Canada, 81
Queen Emma. *See* Rooke, Emma Kalanikaumaka'amano Kaleleonālani Na'ea

Race records, 96–97
Raga, 124, 126, 228
Rainey, Ma, 169–70
Raitt, Bonnie, 200
Rajao, 20
Ramona Café (Honolulu), 217
Ramsey, Frederick, 178
Randolph, Robert, 234
Rathskeller (Honolulu), 313 (n. 18)
Raymond, Alice, 280 (n. 22)
Rea, George Bronson, 33
Reciprocity Treaty of 1875, 39
Red, Tampa, 176
Red Bank, NJ, 154
Reece, Ken, 56
Remington, Herb, 192
Reno, NV, 91
Resonator guitar, 5, 60, 135, 175. *See also* Dobro Manufacturing Company; National String Instrument Company
"Restoration Anthem, The" 36
Reuter, Dick, 80 (ill.), 88, 89
Rey, Alvino, 194
Reyes, Louisa. *See* Ilima, Lei
Rialto Café (Honolulu), 206
Rickenbacker (Rickenbacher), Adolph, 136
Rickenbacker guitars: EH "frying pan," 135–37, 142, 179 (ill.), 202, 228, 293 (n. 40), 293 (n. 42); B6, 205 (ill.). *See also* Electro String Instrument Corporation
Ritte, Walter, 212
Rivière, Madame Claude, 114–17
Roberts, Helen H., 57, 62–63
Rockford, IL, 199
Rock 'n' roll (music genre), viii, 200, 201, 209, 222, 225, 228, 234
Rockwell, Malcolm, 100
Rodgers, Jimmie, 6, 140, 175–76
Rogers, Benny, 219, 223
Rogers, David "Feet" (or "Feets"), 218, 222, 225
Rogers, George, 218–19
Rogers, Roy, 173
Rolling Stones, the, 200, 214
Rooke, Emma Kalanikaumaka'amano

Kaleleonālani Na'ea (Queen Emma), 17, 35, 39
Ro-Pat-In Company. *See* Electro String Instrument Corporation. *See also* Rickenbacker, Adolph
"Rosary, The," 82, 84, 100
Royal Hawaiian Band, 18, 65, 67, 70, 81, 112, 131, 158, 168, 201, 300 (n. 22)
Royal Hawaiian Entertainers (Moe family), 117
Royal Hawaiian Hotel (Waikīkī), 130, 204, 205–6, 209, 290 (n. 2), 313 (n. 18)
Royal Hawaiian Players, 161
Royal Hawaiian Serenaders, 212
Royal Hawaiian Sextet, 75, 99
Royal Hawaiian Theatre, 18, 19, 242 (n. 23)
Royal Samoan Dancers, 115
Royal School. *See* Chief's Children's School
Royal Serenaders, 169
Russia, 13, 117, 228

Sacramento, CA, 89
Sacred Steel, 187, 234, 309–10 (n. 133)
St. Louis, MO, 169, 187
"St. Louis Blues," 124, 176
Salazar, Owana, 221, 232
Salt Lake City, UT, 43, 50, 51
Sam K. Nainoa Foundation of Hawaiian Music, 94
Samoa, 113, 137
Samoan Troupe, 115
San Antonio, TX, 187
Sandbox, the (Honolulu), 216
San Francisco, CA, 6, 9, 19, 45, 64, 70, 72, 73, 74, 75, 76, 77, 79, 84, 92, 93, 94, 95, 97, 98, 102, 128, 131, 132, 136, 173, 186. *See also* Panama Pacific International Exhibition of 1915
Sanine Hawaiian Troubadours, 161
San Jose, CA, 77
Santa Cruz, CA, 74, 75, 88
"Santa Lucia," 124
Santo and Johnny, 197, 225
Sardinha, Greg, 221, 225
Savoy Hotel (London), 112
Schaffer, Eddie, 169
Schenck, Mildred Leo Clemens, 278 (n. 5)
Screen Actors Guild, 143
Screen Extras Guild, 143
Seattle, WA, 78, 89, 101, 102, 134
Secunderabad, India, 124
Selfridge Store (London), 109
Seven Seas, the (Los Angeles), 138, 144
Shanghai, China, 65, 115, 117, 128
Shankar, Ravi, 125
Shastriya sangit (music genre), 125
Shaw, Artie, 217
Shipley, Van, 125
"Show Me the Way to Go Home," 116
Shreveport, LA, 154, 167
Silva, Buddy, 145 (ill.)
Silva, Noenoe, 32
Singapore, 115, 117, 127
Singh, Hazara, 125
Sitar, 125
"Singing the Blues," 132
Skull Valley, UT, 43, 51
Sky Room, the (Honolulu), 217
Slack Key Guitar. *See* Kī hō'alu
"Sleep Walk," 197, 225
Slide guitar, 5, 156–57, 165, 168, 169, 176–77, 200, 298 (n. 14), 304 (n. 50)

Slovakia, 134
Smeck, Roy, 194
Smeeman, Glen. *See* Stanley, Harry G.
Smith, Bessie, 177
Smith, Henry, 88
Song of the Islands, 140, 142
Sonny Cunha's Royal Hawaiian Band, 81
Sons of Hawaii, the, 214, 216–19, 223
Sousa, John Philip, 70, 163
South Carolina, 74, 159, 164, 166
Southern California Music Company, 94
South Sea Rose, 142
Spain, 33, 112, 123
"Spanish Fandango," 27; tuning, 83
Spanish guitar. *See* Guitar
Speare, Gary, 295 (n. 64)
Spottswood, Richard "Dick," 167
SS *Aorangi*, 105
SS *City of Los Angeles*, 133
SS *Sonoma*, 132
Standard guitar. *See* Guitar
Stanley, Harry G., 187, 188, 194, 310 (n. 134)
Stauffer, Robert, 46
Steel guitar. *See* Hawaiian steel guitar
"Steel Guitar Rag," 181–82
Stella guitars, 185
Stevenson, Robert Louis, 41
Stewart, Danny Kalauawa, 179, 206, 295 (n. 64)
Stiffler, Georgia, 132, 133
Stillman, Amy K., 213
"Stone-Eating Song." *See* "Kaulana Nā Pua"
Strand Theater (Fort Wayne, IN), 302 (n. 43)
Strand Theater (Hattiesburg, MS), 161
Strings, guitar: arrival of in the Islands, 10–11, 14; steel, 10–11, 20, 78, 134, 165, 241–42 (n. 3), 246–47 (n. 56), 303 (n. 45)
Strong, Isobel, 41
Stumpf, Myrtle, 94, 95 (ill.), 134, 186
Sullivan, "Big Tim," 88
Sunday Manoa, the, 211, 214
Superior Collection of Steel Guitar Solos, The, 94
Sweden, 10, 112, 117
"Sweet Leilani," 141 (ill.), 211, 216
"Sweet Lei Lehua," 38, 154
Switzerland, 112
Symphony Club (Honolulu), 20
Szego, Catherine, 52

Tagore (music genre), 125, 287 (n. 105)
Tahiti, 114, 137, 211
Tai, Jimmy. *See* Haulani, Jimmy
Takaki, Ronald, 31
"Take Me Back to My Boots and Saddle," 172
Tapia, Bill, 131
Tarab strings, 126
Tarlton, Jimmie, 166, 174, 303–4 (n. 47)
Taro, 45, 46, 47, 48, 49, 50, 89, 104, 113, 232
Taro-patch fiddle, 5, 20, 21, 25, 27, 44, 66, 73, 79, 93
Tatar, Elizabeth, 26
Tavares, Ernest, 205
Tavares, Freddie, 142, 194, 205, 206, 311 (n. 159), 313 (n. 18)
Tawmsen, Keouli. *See* Thompson, Louis
Tawmsen, Luvaun. *See* Thompson, Louis
"Teach Your Children Well," 197
Ten Commandments, The, 142

Tenor guitar, 90
Theater Owners Booking Association, 164
Thomas, Tony, 304 (n. 50)
Thompson, Louis, 81, 88, 112, 159, 280 (n. 23)
Thompson, Lu. *See* Thompson, Louis
Thompson, Lui. *See* Thompson, Louis
Those Who Dance, 140
Thurston, Lorrin A., 42, 64
Tijuana, Mexico, 137, 144
Tin Pan Alley, 2, 79, 85, 90, 96, 101, 138, 150, 151, 163, 178, 208, 226, 296 (nn. 79, 80)
"Tiny Bubbles," 210
Todaro, Tony, 132
Tokyo, 115
"Tomi Tomi," 91, 272 (n. 59)
Tonnessen, Billy, 192
Toots Jones and Her Hawaiian Troupe, 81. *See also* Toots Paka's Hawaiians
Toots Paka's Hawaiians, 76, 78–86, 87, 168; recordings, 85–86; hula repertoire, 86
Transit Hawaiians, the, 313 (n. 18)
Trask, Haunani-Kay, 212
Tricone guitar. *See* National String Instrument Company
Tropics, the (Los Angeles), 138
Trout Farm Road (Kahana, HI), 230, 267 (n. 145)
Tubb, Ernest, 180
Tucker, Sophie, 160
Tuitogama'atoe, Talalupelele Lupe, 113
Tully, Richard Walton, 76, 90, 91, 110, 163. *See also* "Bird of Paradise"
Tupelo, MS, 161
Turkey, 117, 118, 120
Turner, B. K., 169
Turner, Lemuel, 298–99 (n. 16)
Turner and McCoy, 298–99 (n. 16)
Tutwiler, MS, 166, 169
Twain, Mark, 16
Two of Spades, 171
Tyrolean yodelers, 163

"Ua Like No a Like," 91, 100, 154, 209, 272 (n. 59)
'Ūkēkē, 4, 201
'Ukulele, 5, 20, 21, 22, 24, 41, 42, 44, 57, 65, 66, 68, 73, 78, 79, 88, 90, 91, 93, 97, 104, 111, 114, 131, 132, 146, 154, 161, 168, 171, 183, 203, 205, 210, 213, 216, 218, 222, 225, 227, 228, 229, 239 (n. 16)
'Ukulele Bob Williams, 171
'Uli'uli, 4a
United Booking Office, 82
U.S. Atlantic Fleet, 89
U.S. music industry, 96; relationship of genres to racial categories, 7–8, 156–58, 297–98 (n. 13); ethnic and foreign representations, 96–97; impact of the Great Depression on, 102
U.S. Navy, 130
U.S. Patent Office, 137
University of Hawai'i at Mānoa, 114

Valera, Charles Kama, 187
Vancouver, George, 14
Vaqueros, 14
Vichitra vina (vichitra veena), 55, 56, 124
Vicksburg, MS, 161
Victor Talking Machine Company, 91, 96, 100, 101, 179
Victrola, 87, 114, 156, 161
Vienna, Austria, 124
Vierra, Albert, 161
Vierra, Bob, 132. *See also* Vierra Brothers

Vierra, Frank J., 81, 161. *See also* Vierra Brothers
Vierra, George, 88. *See also* Vierra Brothers
Vierra, Joseph, 161
Vierra Brothers, 161, 186, 301 (n. 30)
Vierra's Royal Hawaiian Singers and Players, 161, 162 (ill.)
Virginia, 159

Waiahole Zither and Guitar Club, 64
"Wai'alae," 91, 272 (n. 59)
Waialua, HI, 93
Waihe'e, HI, 53
Waikīkī, HI, 15; hotels as music venues, 8, 34–35, 130, 209–10, 204–6, 204 (ill.), 216–17, 224–25; tourists in, 34–35, 212–13, 216, 220, 225
Waikiki (Los Angeles), 138
Waikiki Beachboys, the, 212
Waikīkī Beach Marriott Resort, 227
Waikīkī Beach Walk, 227
Waikiki Hawaiian Orchestra, 172
"Waikiki Mermaid," 148
Waikiki Players and Singers, 160
Waikiki Serenaders, 100
Waikiki Stone-Wall Boys, 114
Waikiki Tavern (Waikīkī), 142–43
Waikiki Wedding, 140, 142
Waikuiki, Rudy, 174, 175, 185
"Wailana Waltz," 100
Waimānalo, ix, 139, 218 (ill.), 230
"Waimānalo Blues," 211
Waipi'o Valley, 21
Waiwaiole, Benjamin, 88, 90
Walanika, Juliana, 78–79
Wallace, Lizzie, 164
Ward, Helen, 153
Ward Street (Honolulu), 215
Warner Brothers use of Hawaiian steel guitar in cartoon theme, 6–7
Warwick, Dionne, 200
Washington, 77, 78, 81, 89, 101, 102, 134
Washington, DC, 137, 185
Waters, Muddy, 172
Water Valley, MS
Wauke, 46
Wayne, John, 140
WBAP, 162
Weaver, Sylvester, 167, 168, 169, 181, 182, 298–99 (n. 16)
Weissenborn, Hermann, 5, 134, 137, 234, 288, 291–92 (n. 29)
Weissenborn hollow-necked Hawaiian steel guitars, 5, 60, 234. *See also* Weissenborn, Hermann
Weldon, Casey Bill, 169
West, Irene, 81, 99, 100, 112, 127, 179, 185. *See also* Irene West Royal Hawaiians
West, Sam Ku. *See* Ku, Sam
West, Wesley "Speedy," 194
Western swing (music genre), 173, 179–82, 192
West Point, MS, 161
WFAA, 162
Whalers, 3, 7, 10, 11, 14
"While We Were Marching through Georgia," 16
Whistlin's Hawaii (Los Angeles), 144
White's Point, 144
"Wiggle Yo Toes," 160
Wiliama, Albert, 291 (n. 14)
William Atherr's Dog and Pony Circus, 81
Williams, Bert, 84
Williams, Hank, 180
Williams Twins. *See* Parker, Joanne; Crum, Janis

Willing, Julia Anelika, 280 (n. 23)
Wills, Bob, 181, 182 (ill.)
Wilson, Jennie. *See* Kapahukulaokamāmalu, Kini
Wilson, John, 80 (ill.), 159
Windsor, Claire, 138
Winnipeg, CA, 74
Winona, MS, 161
Winston, Bill, 154
Winterhilfswerk, 118
Wittmann, Matthew, 19
WLS, 162
Wonder Bar (Honolulu), 206
Woodbridge, Hudson. *See* Red, Tampa
Woods, Oscar "Buddy," 167, 168, 169
Wooley, Samuel E., 256 (n. 32)
Woolworth Building, 94
World War I, 1, 102–3, 108, 109, 110, 114
World War II, 117–21, 127, 128–29, 148
WRC, 185
"The Wreck of the Old 97," 171, 172
Wright-Prendergast, Eleanor Kekoaohiwaikalani, 67
WSM, vii, 175

Xenia, OH, 91

"Yankee Doodle Dandy," 193
Ybarra, Concepción, 134
"Yes Sir, That's My Baby," 116, 133
Yinusa Dauda, Lai, 289–90 (n. 124)
Yodeling, 15, 44, 62, 164, 174, 175, 176, 242–43 (n. 27)
"You Are My Sunshine," 168
Young, Neil, 197, 200
Young Hotel Roof Garden (Honolulu), 313 (n. 18)

Zablan, Anthony, 80 (ill.)
Zambia, 128
Zimbabwe, 128
Zither, 29, 64, 77, 81, 82